Black Politics Afte.
Civil Rights Movement

Black Politics After the Civil Rights Movement

Activity and Beliefs in Sacramento, 1970–2000

DAVID COVIN

McFarland & Company, Inc., Publishers
Jefferson, North Carolina, and London

LIBRARY OF CONGRESS CATALOGUING-IN-PUBLICATION DATA

Covin, David, 1940–
Black politics after the civil rights movement :
activity and beliefs in Sacramento, 1970–2000 / David Covin.
p.   cm.
Includes bibliographical references and index.

ISBN 978-0-7864-4258-4
softcover : 50# alkaline paper ∞

1. African Americans — California — Sacramento — Politics and government — 20th century.
2. African Americans — Civil rights — California — Sacramento — History — 20th century.
3. African American leadership — California — Sacramento — History — 20th century.
4. Political leadership — California — Sacramento — History — 20th century.
5. Sacramento (Calif.) — Politics and government — 20th century.
6. Sacramento (Calif.) — Race relations — History — 20th century.   I. Title.
F869.S12C686 2009   323.1196'07307945409045 — dc22   2009004515

British Library cataloguing data are available

On the cover: Men assembled for the 1,000 Man March, February 17, 1996.
Photo courtesy of *The Sacramento Observer Newspapers.*

Manufactured in the United States of America

*McFarland & Company, Inc., Publishers
Box 611, Jefferson, North Carolina 28640
www.mcfarlandpub.com*

To Ganga and Big-Momma, who lived their lives
that we might live ours more fully

Acknowledgments

By way of acknowledging the particular form this work has taken, I must first thank Robert Smith for his detailed and invaluable reading of two complete early drafts of the manuscript, including an initial one of almost 700 pages, which was a riot of words. His incisive analysis and honesty made this book not only much stronger, but even possible.

I must also thank Georgia Persons for her support and the thoughtful and valuable editing she has given my work on Black politics in the U.S. for over 15 years.

Next I must thank Sacramento's African-descended population which welcomed me into its midst from the first moment I arrived in the city for a job interview. In those days of the Black Student Movement, hiring of Black faculty was a joint community-university affair, with the B.S.U. playing a prominent role in both settings. I never felt a stranger among Sacramento's African population. I was embraced, supported, and helped as a job applicant, teacher, researcher, colleague, friend, and activist. I also thank them for the inspiration, instruction, friendship, and tolerance they have afforded me over the years. As my presence here has been long, wide, and deep, I owe too much to too many people to be able to cite them individually for fear that with the passage of time and my declining faculties I should forget and slight someone. I may, however, note two people, one a colleague, whose presence affected every dimension of my work as first my student, then colleague, fellow community activist, and ultimately, my boss, Otis Scott; the other, who is a model of the committed activist, is Faye Kennedy. I thank Bill Lee for great generosity with his newspaper's photographs.

At the university, I have learned and gained far more from my students than I have given them. They have been — and are — a delightful and unexpected addition to my life. Again, there are far too many to name individually. My colleagues in Pan African Studies, the Ethnic Studies Department, the Government Department, and the Cooper-Woodson College Enhancement Program, as well as in a number of other settings throughout the university, have been more supporting and rewarding than anyone could hope for.

My ongoing intellectual and collegial sustenance has been afforded by the National Conference of Black Political Scientists (NCOBPS). There I have learned, grown, and benefited from a singular collection of immensely capable scholars and activists. The whole organization has had an indelible impact on me. Among all my valued NCOBPS colleagues, those I regard foremost as my teachers and mentors, though they are all younger than me, are Robert and Georgia, mentioned above, Dianne Pinderhughes, K.C. Morrison, Kathie Golden, Melissa Nobles, William Strickland, Lorenzo Morris, and the U.S. cohort of my colleagues from the Race & Democracy Project that in addition to Dianne and K.C. includes Michael Mitchell, Ollie Johnson, James Steele, Mark Sawyer, Tonya Williams, and Raquel Souza.

I cite three colleagues from my graduate student days at Washington State University, who, to this day, still deeply influence my life: Rutledge Dennis, Johnetta Cole, and Rudy Martin.

The rest leads me back to family, my mother and father, Lela and Odell Johnson; my grandmothers and grandfather; my sister, Jacquie; and my whole host of aunts, uncles, and cousins, Mathilde and Kimenyi, and what is referred to as the nuclear family, Judy, my wife; Wendy and Holly, our daughters; and now — somehow attached to the nuclear family — the grandkids, Nicola, William, and Claire. Life is a collective project; they make possible what I do and give it joy.

Table of Contents

Preface

I once sat on a conference panel where a member of the audience raised the question, "What is our responsibility *as Black scholars* to contribute to the struggle of our people?" In addressing the question, I said, "We have a responsibility to provide the best scholarship our abilities and the state of the art enable us to conduct. We must seek to convey the truth as we know it, as fully, as clearly, and as accurately as we can. We do our people, our activists, our leaders, no service when we provide them less than the best scholarship, no matter how harsh. Delusion is no asset in the dreadful conditions we face."

This is my mantra as a scholar-activist. It is the voice with which I write. I have witnessed and participated in many events described in this work. I have studied Black politics in Sacramento for nearly four decades. Many of my publications arose from the rich field of Black politics in Sacramento. Both as a scholar and an activist I have sought to understand the political world in which I live and work. I believe with Mari Evans that we should "speak the truth to the people." As a result, in these pages I have done my best to produce a book of responsible scholarship. I am persuaded to the position argued by Karl Mannheim that all rational knowledge is based on an irrational foundation. This imposes a limit on the objectivity of any human scholarship. It does not prohibit the scholarship or its utility; it simply recognizes its inherent qualification. As I am both human and a committed activist, my objectivity can be legitimately challenged on both grounds. It is my serious intention that any failings in this work may be due to my human shortcomings, not to any political slant I bring to the effort. I believe all of us in the word of political analysis are best served by the naked truth. Since I believe the limitations of our scholarship prevent us from knowing the absolute truth, I think we should come as close to it as we can. In my enthusiasm, even in this treatise I sometimes comment on the findings. I trust that such spikes of excitement will not lead the reader to lose sight of the findings themselves.

In choosing terminology I have deliberately refrained from using the term African American to refer to persons of African descent in the United States. As a student of the African diaspora, I know that most Africans in the Americas do not live in the United States. I consider the use of the term to refer only to those who inhabit the U.S. as a form of chauvinism.

Introduction

An Alternative to "Received Wisdom"

Some of the most prolific and penetrating scholars of Black politics in the United States have devoted their research and analysis to the post–Civil Rights epoch.[1] For the most part, that work finds neither the Black population nor the period's Black leadership as worthy heirs of the Civil Rights and Black Power legacies.[2]

This book sets forward an alternative proposition: Black politics in the post–Civil Rights era has not been as vacuous as often depicted; it has laid a sound foundation for a Black politics of the future. I suggest that one reason for the intensely negative interpretations of Black politics from the 1970s on has been a fixation on elite politics, particularly at the national level: congressional and presidential elections, national legislation, formations such as the Congressional Black Caucus, the National Black Assembly, the National Black Independent Political Party, the NAACP, the National Urban League, the National Black Leadership Roundtable, and the Joint Center for Political and Economic Studies. Even at the subnational levels most work has focused on elites: mayoral and city council politics in municipalities, gubernatorial and statehouse politics in states. Major studies have also examined national public opinion polls and the judiciary.[3]

The range and depth of Black politics in the elite spheres during the decades 1970 to 2000, compared with the decades 1940 to 1970, suggest that something extraordinary was going on. As Black public education in the 21st century makes exceptionally clear, *Brown vs. the Board of Education*—absent meaningful implementation — was a court ruling. Period. Once its implementing mechanisms were removed, its effects vanished. The 1964 omnibus Civil Rights Act and the 1965 Voting Rights Acts, absent implementation, would have been empty laws; witness Humphrey-Hawkins. In the three decades following 1970 something was going on which continued to implement Civil Rights era gains. Whatever it was, most of the literature does not speak to it. Whatever it was put Black people in significant places throughout the governmental apparatus, sometimes to the point of having significant influences on public policy. Whatever it was produced the structures, connections, experience, organizational and mobilizational capacity that made possible the election of the 44th president of the United States, Barack Hussein Obama. Obama's grassroots experiences in Chicago, his subsequent election to the Illinois Senate, the U.S. Senate, and, ultimately, to the White House were made possible by a deep and dynamic infrastructure created over decades that made the oft-heard "unbelievable in my lifetime," and "historical" election possible. This book is dedicated to the proposition that "whatever it was" derived from the politics of ordinary Black people.

3

By ordinary Black people I mean Black people at large. I do not mean they were less extraordinary in any way than those who represented them in political office and had titles beside their names such as civil rights leader, mayor, governor, senator, congressional representative, judge. I mean they were ordinary in the sense that they were not widely known, and nobody recognized anything about them that set them apart. Some were middle class, some were local officeholders, but in the grand scheme of things, during most of their lives their *political* lives went unreported and unknown. What they did politically and how they did it have remained off the radar screens of the public and academia. This book is intended to establish that this is a critical omission, and that rectifying it will greatly improve our understanding of the great transformation in Black politics that took place between 1970 and 2000. What ordinary people had accomplished by 2000 was the root stock of what shook not only the United States, but the world, in the presidential election of 2008. Like the fall of the Berlin Wall, the "surprise" factors of the Obama election — and the accompanying transformations of the U.S. Senate and the House of Representatives — were surprising because both received knowledge and traditional academic lenses were not attuned to key factors that were involved, factors that were at work among ordinary Black people for three decades. The role that Black politics played in Obama's election is witnessed both by the recognition that with all his broad appeal, Obama did not win a majority of the white vote, and by the incomparable presence of African-descended people at his inauguration in January of 2009.

Black Politics

What do we mean by Black politics? We cannot accept as often happens in studies of Black politics — not explicitly, but implicitly — that Black politics is white politics in Blackface, that it is whatever Black people do in the political world as opposed to what white people do. Though one may certainly describe and analyze what Black people do politically, that no more establishes that there are substantive reasons for doing so than there are for describing and analyzing the politics of left-handed people.

In their award-winning study, *Protest Is Not Enough*, Browning, Marshall, and Tabb indicate that at certain periods in all ten of the Northern California cities they study, there is little which could fruitfully be identified as Black politics.[4] We may make a similar observation about the whole country. But even that assessment presupposes something we may identify as Black politics.

Black politics assumes Black people. Is there any such thing? We conceive of Black people, but does that conception have any analytical utility? We know from current genetics, biology, and anthropology that race, as popularly understood, has no scientific meaning. We know that genetic variation within so-called racial groups is greater than genetic variation between them.[5]

We know race is defined differently in different places and differently in the same place over time.[6] Definitions of race in the U.S. related to people of African descent were at one time subject to the one-drop rule. If a person had any known African ancestry, that person was considered Black. Yet even that rule, dominant as it was for much of the country's history, was only transient. It did not apply throughout the U.S., it was not enforced with equal vigor in all places where it did apply, nor did it exist at all for much of the period when Europeans and Africans settled in North America. Earlier rules specified many racial categories for

Africans, including but not limited to Zambos, Mulattoes, Africans, Creoles, quadroons, and octoroons.[7]

If we consider Africans globally, we are lost. Zora Neale Hurston points to the presence of honorary whites in Jamaica. We know of the Creole fantasy of producing white children throughout the Caribbean.[8] In Brazil and much of South America it is possible for Africans or their descendants to whiten themselves, even to become white. Members of the same family, children of the same parents, can be members of different races.[9] Throughout the diaspora the question of whether race is determined by appearance or ancestry is answered differently.

In the U.S. the phenomenon of passing meant that Black people could pass for white. If that is not an oxymoron, what is? How can a Black person appear white? If Black and white are descriptive terms, the notion of one appearing to be the other is nonsensical. Moreover, it works both ways — white people passed and pass for Black.

Currently, the U.S. census enables one to designate oneself as belonging to more than one racial category. Someone who was Black in 1989 can be something else in 1999. This reveals the unmistakable nature of race as a mutable condition. What race is, indeed, whether it exists at all, depends on time and place. This is partially the recognition that race is socially determined. Yet not only do societies change their collective minds about what constitutes race, no single society is uniform in its definitions of race. Since as far as we know, all human beings originated in Africa, what does it mean to be of African descent?

All these questions seem to have only extremely circumstantial answers. There are Black people in certain times and places. Still others say there is no such thing at any time anywhere. In certain respects we may not be able to say with any utility that there is any such thing as Black people. In so far as that is true, it is absurd to speak of Black politics.

It is in their collective social life, the ways people actually live, the ways they experience life, the ways they feel about their lives, that we can identify not only Black people, but Black politics. Such identifications, nonetheless, are fraught with problems. It is worthwhile examining how they might be made in the U.S. Here we can cite populations which have been historically identified by most residents as Black or African and who have identified themselves in the same way. None of these conditions is absolute. Not all people in the U.S. have characterized others this way. Not all those so classified by others have accepted such definitions. Yet we can say, in the main, in the U.S. there has been a consensus (varying slightly over time in its particulars), both among the population at large and among those generally classified as members of the group, as to the existence of a Black or African population, and as to its members. We may also say there has been a widespread feeling of connectedness among people linked to one another on the basis of such identity. The conceptualization of linked fate incorporates this understanding.[10] Yet is there any scientific or analytical utility in studying such people as a distinct, Black population, and certain manifestations of their lives as Black politics? It is not as if Black people are or ever have been uniform.

Though all Black people in the U.S. have at least some African ancestors, they do not all have the same ones. Many studies have identified various areas and nations in Africa from which people were brought to the U.S. It would be purposeless to list them all, but to indicate the variety of peoples involved, it is worthwhile to note a few: Fanti, Fulani, Ashante, Wolof, Dan, Yoruba, Hausa, Ibo, Mende, Ewe, Dendi, Congo, Bakongo, Mandinke, Ti. They spoke different languages, practiced different religions, lived in separate states, participated in distinct cultures, and were sometimes even at war with one another. They differed greatly in physiognomy, in appearance. Some were agriculturalists, others fisher-folk, some pastoralists.

Some were urban dwellers. This was no undifferentiated population. They did not identify with each other. They felt no emotional attachment to each other. They were, categorically, separate peoples. Therefore, if we limit our consideration of commonality among Black people in the U.S. to African origins, we find those origins offer no basis for commonality.

Whatever their origins in Africa, whatever their travel route, once Africans arrived in North America, they lived in a wide range of settings and circumstances. A major feature of the whole social, political, economic, and cultural system was to circumscribe them, limit them, keep them constrained. As a result, they tended to be parochial, not exposed to the vast extent of their presence here. Most had short life spans and had little ability to develop and perpetuate central social and cultural values and memories.[11] Their life circumstances afforded them little commonality.

Some cohabitated across groups that in Africa would have been separate nationalities and ethnicities, forming among Africans liaisons never found in Africa. Some of their lineages were linked to people from all over Europe, and to a wide spectrum of Native Americans. Yet others continued to reproduce only with members of their own ethnic groups. This hodge-podge of Africans and non–Africans all producing offspring generated a population in the Americas that had existed nowhere before on the planet and containing extraordinary ancestral diversity. There is consequently no single ancestry, no ancient traditions, no common origin to justify their consideration as a single people. They don't even look alike. The veritable rainbow of the Rainbow Coalition exists complete within the Black population.

There is today the further question of how to consider Black immigrants, increasingly significant numbers of people who have come to the U.S. voluntarily from Jamaica, Trinidad-Barbados, Belize, all the Americas, not to speak of Nigeria, Ghana, Senegal, the whole African continent. They came with different national and ethnic identities and with different religious identities. They came with perceptions of the world quite different from Black people who were here before them. Yet almost anyone simply looking at them would say they're Black.

People of African descent in the U.S. number at least 35 million, a larger population than most of the world's countries.[12] They inhabit every region of the country and every state. They are urban, rural, and suburban. They are at every income level and hold and have held almost every occupation including the presidency. They are celebrants of almost every religion in the country, and they range across all educational levels. They engage in diametrically oppositional politics: Republicans and Democrats, Communists and Libertarians, revolutionaries and reactionaries, nationalists and one-worlders. There is no political program or practice which unites them. To talk about the politics in which Black people are engaged is to talk about all politics. What sense does it make to lump such a heterogeneous collection of people into one political category?

The answer to this question is contextual. Black people in the U.S. do not exist just anywhere. They exist in the United States of America with all of its history, customs, culture, and idiosyncrasies. Indeed, it is largely because of the specifics of that context that Black people in the U.S. are perhaps the most race-conscious people in the world. For most of them, for most of their history in the U.S., the character of their existence has been explicitly determined by race. That affects how they conceive of themselves, how they feel about themselves, and how they conceive of and feel about others.[13]

The whole legacy of slave codes with laws addressed specifically to people of African descent, slave or free, was a specific political expression of the attention Europeans in North America afforded Africans. Africans were defined in law as being the same, consecutively, by point of origin, religion, parentage, and eventually, by dint of the presence of any African ancestry. This was an unusual, sustained, and detailed preoccupation with the African presence. Anthony Marx argues that the making of the nation and the making of race in the U.S. were inseparable, part of the same process, and that the making of the nation was based on the exclusion of Africans, an exclusion that formed a basis for uniting a varied European population.[14] In building the country there was a specific project to marginalize Africans, expressly placing them outside the scope of national life, and indeed, of human life. That intention is nowhere made more explicit than in the U.S. Constitution, which did not call on the census to count enslaved persons as human beings. Subsequent opinions of Supreme Court justices also made the national purpose clear — to exclude Africans from the nation.[15] The process which unified a diverse European population into a national population, a white population, also served to unify a diverse African population into a single Black population — excluded from the white nation, and, hence, members of a nation of their own by default. Once so constituted, they set out to provide themselves, by choice, with their own, substantive identity.

Africans in the U.S. live in a political context dominated by others. Those politics have been extremely hostile to Africans. They have sought to define Africans so broadly that censures against them would omit none. The definition of the African was so widely conceived as to leave no chance for Africans to wriggle their way into the national identity, claiming by way of entrance a mother, father, grandfather, or great-great-grandmother. Leaders in the U.S. sought to leave no doubt as to who was an African, to leave no back-door exit, no way out. In doing that, they protected the in-group status of all whites. The definition of the African had to be clear and absolute. That, over time, is what it came to be: anyone with any African ancestry, no matter how remote, was African. Any and every such person was excluded from the nation.[16] The national politics first emasculated Africans by legally assigning them slave status, an accompanying inferior status for those yet free, and after the end of the slave system by *de facto* deprivation of citizenship. The *Plessy* decision made crystal clear the reality that such exclusion had nothing to do with appearance.[17]

What was obvious to others was at least equally obvious to Black people: Black people did not look alike, speak alike, have the same social mores, were members of different social classes, lived in different circumstances, practiced different religions, and harbored great animosities against each other. What they had in common was that they were all labeled, "colored," "Negro," "Nigra," "Nigger," or some other epithet by white people. What they had in common was that they were all treated as inferiors, permanent inferiors, with no hope for themselves or their descendants ever to emerge from that status.

All these policies, acts, conditions imposed upon Black people have meant that most politics Black people have developed have addressed the matter of their permanent oppression. Some have done this by attempting to find ways to escape as individuals. Others have done it by looking for ways to protect themselves as members of special groups. But most efforts have utilized some conception of the mutuality of the Black condition, and have attempted to derive solutions which encompass the group as a whole. Most Black people have, over time, identified with each other, felt a common bond, felt linked to each other. The character of life in this country has created powerful emotional bonding for most of them with those they consider to be of the same race. Black people are wont to speak of "my people" and by that they mean neither blood relatives nor all the inhabitants of the U.S. They mean, specifically, the population they identify with as members of a racial group.

Contextual factors give utility to the study of Black politics. They have determined that in the U.S. most Black people live in areas where the majority of other inhabitants are Black;

go to school, K–12, largely with other Black people; and that most of their friendships are with people of African descent, as are most of their family members. They go to church with each other and even tend to be buried in the same cemeteries.[18] They feel an emotional attachment to each other. It is an amorphous attachment — as vague yet as powerful as appeals to the flag and the national anthem in other contexts. This condition results not so much from deliberate choice as it is an expression of social reality. It makes sense to study Black politics *sui generis* because those politics involve efforts to define and address problems, conditions, emotional attachments, and visions not shared by the rest of the population.

The context within which these politics take place has changed and is changing both domestically and internationally. That does not diminish the importance of such inquiry. Rather the contrary, for changes in context enable new areas of examination. They open new possibilities for political actors, new ways of understanding the world, and new visions of the possible. Change and the ways people create and respond to it open windows on political thought, discourse, and action.

Some contextual changes in the U.S have come from the international environment. They have resulted in a different demographic picture within the U.S: higher immigration rates from Asia and Latin America and higher birth rates among such populations. These immigrants and their offspring have lowered the percentage of the national population that is Black. Ironically, the presence of most such populations was enabled by the Black-led Civil Rights Movement, which among its other accomplishments changed U.S. immigration law.[19] But the change in the proportion of the national population that is Black doesn't change the circumstance that the Black experience in the U.S. is particular. Nor does it mean the country's Black population is decreasing. On the contrary, it is growing. Moreover, as Browning et al. point out, much more critical to the development of Black politics may be critical mass, absolute numbers, as opposed to proportional numbers.[20] This should alert us to the critical role of ordinary folk in the conduct of Black politics. The task is so demanding there has to be a certain base number of people to get it done, a critical mass to make it possible.

In the aggregate the Black experience is qualitatively different from that of any other specific group. Indeed, the experiences of each group differ from the others, and are particular. The presence of Asians and Latinos as part of a changing context offers no grounds for finding less utility in the study of Black politics. It does transform the setting in which such study must be conducted.

Only some contextual changes have resulted from demographic factors. Others, such as Black electoral politics, the tripling of the size of the Black middle class, and the end of Jim Crow, have been significantly influenced by Black people engaging in politics. The study of Black politics offers valuable insights on the full panoply of life in the U.S.

I conclude Black politics exists and that its study is possible and useful. But this is a conclusion reached only under certain carefully specified conditions — which I have attempted to lay out above. I also contend that Black politics is uniquely influenced by the politics of everyday people.

Parameters of Black Politics

In this book, Black politics are to be broadly understood. The work incorporates features of life related to Black people's attempts to affect governance, including conducting that governance themselves. Those features also include conceptualizations, values, and perceptions related to governance. They include emotional (affective) orientations as well as cognitive ones. They include memories of the past as well as visions of the future. This understanding includes electoral politics, along with features of political life usually associated with it — appointments, judicial politics, lobbying, "withinputs," the internal machinations of the governmental apparatus, civil service bureaucrats and appointed officials. It also includes social movements, the internal workings of Black organizations, and what I refer to as pseudo-governmental functions.[21] Many organizations which in the broader population would be regarded as social, cultural, or educational will be considered political. Most of the latter activities are not within the province of elite political actors.

Black people, who were deliberately excluded from the nation's social contract, had no state to look after their interests. They were governed, but not represented. They were taxed but not consulted. Nor, for the most part, were the taxes they paid used for their benefit; rather, they were used for the well-being of their oppressors. They experienced the state as an instrument of oppression, control, and exploitation. This pattern of association between Black people and the state, established in the slavery era, was reinstated, re-enforced and knitted into every fiber of society through the periods of redemption and Jim Crow. In the absence of a benign state apparatus, Black people constructed mechanisms to perform state functions. Churches, fraternal orders and sisterhoods, benevolent and protective associations operated to offer leadership roles and training to weave together positions of influence and power within the community, to offer relief and social welfare, to offer citizenship training, to provide forums for debate and discussion, and to enter the public world. They served as vehicles for mobilization.

These institutions have ever been pseudo-governments. They had and have no compelling authority. They cannot command obedience or the surrender of resources. They have no force to impose sanctions. They operate entirely — much more so than even democratic polities — under the sufferance of those they would have benefit from their actions. They come into being and dissolve altogether according to the dictates of need and capacity.

The Black population in the United States is extraordinarily diverse and complex. The degree of that complexity is highlighted by the circumstance that many people whom others consider Black don't consider themselves Black — the very parameters of the Black population are problematical. To oversimplify this condition leads directly to inappropriate and simpleminded analysis. It leads one woefully astray.

That, too, is true of Black politics. People who are at once reactionary Republicans and revolutionary socialists do not settle easily into the same political category. Certainly, as Mack Jones continually reminds us, every politics Black people do is not Black.[22] Nevertheless, it is critical to survey the range of politics Black people employ as well as popular variations and general tendencies. Only by so doing can we come to sustainable conclusions with respect to which of these myriad behaviors we can appropriately consider as Black politics.

20th Century Sources of Change in Black Life

The collective lives of African descendants in the United States went through unprecedented change in the second half of the twentieth century. In 1940 the aggregate condition of African people in the U.S. remained what it had been during the Depression: abysmal. Economically, they were overwhelmingly an oppressed, terrorized, and exploited peasantry. Politically, the vast majority was denied the franchise. In most of the country's legislative bodies — municipal, county, and state — no Black people served. One Black person, William Dawson of Chicago, sat in the national Congress. Sixty years later, those conditions had been transformed. The Black middle class had quadrupled. The percentage of Black people in poverty had markedly declined. These conditions alone freed much greater proportions of the Black population for political work. Thirty-nine Black people occupied seats in the national Congress, one of them in the Senate. Black people throughout the country exercised the franchise. A Black person had been elected governor of the seat of the former Confederacy, Virginia. African descendants were city council members, mayors, sheriffs, judges, and police chiefs in every part of the country.

Many of the differences can be attributed to changes in the country as a whole. The U.S. had become the dominant economic power in the world. By the early 1950s it accounted for more than 50 percent of the world's wealth. Court decisions, executive actions, and legislation had also contributed to substantive changes in Black life, as had pressures from the international environment.

That African descendants themselves were significant change agents is recognized almost universally in the attention given to the Civil Rights Movement, and to a lesser extent the Black Power Movement. Nevertheless, in those treatments, much more attention is given to national and elite work than to that of the Black population at large.

Even during the 1960s, resistance to change remained intransigent. The Ku Klux Klan revived and revitalized. The Aryan Nation and White Citizens Councils emerged. School districts throughout the South were privatized. George Wallace's candidacy for the presidency, Nixon's Southern strategy, the reinventing of the Solid South from the Democratic Party to the Republican Party were all representative of that resistance.

Following the '60s, despite deep and organized opposition, and despite the diminution of the Civil Rights and Black Power movements, Black material and political gains persisted. The changes which continued after the 1950s and '60s cannot be accounted for solely by the macro-world outside the Black population or even by the "big picture" examinations within the Black population. To understand what transpired we must look at what Black people outside the national elites were doing politically in the '70s, '80s, and '90s. That is what this study does.

Black Politics in Sacramento

While this book examines the national phenomenon of Black politics, I pay particular attention to Black politics in Sacramento, California. In 2002 *Time Magazine* recognized Sacramento as the most diverse and integrated city in the U.S., unwittingly enhancing the heuristic potential of this work. One reason for looking so closely at Sacramento is that by doing so, we are looking at the country's population writ small.[23]

Any serious student of Black politics is aware of the extraordinary demographic, structural, and procedural challenges any transformative Black politics faces. The failing in the literature is that Himalayan obstacles are treated the same as the rest of the political landscape: voter registration, campaign strategies, and internal squabbles among organizations, leaders, and social classes. *The specific challenges confronting Black politics are not comparable to generic features of politics.* They are of a different order. To understand what actually transpired in Black politics from 1970 to 2000, we must look at the terrain — the real terrain in which the battles were waged — and at the specific character of the battles.

Such an examination requires a dense reading of conditions. Currently, we have the capacity to do this only in very limited contexts, i.e., by *limiting* the field of investigation. This can be done by subject, time, location, or a combination of factors.[24] In this book the principal limitations I use are time and location. The implications are national, but to bring the stupendous array of variables into relief, the focus is on one place, Sacramento, California, between 1970 and 2000.

In some cases we can make direct extrapolations because what was going on in Sacramento was going on throughout the country: the War on Poverty and its attendant structures, the Rainbow Coalition, the National Black Assembly, the National Black Independent Political Party, the Anti-Bakke Coalition, national election campaigns, the nationalization of the Harold Washington campaign. Likewise, specific organizations such as Black Student Unions, the Panthers, the NAACP, the Urban League, and the All African People's Revolutionary Party were found not only in Sacramento, but all over the country, often engaging in similar or coordinated policies, strategies, and tactics.

Municipalities all over the country experienced conditions such as police violence, a biased popular press, and hiring and housing discrimination. Black people throughout the United States faced comparable circumstances. In Sacramento, because we can look in detail at the whole range of Black politics, we can see how deep changes transpired in a hostile environment.

Sacramento's population, as in almost every contemporary urban setting, is not static. People move in from all over the state, the country, and the world. People move out. People die and others are born. The politics of Sacramento over the 30 years considered in this study speaks to a Black population of over 120,000 at its end but involved far more Black people than that, including people who moved in and out, and who died.

Method

While the focus of this book is "the little people" in Black politics, it necessarily incorporates the total Black political environment: local, state, national, and international; historical, cultural, social, and economic; and racial, class, religious, and national origin. It looks at beliefs, perceptions, emotions, and values, and procedures and structures of the state and the mass media. It uses many sources: secondary, newspapers, census and precinct data, government documents, organizational records, newsletters, official correspondence, organizational correspondence, personal correspondence, court transcripts, surveys, interviews, maps, and participant-observer experiences.

The engine of this work is its conceptual apparatus. The *sine qua non* of political study is the necessity to simplify, focus, and analyze extraordinary complexity, because, ironically, extraordinary complexity is not extraordinary at all in politics. It is the norm. To make sense of politics, we have to — routinely — conceptualize phenomenal complexity in a comprehensible way.[25] To accomplish this goal the book is constructed around manageable units of description and analysis.

Use of Time-Frames

The first and over-arching method of construction is to divide the study into three decades. This achieves two important objectives: it organizes the data into manageable portions, and it enables subsequent description and analysis to build on the examinations of preceding decades.

Social Spaces, Social Narrative, and Social Memory

The second method is a heavy reliance on the constructs of social spaces, social narrative, and social memory.[26] This focus enables us to examine the political environments in which Black people operated.

SPACES. By social spaces I mean places in society where people come together for social activities. They may be actual physical places such as theaters, churches, nightclubs, public squares, homes, governmental buildings, parks, buses, automobiles, workplaces, sports fields and stadiums, as well as a host of others. They may also be virtual places, which people may or may not share in real time, but where they do not share the same physical space. These may be radio and television broadcasts, newspapers, books, publications of all kinds, films, conference calls, and cyberspace, to cite the more evident forms.

Social spaces vary not only by location, but also by size, time, accessibility, durability, purpose, and control. They also differ by format. One cannot, for example, communicate musical sounds through newspapers and books. One cannot communicate pictures on the radio and conference calls. One cannot enter cyberspace without a computer or a computer-like device.

They differ by size. A large hall offers different space than a cramped room. A mass demonstration in a public space provides a different size space than a complaint counter at a public utility. Some spaces — streets, phone lines, cyberspace, books — are open virtually all the time. Others, such as offices, places that require permits, nightclubs, and governmental departments, are open only at specific times. Some spaces are accessible only by those who have a ticket or a membership, a specific rank, celebrity, or point of view. Others are open to almost anyone.

The purposes of social spaces are myriad, from entertainment and exchange of information to civic action, war, revolution, and treason. Some, such as gatherings of friends, may have no purpose beyond simply sharing the space.

Nevertheless, almost all social spaces are controlled. Someone, some values, some rules determine who may enter and participate in them. Entering and participating are not the same thing. Many people may enter legislative chambers, but not everyone who enters can speak, and even fewer can vote. In this study the primary space distinctions are between hegemonic and Black spaces, between Black and non–Black spaces. Hegemonic spaces are controlled by the leading elements of society and politics. Hegemonic and non–Black spaces are not controlled by Black people. Most participants in hegemonic and non–Black spaces are not Black people. Black spaces are controlled by Black people and most participants are Black.

Some spaces — a conference call, or a riot — may be a one-time occurrence. Others, such as organizational meetings, legislative and judicial sessions, may take place at regularly scheduled times over years, decades, and even centuries.

Spaces can be fungible. Who controls them can change. When Democrats are the majority in Congress, they control the legislative spaces. When Republicans are the majority, they control them.

NARRATIVE. Social narrative consists of messages exchanged in social spaces. Different kinds of messages tend to be exchanged in different kinds of spaces. The substance of the narrative at a physics colloquium is likely to be decidedly different from the narrative at a family gathering or a caucus of a political party. The narrative at a caucus of the Republican Party is likely to be different from the narrative of a caucus of the Democratic Party. I am concerned primarily with narratives within Black spaces. I sometimes compare them with narratives in hegemonic or non–Black spaces, but my central concern is with the narratives within Black spaces. I look at what Black people said to each other and how they said it.

MEMORY. By social memory I mean perceptions, information, interpretations, and memories which members of social groups share. They are social in that they are group memories. Within the same society there are some memories which are broadly shared across groups, and others which are not. In the U.S., for example, though no one alive now was alive at the time of the Civil War, there is a widespread memory that it was a catastrophic event. Yet the nature of the catastrophe tends to differ among Northern whites, Southern whites, and Black people (wherever the Black people are). Slavery is generally a much more powerful and prominent memory among Black people in the United States than among whites. Both white and Black South Carolinians have social memories connected with the Confederate battle flag, but the substance and the meaning of those social memories are starkly different. Social memory tends to be spread by means of social narrative within social spaces. Social memories can be quite specific at the local level which can be critical to the socialization of newcomers both to the area and to politics.

Throughout the text these conceptions are used to help us understand more clearly how Black people were able to operate in exceedingly problematic circumstances, and how with extraordinarily limited resources, facing adversaries with comparably stupefying resources, they were able to effect transformative change.

Plan of Organization

Following this introduction, the book is divided into five chapters: chapter 1, a condensed history of Black people in Sacramento; chapter 2, the decade of the 1970s; chapter 3, the decade of the 1980s; chapter 4, the decade of the 1990s; and chapter 5, the conclusions. Following factors with national implications over 30 years enables substantive assessments of elements of resistance, change, continuity, and stability, as well as an assessment of how Black politics was able to accomplish anything at all, given the odds it faced.

In each decade I have followed specific features of national political life as they were expressed in Sacramento. Some were not present in all three decades. Others were. In many instances the circumstances associated with the presence or absence of such features are just as illuminating as comparisons of those which persisted throughout the entire period. Each examination includes a broad discussion of the national or international contexts within which the features developed, as well as a detailed depiction and analysis of their expressions in Sacramento. Specific features treated are the war on poverty; collective mobilization, both general and activist; Black organizations; Black electoral politics; and the role of the state capital in Sacramento politics. Sacramento is neither a proxy nor a substitute for the broader polity, but because of its unusual demographic (it uniquely mirrors the national population), it serves as a useful model. The close scrutiny afforded by the study reveals explicit and detailed connections between national and local politics across a wide range of political phenomena — instead of the typical situation in case studies where the connections are visible only in a very limited policy area, such as health or educational policy.[27]

What emerges from a work with this degree of focus and at this level of complexity is a new picture of Black politics not only in Sacramento, but also in the U.S., one which requires us to abandon much of the conventional wisdom of political science, and brings us closer to what Bill Strickland calls "a revolutionary Black research agenda in the 21st century."[28]

CHAPTER 1

Origins of Black Sacramento

This study explores national phenomena. Yet the ground for examining their detailed manifestations is Sacramento, California. While most readers may have some general familiarity with U.S. history and politics, few have a similar acquaintance with Sacramento's. This chapter provides a minimal contextual background for the aspects of the discussion grounded in Sacramento.

Early History

As is true all over the country, the politics of unheralded Black people in Sacramento is scarcely known; i.e., in the public mind it does not exist. But it has existed, and for a very long time.

Native American peoples had inhabited the Sacramento Valley for thousands of years before European conquest in the 18th century made the valley part of Alta California, a province of Mexico. Alta California had many residents of African descent. The Spanish, like the Portuguese, French, Dutch, and English who followed them, enslaved Africans and brought them to the western hemisphere. In the 16th century there were more Africans — 60,000 — than Spaniards in Mexico.[1]

Throughout Alta California African descendants were engaged in agriculture, commerce, the military, and politics. An African descendant had been mayor of Los Angeles, another governor.[2] The largest landowner in the area that became Sacramento was Alexander Leidesdorff, an African descendant from St. Croix in the Virgin Islands. He had received a 35,000 acre land grant from the Mexican government in 1845.[3] After Leidesdorff, however, African descendants came to California from social strata closer to the norm in the U.S. even while the area was still part of Mexico. A significant number came because it was Mexico; i.e., it was *not* the United States. Some had escaped slavery. More were free people of color who simply wanted to get out of the abominable conditions even free people of African origin faced in the U.S. Opportunities such as Leidesdorff's were not available to them in the land of their birth.

Leidesdorff died in 1848, right after the Gold Rush began; soon after, Alta California, as a result of the U.S.-Mexican War, became part of the United States.[4] His land incorporated a river bed literally paved with gold. His estate was purchased from his mother at a reasonable price for the time but at a pittance of its actual worth. With the gold rush, the few African people in the area flocked to the mother lode, the sources of gold along the American river and its tributaries. Their presence was documented by the place names assigned to topographical features — Nigger Hill, Nigger Bar, Nigger Gulch. No fewer than 65 sites in the mother lode have names which mark the presence of Black miners.[5]

Many Black people who came to California with the Gold Rush settled in San Francisco and Sacramento. In 1852 the two towns accounted for 80 percent of the state's African inhabitants. Most of the others were in the surrounding area — the mother lode.[6]

In the early days of California's statehood, Sacramento became a center of the state's Black life. The first Black church west of the Mississippi, St. Andrews A.M.E. Church, was founded in Sacramento in 1851.[7] It still exists today. Black women, though only 19 percent of the city's Black population, were instrumental in its founding.[8] The city's first Black secular organization, Philomethan Lodge, # 2, Free and Accepted Masons, was founded in 1853.[9] St. Andrews and the Philomethan Lodge formed the organizational base that enabled Sacramento to host the 1st and 2nd state conventions of Black people, in 1855 and 1856 respectively.[10] Though the region accounted for almost all the state's Black population, the numbers of Black people were small. In 1852 80 percent of the state's Black population were accounted for by 464 people in San Francisco and 338 in Sacramento.[11] The 1850 census listed California's population at 92,579. Only 962 (1 percent) were Black.[12]

Although California was admitted to the U.S. in 1850 as a free state, many whites who staked claims in the gold country brought enslaved Africans with them to work their claims. Others brought their personal and household enslaved persons. The free state of California turned a blind eye to these practices.[13] Free people of African descent were attentive to the number of enslaved Black people in the mother lode and throughout the state. They supported an extensive abolitionist movement. The state was home to an active underground railroad in which Sacramento's Black population played a significant role.[14]

Due to the refusal of the city's school system to admit Black students, Black residents founded the first school for children of African origin in 1854.[15] Perhaps shamed by the initiative of its Black citizens, the Sacramento School Board assumed support for the school in 1855.[16] The support was minimal, not enough to sustain the school. Black women filled the gap, forming school committees to raise supplemental funds.[17]

Most Black people in the city were cooks, barbers, and boarding house keepers. They established residence along the banks of the Sacramento River.[18] Theirs were the least favorable housing sites as the river was highly prone to flooding during the winter. In general, the African descendant population of Sacramento consisted of poorer and less educated people than their counterparts in San Francisco.[19] They were similar to most of the country's Black urban populations.

After 1860, Sacramento's Black population grew very slowly: 394 in 1860, 455 in 1880, 402 in 1900, 486 in 1910.[19] It became insular and self-contained. Everybody knew each other. It was centered in the lower end, the slum community along the river's flood zone where the neighbors were Mexicans, Chinese, and other undesirables. All were targets of sporadic violence from white men and boys.[20] The lower end also housed the wide-open red-light district which befitted a town founded during the gold rush. Honky-tonks and bawdy houses ran all night.

The Anchoring Period

During the early 20th century, most Black Sacramentans were service workers: cleaning women, maids, cooks, household day workers, janitors, yard men, dish washers, redcaps, doormen. A few were farm laborers. Some operated small businesses — restaurants, catering serv-ices, barber shops, tailor shops.[21] The African population wasn't large enough to support a full-time Black funeral service. Public employment was largely out of bounds. Racial discrimination was widespread, not only in hiring, but also in service by public establishments of all kinds, such as restaurants, bars, clubs, hotels, bowling alleys, golf courses, public swimming pools, and boarding houses.[22] Even the public hospital, the only hospital which accepted Black patients, was segregated. The Black ward was housed in the basement with no staff regularly assigned to the patients.[23] Renting and selling property to African descendants was strictly lim-ited. Restrictive covenants were widespread.[24] While there were too few Black people to enable strict segregation of the public high school, elementary schools that served the lower end tended not to include students from other neighborhoods. In short, the general *de facto* con-ditions found in the non-slaveholding states after the Civil War were present in Sacramento.

A few pockets of Black people developed outside the lower end, most notably in Oak Park and Del Paso Heights, but these were outside the incorporated area of the city for many years. In Oak Park, as the area began to grow into a thriving suburb, further Black residence was prohibited. Del Paso Heights remained a sparsely inhabited rural area. The few Black residents in both areas were scattered individual families, isolated from the vibrant daily life of most of the city's Black population. While there were occasional Black professionals — a teacher here or there, every now and then a physician, once and again a dentist or a pharma-cist — there was no Black professional class.[25] The first Black person was not hired as even a street sweeper until 1912.[26] Black men were not hired as city garbage workers until the 1920s.[27] When that happened, the Black garbage workers became a privileged group in the African population — with regular, steady employment, wages, and benefits. The hiring was a triumph, spearheaded by the NAACP. It was commemorated every summer by a Garbagemen's Picnic, widely attended by Black Sacramentans. Black people came to it from as far away as the Bay area and Los Angeles. To Black Sacramento it was the year's greatest communal celebration.[28] This pattern of slow entry into public employment, often only after dogged struggle, played out during the Jim Crow years in every part of the "enlightened" North.

That Sacramento was the seat of the state government had virtually no effect on the eco-nomic, social, cultural, and political conditions of Black residents. The singular exception to this situation was Virginia Cater, who was hired as an attorney by the Office of the Legisla-tive Council in 1935. This was not a civil service post.[29] Attorney Cater was a 1929 J.D. grad-uate of Berkeley's Boalt Hall Law School.[30] She passed the bar the year she graduated and established a private practice in Sacramento.[31] Although she was a Sacramento native, she played no appreciable role in the collective life of Black Sacramentans.[32] Occasionally the state hired Black workers for temporary jobs. Aside from Attorney Cater, it hired none as permanent employees. A few Black businesses were patronized by state officials: the Dunbar's Restaurant in Oak Park, the Canson barbershop, and a few caterers.[33] Throughout the first half of the twentieth century Black Sacramentans found a whites only sign on the doorway to state employment and contracts.

Black Civic Life

Almost from the outset Black Sacramentans had an active civic life. In the period before the Civil War it was concentrated on supporting the Underground Railroad, the rights of formerly enslaved persons in a free state, and public education for Black children. Particularly after the late 1800s, Black civic life was internal to the Black population and only rarely directed externally to the white world. Indeed, while the Black population didn't exceed 1,000 until 1930; the white population had exceeded 100,000 by then.[34] As such an infinitesimal part of the area's population, and also as a small population in absolute numbers, Black people had little ability to affect Sacramento's broader civic and political life. This was a period when Browning et al. indicated that nothing resembling politics could be associated with Black life in Sacramento. The Black population consisted entirely of "little people." They were at the absolute mercy of the powers that be.

In the 1920s Black women formed colored women's clubs, which from the start functioned as self-help groups for women, churches, and the African population at large. The principal clubs were the Ladies Monday Club, the NUG (Nothing Unless Good) Art Club, and the Sorosis Club.[35] In 1936 these clubs merged into the Negro Women's Civic and Improvement Club.[36] They were part of the Colored Women's Club Movement then spreading throughout the country. The merger was blessed by a personal visit from Mary McLeod Bethune.[37] Within these structures individual women emerged as formidable leaders.[38]

Black Sacramentans were well aware of what was going on elsewhere in the country and the world. The Sacramento chapter of the NAACP received its charter in 1918 with 73 members.[39] At the same time there was an active and aggressive Ku Klux Klan chapter in the city. In 1922 it had 144 paid members.[40]

Black civic life centered around the churches, fraternal and sisterhood organizations, women's clubs, and men's clubs. Though people moved out and in, were born, and died, there was a 60 year period during which Sacramento's African descended population was virtually static in terms of growth.[41] During those six decades the foundation organizations and the networks between them became the pillars of the small Black settlement.

When the Depression began in 1929, there were four Black churches: St. Andrews Chapel A.M.E., founded in 1851[42]; Shiloh Baptist Church, founded as Siloam Baptist Church in 1856[43]; Kyles Temple A.M.E., founded in 1917[44]; and New Hope Baptist, founded in 1922.[45] Churches were the Black population's cornerstones, but the other organizations were mortared to them.

Civil Rights

The NAACP was Sacramento's leading Black organization in the struggle for group rights and employment. The city had refused to hire Black men to work on the city's horse-drawn garbage wagons. During a garbagemen's strike, the NAACP convinced the city it should expand the labor force eligible to work on the wagons. When the strike was over, the city began hiring Black workers.[46] They did not, however, pay them the same wage as white workers. The rationale was that white workers drove the garbage wagons, while all Black workers did was tote the cans. Once again, the NAACP intervened, and the city adopted the policy of rotating the duties of a truck crew between driving and hauling. It paid all crew members equal wages.[47] The NAACP instituted voting classes for the city's Black residents, particularly recent immigrants from the South where Black voting was prohibited.[48] The narratives which led to these initiatives did not arise on the golf links or in city hall. Those were spaces closed to Black people. They came from the organizations Black people had established for themselves — the lodges, the clubs, the churches, the NAACP.

In the arena of health care, the Sacramento Health Department accepted Black patients, but would not hire Black doctors, nurses, or any health care workers. Black patients were the only ones placed in the hospital basement. There they were largely neglected by the hospital staff. The NAACP sent in visitors who took photographs of the medieval conditions imposed on Black patients, including many immobile patients lying in their own wastes. The organization was able to get the pictures into a local newspaper. The branch used the newspaper exposure to drum up public pressure against the county and its despicable treatment of desperately ill people, all of whom were African descendants. The public outcry led the county to hire Black nurses' aides and orderlies to care for Black patients — still housed in the basement.[49] All this was accomplished without the benefit of any Black elected or appointed officials, and with very few Black voters.

In Sacramento, as much as any other place, the Depression hit the Black population hard. It derailed the Black women's organizations and the NAACP. People could not afford to maintain their memberships. The three Black women's clubs merged because they were not able to continue as individual organizations. One distributed all of its remaining treasury by spreading its total of nine dollars among the city's four Black churches. The clubs survived by unifying. They named the new organization the Negro Women's Civic and Improvement Club. In 1930, due to insufficient membership, the NAACP chapter lost its national charter. Even in the economic trauma visited upon the community, Black leaders fought to get the charter back. They launched an aggressive drive to recruit new members and get old members back in the fold. Their efforts paid off. The local chapter charter was restored in 1931.[50]

The effort to reconstitute the chapter revitalized it. In the early 1930s it was the NAACP which got the signs removed from local businesses which said, "No Negroes & Dogs."[51] While removal of the signs did not require the establishments to serve Black people, as they still maintained, "We do not solicit colored trade," the visible declarations of their policies were banned.[52]

In the early '40s it was the NAACP which was able to get a Black woman, Iverna Anderson, hired as the first full-time Black employee in the California State Civil Service system.[53] About her case, we may say in retrospect, *vis-à-vis* affirmative action and arguments against it, though she had passed the Civil Service exam with the highest score, she was offered only temporary employment, while white women with lower scores were hired for full-time, permanent jobs. That had long been the established policy of the California state government. Black people were not to become full-time, permanent employees, regardless of merit measured by objective standards.[54]

Social Spaces, Narratives, and Memory

Black people were excluded from most public and private spaces — which were also hegemonic spaces and white spaces. As in most of the North, while they could vote, their votes had virtually no impact on public officeholders or policies. In Sacramento, the numbers of Black people were too small to enable the construction of all-Black schools. There were so few Black children they were almost invisible among the white children in the schools. As a result, they were allowed within the important space of public schools. This situation was replicated in localities with small Black populations throughout the North. Except as domestics, Black people were not allowed in most private homes. They weren't allowed to buy or rent in white neighborhoods; i.e., they weren't allowed *to live* in certain neighborhoods. They weren't allowed into the public work force, except belatedly, and then only as street sweepers, garbage collectors, and one lone lawyer within the vast state government. Likewise, they had no voice in public places. Ku Klux Klan voices outnumbered theirs. The public was deaf to what they had to say, their narratives.

The social memories they shared with their white counterparts were only the broadest: the Fourth of July, the glory of the Declaration of Independence and the Constitution, Christmas, Easter, World War I and the doughboys; flappers and the Roaring '20s, the Depression, Franklin Delano Roosevelt, the New Deal, and fireside chats. Not slavery, not penury. Not dim hopes for their children. Not Jim Crow. Not endless, relentless discrimination, prejudice, and contempt. Not the meanness and wickedness of white people or dreams dashed to earth by the hard realities of race.

Instead, they developed their own spaces. Their living spaces were separate from whites. Most were rented, some they owned. They cultivated their own neighborhoods. They built their own churches. They rented and bought their own lodge buildings. Some occupied their own businesses. These were spaces they controlled — where they could go for rest and succor, for celebration, places where they could talk over the events of the day.

Almost the only substantive conversations they had were with other Black people. They developed their own narratives, their own understandings of the world they inhabited. They published their own small newsletters and newspapers, spaces they filled with their concerns, their hopes, their aspirations. They read the *Chicago Defender*, which porters brought back from their days on the rails. In those spaces, those narratives, they learned about the NAACP, the Colored Women's Club Movement. They heard about Garvey and DuBois, Booker T. Washington and A. Philip Randolph. They learned about Ida B. Wells, Mary McLeod Bethune, and the deeds of Mary Ellen Pleasants.

The park they reserved for the garbagemen's picnics became a Black space. Their voices expressed the sole narrative there. *These stories were present in no other population.*

Their social memories contained the daily affronts they faced, the dinners they sold to raise money for their churches, lodges, and social clubs, the viciousness of their white neighbors, employers, and public officials. Their social memories celebrated Jesse Owens, Joe Louis, and Marianne Anderson.

The Negro Women's Civic and Improvement Club bought a house and turned it into a home where single, Black women could rent rooms and enjoy kitchen privileges. The only other places they were allowed to rent rooms were in houses of ill-repute. Through subterfuge the club purchased a Victorian mansion which became an elegant residence for young Black women, and whose public spaces became a Black community center. All this became part of the community's social memory.

These spaces, narratives, and memories enabled Black people to prepare themselves to live in a harrowing world and to seek collective ways to improve their places in it. Without these protected venues the cruel land of their birth would have been not only sterile, but also eviscerating. They were doing what others of their race were doing in every village and hamlet in the United States.

Black Sacramento Reconstructed

Two significant events served as catalysts to disperse Sacramento's Black population. The first was World War II. With the war came the construction of two major air bases, McClellan and Mather. The demand for workers at the bases pulled in thousands of Black workers, mostly from the South. Many settled near the bases. In the case of McClellan, that meant living in Del Paso Heights and North Highlands. In the case of Mather they came to Lincoln Village and nearby parts of Rancho Cordova.

The second development was urban renewal. The lower end was destroyed. It was replaced by massive, D.C.-like malls west of the state Capitol building, state office buildings, freeways, and freeway interchanges. Three major freeways — I-80, I-5, and State 99 — met where the lower end once flourished. This was a fate simultaneously visited upon poor Black neighborhoods all over the U.S., the infamous urban renewal, often categorized in Black narrative as Negro removal.

The air bases brought more salaried employees. Though many were temporary workers, some were not. Additionally, some temporary workers sought regular employment in the area, a few opening their own businesses, such as barber shops, beauty shops, restaurants, and yard services.[55] The war also brought a series of ill-gotten gains to scores of Black Sacramentans. When Japanese-Americans were rounded up, packed up, and shipped off to concentration camps, many Black Sacramentans who were in a position to do so bought their houses and businesses at cut-rate prices. This was also a means by which Black Sacramentans moved into areas where they had earlier been excluded, including Oak Park.[56]

All these developments meant that Sacramento's Black population was no longer concentrated in any single neighborhood. It was located in pockets. Most notable were Del Paso Heights, Oak Park, North Highlands, Lincoln Village, and a bit later, Glen Elder. Black mobility was limited. Many neighborhoods banned Black people. Restrictive covenants remained. So while Black people were not centered in any single neighborhood, there were areas without a single Black resident. Indeed, almost all of the city's Black population resided in a few widely separated neighborhoods.[57]

Sacramento, like many California cities, had irregular boundaries. There were places where parts of the city were merely pockets inside unincorporated areas of the county. School districts were often partly in an unincorporated area, and partly in the city. When Black people started settling in Del Paso Heights it was an unincorporated area. So were Lincoln Village, Rancho Cordova, and other enclaves where Black people located. This dispersion was not only geographical, it was also jurisdictional, and had significant political consequences.[58]

By the late 1960s comparatively few Black people remained downtown. Two small areas of new housing projects, one at the southern edge, and the other at the northern edge of downtown contained the bulk of the area's Black residents. Of all the Black neighborhoods, Del Paso Heights and Oak Park were the most established, the most widely known, and had the largest Black populations. As might be expected, young people from the two neighborhoods saw each other as rivals.[59] While in the post World War II era these neighborhood rivalries did not result in gangs as they did in many older cities, they frequently resulted in fights and threats between neighborhoods, a phenomenon representative of many cities of similar size in every national region.

The character of the two neighborhoods reflected interesting differences. Oak Park was older. It had been Sacramento's first suburb. A few of the earliest Oak Park residents were Black, but no Oak Park realtor or contractor, and very few homeowners, would sell to Black people. The earliest Black Oak Park residents were there simply because they were the first people to arrive.[60] As the Black population of the Sacramento area increased, and the lower end was destroyed, the pressures driving Black people to find new housing pushed heavily on Oak Park. Over the years the city had incorporated it and grown beyond. It had become a

SACRAMENTO COUNTY STATISTICAL AREAS

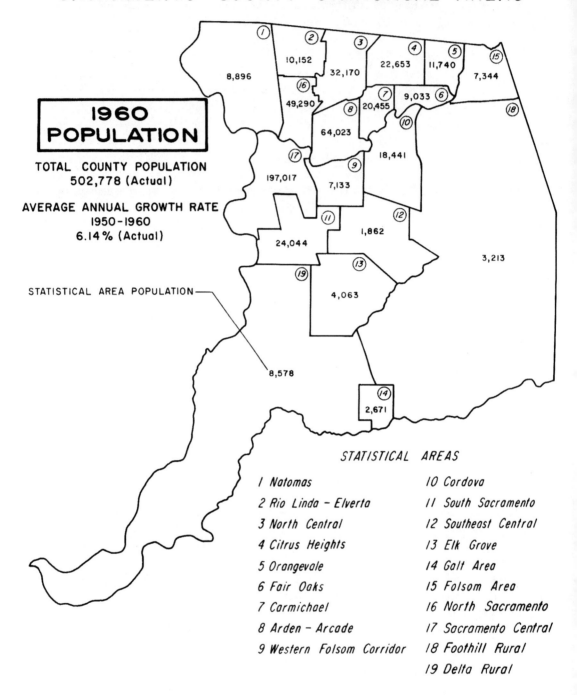

1960 POPULATION

TOTAL COUNTY POPULATION
502,778 (Actual)

AVERAGE ANNUAL GROWTH RATE
1950-1960
6.14% (Actual)

STATISTICAL AREA POPULATION

STATISTICAL AREAS

1 Natomas	*10 Cordova*
2 Rio Linda – Elverta	*11 South Sacramento*
3 North Central	*12 Southeast Central*
4 Citrus Heights	*13 Elk Grove*
5 Orangevale	*14 Galt Area*
6 Fair Oaks	*15 Folsom Area*
7 Carmichael	*16 North Sacramento*
8 Arden – Arcade	*17 Sacramento Central*
9 Western Folsom Corridor	*18 Foothill Rural*
	19 Delta Rural

PREPARED BY THE SACRAMENTO COUNTY PLANNING DEPARTMENT – JUNE 1971

Sacramento County Statistical Areas, 1960. The map shows Sacramento County population distribution at the time of the 1960 census.

close-in neighborhood. As more Black people moved in, white people fled. Many of them did not sell. They rented their former homes to the dark-skinned migrants.

Del Paso Heights was altogether different. North of the American River, it was not only outside Sacramento, it was in the opposite direction from the city's course of growth. Black people first started moving there because there was no competition for the land. They could buy lots, and they did. Many Black buyers built their own houses. There were no streets. There were dirt roads or ruts people built their houses beside. Many Black migrants said the Heights reminded them of the rural areas or small southern towns they came from. Most of the area consisted of uninhabited, open fields. People hunted rabbits and fowl. There was no electricity, no plumbing, no city water. But a feeling of ownership and community developed. By the time McClellan Air Force Base was built in the open spaces to the north and east of Del Paso Heights, many of the Black people who worked at the base saw Del Paso Heights as a nearby place where they could not only live, but where they could own their own homes. Many built their houses from the heavy, well-built wooden crates used to transport airplanes and airplane parts. Because the Heights was largely Black and unincorporated, the county provided few services. As the population grew, Heights residents, feeling ownership of their neighborhood, began the drive to have the area incorporated into the city as a means of acquiring municipal services. They were successful. Del Paso Heights had its own elementary school district, a feature of *de facto* segregation. It was served by the Grant Joint Union High School District. Both Grant High School and its headquarters were located in Del Paso Heights. The Heights was a community which not only felt empowered, but which also was vested in many of its own public institutions.[61] This condition was to have significant repercussions for Black politics in the city.

The Birth of a Black Middle Class

The developments associated with WWII contributed to the growth of a marginal Black middle class. It was extremely small and fragile, yet it exceeded by orders of magnitude what had preceded it. In the post war years it was joined by an increasing professional class. As late as 1947, though attorney Virginia Cater worked in the Legislative Counsel's Office, there was not a single, Black attorney in Sacramento private practice. That changed with the arrival of Nathaniel Colley in 1948.[62] He moved to Sacramento because his wife's family lived there. Colley graduated from Yale Law School that year. As soon as he passed the California State Bar, also in 1948, he opened his practice. He was an exceptional litigator. Buoyed by a bevy of Black clients who had longed for a local Black lawyer, Colley instigated a series of lawsuits which began to dismantle the structural segregation of Sacramento life.[63] Similar cases were having impacts all over the North.

After the gold rush Sacramento had been the home to only one Black medical doctor.[64] That, too, changed. Black Sacramentans opened pharmacies and funeral parlors. They became insurers, real estate agents, and brokers. They helped Colley's clients find homes where they had hitherto been excluded. Spurred by the combination of legal actions and burgeoning numbers of applicants, increasing numbers of Black people were hired by the state. As in most places in the U.S., the public sector was the first to open significant occupational spaces to Black people. In Sacramento that was particularly significant because it was the seat of state government. The numbers of Black employees in state government increased to the point where some began to attain supervisory ranks. Black teachers began to enter the public school

Nathaniel Colley, first Black attorney to establish a private practice in Sacramento, pioneered law-suits breaking down residential segregation in Sacramento and served on the National Board of Directors of the NAACP. Courtesy of the *Sacramento Observer Newspapers.*

system. Black churches began to increase in number and size. Nationally, such developments coincided with the development of the Civil Rights Movement.

The NAACP, with its long history in Sacramento and many significant achievements, was revitalized by the influx of new professionals, Colley among them. Indeed, he was elected to the National Board of Directors in 1961 and remained on it for most of the rest of his life. A branch of the National Urban League was established in the city.[65]

The Johnson administration's poverty administration brought a level of mobilization to Sacramento's Black poor and to attendant Black professionals that was a novelty — a novelty accompanied by funding (however minuscule). The poverty program also brought the Black poor as well as the Black professionals they hired into interactions with decision makers at the local, state, and national levels; it also brought them a sense of competence, and the trappings of power. These occurrences within the local war on poverty paralleled what was going on in Black communities in every part of the country.

By the late 1960s, bolstered by arrivals from all over the country, and indeed the world, Sacramento's African descended population increasingly associated its identity with the aspirations of the Civil Rights and Black Power movements, an identity incorporating political dimensions. It had a secret weapon that helped crystallize its identity, *The Sacramento Observer*, the community Black newspaper founded in 1964 by William Lee, John Cole, and Geno Gladden.[66] The *Observer* played a role in Sacramento that the Black press played in almost every metropolitan area in the country with populations of 30,000 Black people or more. It was a voice, a sounding board, and the unique dispenser of a regular, published set of Black narratives for African descended people in the region. It kept Black people in Sacramento alerted to what many of their counterparts were doing, not only locally, but statewide, nationally, and internationally.

The Black Panther Party for Self-Defense made its first public appearance in Sacramento in 1967. They came because a Bay Area legislator, Donald Mulford, had introduced legislation targeting the Panthers. It forbade the populace from bearing arms in public. Protesting the legislation in their inimitable way, the Panthers exercised their rights of free speech, assembly, and petition — as well as the right to bear arms — by marching up the Capitol steps and into the building during a legislative session, carrying (while it was still entirely legal to do so) shotguns, rifles, and pistols. The Capitol Building and Sacramento were thrown into confusion. The state police didn't know what to do. Legislators and staffers ran and hid. They called the Sacramento police. They didn't know what to do, either. The Panthers, having, as it were, made their statement, left. Some were arrested before they left Sacramento. Others made their way back to the Bay Area. The ban against carrying fire arms in public was passed with amazing bipartisan support. Black youth from throughout California flocked to Oakland. In Sacramento a number of young people, inflamed by the Panthers' daring and bold programs, left their hometown to participate in a new vision of the future.[67] Others in Sacramento, like young Africans all over the U.S., wanted the Panthers' imprimatur to start their own chapters of the party. Press coverage of their bold visit to the Capitol brought inquiries about forming chapters from every part of the country.[68]

In 1968 Eldridge Cleaver of the Black Panthers came to speak at Sacramento State College.[69] Black students at the college formed a Black Student Union. They formed a coalition with Chicano, Native American, and Asian American students. The coalition rounded up allies from faculty, staff, and the community. They demonstrated, and they pressed the administration. They held rallies and marches and brought in guest speakers. The college yielded an Ethnic Studies program with the authority to grant degrees. It was composed of separate programs of Black Studies, Chicano Studies, Native American Studies, and Asian American Studies, each of which offered a concentration in the Ethnic Studies major, and a minor. The college created an Educational Opportunity Program to provide transitional support to students represented by the coalition. The college reached out to the under-represented populations, recruiting students. It hired and prepared to hire many more under-represented faculty and staff.[70] The Black student movement, national in scope, fully materialized in Sacramento. Its mobilizing and energizing of Black students and the communities they were associated with, and its impact on local educational institutions, was dramatic, with consequences as enduring as anywhere in the country.

Perhaps Sacramento's most significant Black Student Union (BSU) was formed at Sacramento City College (SCC), one of two junior colleges then in the Los Rios Community College district which incorporates the Sacramento area. Many of the BSU members from SCC eventually transferred to Sacramento State or UC Davis (UCD), just eleven miles west of Sacramento. On both campuses the SCC transfers were instrumental in founding and energizing the BSUs. At SCC the BSU organized BSUs in local high schools, establishing a citywide council of high school BSUs. The Black Student Union at SCC drew on a rich blend of people. Many of its members were veterans or people returning to school after having been workers, job seekers, or full-time mothers. They were an eclectic mix of locals, migrants from other parts of the country, street hustlers, ingénues, the inspired and the obscene. Sacramento City College was the city's most urban campus. It was hit by a sudden influx of Black students such as it had never seen. The students rejoiced in each other.[71] The pattern was representative of what was happening in this Black age cohort in every part of the country. Somewhat belatedly, perhaps, the door opened for many of them, and they seized the opportunity to charge through it.

With the support of Black faculty and staff as well as community activists, the Sacramento City College BSU was able to wrest an independently operated center from the college administration. It was called the Oak Park School of Afro-American Thought. It consisted of portable classrooms erected on a site in Oak Park owned by the Sacramento City Unified School District. The Oak Park School, as it was popularly referred to, had its own administrator. It offered evening classes in Black Studies for SCC students. The classes were open to the public. Through the Oak Park School the BSU engaged in community outreach and organizing, hosted speakers and seminars, and staged theatrical performances. When not in use by the school itself, its rooms were available for community meetings. This was dedicated community organizing pursued by members of the same generation who had participated in the Civil Rights Movement and had launched Black Power initiatives in the South and the North, the East and the West.

By 1968 the Black Panther Party (BPP) had also established itself in Sacramento. As in the Bay Area, Los Angeles, and elsewhere, the Panthers saw central city college campuses (as well as the streets) as fertile recruiting grounds. Central city community colleges were prime grounds because there one was likely to find both idealistic students and thugs on the same campus, and the Panthers wanted both. This combination was particularly present at SCC. There the Panthers came on campus with an ultimatum — either the BSU or the BPP. You can't have both. You must choose. As they did elsewhere, the Panthers backed up their declaration with cold steel and other forms of brute force. The BSU at SCC, however, had as many thugs in it as the BPP. Only a courageous sister, Margaret Washington Creel, prevented them from shooting it out in a city park.[72] The Panthers never took over the SCC Black Student Union. Except for Maggie Creel, what happened at UCLA could well have happened in Sacramento.[73] If anyone

Offices of the *Sacramento Observer*. Courtesy of the *Sacramento Observer Newspapers*.

in the late '60s still needed evidence that the Black population was not monolithic, that the Black activist population was not monolithic, young Black people were providing that evidence prodigiously every day of the week, in every part of the country, including Sacramento.

Ultimately, Sacramento became a site for a Temple of the Nation of Islam, organizers of the Republic of New Africa, and, as indicated, the BPP.

In the NAACP, the *Sacramento Observer*, the poverty program structure, the Sacramento Urban League, the BSUs, the Black Panther Party, the Nation of Islam, and the Republic of New Africa, Black people utilized established Black spaces, created new ones, developed potent narratives, and both formed and drew on powerful social memories to forge new paths for political action. Their actions were informed by what was going on all over the country and throughout the African world. They were also part and parcel of those national and international developments. The late '60s were explosive times, years of social movement, political confrontation, and rebellion. People called themselves revolutionaries. Political science research has shown that periods of regime contestation open political spaces for marginalized groups.[74] That proved true for everyday Black people who rushed into those spaces in an effort to create new possibilities for themselves.

Black Sacramento as an Embodiment of National Patterns

We find in Black Sacramento's history much of what we find in the rest of the country: an early African population of the enslaved, the escaped, and the free. We find also in Sacramento the Underground Railroad, the Black Convention Movement, the Black Church, and Masonic Lodges. What we find throughout the North after the Civil War we find in Sacramento: segregated schools and residences, widespread racial discrimination, the Ku Klux Klan. Place names designated the demeaned status assigned to African descendants. Black people resisted in the ways they did throughout the union: the Colored Women's Club Movement and the NAACP. Yet in none of that can we name a person of national, regional, or even local stature as measured outside the local Black population.

In Sacramento the NAACP had impacts similar to what it had in other parts of the country. Public employment was desegregated battle by battle. With the onset of World War II the employment picture for Black people was dramatically impacted. New Black people came to town from all over the country and the Black population exploded. The newcomers brought with them the full variation of experiences they'd had in their places of origin. As in much of the North, many of the new residents were from the South. When the war was over the NAACP and a new cadre of Black lawyers went to court. Sacramento developed a Black middle class, representative of a national pattern.

When the Civil Rights Movement and the Black Power Movement came to Sacramento, the former helped give birth to the War on Poverty, and the latter allied with it. Sacramento's Black press became a major influence in the expanded Black community. Black Panthers, Black Student Unions, Black Studies in Sacramento became what they were throughout the United States. In many ways the history of Black people in Sacramento prepared them to serve as surrogates for the country's African descended population. How deeply this is the case we will see subsequently.

CHAPTER 2

The 1970s

This chapter begins with the War on Poverty. The poverty program serves as a convenient transition between the turbulence of the 1960s and the post–civil rights era. The '60s — even 1968 — did not consist of omnipresent dynamism and drama, nor were the following decades completely staid. The War on Poverty spans Democratic and Republican administrations, assassinations and presidential resignations, burning cities and impeachment proceedings. In Black politics it bridges the movement and electoral eras. Because of its target populations the War on Poverty also serves as an informative introduction to everyday Black people. We get to see them in all their variety. It is a caution against stereotypes.

From the War on Poverty we move to collective mobilization, which makes plain that much of the early '70s was like much of the late '60s. Black organizations, electoral politics, and the role of state government in local politics complete our examination of the decade.

The War on Poverty

By 1970 the social movements which had thrown the country into turmoil during the late 1960s were winding down, but they were not spent. They still harbored powerful energies. Richard Nixon was in the White House, but the war in Vietnam raged on. Dr. King was dead, but the Poor People's Campaign had continued. SNCC had disintegrated. The national Panther leadership was in disarray. But the first meeting of the National Black Assembly lay two years in the future. Throughout the country powerful and creative forces had been released which were far from exhausted. Some of them had coalesced within the War on Poverty.

When President Johnson introduced the War on Poverty, the Vietnam War had not yet seized the reins of the national government. The Civil Rights Movement was at its zenith. The Black Power Movement was in gestation. The conditions which were to lead to the Long Hot Summers were simmering. Race and Black people were on the top of the national agenda — and driving policy. Increasingly, Black people mobilized and took action. It was "the Negro Revolution."[1] In many important respects, "the Negro Revolution" drove the War on Poverty. We can see what this meant in very concrete terms by looking at the specifics in Sacramento.

The Shape of the War in Sacramento

The War on Poverty consisted of structures and procedures designed to operate at the local level for the maximum participation of ordinary people, including the poor. In Sacramento, as in every other locality, it arrived in many forms. There was the over-arching anti-poverty organization; in Sacramento it was named the Sacramento Area Economic Opportunity Council (SAEOC). Associated with it and directly funded by it were the Neighborhood Councils, delegate agencies of SAEOC, intended to drive implementation of the president's policies in the war zones. There was the collective, collaborative body of the Neighborhood Councils, the Federation of Neighborhood Organizations (FONO). There was Head Start, implemented through various programs around the county, and also through its delegate agencies. Additional components included Legal Aid, Planned Parenthood, addiction rehabilitation (7th Step), Emergency Food and Medical Services, OJT, and summer work programs. There was a unified Chicano agency, Sacramento Concilio. Neighborhood development was another facet of the national program. In Sacramento it was administered by the Sacramento Redevelopment Agency. At the community level neighborhood development was represented by the Project Area Committees (PACs). Many of these organizations were initiated by acts of the City or County of Sacramento. National legislation required the whole set of enterprises to engage the maximum feasible participation of the poor.[2]

Three social sectors were mandated by federal law in each poverty council: (1) public representatives, (2) private representatives, (3) representatives of the poor. Public representatives meant the state, and local governments such as city councils, county boards of supervisors, and school districts. Private representatives were organized private interests, e.g., businesses, including neighborhood businesses; non-profits; and labor. Representatives of the poor were elected from neighborhoods through procedures established locally and implemented through organizations such as Neighborhood Councils and PACs.[3]

Whatever the intention of the federal legislation, Black people throughout the country and in Sacramento tended to see the War on Poverty and its specific manifestations in Sacramento as theirs. This was part of the narrative afoot in Black spaces. One of the results of the Civil Rights and Black Power movements was the politicization of Black people to a much greater degree than ever before. That coupled with the feeling among Black leaders that they had a mission to use politics to serve the interests of the broad Black population, two-thirds of whom were poor, constituted Black people as the most politicized component of the country's impoverished population, i.e., the Negro Revolution.

In order to be eligible for the anti-poverty program, neighborhoods had to meet low income requirements. Nationally, due to racial residential patterns, neighborhoods which met the poverty criteria tended to be racially homogenous. This was less true in Sacramento, where non-white groups tended to be clustered in scattered pockets, rather than each concentrated in a single neighborhood. While there were mostly Black census tracts, they were present in neighborhoods with mostly non–Black census tracts. There was no poverty neighborhood with a majority Black population. Nevertheless, in neighborhoods with comparatively high percentages of Black residents, Black people conceived of the neighborhoods as their own and acted accordingly. They saw the neighborhoods and the poverty agencies as Black spaces.

A survey directed by faculty from Sacramento State College looking at general participation in neighborhood poverty organizations found that in Del Paso Heights almost three times the number of Black people as white had heard of the neighborhood council, though a majority of residents was white. The numbers of Latinos and Asians who had heard of the council was minimal. Eighty percent of those who actually participated in the local council were Black, 20 percent were whites, and no Latinos or Asians surveyed had participated.[4]

TABLE 2.1 DARYL ENOS SURVEY RESULTS: PARTICIPATION IN NEIGHBORHOOD COUNCILS— DEL PASO HEIGHTS

Response category	White	Mexican-American	Negro	Oriental	Total
Have not heard	7	2	23	0	32
Have heard	11	3	28	1	43
Heard through news media	8	0	6	1	15
Heard, but no personal contact	1	3	12	0	16
Friends	2	0	5	0	7
Church	0	0	3	0	3
Contacted, no participation	0	0	2	0	2
Participated	1	0	4	0	5
TOTAL	30	8	83	2	123

In Glen Elder, where, again, a majority of the population was white, more whites than Blacks had heard of the Neighborhood Council, few Latinos had, and no Asians had, yet *all* of those who actually participated in the council were Black.[5]

TABLE 2.2 DARYL ENOS SURVEY RESULTS: PARTICIPATION IN NEIGHBORHOOD COUNCILS— GLEN ELDER

Response Category	White	Mexican-American	Negro	Oriental	Total
Have not heard	29	4	8	0	41
Have heard	16	4	14	0	34
Heard through news media	3	0	0	0	3
Heard, but no personal contact	6	3	1	0	10
Friends	4	1	4	0	9
Church	0	0	0	0	0
Contacted, no participation	3	0	1	0	4
Participated	0	0	8	0	8
TOTAL	62	12	36	0	108

In Oak Park, again, an area whose majority was white, Black people were 30 percent more likely to have heard of the Neighborhood Council than whites, 70 percent more likely to have heard of it than Latinos, and no Asians had heard of it. All who actually participated in it were Black.[6]

TABLE 2.3 DARYL ENOS SURVEY RESULTS: PARTICIPATION IN NEIGHBORHOOD COUNCILS— OAK PARK

Response Category	White	Mexican-American	Negro	Oriental	Total
Have not heard	9	2	3	0	14
Have heard	25	2	34	0	61
Heard through news media	15	1	5	0	21
Heard, but no personal contact	6	1	2	0	9

Response Category	White	Mexican-American	Negro	Oriental	Total
Friends	2	0	11	0	13
Church	2	0	0	0	2
Contacted, no participation	0	0	0	0	0
Participated	0	0	16	0	16
TOTAL	59	6	61	0	136

In the Southside neighborhood, which was predominantly Latino, whites were more likely to have heard of the council than either Latinos or Blacks, Blacks and Latinos were equally likely to have heard of it, and Asians 50 percent as likely as either Blacks or Latinos to have heard of it. However, no whites or Asians had actually participated in the council, and Blacks were twice as likely to have participated in it as Latinos.[7]

TABLE 2.4 DARYL ENOS SURVEY RESULTS:
PARTICIPATION IN NEIGHBORHOOD COUNCILS—
SOUTHSIDE

Response Category	White	Mexican-American	Negro	Oriental	Total
Have not heard	13	12	8	16	49
Have heard	11	6	6	3	26
Heard through news media	6	1	1	0	8
Heard, but no personal contact	2	2	1	2	7
Friends	1	2	2	0	5
Church	1	0	0	1	2
Contacted, no participation					
Participated	0	1	2	0	3
TOTAL	34	24	20	22	100

The Washington neighborhood was another predominantly Latino neighborhood. Latinos were more likely to have heard of the organization than whites, Blacks, or Asians. Whites were next most likely to have heard of it, Blacks third, and Asians least likely. Yet with respect to those who had actually participated, 25 percent were Black and 75 percent were Latino.[8]

TABLE 2.5 DARYL ENOS SURVEY RESULTS:
NEIGHBORHOOD PARTICIPATION—
WASHINGTON

Response Category	White	Mexican-American	Negro	Oriental	Total
Have not heard	25	19	4	2	50
Have heard	8	11	5	1	25
Heard through news media	2	1	1	1	5
Heard, but no personal contact	2	0	0	0	2
Friends	3	4	1	0	8
Church	1	0	0	0	1
Contacted, no participation	0	3	2	0	5
Participated	0	3	1	0	4
TOTAL	41	41	14	4	100

In every instance the percentage of the Black population participating far exceeded the rate of every other group. This pattern was repeated at the central agency. The first executive director of SAEOC, Marion Woods, was Black. So were three subsequent directors, Naaman Brown, Essie Brown (no relation), and John Robinson. Additionally, significant numbers of the central board members were Black, and the president was often Black. FONO had a Black president, O.W. Clanton, and ultimately appointed a Black executive director, Harry Steele.[9]

It is surprising that in only one neighborhood, Del Paso Heights, did any of the Black people who heard about the neighborhood poverty organization hear about it from the church. And even then, more heard about it from every other source than from the church. In short, the Black domination of poverty organizations was not church based. On the contrary, the church seems to have played a negligible role in that engagement.

Black people who captured parts of this organizational structure felt entitled to run them and reap the benefits. They operated them as Black spaces. They hired and contracted with Black people. Some entered into arrangements which benefited them personally. While Black people generally saw the spoils of the agency as theirs to control and disperse, this did not mean they were in collusion or even cooperative with each other. They certainly were not co-conspirators. On the contrary, they often were in heated conflict. Almost every conceivable animosity arose between them: between board members on a council, between board members and the council's executive director, between one agency's board and another agency's board, between one executive director and another, within an organization's staff, between staffs of different organizations, and various permutations of all of these. Such unending conflicts were features of the anti-poverty agencies which made them fun for the press.[10]

Black Presence in the Polity — A New Dimension

The anti-poverty programs derived from national legislation, accompanying state and local legislation, and implementing regulations at each level. Once the structures required by law and regulation were peopled, the extensive body of rules required continuous interaction between the incumbents of the poverty structure and the incumbents of the constitutional or charter government structures at every level, and in every segment of the state — elected, appointed, and civil service, including the courts. The anti-poverty apparatus itself was an arm of the state. All this meant that the poor, and representatives of the poor — especially the Black poor and their representatives — became more incorporated into the machinery of the state and mandated to interact with that machinery than ever before. Short of Radical Reconstruction, there had never been a remotely comparable compulsion for Black inclusion in the governmental process.

In Sacramento almost all Black people involved in the War on Poverty identified with the Democratic Party, as they did nationwide. This gave them access to Democratic power wielders and power brokers. It gave them inroads to career paths facilitated by the Democratic Party. They worked in Democratic campaigns, sometimes in salaried positions. They were hired to legislative and executive staffs. They became mini power brokers in their own communities. They had access to facilities — offices, phones, mimeograph machines, staffs — and to insider information. All these resources became valuable to them as individuals, to the constituencies they represented, and for the causes they favored. College-trained and professional school graduates worked as executive directors and in high-ranking staff positions as accountants, program analysts, and executive secretaries. Others just entering the job market occupied entry level professional positions. Still others, taking basic clerical roles and custodial positions, found themselves employed when otherwise they would have been entirely without work. The percentage of the Black population benefiting from these positions was small, but to the individuals, the opportunities were invaluable.

While it is often argued that the War on Poverty was stillborn, the Sacramento example does not support that position. It was truncated. It was short lived. But its impact was significant, and in some ways, transforming. Throughout the latter half of the 1960s and the whole decade of the 1970s, the War on Poverty, its structure, procedures, and the people in it were highly visible and significant components of public life nationwide. In most of the country, including Sacramento, the majority of the War on Poverty's actors who received widespread press coverage, and who were popularly identified with the program, were Black. In Sacramento most notably they were the SAEOC directors. But other Black people were also often noted in the press: Willie Hausey, board president of SAEOC; O.W. Clanton, chair of FONO; Callie Carney, from Oak Park; George Heard, from Glen Elder; Charles Bradley, from Del Paso Heights.[11] They were all people who a decade earlier would have had no substantive interactions with the state, but all of whom, under the auspices of the War on Poverty, became significant political role players in the region. They were unknowns in the wider world, but in their world they were agents of transformation.

Wars Within the War

While the War on Poverty had many substantive and long-lasting effects, it was not what anybody wanted. The right saw it as too vast a meddling of the government in the economy and in the society at large. The left saw it as far too little and misdirected. As one wag put it, "We don't need a war on poverty, we need a war on the rich." Even for its formulators and promoters, its promise was never realized. It was drained away by the hellhole of the Vietnam War. The War on Poverty never became more than a pilot program, and all too soon simply withered away. Partially because of its altogether unsatisfactory character for everybody involved — and even the uninvolved — it was throughout its existence a fiery caldron of antagonisms and contestations, rivalries and fears, hates and eruptions.

One Sacramento episode illustrates the bewildering and often chaotic character of the program at the local level. In that incident the BPP sided with the Brown Berets and the Chicano community against organized representatives of the Black population.

On August 13, 1969, the FONO Board met at the Lincoln Christian Center, a Community Outreach Center of the United Christian Centers of Sacramento. The purpose of the meeting was to consider delegate agencies' budget proposals for the following year and recommendations from the SAEOC director of Housing and Economic Development, Peter Hill. In an earlier meeting Hill had indicated he supported all of the proposals except two: the Washington Neighborhood Center and Cabinet, Inc., a youth program headed by George Choung.[12] The Washington Neighborhood Center was in a Chicano neighborhood and largely run by Chicanos. George Choung was Black.

In order to offer support to the Washington Neighborhood Center, a large number of Latinos attended the meeting. Among them were members of the Junior Brown Berets, aged

Opposite: **Black Population Distribution 1975. This scatter diagram represents the pattern of Black residential distribution in Sacramento County. With each dot representing 25 African descendants, it is clear that while Black residents are sprinkled in many areas of the county, they tend to cluster in specific census tracts, and most densely in Oak Park. It is also evident that there are large areas of the county with virtually no Black residents.**

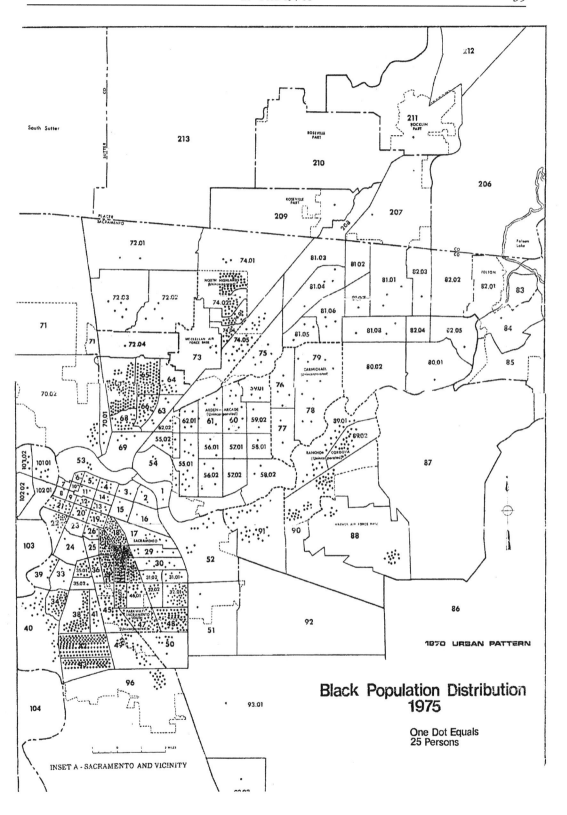

Black Population Distribution
1975

One Dot Equals
25 Persons

1970 URBAN PATTERN

INSET A - SACRAMENTO AND VICINITY

14 to 17. Twenty minutes into the meeting George Choung and nine other young Black men walked in. One carried a baseball bat and another carried a sawed-off golf club. They pushed the Junior Brown Berets around and spit on them. They yelled at the chairman, O. W. Clanton, a Black man. Clanton finally adjourned the meeting.[13]

As people left, Choung's gang erupted. They beat everybody they could reach. Shots rang out. Choung shouted, "The Browns are going to die!"[14]

By the time the police arrived, most of the people had fled. There was nothing for the officers to do. They left.[15]

The next day Choung was seen in a convoy of cars filled with Black youth, many pointing gun barrels out of their windows as they cruised through the Washington Neighborhood.[16]

Members of the Washington Council sent telegrams to everyone from the FBI to the BPP. On September 15, the National Black Panther Party, represented by Bobby Seale, and the Brown Berets, represented by Fred Rodriguez, held a joint press conference. They condemned George Choung for his disruptive behavior, and accused him of attempting to split the Black and Brown communities.[17]

Though more dramatic than most, the scenes represented the level of acrimony that often permeated SAEOC and its delegate agencies.

The War on the Ground

These outbursts and others like them, however, constituted the static, the background noise. SAEOC priorities for 1971 were: employment and job training, family health and planning, child care, improved knowledge of programs, coordination among programs, combating economic deterioration, disorganization, and lack of consumer education.[18] Problems it associated with poverty were: emergency food, credit, housing, nutritional education, and justice. SAEOC established 13 targets. They included: 1,000 permanent jobs, 600 part-time jobs, family planning for 3,000 low-income residents, 700 children in Head Start, and 10,000 residents receiving information on how to get assistance from health services.[19] SAEOC, through FONO, was particularly effective at developing low income housing. FONO initiated two low income public housing projects: Ralph Kennedy Estates, and O.W. Clanton Estates.[20]

SAEOC identified coordinating with existing agencies and services through referrals and joint projects as one of its important functions. There were 24 agencies and services with which it coordinated services on a regular basis. These tasks were monumental, because SAEOC not only had to coordinate with exterior agencies, it had its own formidable infrastructure to manage.[21]

While the poverty program legislation called for "maximum participation of the poor," maximum participation in Sacramento was almost an oxymoron. Studies showed that seven impoverished neighborhoods each contained a minimum of 2,000 families. Some had up to 9,000. Only three had 100 or more residents voting for representatives on neighborhood councils. They were Del Paso Heights with the highest number of voters (136), Washington Neighborhood with the 2nd highest (106), and Oak Park with the third (100). No other neighborhood had more than 80 voters.[22]

TABLE 2.6 TARGET AREA RESIDENTS PARTICIPATING IN THE ELECTIONS
AND VOTING PROCEDURES OF NEIGHBORHOOD COUNCILS

Neighborhood Council	# of low income in target area	Target area council membership	# voting in last election
Delta	3,156	150	60
Cosumnes	5,080	750	80

Neighborhood Council	# of low income in target area	Target area council membership	# voting in last election
GEECIA	2,036	444	50
Southside	9,000	500	59
Oak Park	4,200	370	100
Washington	4,000	360	106
Del Paso Heights	3,156	400	136
Grand Total	30,628	2,974	591

Milton McGhee, the first Black person elected to the Sacramento City Council, was elected at large in 1967. Courtesy of the *Sacramento Observer Newspapers.*

WARRIORS WHO CAME OUT OF SAEOC.　SAEOC developed many Black warriors for the War on Poverty. Some went on to leadership positions within the organization. Others contributed significantly to politics in the city, the state, and the country. A good case in point is Marion Woods, the first executive director of SAEOC. Marion was a graduate of Morehouse College. His role model and the biggest influence on him was his mother. She was a civil rights pioneer in Marietta, Georgia.[23]

When Marion was in the Air Force he was stationed at Mather Field. He liked Sacramento. Not long after he was discharged in 1956, he returned. He got a job with the state, and spurred by his mother's example, he looked for something to do in the community. It struck him that there was no Urban League in Sacramento. He believed the absence was a major shortcoming. Along with Bill Lee and Oliver Sims, he worked to build a local chapter. He was shocked to learn that the Sacramento Community Chest (the forerunner of the United Way) had never heard of the Urban League. Nevertheless, the three men put together a branch. Marion finally left the league because the board of directors was all white.[24]

Marion was director of a State Minority Specialist Program when Virna Canson came to his house and told him about the Equal Opportunity Act. She said, "I think you ought to run this for us."[25] "Us" meant Black people.

Virna's vision was that the Equal Opportunity (poverty) program was a way for Black people to get job experience. They could transition from it to a wide range of positions in government and private employment. Generally, whatever their educational backgrounds, Black people had trouble competing against white candidates with experience. Black people couldn't get the experience because white people wouldn't hire them. It was a catch-22 situation. Virna saw the Equal Opportunity Program as a way to build up an experience bank for Black workers. She thought Marion would be just the person to keep the local program focused on that goal.[26]

Marion applied. Milton McGhee, the Black city councilman, lobbied heavily for his appointment. Marion was named SAEOC's first executive director.[27]

A community of interest in support of Marion and SAEOC arose among Black professionals. A newly patented attorney, Clarence Brown, became the first director of Legal Services for the Poor.[28] This is a striking representation of linked fate — that middle class and poor Black people were both invested in the War on Poverty, but for different reasons.

Without that job Marion would have had no *bona fides* as an executive manager. When he left SAEOC he went back to state government as chief of the management and Demonstration Branch of the State Government. He was subsequently appointed director of the State Services Center by Governor Pat Brown. When Jerry Brown was elected, Marion was appointed director of the Department of Benefits Payments. SAEOC was the first step in a path that moved him from director of the local poverty agency to the director of the California Department of Benefits Payments.[29] Naaman Brown, Essie Brown, and Callie Carnie all had remarkable careers nurtured by their tenures at SAEOC.[30] Yet beyond Sacramento they were invisible.

The War on Poverty — An Intriguing Anomaly

The War on Poverty never had a chance of eliminating poverty in Sacramento or anywhere else. Nor is that solely because of the war in Vietnam. It *is* because of the war in Vietnam that the War on Poverty never became more than a pilot program. To entertain a counter-factual conjecture, it is likely that without the Vietnam War, President Johnson, with an overwhelming Democratic majority in the Congress, as a centerpiece to his legacy, would have pushed through a fully funded campaign to wipe out poverty. It is also likely that the alliance between Johnson and Dr. King would have continued and produced remarkable results. But even a fully funded war on poverty — as conceived — would not have eliminated poverty in the U.S. The War on Poverty did not address the central dynamic of poverty in the U.S.— the distribution of wealth.

The War on Poverty addressed the products of poverty: absence of job skills and employment opportunities, bad health and unstable families, bad housing, absence of child care, lower levels of education, low levels of information about the state and its operations, lack of understanding about the economy, and low levels of nutrition.

Fully funding the elimination of all these deficits would require a significant redistribution of wealth through higher levels of taxation. The military expenditures associated with the Vietnam War *did not* result in wealth transfers. The same amount of spending funneled into the poverty program would have resulted in wealth transfers. In short, without the Vietnam War, taxation levels probably wouldn't have been any higher than they actually were, but the impact of the taxes on wealth distribution would have been substantial.

If we look at what wealth transfers can accomplish — many of the New Deal programs, the G.I. Bill, the Marshall Plan — we see that they can result in not insignificant changes in demographic profiles. None of them, however, eliminated poverty.

The War on Poverty, moreover, was never conceived of as a wealth transfer program. It was seen as, "give 'em crutches, give 'em a cane, give 'em an artificial hand." Help them to help themselves in the most rudimentary ways. Nevertheless, there was one aspect of the War on Poverty which was a wild card factor.[31] It was "the maximum feasible participation of the poor." One responsibility of that aspect of the program was to organize the poor, to mobilize the poor to work for their own benefit — to politicize them to engage the political process on their behalf. Had that part of the program been implemented on a wide scale for the long term, *it could have resulted in significant wealth redistribution.* All of the key players knew that, which is why "maximum feasible participation of the poor" was the most fiercely resisted component of the program. With all the reports, forms, and reporting mechanisms imposed on the program, the goal of organizing and mobilizing the poor was starved of resources. Political organizing, which the mandate to engage the poor amounted to, had to be taken out of the hides of program workers. The poverty agencies simply were not funded to accomplish it.

The Civil Rights Movement had shown what mobilized constituencies of the disenfranchised can do. The War on Poverty had no intention of spawning an economic rights movement. On the contrary, it wanted to enmesh the potential junior officers and non-coms of such a movement in a system of structures and procedures which would prevent them from leading their troops, which would lead them and their picked troops to envision joining the officer corps as a preferred alternative. By and large, *without consciously choosing to,* that is what Marion Woods, Naaman Brown, Essie Brown, Callie Carney, and many others did.

SAEOC survived the decade, but barely. As a new decade rolled around, SAEOC had lost its vibrancy, its initiative, its hope, and its funding. But it had made a significant impact on Sacramento, and it had introduced many descendants of Africa to the political world.

Summary

The Civil Rights Movement enabled the war on poverty to organize and mobilize poor Black people to unprecedented levels. The Black Power Movement sustained that capacity.

As a result, even in Sacramento Black people captured most of the War on Poverty infrastructure and turned their spoils into Black spaces. In part the takeover was a product of the narratives present in broader Black spaces. It was not so much that the War on Poverty produced a particular Black narrative as that a national Black narrative allowed Black people to privilege themselves within the War on Poverty. They — more than any others — were the anointed poverty warriors.

The War on Poverty also made explicit the linked fates of Black people across class lines — middle class Black people benefiting from upper echelon War on Poverty employment, and poor Black people benefiting from poverty programs and lower echelon employment in the war. Both sets of people were linked to the same social program, but for entirely different reasons. Their work and their triumphs were the substance of the Negro Revolution.

Collective Mobilization

By collective mobilization I mean the processes to involve as many Black people as possible in collective action. I consider two categories of collective mobilization: community and activist. By community mobilization I mean the activation of a wide spectrum of Black organizations, leaders, and unaffiliated persons. By activist mobilization I mean the activation of a wide spectrum of organizational and individual *leaders*. Some collective mobilization involved electoral politics. Collective mobilization, both community and activist, was a hallmark of Black politics in the 1960s and '70s in the United States. Yet most of what people know about them is what was reflected on the national stage: the March on Washington, the March on Montgomery, the Panther appearance at the state Capitol in Sacramento, the National Black Assembly.

None of those dramatic events, however, would have been possible without deep stirrings within local populations in every section of the country. By the same token, what transpired nationally often inspired local developments. The trends were mutually re-enforcing. The notions of social spaces, narratives, and memories render the dynamic milieus in which they transpired more accessible. In order to look at these complex relationships in detail, I consider five instances of community mobilization and two instances of activist mobilization in Sacramento. In the electoral arena I note seven instances of community mobilization and two of activist mobilization.

Community Mobilization

THE OAK PARK 4. On June 16, 1969, officers of the Sacramento Police Department (SPD) invaded Oak Park.[32] They sped down neighborhood streets in single file columns, converging on a first floor office on 35th St. They cordoned off the area. Heavily armed policemen charged the headquarters of the Sacramento chapter of the BPP, responding, they said, to reports of shots fired from inside. No one was there. They tore up the place. They scattered organizational files and pamphlets. They smashed typewriters, the telephone, and refrigerator. They trashed food for the Panthers' breakfast program. They knocked out all the windows.[33]

The police, operating as an agent of the hegemonic powers, took over and destroyed a vibrant space Black people had created. While the space was used to carry on activities its creators deemed vital to Black people, it was also used to articulate vehemently anti-hegemonic narratives and foment anti-hegemonic actions.

Thirty-fifth Street was the heart of downtown Oak Park. Black people who frequented the street and McClatchy Park a half a block away had heard about the raid. When they walked by the office they saw the smashed glass and came to the conclusion that the police had shot out the windows in an attempt to kill Panthers. Throughout Black Sacramento that story became the accepted version of what had happened. The raid was a deliberate attempt to kill Panthers.

The police siege of Oak Park was part of the national war against the Panthers by police departments, the FBI, and military intelligence agencies. In Sacramento the chief targets were young Black men, particularly anyone who could be tagged as a militant. On Saturday, May 2, 1970, in their ongoing policy of harassing Black Oak Park residents, the SPD broke up a party in McClatchy Park.[34] They charged young people listening to amplified music, drew their guns, pointed them at people, and used them as cudgels to beat the youngsters who scattered and fled.

Later that evening officers Bernard Bennett and Lloyd Smothers patrolled the same area. A single shot rang out. It hit Bennett in the back of the head and lodged in his brain. He was rushed to the Sacramento Medical Center. Smothers said he thought the shot came from the roof of an unoccupied building on the other side of the street from the Panther office.[35]

Police descended on Oak Park. They stopped, harassed, intimidated, interrogated, and threatened every Black man and youth they saw. They sealed off the area. Sunday and the days afterward they continued to terrorize the neighborhood.[36] The city council offered a $5,000 reward for information leading to an arrest.

On Wednesday morning, May 6, at 10:15 A.M., officer Bennett was pronounced dead.[37] The SPD became a revenge machine. Stops, harassments, threats, and intimidations multiplied and intensified. People were locked up and subjected to jailhouse questioning. One patrol car pulled over a vehicle containing Black teenagers. The officers terrorized them and then placed a placard in the rear window of the car. It read, "Fuck Niggers."[38]

The events of June 16, 1969, triggered Sacramento's entry into a national clash between police departments and urban Black populations originating in 1965 with the Watts uprising and the country's "long hot summers." A smaller rebellion had occurred in 1964 in New York City, but the larger conflagrations began with the Watts uprising, and were repeated in the summers of 1966, 1967, and April of 1968, following the assassination of Dr. King. From 1968 on, police featured crackdowns on the Black Panthers, beginning on the West Coast where the Panthers originated. Sacramento came late to the party, but it came as a full-fledged participant.

POLICE JUSTICE. On May 13, 1970, the Sacramento District Attorney's Office held a press conference to announce that seven Black suspects were being held in connection with officer Bennett's death. They were charged with conspiracy to commit murder. Conviction on the conspiracy charge was subject to the same penalty as conviction for murder: the gas chamber.[39]

Held were Lamont "Buster" Rose, 21, unemployed; Mark Anthony Teemer, 22, Vietnam veteran, SCC student, and artist; Jack Strivers, 19, SCC student; Booker T. Cooke, 20, SCC student; Dale McKinney, 20, SCC student; Ceariaco Cabrillo, 23, married, father, felon, unemployed; Jeffrey Howell, 17, Sacramento High student. Their friends and fellow students labeled them the Oak Park 7.[40]

The next day one of the arrested suspects, Booker T. Cooke, was arrested again, while in custody, in connection with an armed robbery of the Oak Park branch of Bank of America. His link to the robbery was extremely tenuous. He had been stopped during the year-long campaign of police terror. The police said they stopped him because a bank robbery had occurred in the area. They released him because he had *no physical resemblance* to the suspect. That stop constituted the only grounds for his later *arrest and indictment for bank robbery.* From the SPD point of view, the arrest and indictment for bank robbery would be good to have on his record when he went on trial for conspiracy to commit murder.[41]

By early June the Oak Park 7 had dropped to five. Lamont "Buster" Rose, drug addicted felon, was released, as was the high school student, Jeffrey Howell.[42] The now Oak Park 5 was a remarkable collection of young men. All were, or had been, students at SCC. Two, Cooke and McKinney, had been president of the BSU at SCC. All had been active in the BSU. Teemer was not only a Vietnam vet who had been wounded in Vietnam and received the Purple Heart, he was a natural leader. He had been lieutenant of Culture in the BPP, and was one of the party's artists. He had been active in the Panthers' Breakfast Program. Since leaving the Panthers he had dedicated himself to converting an abandoned Oak Park building on the same block as the Panther office into a community art center for children. He had completed the physical labor himself, with the help of friends, including Cabrillo. Teemer was so ardent and articulate in his zeal for the center he had secured funding from white patrons to launch the center as a full-scale operation with a paid staff. The grand opening had been scheduled for what turned out to be the week following his arrest.[43]

Striver was raised as an army brat and had lived all over the world. He was a gifted and eloquent student who had joined the Panthers out of a deep commitment to Black people. He was a leader in the SCC Black Student Union and was actively involved in racial uplift. Cabrillo was married with a daughter to support. He too had a passion to work for the betterment of Black people. He had labored beside Teemer to renovate the site for the proposed art center. He was looking forward, following the grand opening, to assuming a paid position in the center.[44]

Almost as soon as the initial seven were arrested, SCC students and other community activists started a legal defense fund for the defendants. Under the name of the Oak Park Community Legal Defense Fund, they immediately began to pursue two objectives: (1) raising money for legal representation of the defendants, (2) educating the public about the actual circumstances involved in the charges and arrests. The Defense Fund held fundraisers, collected contributions, sponsored rallies, accepted public speaking engagements, visited the defendants in jail, encouraged others to write and visit the defendants, and published information bulletins on the ongoing procedures.[45] This process created Black spaces and narratives for the defense of the Oak Park 5.

A series of lawyers represented the defendants. Two who were hired early and never left the defense team were young Black men who had finished law school and passed the bar just the previous year, James L. Long and Joseph Cooper. One other Black lawyer, Doug Grier, one of Sacramento's most established and respected lawyers, joined the team. The other attorneys associated with the defense were white: Donald Buchman, Christopher Longaker, John E. Virga, and Robin Yeaomans, the only female defense lawyer.[46]

DOWN TO FOUR, WHAT'S GOIN' ON? By early July charges had been dropped against Dale McKinney and the alleged conspirators had been reduced to four.[47]

At the same time one battle was going on in the courts, another was going on outside the courts. Because of the racialized nature of spaces and narratives in the U.S., only one side was aware of the second combat zone. On one side was the white press: the *Sacramento Bee,* the *Sacramento Union,* the radio and television stations; on the other, the Black press, represented by the *Sacramento Observer*, and the Oak Park Community Legal Defense Fund. This out-of-court battle was an attempt to frame the contested issues. It was a battle in Black spaces and Black narratives which invoked the question raised by the popular Marvin Gaye song of the period, "What's Goin' On?"

The *Bee*, the *Union*, and the electronic media recognized no perplexity. They *knew* what was going on: the search for justice. Their narratives were concerned with describing what was involved in the cold-blooded murder of a young white police officer, and the violent, depraved, and despicable world from which the killer came.

While everybody in Sacramento was exposed to the description proffered by the popular newspapers, radio, and television stations, only Black people — and far from all of them — were privy to the discourses suggesting there was any perplexity involved in the search for justice. On October 1, the *Observer*, a weekly, put out a supplement which examined the case in detail. The *Observer* covered the case in every issue, a coverage amplified by letters to the editor from its readers, letters which described what was happening in their neighborhoods, to them, and their children. The Defense Fund published and distributed its bulletin and spoke before innumerable meetings. The people reading the *Observer* and the bulletin, the people listening to the speakers for the Defense Fund, were almost exclusively Black. In frequenting Black spaces, they were exposed to the narratives present there.

Neither Marvin Gaye's question nor the population from which he and it arose, spoke to other Sacramentans. Neither the persons nor neighborhoods (social spaces) of non–Black Sacramentans were subject to police terror. Nor did the mainstream media report it. Other residents were not exposed to the police contempt for and rage at so-called militants. They were not witnesses to, nor were they provided witness of, the blatantly illegal actions of the SPD. They had no frame of reference, nor were they provided one, whereby they might see the young men on trial as heroes and role models. Spatially and perceptually they lived in a different world from their Black counterparts. In Black spaces the case was covered continuously. In mainstream spaces it appeared sporadically.

The paradoxes at play were on broad display before substantial proportions of the Black population. Many who did not read the *Observer*, the Defense Fund Bulletin, or hear speakers from the Defense Fund, were nevertheless exposed to those views through conversations of relatives, friends, and acquaintances. Many had no need for external reports. They themselves were witnesses or even objects of stops, searches, pestering, of groundless questioning. Black people were aware of the superficial nature of white views on the case — they were exposed to them every bit as much as white people were. White people and others (Latinos, Asians, Native Americans) had not a clue of the framing of the case employed by Black people, nor of the detailed information which substantiated it. While one group was not aware there were any grounds for challenging the justice of the process, the members of the other group were not only aware of the grounds, they also knew why whites had no such suspicions. They lived in a world dominated by white narratives.

The *Observer* and the Oak Park Community Legal Defense Fund, in asking, "What's goin' on?" were saying that almost every young, Black male in Oak Park had been harassed, intimidated, roughed up, threatened, arrested, jailed, or all of the above. Did this constitute an impartial investigation? Of the original Oak Park 7 only one was not a Black militant, Lamont "Buster" Rose, and he was the first one released, although he had an extensive criminal record and documented mental instability. They raised the question of whether the police made a deal with him for incriminating testimony against the others. Did the $5,000 reward enter into the picture?

They pointed out that the young men being held were industrious, personally responsible, and seekers of justice. In addition to being college students, they devoted much of their time to community uplift.

Why were the police allowed to break the law with impunity while it appeared the only offense committed by the Oak Park 4 was that they were all Black militants? Had being a Black militant become a capital crime? Only the Black public was exposed to this counter-narrative.

In the pretrial proceedings the prosecution identified its key witness, Lamont "Buster" Rose. Prosecutors indicated he had spilled the beans on his once alleged co-conspirators.[48]

The defense said there were no grounds for the prosecution to proceed. Mr. Rose was a known drug addict. He had been arrested for both possession and sale. Defense investigators had uncovered findings of brain damage and mental incompetence. Since Rose's testimony was almost without supporting evidence, and he was the only self-identified witness, there were no grounds on which to proceed. As the Community Defense Fund bulletin pointed out, there is no gun, no fingerprints, no competent witness, in fact, no evidence. Additionally, though on the night of the killing, officer Smothers had said the shot was fired from a building across the street from the BP headquarters, by the time of the trial the location of the shooter had moved to the roof of the BP building.[49]

In pretrial testimony Rose said he overheard the four defendants plan the murder of a police officer. He also said he saw the shooting, though it was night and at a distance and he could not identify the shooter.[50]

The district attorneys arraigned one of their own witnesses on felony charges. They delayed his arraignment, keeping him in jail, and set his bail at $3,300. The alleged felony arose from an exchange between the prosecuting attorneys and the witness. The prosecutors asked, "Did you tell the police that you heard people talking about sniping at policemen that night?" The witness replied, "No." The witness was then charged with lying under oath (a felony). Defense counsel argued this was a blatant attempt to intimidate witnesses, not only the extant one. Other witnesses who heard about what had happened to him would be intimidated from saying anything other than what the prosecution wanted to hear. The judge took no action and the trial continued.[51]

The police and the D.A.'s office were concerned about resting the case on the back of their felonious, drug-addicted, and mentally unbalanced star witness. As a result, from the scores of Black men and teenagers they had rousted in the twelve days following the murder of officer Bennett, they took aggressive measures to identify other witnesses. They came up with four.

The problems with the prosecutors' case began when they presented Rose. Because of the centrality of his testimony, he was on the witness stand for more than a week.[52] He indicated, somewhat less confidently than his pretrial testimony indicated, that he had both heard the conversation which was evidence of a conspiracy, and had witnessed the conspirators firing the shot. That was not all he testified to. Under cross examination he testified that he was using drugs the week of the shooting, that he was prone to lapses of memory, that he sometimes lied, and that he had once — while not high on either drugs or alcohol — seen a giant walking across a street, and that on another occasion he had seen brains jumping in the street.[53] To have any credibility, Rose's testimony would require corroboration.

The first of the corroborating witnesses, Joseph "Jody the D.J." Ramey, told the court he wanted to recant the testimony he had given to police on June 25. When the judge asked why, Ramey said because it was involuntary. The judge excused the jurors from the courtroom. He held hearings to determine whether the initial testimony was voluntary or involuntary.[54]

Ramey said he woke up on May 29 looking into the barrel of a police shotgun. That shook him up because one of his Chicago high school friends, the Black Panther leader Fred Hampton, was killed by police the year before.[55] One of Ramey's friends, Ray Sylvester, said when he came to visit Ramey on the morning of the 29th, he was met at the door by shotgun wielding police.[56]

Police officers denied they had used any weapon to threaten Ramey. The chief deputy D.A., Edward Garcia, denied he had ever offered Ramey a $5,000 reward, safe conduct out of Sacramento, and spending money in exchange for his testimony.[57] A Youth Authority parole agent, who was on the raid on Ramey's house, when asked whether the police pointed a shotgun at Ramey and threatened him, answered, "I don't recall."[58] This was extremely weak support for the prosecution from a law enforcement witness.

On January 9, 1971, Judge DeCristiforo threw out Ramey's testimony.[59] He said the police simply had kept after the witness "until he produced a result acceptable to them."[60] One of the four legs upholding Lamont Rose's shaky testimony was kicked away. The defense moved for a mistrial, but the judge denied it.[61]

The next prosecution witness, Kenneth Diagre, also wanted to recant. He said he was afraid "if I didn't tell 'em what they wanted to hear they would book me for conspiracy."[62] DeCristoforo disallowed his earlier testimony as coerced. Two legs of the stool were gone.[63]

The third witness, Lee Hawkins, refused to testify. He pleaded the Fifth Amendment. DeCristoforo held him in contempt. It made no difference. He would not testify.[64] The third leg fell. One leg could not support a stable stool, much less the rickety one Lamont Rose sat on.

The prosecution moved to abandon the case. The judge accepted the motion. He dismissed the case against all four defendants.[65] Teemer, Cabrellis, and Striver were immediately released from custody. Sadly, Booker Cooke was kept in jail because the egregious charge of armed bank robbery was still pending against him — a charge made only to strengthen the flimsy case the judge had just thrown out of court.[66] Showing his true law enforcement colors, the sheriff immediately threw Cooke into the hole.[67]

AFTERMATH. The Oak Park 4 case represented a pattern of relations between Sacramento's Black population and Sacramento's white population, between the Black population and the police department, and between the Black population and the mainstream media that persisted through the decade. It also prefigured tendencies *within* the Black population which reappeared throughout the next ten years. This is not to suggest that any of these relationships arose in 1970 with the Oak Park 4, that they were not of much earlier derivation. It is to assert that the Oak Park 4 case serves as a revealing metaphor for many long-term features of Black political life in Sacramento. Because of similarities with what transpired in other municipalities at the same time, it is also suggestive about dynamics at work all over the country.

While the wider public viewed the police investiture of the Panther headquarters in June of 1969 as an attempt to apprehend a dangerous gunman who was shooting from the Panther office and endangering the public safety, most Black people in the city remembered it as cowboy policemen attacking and shooting up the Panther office in an attempt to kill Panthers. While the broader public viewed police activity in Oak Park on May 2 and subsequent days and nights as a manhunt for a cop killer, most Black people experienced it and remembered it as a demented police force unleashing blind fury on the Black population. The same thing had happened in Oakland with the police murder of the Panther, Little Bobby Hutton. The same thing had happened in Chicago with the police murder of Fred Hampton and Mark Clark. This trauma was happening to Black communities all over the country and the attendant Black populations reacted to it in similar ways.

To Black people the kind of police and prosecutory behavior they experienced was capricious and arbitrary. It did not contribute to their greater security and public order; rather it fostered disorder and great feelings of insecurity. African descendants felt themselves assaulted as a people and responded accordingly. They developed and strengthened existing organizations and institutions, mobilized them, and found ways to operate them in cooperation with each other.

The Oak Park 4 is a marker of polarization based on race. It was a polarization between Blacks and whites. Chicanos (as politically conscious Latinos in Sacramento called themselves then), Asians (almost exclusively Chinese and Japanese then), and Native Americans did not figure in this specific racial polarization. The white population, in the main, believed the SPD and the D.A.'s office were in the right. The Black population, in the main, believed the SPD and the D.A.'s office were in the wrong, and whether the Oak Park 4 were in the right or not, *they had been wronged.* Despite the final outcome, it had been an injustice for them to have been arrested, held without bail, indicted, and tried in the first place. Many Black people believed not only had the SPD and the DA lied and acted illegally (as was established in court), but also that they did so with wanton disregard for any semblance of the truth or justice for Black people. They were not to be trusted.

Many Black people also believed *the white media* had acted without regard for the truth or any semblance of the truth, and that they, too, were not to be trusted. Significant aspects of the Black population believed that white people in general were hopelessly out of touch with life, particularly as Black people experienced it.

Black narrative and social memory drew clear lessons from the Oak Park 4. *White people are afraid of competent Black people. They freed the drug-addicted, brain-damaged man. They want to send the leaders, the artistic, articulate, intelligent, activist, courageous young Black men with social consciences to the gas chamber. They want to kill us if we are going to realize our potential.*

Nor did the final outcome of the Oak Park 4 make the SPD better disposed toward Black people. The police put how they felt in writing: "Fuck Niggers." They believed "the niggers" got away with murder. The SPD launched an unending vendetta against every member of the Oak Park 4. The spaces occupied by the SPD developed and retained a specific and vengeful narrative pointed at the Oak Park 4. It shaped a powerful and sustained social memory centered around retribution. That kind of deep-seated animosity among police officers and criminal justice officials around the country attached itself to those perceived as rioters, militants, trouble-makers, and others of their ilk. In Sacramento as elsewhere it did not bode well for future relationships between those pledged to protect and serve, and those whose initial and long-standing role in the country had been solely humility and service. The social memory of past years remained for Black people, but their new narratives called on them to reject that place out of hand.

A CRITICAL CATALYST FOR BLACK SACRAMENTANS. When the Oak Park 4 occurred the *Sacramento Observer* was 7 years old. It was a fledgling newspaper. The *Observer*'s editor and publisher was just as upset by officer Bennett's murder as most Sacramentans. He wanted the guilty party found and punished. In a way, the *Observer* was a voice of Sacramento's new Black middle class. Bill Lee and his wife, Kathryn, were by 1970 the sole owners of the publication. Lee worked in real estate. His father was a minister. Kathryn came from one of Sacramento's leading Black families. Like *Ebony* magazine, the *Observer* generally portrayed upbeat, positive features of Black life. Its pages featured pictures and articles about the Alphas, the Deltas, the Links, and Les Belles Artes Club. Church celebrations, newly appointed executives, successful business owners, outstanding students, and women's club events were all regular fare. It was a chance to say something good about Black people. Articles and columns written by the executive director of the national NAACP, the National Urban League, and Black members of Congress celebrated Black leadership and Black ideas. These were all spokespersons of the Black middle class.[68]

SNCC, the Panthers, Angela Davis and Jonathon Jackson appeared in the *Observer*. Frequently, along with Malcolm X, the Nation of Islam, and H. Rap Brown, they were highlighted. But the staple fare was provided by the ideas, the photos, and the aspirations of the Black middle class.

Whatever else the Oak Park 4 were, they were not the middle class ideal. Two had been Panthers. One, Cabrillo, had a criminal record. All were militants. All were members and leaders of the B.S.U. They were poor. They wore Black berets and leather jackets. As Panthers they had carried guns. One could hardly say they were genteel. They were college students, and that was laudable, but they were college students in a way not preferred by most of Sacramento's Black *bourgeoisie*. They were not at Berkeley, not at Spelman or Morehouse, not even at Sacramento State College. They were at City College, a junior college. They were admirable young men for what they had overcome and against what odds. They were highly motivated. Their values of service and social commitment met the highest standards of the Black population. But if you were a physician, a dentist, a lawyer, an administrator for the state, a successful real estate broker, would you want your daughter to marry one?

Bill Lee wanted the murderer captured. He looked at the arrests. He looked at the life stories of the indicted young men. He looked at the rousting by the police department. He looked at the $5,000 reward money, and he looked at the evidence. He witnessed the founding of the Oak Park Community Legal Defense Fund. He read what they had to say. Lawyers talked to him. In a sense, Marvin Gaye's question formulated in his mind: "What's goin' on?" He decided to look at the case more closely. He wanted others to look at it more closely, too. Ultimately his examination led him to come out on the side of the Oak Park 4.

This position, reached by the penultimate spokesperson for Sacramento's Black middle class, preshadowed a tendency that was to appear again and again: cross-class collaboration among Black people, cooperation between politically moderate Black people and politically militant Black people, and linked fate.

The Oak Park 4 united Black people in Sacramento. They did not achieve unanimity, but people of quite different persuasions and vastly different social backgrounds joined in common sentiment and sometimes in common action. Young Black men just out of law school made cause with young Black men indicted for capital crimes and held for trial without bond. College students raised money to pay lawyers and developed information to persuade Black people to support their cause. The college students forged bonds with the broader Black population and with activists from that population. This pattern, too, unfolded throughout the '70s. It provides substantiation for the proposition of linked fate concerning African descended people in the U.S., widely examined by Black political scientists. Perhaps the most succinct expression of the linked fate proposition is provided by Michael Dawson: "The historical experiences of African Americans have resulted in a situation in which group interests have served as a useful proxy for self-interest."[69]

The Oak Park School of Afro-American Thought, founded by the BSU at SCC, served as the headquarters for the Oak Park Community Legal Defense Fund. That marked an important component of Black politics throughout the '70s — the capture of a public space by Black people, turning it into a Black space. In this case Black students captured a segment of a public educational institution and used its resources to help realize their own objectives. It was turned into a Black space. The pattern was that Black people, students *as well as others*, captured public spaces, public resources, and used them, specifically, to benefit Black people.

The same thing had happened in the War on Poverty. This was a way that Black people all over the country were waging successful struggle, capturing state resources (although modest, far more than anything they possessed) and using them for their own purposes. What was most gratifying to Black people about the Oak Park 4 instance was that the Black students won. Equally satisfying was that this was not a solitary victory. Against all odds, against the entrenched powers that dominated and controlled public spaces, time and time again, Black people found ways to prevail. Such triumphs were expressed through narratives in Black spaces and became incorporated into Black social memory.

The Police Murder of Raymond Brewer

In 1972 there had been a series of armed robberies of bars in North Sacramento, a working class white neighborhood, contiguous with the Heights. The robber was described as a young, Black male. Undercover police officers had staked out bars in the area. Raymond Brewer was fifteen years old, an outstanding student and an athlete at Grant High School. His parents worked at McClellan Air Force Base. One evening he was walking through North Sacramento with companions on his way home. He was carrying a stick which he used to fend off the stray dogs endemic to the area. *Not many young Black males ventured through North Sacramento in the evening hours.* Several plainclothed officers leaped from their hiding places, weapons drawn. They shouted for the boys to halt. They took off running. The police opened fire. Raymond Brewer died in the street.[70]

In their defense, the police said Brewer was armed. Yes, it was true, it was only a stick, but when they first saw it, in the dark, they thought it was a gun. Also, if he were innocent, why did he run? They told him to halt. Didn't he see they had drawn their guns? They finally admitted killing him was a mistake. He was not the armed robber. But it was an honest mistake. Anyone could have made it. Tensions were high. It was a regrettable incident.

When the city council met after the killing, the 2nd floor chambers were filled with furious Black people. The hall outside the chambers was filled, as was the stairwell down to the first floor, the lobby, and further steps outside the building, leading to the street, where enraged citizens poured all over the sidewalks. When the floor was opened for the apoplectic residents to speak, they all but tore the roof off. They said there was no defense for the PD. It was dark; they couldn't see Brewer clearly; they couldn't even tell that what he was carrying was not a shotgun, but a stick. He was a boy, not even a big boy, a fifteen year old. He was not a man. They had jumped at him out of the darkness, shouting, waving, and pointing guns. In his terror it was unlikely he even understood what they said. They were a lot of angry white men, making a lot of noise and waving guns.[71] They were not wearing uniforms. *They were undercover.* They were in street clothes. To Brewer they were probably the kind of hooligans who frequented North Sacramento, which was one of the reasons Black people usually avoided it. They victimized Black people. *And he was not supposed to run?* Were they absolutely crazy? They opened fire. They shot him down in the street as if he were a mad dog. He was a kid, a good kid, a role model, the kind of kid we need more of, and they took him away from us. They didn't even give him a chance to identify himself. They could easily have taken him into custody. There were several of them, grown men, and he was a boy.[72]

That night the mayor, Richard Marriot, said he would appoint a citizens' commission to investigate SPD practices, and to make policy recommendations to the city council. It would be provided with funds, complete police cooperation, and open access to the police department and departmental records. Once appointed, the commission included a cross-section of the city, including, specifically, residents of the Heights and Black organizations.

In this instance, a city council meeting, a hegemonic space, was converted into a Black space. It became a Black space in which Black narrative prevailed. There was no countervailing narrative. No member of the city council and no member of the city staff brought to the dais challenged the belligerent Black speakers. And while the police chief did not capitulate, he admitted the terrible, regrettable tragedy of the night Raymond Brewer died at the hands of his officers and promised complete cooperation with the citizens' commission.

The Sacramento Police Officers Association was not in agreement with what transpired in city hall, but they did not step forward into that forum to challenge it. On that night the city council had become an alien space for them, and they kept their presence and their narrative out of it. After all, their charge was preserving the public peace, and their entrance into that arena could have produced an unpredictable and uncontrollable reaction.

The Nation of Islam

In late April of 1974 Sacramento experienced a rash of shootings. This was during the same time that the so-called Zebra murders were going on in San Francisco. The San Francisco police had alleged connections between the Zebra murders and the Nation of Islam. In Sacramento, within a one week period, two citizens and a police officer, Bakarich, were shotgunned. The police officer was hospitalized, as was one of the civilians. The second civilian, Joseph H. Belmore, was killed. Within an hour after Belmore's murder, police arrested three young, Black men, all members of Sacramento's Temple of the Nation of Islam, number 73. They were driving a car which police said fit the description of a car seen at the murder scene. A number of weapons were found in the car, including a shotgun police believed was the murder weapon. A fourth suspect, also a member of Temple number 73, was arrested the following day and charged with the shooting of Officer Bakarich.[73]

The SPD cordoned off the 35th Street area, where Temple number 73 was located across the street from the former Black Panther Headquarters. They saturated the whole neighborhood with police cars, blocked off streets, put officers on foot up and down both sides of 35th Street where the temple was situated, and with a massed force of heavily armed police troopers, broke into the sanctuary, breaking doors, knocking out windows, smashing furniture, ransacking and trashing the worship place in their search for evidence. The organized Black community rose up in unified support of the Nation, castigating the PD for its blatant desecration of the religion's inner sanctum. How many times had police departments in the U.S. violated Christian churches, especially white, Christian churches, when members of their congregations had been suspected of committing crimes? The raid set off a flash point for

African people in Sacramento. Black spokespeople held press conferences, went to city hall, and jammed the police chief's office, demanding apologies and restitution.[74]

The Nation of Islam was a national institution. What happened to it in Sacramento had happened to it elsewhere — in Chicago, and in Los Angeles. Nowhere did Black people sit idly by. Though almost all Black people were Christians, they wasted no time rushing to the defense of their Muslim brothers and sisters. Their reactions were generated by the national context, the national atmosphere. Invasions of homes and temples of the Nation of Islam were invasions of homes and temples of Black people. That was intolerable. For the whole history of the country white people had carried on such raids with impunity. The Civil Rights Movement and the Black Power Movement had led Black people to proclaim, "Never again!" You may still do it, but now — every time — there will be a price to pay.

MILTON BAKER, JR. The Milton Baker, Jr., Community Coalition for Justice resulted from the murder of a young Black man.

> On July 25, 1979, at 3:30 PM, 17-year-old Milton Baker, Jr. was stabbed in the heart and then beat on the head with the top of a garbage can as he ran down the street fleeing his assailants.
>
> Dennis Glenn Fisher, 22, and Brett Conway, 18, the two men responsible for Baker's killing were not even arrested.[75]

Black residents and activists called a protest rally which resulted in the formation of the Milton Baker, Jr., Community Coalition. The coalition organized Black people throughout the county to join and participate in its activities. It sponsored neighborhood meetings, countywide rallies and demonstrations, and initiated letter-writing campaigns to the local newspapers. It met with the County Board of Supervisors, with police department and sheriff's department officials, and with local prosecutors. The committee's work brought intense attention to the operation of the county sheriff's department.

One of the assailants, Brett Conway, was the son of a California Highway Patrol employee. The committee demanded: (1) That the sheriff be ordered to re-open and conduct a proper and thorough investigation of the case; (2) The district attorney be ordered to properly investigate and evaluate probable criminal conduct and prosecute if the facts warrant; (3) The assailants be required to guarantee their presence in the county; (4) That the Board of Supervisors recommend the grand jury investigate the case; and (5) The establishment of a community advisory council for the sheriff's department. This flagrant dereliction of the police authority was another occasion when many sectors of the Black population stood together long enough and effectively enough to result in a public condemnation of law enforcement's complicity in the slaying of a Black person. As a result of the demands and public pressure, the county took steps 1, 2, and 4.[76]

DR. KING'S BIRTHDAY. The Committee for the Commemoration of Dr. King's Birthday was begun by a Del Paso Heights Black activist, George Smith, and his wife. They enlisted the support of Grant High School students who were backed by teachers and administrators. Smith led the students and other supporters on a six mile march from the Grant High School campus to the state Capitol. They were joined at the rallying point and along the march by thousands of participants. The march launched the effective phase of the statewide campaign to recognize Dr. King's birthday as a state holiday. The legislation was backed by the California Legislative Black Caucus.[77] The Committee for the Commemoration, along with a host of organizations statewide, supported the caucus in passing the holiday legislation in California long before the national holiday was signed into law by a reluctant former California governor.

Activist Mobilization

Bob Tyler. As the 1970s began, the executive director of the Sacramento Human Rights Commission was Bob Tyler. He was a Black man who had been active in the Sacramento Civil Rights movement. As chair of the local CORE (Congress of Racial Equality) chapter he had led a successful boycott protesting the hiring practices of a local retailer. He was a vested member of Sacramento's Black leadership. The Human Relations Commission dismissed him from his post as executive director without cause.

The Black Civil Rights community was incensed. The Sacramento Area Black Caucus, the NAACP, the Urban League, Black Professional Associations, the Black city councilman, local school board members, Equal Employment Opportunity directors, and poverty program warriors, telephoned each other, met, and decided to express their collective indignation at the next Human Rights Commission meeting.

The Human Rights Commission meeting was packed with Black faces. Each Black speaker was greeted with thunderous applause and shouts of approval. The meeting became a Black space. The sole narrative was Black. It castigated the commission for taking an unwarranted action and doing it in the most callous and precipitous way.

The commission rescinded its earlier action and reinstated Tyler. Sacramento's Black leadership had operated as an impromptu committee of the whole. Acting as a quasi-government of the Black nation, they delivered a pronouncement condemning the commission's earlier action and calling on the commission to do the right thing. In this instance, they carried the day.

The Formation of the Sacramento Area Black Caucus. In 1972 Bill Lee sent out invitations to organizational and individual Black leaders to meet in his conference room. On meeting day the room was filled and the group decided to keep meeting, without Lee. As a journalist he felt his responsibility was to act as a catalyst, not to be part of the organization. His intention, later adopted by those who continued to meet, was to establish a council, a governing Caucus which would speak as the united voice of the Black population. As originally constituted, with both organizational and individual memberships, the Caucus represented the voice of the organized Black community. It led a successful boycott, challenged the dearth of Black appointees on the city's boards and commissions, induced the county to create the office of director of Affirmative Action, and selected the first occupant of the position. It had one of its members appointed to the Citizens' Commission on Police Practices after the police murder of Raymond Brewer. The whole range of Black organizations and incumbents of important civic positions consulted with each other, joined hands, and collectively constituted this active and aggressive organization. It legitimately spoke on behalf of the broad Black population, and it wielded considerable clout.

After its first two years the SABC no longer functioned as an umbrella organization. Most of the non–Black political community did not know that. The Caucus continued to exercise disproportionate influence for years, a condition enhanced by its annual capacity to draw over 10,000 African descendants to the Black Unity Festival. The collective mobilization of Sacramento's Black leadership made the creation of this formidable organization possible.

Community Intervention at CSU Sacramento. Two instances of activist mobilization occurred at California State University. The first arose following the removal of Albert Shockley from a speaker's platform by the Pan African Student Union. The university moved to expel all PASU members. The Pan African Student Union and the program's faculty went to Black leaders — organizational and individual. They called on the leaders to use their collective influence to make a significant impact on the university. Leaders encompassing the whole spectrum of the Black population present in the initial SABC agreed to act on behalf of the students. Some were members of the University President's Council (a group of local grandees invited to meet with the president at regular intervals in an advisory capacity). A compromise was reached whereby some PASU members involved in Shockley's removal were allowed to transfer from the campus in good standing and others received no penalty.

The second instance arose when the university decided Pan African Studies was passé and should be terminated. PASU and the Pan African Studies faculty returned to the same spectrum of Black leaders to save the program. The leaders met with Black students and faculty to develop an understanding of the characteristics of the Pan African Studies program, its roles in the university and curriculum, its strengths, its weaknesses, and its unique attributes. Afterwards, they met among themselves and subsequently scheduled a meeting with the university president. When they met with him and his cabinet their position was unequivocal: *The program must continue, with the wholehearted support of the university and the president.*

The president acceded to their wishes. Neither he nor any other member of the university administration raised the question again. In each instance an array of Black leaders mobilized for what they believed to be the best interests of the wide African-descended population, within and outside the university.

Around the country the instances where this kind of activity by Black student organizations took place were legion. Some of the more noted were at San Francisco State, UCLA, Cornell, Northwestern, and even Howard. There were also many occasions when mobilized Black communities supported Black student organizations in their struggles with university administrations. Cities where such struggles took place included New York, Detroit, Chicago, Los Angeles, and Berkeley.

Electoral Mobilization

Nationally, Black electoral mobilization received a great deal of attention. Most widely publicized were Shirley Chisholm's run for the Democratic presidential nomination, and mayoral elections such as Carl Stokes in Cleveland, Richard Hatcher in Gary, and Kenneth Gibson in Detroit, as well as the later triumphs of Black mayors in Atlanta and New Orleans. The same processes which made those flagship electoral challenges and victories possible took place in places where they were less expected — in the case of municipal elections, in places where Black people were far from a majority, such as Sacramento.

COMMUNITY. A number of elections in the 1970s involved mass Black collective mobilization. They were Robbie Robertson's campaign for the Sacramento City Council from District 2 in 1971; Charles Bradley's campaigns for the District 2 seat in 1975 and 1979; Callie Carney's and Dan Thompson's campaigns for the District 5 seat in 1977; and campaigns in the Del Paso Heights Elementary School District and the Grant Joint Union High School District.

Robbie Robertson's and Charles Bradley's campaigns involved extensive mobilization in Del Paso Heights — door-to-door efforts concentrated on increasing the number of Black registered voters and turning out Black voters for the primary and general elections. In the case of Charles Bradley's campaigns, workers and contributors were recruited from throughout the region. They were brought in to help mobilize Black people in the Heights. During the 1977 campaign these efforts were augmented by Black activists in the Heights who organized and ran a Black political convention which chose Bradley as the single Black candidate to run for the seat.

Both Callie Carney's and Dan Thompson's campaign for the same seat in 1977 mobilized Black voters and activists within District 5 and throughout the region. Both campaigns ran voter registration efforts targeting Black voters in Oak Park.

In the Del Paso Heights Elementary School District, there were multiple elections during the '70s and multiple candidates in each election. I consider mobilization in the district, however, as one collective mobilization event because of the narrow focus of the campaigns — restricted to Del Paso Heights. While they were significant political efforts, they were less intense than city council campaigns which included the Heights. The Black mass collective mobilization effort for the Grant Joint Union High School District was also restricted to the Heights, though the election encompassed the whole Grant district of which Del Paso Heights was only a small part.

ACTIVISTS. In both District 2 in 1973, and District 5 in 1976, Black activists from throughout the Sacramento area lobbied the city council to fill council vacancies with a Black person.

Summary

The most dramatic mass collective mobilization efforts arose directly from conflicts with the police department. No other segment of the national population had been under such relentless police assault as people of African descent. As a result, no other population had to organize, mobilize, and defend itself as ferociously. In the past predation of Black people had been routine, the norm. By 1970, however, Black people had determined to change what was routine, what was normal. It could no longer be normal to charge the pride of the population with capital crimes without evidence. It could no longer be normal for police to murder promising Black youths for walking through white neighborhoods. It could not be normal for the police to break into Black houses of worship, smash and trash them, take the congregation's records. It could no longer be normal to release without charge white youths who were family or friends of the police who had been witnessed beating a Black man to death. This wasn't happening to any other group of people. Black people were under tremendous pressures to galvanize themselves in unprecedented ways. They did.

With the exception of the formation of the SABC, activist collective mobilization tended to arise in instances involving offences against individuals, usually high profile individuals. Black people saw themselves under attack, not only by the police, but by the society at large: being fired without cause from leadership positions, being thrown out of the university, having fields of study devoted to them targeted for closure. That had been the norm for over 350 years. No more. Continually, Black people sought collectively to teach the society that the string had run out.

If these tendencies of onslaught and resistance were found in Sacramento, and we see quite clearly they were, it doesn't take much imagination to project what was going on in Oakland, Los Angeles, Dallas, Houston, Cleveland, Chicago, Boston, New York, Newark, Atlanta, and Mobile.

Electoral collective mobilization transpired under different circumstances than other expressions of collective mobilization. In the case of electoral mobilization we witness what transpired in the arena of routine political change, where political change was formalized, and from which except for the brief experiment of Reconstruction, Black people had been routinely excluded. In this field, Black people organized and mobilized at unprecedented levels — at the mass level for elections and the activist level for appointments.

Black Organizations

This initial consideration of Black organizations undertakes three principal tasks: (1) a discussion of Black organizations in the U.S. generally and pertinent propositions in the literature; (2) a description and analysis of the universe of Sacramento's Black organizations during the '70s; and (3) a detailed examination of a single Sacramento Black organization during the decade.

Black Organizations in the U.S.

In the U.S. there are so many Black organizations, and they have such a vast range, complexity, and density, that what they do collectively is something we see only fleetingly in the literature. They make appearances in the work of Bush, Cruse, Jennings, Smith, Walters, Morris, Morrison, Payne, McAdams,[78] as examples, but as these are appearances, they are not detailed treatments. As Sidney Tarrow reminds us about the social movement literature, "Individual and group decisions depend on a chain of intermediary structure."[79] Data sets and rational choice literature look at individual decisions and aggregate them into group decisions, but they do not focus on the intermediary structures, nor do qualitative studies which tend to look at relationships between organizations or categories of organizations and roles individuals play in organizations. They don't provide much description, much less analysis, of intermediary structure.

The study of groups is extensive in political science; some even believe there is too much of it.[80] There is also an extensive literature on groups in sociology — large groups, small groups, groups *ad infinitum*.[81] There have been almost innumerable studies of specific groups (organizations), including many Black organizations.[82] What we lack is a base of dense examinations of multiple groups acting within single settings — how they interact and how they engage other political actors over time.

Tarrow says,

> The evidence is overwhelming that (these intermediary structures) intervene differently to produce many different degrees and patterns of collective action. If we ignore these intermediary processes, we have no way of knowing how structure is translated into action.[83]

The manageable yet substantial world of Black organizations in Sacramento affords a laboratory for looking at how structure is translated into action, and what we find in Sacramento is reflective of what we see elsewhere in the United States.

Black Organizations in This Study

I classified Black secular organizations as ones whose membership was composed of at least a majority of Black people, whose leadership was dominated by Black people, and which expressly pursued interests and aspirations of Black people. If a secular organization met all three criteria, I categorized it as a Black organization. These criteria mean that many organizations I classified as Black were not exclusively Black. Many Black churches, the paradigmatic Black organization, do not have solely Black members. They are, nevertheless, dominated by Black people. I intentionally focused on secular organizations because I wanted to look at Black churches as a separate subject, and I wanted to see what Black organizational life looked like *sans* the church. In a later portion of this chapter I look specifically at the Black church.

I identified both private and public Black organizations. By private I mean organizations which were not created by an act of the state at any level, whose employees were not state workers, and which were not directly financed by the state. They may have received state funds, but those funds were acquired through contractual arrangements. By public organizations I mean elements of government which Black people captured to the extent that the majority of the employees were Black, the chief decision makers within the organization were Black, and the organization operated to serve the interests and aspirations of Black people. They were organizations Black people turned into *de facto* Black spaces.

Matthew Holden tells us in *The Politics of the Black Nation* that within each Black community in the U.S., there is "a wide variety of institutions."[84] He says, "These institutions are manifold.... That they differ with respect to size, permanence, resources, appeal."[85] His statement identifies spaces used by ordinary Black people throughout the U.S.

Milton Morris in *The Politics of Black America*, says,

> Some attempts have been made to compare the level of overall participation in organized social groups for blacks and whites. The results are not altogether consistent but they strongly suggest that the rate of this form of activity among blacks may be higher than among whites.[86]

While Harris et al. remind us that Black people in the U.S. are less involved organizationally and politically than whites,[87] that observation is not revealing either about whether Black people who are involved are more or less involved than whites who are involved, nor does it tell us how the *number of organizations* of both groups compare. On the basis of socio-economic status alone we might expect Black people to be less involved organizationally and politically.

Morris tells us, "Black involvement in organized groups is widespread, long-standing, and directly related to the distinct character of the group and its subordinate status."[88]

What Morris says suggests a different condition from that indicated by studies showing lower levels of organizational or political activity among Black people than whites. Morris's statements imply an over-organized Black population. Nor is he alone. Hanes Walton reports a community leader in Savannah saying, "There was great frustration"[89] and that "all of the different organizations ... ought to get together."[90] The implication is there were *so many* organizations they caused frustration because *all of* them couldn't get together, i.e., there were too many.

In 1975, Charles Hamilton said, "Within a 4½ square mile area in Harlem ... I counted 212 different organizations serving the community." He continued, "Yet programs within blocks of each other will not get together."[91]

Anyone who has done any detailed study of Black organizations in the field or who has been active in Black organizations, is familiar with the continual chorus calling for Black unity. These refrains erupt in many and sundry settings over the recognition (seemingly made anew every time) that despite the large number of Black organizations they often disagree with one another and do not work together.

Robert Smith, in his decades long study of the post–Civil Rights era, characterizes these features most pointedly. He says,

The black community in the United States has always had an extensive and diversified structure of organization, paralleling that of white America but in some ways *more extensive* [italics mine].[92]

He says, more explicitly,

The problem of *hyper black organization* has in the past been identified and is today to some extent a problem itself in black society and politics.[93]

Summarizing all these tendencies, Smith states,

Blacks, who probably have more organizations (at least on paper) per capita than any other group in the United States, are nevertheless not effectively organized.[94]

Another feature of community organization is that membership is often overlapping. The same people belong to a number of organizations. The same individuals operate under different organizational names. Also, when one organization folds, the same people will be involved in creating a new one which may carry on the mission or a modified mission of its predecessor. Leland T. Saito, *Race and Politics,* comments extensively on such characteristics among Latino and Asian organizations in a Southern California community.[95]

Matthew Holden cites another organizational characteristic in the Black population.

The system becomes a system of influence (or powers) ... the constant interplay between the elites of these various institutions produces a central tendency which becomes the judgement of the black community.[96]

In short, the people active in these organizations know each other, interact with each other, communicate with each other, and produce collective judgments which serve as the standard for the Black population. They are elites, but only among their own local Black populations.

Many people who belong to Black secular organizations belong to more than one. Many belong to Black churches as well, and many to organizations within Black churches. Many of the people most active in Black organizations and active in the largest number of Black organizations, including churches, also belong to non–Black organizations: professional, recreational, youth-related, school-based, and civic.

Given what it takes simply to live a life, it seems unlikely that Black people would join, create, and participate in such an extraordinary array of Black secular organizations — in addition to their participation in other organizational life — for frivolous reasons. They must feel a need for this organizational life. Otherwise, why do it?

Black people need each other. They need each other in organizational settings. This representation of need is perhaps one of the most powerful indicators of the hostility of their environment. They have a need to create counter-environments, counter-spaces in which they can have some respite from the vicious onslaught of the rest of the world, from which they can launch their own defensive measures, counter-attacks, and initiatives. This is warfare vocabulary, but Black organizational presence gives evidence of a people who see themselves in a state of war.

The sheer numbers of organizations afford us the recognition that Black organizational life is not nearly so inbred, overlapping, incestuous, and narrow as much of the scholarship and popular commentary imply. While one person may belong to two or three Black organizations, and very active people may belong to ten, as well as to Black churches and non–Black organizations, no one belongs to 30 or 40 Black organizations. There are certainly not collections of Black people who jointly belong to the same 30 or 40 Black organizations — not to speak of 200+ (Hamilton's figure)! The number of organizations dictates that membership is broader than generally surmised.

Walton said,

> As social, economic, and political fortunes changed in the Black community, they developed a diversity of interests.... The result was the emergence of functional leaders. [These leaders arose] naturally from a diversity of needs and aspirations within a particular community.[97]

He also makes the astute observation that

> these individuals wanted to be leaders and given the avenues available, they tended to gravitate toward organizations where they could emerge and make the most and greatest contribution.[98]

Milton Morris also notes that "black involvement in organized groups is ... directly related to the distinct characteristics of the group and its subordinate status."[99]

He also associates Black organizational behavior with the fierce character of the environment Black people inhabit.

> A variety of all-black organizations — churches, fraternal, economic and cultural organizations emerged as a direct result of white hostility and the need for collective struggle against oppression.[100]

Matthew Holden was also right on the mark when he said the institutions among Black people were "manifold as to ... size, permanence, resources, degree of social responsibility, appeals to different social classes, and legal status."[101]

Katherine Tate tells us Black organizations are not broadly representative. "It appears they recruit and involve solely the members of the Black middle class."[102] Further she finds, "Poor and less educated Blacks are not to be found."[103] This, however, is not a literal interpretation of her data, which do, indeed, show 10 to 14 percent of low income people and people with low levels of education with organizational memberships.[104]

Her narrative tells us young Black people were not likely to be organizational members.[105] Finally, she does not believe organizations which can mobilize new Black voters at the grass roots level are likely to operate for long because of the economically and socially disadvantaged characteristics of their memberships.[106] This is an interesting assessment, given her statements that (mobilizing) Black organizations "are not likely to be at the grass roots level,"[107] and (within them) "poor and less educated Blacks are not to be found."

Tate, however, does offer one caveat to these findings. The questionnaire on which her study is based identified primarily membership in national organizations.[108] Therefore she cannot speak authoritatively to the population's membership in grassroots organizations — which is the specific subject of the instant study. Nor, despite her speculations, does she have evidence for saying whether grassroots organizations persist.

Michael Dawson documents the politicization of Black racial interests. His Black utility heuristic is designed to identify specific indicators which represent that politicization.[109] I'm interested in whether an examination of Black *organizations* will also provide indicators that Black racial interests have been politicized.

In their study of ten Northern California cities, including Sacramento, Browning et al. find that demand-protest activity among the Black population was "very closely related to absolute size of the minority group."[110] They find such demand-protest activity much more dependent on numbers of people rather than the group's percentage of the population.[111]

Dawson says, "The 75 year legacy of continuing organizing made available trained, experienced cadres with a strong sense of historical missions."[112]

Along the same lines he adds,

> During key periods, the institutions that were formed in the South and often reproduced in urban areas across the country provided a network for politically mobilizing African Americans.[113]

Home

How do these national observations play out in Sacramento among ordinary folk? How do Black people moving into Sacramento from all over the country, and indeed from all over the world, develop a collective identity which could enable them to coalesce and act in concert with their Black neighbors as Black people? This question is all the more intriguing in Sacramento because of the Black population's dispersal. Parts of the city and county are more likely than others to have Black residents. Others are very unlikely to have Black residents. Yet even in areas with comparatively high levels of Black inhabitants, except for a limited number of census tracts, Black people are interspersed among members of other population groups.[114] In areas with few Black people there are nevertheless scattered Black residences. How do these immigrant Black people (immigrants to Sacramento) find a home with each other? What we learn about Sacramento in this respect is likely to be true for Black people all over the nation.

This is a problem which confronts not only Black people, but any internal migrant population which is not white, and some others, such as specific religious populations, but I'm restricting this consideration to African-descended peoples. Most white residents who move into a neighborhood do not have to worry about how they are going to find other white people and identify with them as a population and as a *political* population. They may wonder about how they're going to find other Democrats, or Baptists, or what they may enjoy with their neighbors, or where the barbershop is, or the bookstore. They don't have to worry about where they're going to find *Black* Democrats, *Black* Baptists, *Black* neighbors, *Black* barbershops, or *Black* bookstores, on *ad infinitum*. In fact, only recently did I learn that the bowls of business cards and boards displaying business cards that I've seen around the country for years, in Black businesses of all kinds, are not simply business courtesies. They are there because of the continual requests from Black clientele about where they can find an AME church, a Black beauty shop, a Black boutique, a Black insurance or real estate agent, a mosque of the Nation of Islam, the NAACP, *without end*.[115]

How Black people find a home in a new place certainly is largely explained by perceptions, conceptions, beliefs, feelings, and mental and emotional orientations they bring with them and maintain. The Black population is, after all, a national population, and that is why we are as likely to find concerns about finding a new home elsewhere as in Sacramento. As Michael Dawson puts it,

> The collective memory of the African-American community continued to transmit from generation to generation a sense that race was the defining interest in individuals' lives.[116]

What puzzled me was whether there were physical, material interests, which could reenforce such mental and emotional dispositions. The church is certainly one way Black people use to establish contact. The first thing many Black people do upon moving to a new area is to establish a new church home. Black newspapers, radio stations that cater to Black audiences are other ways for people to feel at home. Family or friends in an area help bolster a common racial identity. New friends can serve a similar function. *What about secular organizations?*

The Black Organizational Universe in Sacramento

I counted Black secular organizations in two ways. By one, I identified 125 Black organizations in the 1970s. They did not include churches or criminal organizations. They did not include youth gangs, criminal or not. By the other, also excluding churches, criminal groups, and youth gangs, I counted 136 organizations. I placed the organizations into 15 categories. Many fit more than one category, even though there was a specific category for multi-purpose organizations.

The overwhelming number of organizations were private, but significant state organizations were captured by Black people, particularly during the poverty program, as well as in aspects of higher education. Membership figures are available for some organizations, but not for most. Very little information is available longitudinally with respect to membership. There are not enough reliable data on membership numbers to include them.

With respect to longevity, some organizations existed prior to the 1970s and continued throughout the decade. Others arose in the '70s and lasted past them. Still others began during the '70s and ended before the close of the period, some lasting only weeks or months.

FUNCTION. Most organizations had multiple purposes. Organizations such as fraternities and sororities which are primarily designed for socializing, may also offer scholarships, provide mentor programs, and participate in political campaigns. To classify organizations, I identified each by its principal purpose. What is each organization's *raison d'etre*? In most cases I was able to identify one principal purpose. But in some cases no priority could be made between two or more. In such cases I identified the organization by more than one function. As a result, some organizations counted in the functional tables at the end of this chapter are in more than one category. The *functional* tables do not count organizations individually, but by function. There were, for example, 40 separate organizations whose primary purposes were social. Some had one or more other primary purpose as well. A single organization, as a result, could be included in the social, service, and professional categories. The total counts are therefore higher than the total number of organizations. The total number of categorical counts for the 1970s is 166, but because some organizations are listed in more than one category, the actual number of routine organizations is 125. Some organizations are *designed* as multi-purpose organizations. There is a separate category for them.

I identified fifteen functional organizational categories for the 1970s. They are listed below in descending order of the number in each category using the first method of counting: (1) social, (2) service, (3) political, (4) professional, (5) economic, (6) educational, (7) multi-purpose, (8) culture, (9) youth, (10) informational, (11) health, (12) religious, (13) student, (14) recreational, and (15) mobilizing. The overall numbers for the categories and for each decade are listed in Table 2.7. Additionally, I identified women's organizations and men's organizations. Each set was initially gender exclusive. I do a more detailed comparison of gendered organizations below. They are not included as separate categories. They are incorporated into the 15.

The distributions affirm a lot of the early research describing conditions in the early 1970s, '60s, and even before. That research identified most Black organizations as social. These data, however, indicate that in the case of Sacramento, while there were more social organizations than any other kind (24 percent), as compared with 13.3 percent for the second ranking (service organizations), social organizations did not constitute a majority. Social organizations combined with social and political organizations equaled 48.7 percent. Add the fourth double digit *n* category, professional organizations, and one has 55.3 percent of the total. The other eleven categories combined constituted only 44.7 percent.

POLITICAL ORGANIZATIONS. Political organizations have provided the rationale for two methods of counting organizations. The first method, discussed above, counts Black organizations which were routinely present in Sacramento. The method omits one significant kind of political organization. California's electoral process has created a form of organization which exists primarily in election years only. It is the campaign committee. Municipal and special district elections in California are non-partisan. Campaign committees in those elections are not creatures of political parties. They are the candidates' instruments. Their members are usually chosen by the candidates, as are the campaign managers. For most special district elections there is no paid campaign manager. A volunteer plays the role. Such volunteer work is a good way of getting campaign experience. The same situation applies for some municipal elections. The volunteer campaign manager was the rule in Sacramento as the 1970s began. That changed over time, but it was characteristic of most of the '70s. While party activists get involved in the campaigns, and candidates are often party activists, the parties don't run the campaigns. Campaign committees do.

For our purposes this means campaign committees for Black candidates are almost always Black organizations. Other people may belong to them and even play significant roles in them, but they are dominated by the candidates. Most people who play significant roles in them are people of African descent. Even in the case of professional campaign managers the candidates hire and fire them; and there have been Black candidates who fired white professional campaign managers, underscoring the role of the organization as the *candidate's* organization.[117] As a result of this election year peculiarity, I have added the second method of counting organizations to include Black campaign committees. That is the sole difference between the two methods of counting. Campaign organizations significantly increase the number of Black organizations, and, specifically, Black *political* organizations. In the city of Sacramento before the 1971 election, city council members were elected at large. Generally, there were only one or two Black candidates. With a district system, the number of Black council candidates increased. Seven ran serious campaigns in the '70s. Two of those were elected. Many more put their names up for office, but did not run serious enough campaigns to have legitimate campaign organizations. If this study had included the decade of the '60s, the omission of Black campaign organizations would have had virtually no impact on the number of Black organizations. But by the 1970s significant changes in this aspect of Black politics were under way.

By the first method of counting, political organizations were 11.4 percent of the total for the '70s, third in number, with 19. Using the second method, political organizations increased to 30, which is 16.9 percent of the total, numbers and percentages which rank them in 2nd place.

If we look at political organizations under the first method of counting, the measure of salient political organizations, we may argue that constituting only 11.4 percent of the total, they do not compose a major portion of Black organizations. That observation cannot be denied. By itself, however, it obscures more than it illuminates. First of all, although representing only 11.4 percent of Black organizations, political organizations ranked *third* in number.

Secondly, counting political organizations as a distinct class is in some respects misleading when considering Black organizations. When Matthew Holden says, "Black politics actually takes place through a fairly well-defined and stable set of relationships which one may call the black 'quasi-government,'"[118] he is not referring exclusively to political organizations. Indeed, he postulates the following organizational categories: service, mutual-aid, self-interest, and recreational. He doesn't even include political organizations.[119] To him, they all become part of a system of influence or power through the constant interplay of their elites. That system produces a central tendency which becomes the judgment of the Black community. There are times when these judgments are expressed collectively — when Black organizations of all kinds come together to articulate points of view intended to represent the group as a whole, speaking with one voice. There were a number of such occasions in Sacramento during the '70s.

Other times the Sacramento African descendant population expressed a united front, but without a single organizational voice. That happened when Raymond Brewer was murdered by the SPD and Black people stormed the city council meeting. Another was when the Sacramento Human Rights Commission voted to dismiss Robert Tyler.[120] These were both manifestations of a collective judgment of the Black population by a number of organizations, quasi-government, in Holden's terminology.

Black organizations may also perform functions elsewhere and for others performed by the state. Such organizations don't necessarily have explicit political purposes. In so much as they perform state functions as substitutes for the state, however, they are every bit as political as the state. Examples of functions include, but are not limited to: informational, educational, health, and economic. I label this Black pseudo-government, distinct from Holden's quasi-government.

Additionally, other organizations, which do not have a purpose that is principally political, can be mobilized to participate in conventional politics: fundraising, canvassing, government, lobbying. They can be turned out to appear at city council meetings, school board meetings, board of supervisor meetings, and press conferences which are political in intent. Multi-purpose organizations consistently engage in political activities. The 11.4 percent of the organizations specifically identified as having politics as their central purpose do not comprise the total proportion of the organizations involved in politics.

Black organizations which had politics as their primary function did not have a politics in common. They were as diverse as the Republican Party and the Republic of New Africa. Black political organizations did not agree on a political program. While they could and did join forces with each other and with other kinds of Black organizations, they did so at best to realize a minimum program, for episodes deemed crises for the Black population at large, and for occasions of singular opportunity. When wide scale cooperation occurred, it was more an expression of the generally hostile environment inhabited by Black people and the need for allies to mitigate its worst effects than an agreement on common strategies or objectives.

While these divergent political organizations could and did come together for specific purposes, they could not and did not develop a common political agenda. That is precisely why there were so many different political organizations, why people didn't all join the same ones, and why they formed new ones. The population was diverse and required a wide range of organizations to constitute its infrastructure. It also required a broad organizational infrastructure to be able to mobilize its various constituencies. The Republic of New Africa could engage people not reachable by the Urban League and vise versa. But *both* constituencies might be mobilized by *separate* organizations in support of a community center, or justice in the case of a police shooting. Absences of common agendas notwithstanding, there is utility in hyper-organization.

Katherine Tate proposes the possibility that Black organizations for the period she considered, the 1984 and 1988 presidential elections, recruited only from the middle class, and that members of the lower class were not to be found among them. Tate's generalizations well might hold, though not explicitly representative of her data, for members of the so-called underclass. The underclass presence in '70s organizations I studied is not detectable. But if we look at the category of the poor in general, and for the decade of the 1970s, the one prior to the period she surveyed, the proposition is not supported by the instant data.

I have sorted organizations into middle class, mixed, and working class. The very poor, or *lumpen proletariat*, do not appear in either of these groupings. That is not to say they were entirely absent, but that I found no organizations which were led by lumpens, composed entirely of lumpens or mostly lumpens.

This was true even of the Black Panther Party in Sacramento, which contained a few members whose status was so demeaned as to be *déclassé*. Most Panthers were from the working class or Black middle class (not to be confused with the white middle class). Most Sacramento Panthers were college students. The presence of the underclass was so marginal in all the organizations as to be invisible. I based class designations on a combination of income, education, and occupation. In the 1970s middle class incomes were those consistent with middle level civil service incomes, $10,000 and above.[121] Middle class educations were associated with at least a high school education. Middle class occupations were associated with mid-level civil service classifications and higher, with working in the professions, middle level management and above in the private sector, and business ownership which generated an annual income equivalent to mid-level civil service employment. To be categorized as middle class a person had to meet all three criteria: income, education, and occupation. The exception was extreme wealth which automatically placed a person in the middle class. Working class designation was associated with people whose incomes ranged from low to middle, reaching a high of $10,000 in the 1970s; whose educational level was high school or less; and whose occupations were skilled and unskilled laborers, and the lower ranks of the civil service. For a person to be categorized as working class, he had to meet all three criteria. People who did not meet all three were designated underclass. For an organization to be either middle class or working class a majority of the organization's members were in that class, and the leadership was dominated by that class. Mixed organizations had relatively equal proportions of middle and working class membership and leadership. While identifications were not rigid, it was possible to characterize organizations by overall membership and leadership.

Out of 125 organizations in the 1970s, 24 were working class. There were 52 mixed organizations. In short, 76 organizations had substantial working class memberships, over half the total. There were 49 middle class organizations. If we equate working class with Tate's lower class, these results do not confirm her proposition that there are fewer lower class organizations. They do not confirm her position that Black organizations are exclusively middle class, or that the lower class is not represented in Black organizations. If we look exclusively at political organizations, which is Tate's concern, they were not exclusively middle class or devoid of working class representation, as a number of them were mixed. Five were working class. All five were war on poverty organizations. If we take Tate's lower class to mean the truly disadvantaged or the underclass, her proposition holds. While there were underclass members of some organizations: in the poverty agencies, and in organizations such as the Panthers and the Republic of New Africa, none of the organizations were dominated in numbers or leadership by underclass members. Dr. Tate says Black organizations are not likely to be at the grassroots level. What she means by the grassroots level, is not clear. Since she is looking at national organizations, one must assume she means organizations such as the NAACP and the Welfare Rights Organization. If she does, on the basis of the existence of those organizations and ones of similar membership characteristics, such as C.O.R.E. or the A. Philip Randolph Institute, I do not find the assertion tenable. She may intend to exclude middle class organizations as representative of grassroots organizations. I do not understand the basis on which that would be a reasonable exclusion, particularly from a sampling of national organizations, but even if we restrict our grassroots organizations among those identified here to mixed and working class organizations, over half the organizations would be grassroots. If we include only mixed and working class *political* organizations, at least 30 percent of the political organizations (excluding campaign organizations) would qualify as grassroots. For the seventies, the absence of grassroots organizations cannot be supported.

Professor Tate questions the durability of grassroots organizations. To assess that proposition in Sacramento, we shall have to consider more long-term evidence. We may say, however, that 125 local Black organizations were present at the beginning of the decade and 112 of them persisted beyond the end of the decade. A full majority were mixed and working class.

She indicates that young people are not likely to be found in Black organizations. For the '70s that was not the case. The Panthers were almost exclusively young, as were other organizations, such as Black Student Unions, college fraternities and sororities. The greatest number of participants in the effort to make Dr. King's birthday a state holiday were high school students. While the student fraternity and sorority categories were generally not political, Panthers and BSUs had politics as their principal foci.

It is important, however, to reaffirm that Dr. Tate has made clear on all these questions that the survey instrument did not allow her to investigate these possibilities with respect to grassroots organizations. Her data also did not include the 1970s, hence, the above findings have no direct bearing on her results, except to establish, for chronological comparison, that the national description she conveys for the 1980s was not representative of Sacramento during the 1970s. It is entirely likely — due to the data source — that they do not represent the national picture for the '70s when taken to the level of detail present in this study.

Do these data offer any illumination on Dawson's assertion concerning the politicization of Black life? If one refers to the quasi-governmental, systematic agenda prescribing that Holden discusses, virtually all these organizations have been politicized. On the other hand, if one means the extent to which organizations take interests to the state apparatus, one is looking at another phenomenon. The 19 organizations identified as specifically political represent politicization in the second, more formal sense, as do the eleven campaign committees, for a total in the enhanced count of 30 strictly political organizations. The four multi-purpose organizations also engaged in political activities as part of their purposes. The eight Black student organizations also had formal political purposes, as did the four mobilizing organizations. On the basis of these organizations alone, there were 33 routine political organizations, and 44 including campaign committees. A much larger number and proportion engaged in the formal politicization of Black interests at some time. This examination confirms Dawson's postulation of a politicization of Black racial interests.

Dawson's concern, however, is deeper than the politicization of Black racial interests. He is concerned, in the end, with Black identity. He declares it is deeply racial. That perception undergirds his Black heuristic. I attempted to examine one aspect of this perspective by identifying Black organizations which, from their inceptions, were intended to be specifically and explicitly racial — founded as organizations of Black people to serve the purposes of Black people. Eighty-seven of the organizations, 69.6 percent of the total, met this test. In the 1970s Black organizations in Sacramento included a majority cohort rooted deeply in a specific, Black, racial identity. These data support Dawson's primary postulates concerning the salience of Black racial identity.

With regard to Browning et al.'s finding that Black protest mobilization is associated with absolute numbers rather than proportions of the population, it is evident that a minimal population base is necessary to sustain the kind of organizational infrastructure documented here. Keep in mind that these organizations do not include Black churches. In the 1970 to 1979 decade, a time when there were at least 125 routine Black organizations — and 136 including campaign organizations — non–church-based Black organizations in Sacramento, there was a Black population ranging from 37,000 to 58,000+ people. Even given such a population base and such an organizational infrastructure, protest mobilization activity was infrequent, and most concentrated in the first half of the decade. Electoral mobilization activity, though often intense, was limited to very specific jurisdictions which had high Black populations with established institutional bases. These conditions would suggest that the population necessary to support a level of organizational structure and continuity to sustain mobilization efforts is substantial, all the moreso when the Black population is comparatively dispersed. The relatively high level of mobilization in the early 1970s, however, is a reminder that local conditions cannot be understood apart from their broader contexts — not only in space, but also in time. The Civil Rights and Black Power movements were the backdrop of this decade. Their effects were realized not only in Sacramento, but also throughout the United States.

There was also the question of whether secular organizations form a base for racial identity for people coming into the area from the outside. What these data reveal is illuminating. Forty-one of the 125 organizations had national or international affiliations, 30.1 percent of the total. People could come to these 41 organizations from afar and identify with them, find a physical re-enforcement of their mental and emotional self-identifications. Whether they belonged to the All African People's Revolutionary Party, the Order of the Eastern Star, Delta Sigma Theta, the Prince Hall Masonic Lodge, the National Urban League, or 35 other national or international organizations, they could find an organizational home in Sacramento.

There were other organizations, which, while not national in scope, were counterparts of organizations found elsewhere. They were relatively easy to find for people operating in the circles where they were present. Primarily they fall in a number of categories: student organizations, such as Black Student Unions; professional organizations, such as the Sacramento Black Nurses' Association and the Sacramento Black Police Officers' Association; and cultural organizations, such as the Sacramento Kwanzaa Committee and the Sons/Ancestors Players. Political junkies are drawn to campaign organizations. Many people who belonged to counterpart organizations elsewhere found organizational homes for their specific interests in Sacramento.

ORGANIZATIONAL ACTIVITY. Categorizing organizations — even by function — did not tell me what they were doing. Were they, as Robert Smith hints, primarily paper organizations? Were they doing anything? If they were, what? Were they doing different kinds of things? For example, the UNIA published a newspaper, held mass rallies and parades, purchased steamships. Few of its contemporary Black organizations were doing anything like that. At the time the NAACP was filing lawsuits on behalf of Black people which led to major court victories, the strategy was rarely adopted by other Black organizations. I wanted to see whether there were similar divisions of labor in Sacramento.

There was a good deal of dramatic activity. A lot of it was associated with organizations such as the Republic of New Africa, the Black Panther Party for Self Defense, and the Black Student Unions. These organizations were more likely to engage in activities such as (1) disrupting public events; (2) hosting events which were themselves disruptive; (3) taking over classrooms; (4) interrupting speakers; (5) using inflammatory words in large public gatherings. Additionally, a significant collection of organizations: (6) conducted boycotts; (7) engaged in picketing; (8) held mass demonstrations; (9) staged mass rallies and marches; and (10) mobilized mass turn-outs at regular governmental meetings.

Most organizational activity was much more routine. It consisted of networking, hosting conferences, meeting regularly, sponsoring cultural events, publishing newsletters, brainstorming, fund-raising, participating in press conferences, and operating by *Robert's Rules of Order.*

Some organizations were designed to perform specific activities: awarding scholarships, publishing a newspaper or a magazine, producing theatrical events, providing education, providing meals, or fostering skill development. In those cases, the organizations performed their specialized activities in addition to the generic activities almost all organizations carried out. But most organizations did not have specialized missions. They were *broadly* political, economic, service, or other organizations.

Black organizations were not paper organizations. They were active. There was a division of labor with some particularly productive specialization. There was a rich variety of performance — of *what* they were doing.

WOMEN'S AND MEN'S ORGANIZATIONS Black women's and men's organizations shared many characteristics with other organizations. They had social, cultural, and civic purposes. They used similar procedures to conduct business. They sponsored many of the same activities. They differed from all others, however, in that their memberships were (at least initially) limited to one gender.[122]

During the 1970s Sacramento had 27 organizations which originated as exclusively female and 17 exclusively male. The difference in number of organizations between the two genders is not accounted for by a larger population of women than men. The 1970 census lists the Black male population at 19,023 and the Black female population at 18,888.[123] These gendered populations, while counting slightly more men, were basically equal. Sacramento Black women appeared to have a greater propensity for forming single gender organizations than their male counterparts.

There were significant differences in the kinds of single gender organizations that Black women and Black men founded. See tables 2.3 and 2.4. Sororities outnumbered fraternities 6 to 5, yet, interestingly, all the male Greek letter organizations were college-based, and only 3 of the women's were. Men's clubs and women's clubs each numbered 6. Men's and women's Masonic orders each also equaled 6. There were three categories of women's organizations which had no male counterparts — auxiliary, health, and civic. No men's organizations were founded as auxiliaries to women's organizations. Three women's organizations were founded as auxiliaries to men's organizations. Women also created one health organization. Men did not create any. There were five women's civic organizations and no men's civic organizations. Three of the women's civic organizations were also clubs, which requires each to be double counted, one in each category. Most clubs, male and female, were social organizations. But the women's clubs, on the whole, had a much greater bent in the direction of social responsibility.

These data suggest some intriguing possibilities. The historical record unmistakably indicates that Black organizations which are not gender-specific are heavily dependent on Black women. While men often hold the peak leadership positions, women actually make the organizations work.[124] We may find a reflection of this circumstance in the numbers count among single-gender organizations. Women didn't need men to make their organizations go. On the other hand, men needed women so much they sometimes encouraged auxiliary organizations to support them. Women never had need of male support organizations. Men also could not seem to found exclusively civic organizations on their own. The ones they belonged to had female members. Women, on the other hand, were quite capable of starting and running civic organizations composed entirely of their own gender. These findings will be interesting to track over the decades.

STUDENT ORGANIZATIONS. During the 1970s Black student organizations, primarily BSUs, were collectively the most dynamic and dramatic Black organizations in Sacramento. Earlier I discussed the role of the BSU at SCC in its contestation with the BPP, in the development of the Oak Park School of Afro American Thought, and in support of the Oak Park 4. It also sent significant contingents on to energize the BSUs at Sacramento State College and UC Davis. The BSU at ARC was also active — though not as headline-grabbing as the one at SCC. As with SCC, the BSU at ARC sent significant cadres to the area's four year schools.

Black student organizations were major players in Sacramento's Black political life during the 1970s. A number of people who learned their first political lessons and won their spurs in political battles of BSUs and PASU took those experiences as bases for significant political careers in Sacramento and elsewhere.

Black Faith-Based Communities, 1970–1979

PATTERNS. During the 1970s not many Sacramento Black churches were politically engaged. *Members* of a wide range of congregations were, but few entire congregations could be considered activist. Those that were tended to be one of two kinds: (1) churches with a long history in Sacramento and an established tradition of political leadership; and (2) those whose ministers had a pronounced commitment to making their churches meaningful contributors to social uplift. In some rare instances the two features combined in one church. That was true of Shiloh Baptist Church under the Reverend Samuel Cooke. Shiloh was the church home of the West family, including their well-known son, Cornel. It was also true of St. Andrews A.M.E., led by the Reverend Cyrus Keller, the best known and most politically influential Black minister in the city.

A.M.E., A.M.E. Zion, and C.M.E. churches were more likely to be both older and have social uplift missions. One may cite Kyles Temple, A.M.E. Zion; St. Andrews A.M.E.; Allen Chapel, A.M.E. Zion; and Hollins Chapel, C.M.E. For most of the decade, the two Baptist churches with the most activist congregations were Shiloh and St. John's Baptist Church. Toward the end of the seventies, St. Paul Missionary Baptist Church, under the leadership of its minister and founder, Dr. Ephraim Williams, emerged as a font of political and social initiative.

FOCUS OF ACTIVISM. Active churches and activist ministers tended to lend their support to established organizations, such as the NAACP, Black candidates' campaigns for local office, to the push for Dr. King's birthday as a state holiday, and for crises that arose involving the whole Black population. Most Black churches were small. Some had a dozen congregants or fewer. Many had 30 to 40 worshipers. Churches with 200 members or more were considered large. Only toward the end of the decade did one or two churches attain memberships above 500.

The bulk of the congregations, politically active or not, provided support for the destitute by operations such as Christmas and Thanksgiving baskets, meal programs, food closets, and second-hand clothes closets. They performed pseudo-governmental functions.

NATION OF ISLAM. The local temple of the Nation of Islam made a political statement simply by its existence. Its presence asserted the need, desirability, possibility, and actuality of Black people operating in a relatively autonomous fashion across a wide range of human activities. The Nation actively solicited in Oak Park, and to a lesser degree in Del Paso Heights. The temple was located in Oak Park, across the street from the Panther Headquarters. Almost directly next door to the temple, the Nation ran a restaurant which specialized in the Nation's famous bean pies. The Nation also became a *cause celebre* when the SPD broke into the sanctuary, violating it in its search for evidence. The organized Black community rose up in unified support of the Nation, castigating the SPD for its blatant desecration of a holy place.[125]

GENERALIZATION. Most Black churches saw their roles as primarily spiritual, saving souls. Saving bodies, when it was an objective at all, was secondary. The roles Black churches play as alternative public spaces, including providing opportunities for service, training, leadership, self-esteem, mastery of competencies, and fulfilling lives, have been discussed extensively in other studies. Such features of Black religious life were ways Black church participation strengthened Black people for political participation as well. As Smith and Seltzer have shown, Black church members are more likely to be politically active than non-churchgoers.[126]

All in all, Black churches were not driving forces in Sacramento's Black political life during the 1970s. Some played critical roles. But the most active players and voices in Sacramento's Black politics were secular.

EXCEPTIONS. The exceptions were noteworthy. Shiloh, for example, developed an extensive low-income housing project, Shiloh Arms. The activity was both overtly political — it took considerable political resources and skills to put into place — and representative of the pseudo-governmental role of Black organizations. It provided housing for those who most needed it. Shiloh Arms included a day care center.

The Reverend Keller of St. Andrews was twice elected president of Sacramento's NAACP branch.

Allen Chapel, the seat of the Good Neighbors Club, also developed and housed a child care center. The incorporation of the center into the poverty program was a work of abiding skill. The same holds true for the Macedonia Baptist Church's Senior Food Program.

The indispensability of Black communities of faith for the well being of Sacramento's African-descended population cannot be denied. In the 1970s its political impact was minimal.

The Sacramento Area Black Caucus

In order to get a less global and more focused picture of Black political life, we look in detail at the origin, development, and operation of a single Black organization specific to Sacramento, the Sacramento Area Black Caucus (SABC). With respect to the range and complexity of its operations, the Caucus generally represents the area's more engaged Black organizations for the '70s. In it we can see the minute operations of a local Black organization. While there are significant differences between all Black organizations in Sacramento — between what they did, and how they did it — the Caucus represents the intensity, the complexity, and the range of such activities. It is also representative of single-location organizations which arose in many other places.

ORIGINS. Bill Lee had a unique perspective on the dynamics and intricacies of Black politics in Sacramento. Each week's reporting showed him what different Black organizations and individuals were doing. He saw the range and number of organizations at work. From his point of view, though there was tremendous diversity among them, they all seemed to share the same mission: to improve the condition of Black people. He believed there was a tremendous amount of energy and ability being devoted to the task, but inefficiently, frequently ending up in unnecessary redundancy and even undercutting mutual goals. He wondered why all these actors couldn't come together, develop joint, or at least complimentary strategies, decide what they agreed on and disagreed on, and implement approaches that would maximize rather than minimize their collective efforts. He had experienced success working with Marion Woods and Oliver Sims starting the Sacramento Urban League. Why couldn't he do it again? In early 1972 he invited a wide range of people to a meeting in his conference room. They were all leaders. Without his initiative, they were unlikely to have come together in the same space. They included representatives of Black Student Unions, the NAACP, the National Urban League, the Republic of New Africa, Panthers, influential school district administrators, a board member of the Los Rios Community College District, church leaders, union representatives, poverty warriors, boycott organizers, the head of Sacramento's Human Rights Organization, and others. Bill Lee shared his idea with them, the creation of an umbrella organization. Then he opened the floor for discussion.

Many found themselves surprisingly impressed by the others. They were dealing not with stereotypes, but with the flesh-and-blood people whose informed and clearly articulated opinions could not be easily dismissed. Lee told them he saw his role as calling the group together, a catalyst. Most of those present agreed they would like to meet again, without Bill, to see whether they could find a way to operate as a kind of committee of the whole for Black Sacramento. This intention is akin to Matthew Holden's *quasi government*.[127] It's like what Harold Cruse discussed as a "Negro Sanhedrin."[128]

ORGANIZING THE SABC. The people who had first been summoned by Bill Lee met regularly and quickly decided to constitute themselves as an organization. They envisioned an umbrella organization for all of Black Sacramento. They named it the Sacramento Area Black Caucus (SABC). A minister, the Rev. S.L. Higgins, was elected as chair.

The SABC developed a once-a-week meeting schedule on Thursday evenings. It adopted articles of incorporation and bylaws, and received recognition as a 501 (c) 4 organization, a social welfare organization. There were two categories of Caucus membership: organizational and individual. While the SABC met once a week, most of its organizational members met once a month. Matters proposed for action were voted on within a month of their introduction. That enabled organizational representatives to take action items back to their respective organizations for voting instructions.

Generally, 15 to 20 people attended the weekly meetings. Standing committees were established: political, education, and financial. *Ad hoc* committees were also used. About half the members were organizational representatives and the other half joined as individuals. Many who were individual members had organizational affiliations but did not represent their organizations in the Caucus.

While the NAACP and the Urban League were organizational members, many individuals had joined the Caucus precisely because it was not the NAACP or the Urban League. By 1971, influenced by the Nation of Islam, Malcolm X, SNCC and Friends of SNCC, CORE, BSUs, the Black Power Movement, and even SCLC, many people drawn to political activism across the country, including Sacramento, had come to see the NAACP and the Urban League as too staid and conservative, too wedded to the status quo. They were looking for alternatives. The SABC was one.

The dynamics of differing political perspectives and loyalties worked out in unexpected ways. Often, to everyone's amazement, long-term NAACP and Urban League stalwarts found themselves agreeing with members of the Republic of New Africa and Black Student Unions. Though most members were men, women played active roles. There was significant age variation, from people in their early '20s to their early '50s.

Early on the SABC had an organizational crisis. The chair, the Rev. S.L. Higgins, had become a one-man band. He went around town speaking at meetings and gatherings on behalf of the Caucus, articulating policy stances the Caucus had never discussed. He made commitments on matters the organization had never considered. When Caucus members queried him he disparaged them. He canceled meetings to prevent interference with his personal agenda and continued speaking and acting for the organization without authority.

Because the impeachment process was long and required deliberation from member organizations (each deliberation requiring another month), the body empowered the executive committee acting *sans* chair to call meetings, void acts of the chair, and in the absence of the chair, assume the chair's responsibilities. The Rev. Higgins resigned. Morale within the organization, never low, heightened as members recognized the deftness with which they had handled a potentially fatal organizational crisis.[129]

THE SABC ACTS. The first Caucus action was a boycott against a furniture store, Breuner's. The store had refused good-faith negotiations with Caucus members who wanted to discuss the store's failure to hire Black people despite a number of Black applicants, many with qualifications comparable to those of white people who had been hired. To support the boycott, the Caucus organized and maintained picket lines. Eventually the store submitted to intervention by the City and County Human Rights Commission.

The first high-profile public appearance by the Caucus was at the Sacramento City Council. There the SABC presented its study of city-appointed boards and commissions. It found that among a plethora of boards and commissions, Black people were present on only two, and none on the most important, such as the Personnel Board, the Planning Commission, the Transit Authority Commission, and the Housing and Redevelopment Commission. The Caucus called for an immediate end to this condition, the appointment of Black people, and presented lists of qualified Black people who were prepared to serve.[130]

To appreciate the impact of this debut, one must revisit 1972. "Negro" was still the generally preferred term for African-descended people, including the press. To most people *Black* power and *Black* Panthers were threatening and explosive terms. The NAACP was, after all, the National Association for *Colored* People. The National Urban League's name did not even mention race. Neither did SNCC's or the SCLC's. For an organization to appear at a city council meeting proclaiming its name as the Sacramento Area *Black* Caucus drew on the deepest fears of the populace. It was a dramatic performance. It ratcheted up Black pressure on local policy makers.

ORGANIZATIONAL ADJUSTMENTS. Because the SABC met once a week, and its committees and subcommittees more than that, it was able to engage a much wider range of issues than other Black organizations. It could not, however, *act* any more quickly because it had to have the consent of its organizational members to act. As pending business piled up, the built-in procedure of organizational delay became increasingly frustrating to SABC members, even those representing their own organizations. Eventually, after much discussion, the membership voted to amend the bylaws to eliminate organizational membership and restrict membership to individuals. Members were able to deliberate and act without referring decisions back to organizations for approval. The SABC stopped being an umbrella organization and a collective committee of the whole for the area's entire African-descended population. It became simply one more Black organization in Sacramento's dense Black infrastructure. The pace of the Caucus' actions rapidly accelerated.

Another organizational conundrum faced the Caucus. Because of the organization's visibility, its presence in so many arenas, and its reputation as task-oriented, many political officeholders and candidates sought its support. The organization's social welfare status, 501 (c) 4, enabled it to support issues, but not candidates. Most Caucus members, however, were very interested in political races. They resolved the dilemma by starting another organization, the Sacramento Area Black Political Caucus, which was a private association, not a 501 (c) 4 organization. The Sacramento Area Black *Political* Caucus could and did support political candidates. Since most of the Political Caucus's members were also members of the SABC, the Political Caucus meetings were held either before or after SABC meetings, but usually only during election seasons, and then only once or twice a month.

One other SABC organizational concern was a permanent meeting place. Les Gary, a Caucus member, offered the use of the facility he administered, the Lincoln Christian Center, one of the United Christian Centers, whose top administrator was Black, Rosenwald "Robbie" Robertson. The Lincoln Christian Center was located on a busy corridor not terribly distant from Oak Park. For quite some time the Caucus met exclusively at the Lincoln Christian Center. Some members, however, complained that while it was relatively easy for Oak Park residents to go to the center, people from other neighborhoods had to travel long distances. As a result, a rotating schedule was developed. Some meetings took place in the Lincoln Christian Center, others in locations in Del Paso Heights, and infrequently in other neighborhoods.

The advantage of the Lincoln Christian Center was that it was a stable meeting place. Everyone — regardless of where he or she lived — knew where the meetings would be. Since the meetings were every Thursday, everybody knew when the SABC met. If you missed one meeting, no matter, you knew where and when the next would be. With the rotating meetings, while attendance increased from residents of the neighborhood where the meeting was held, attendance from other neighborhoods dropped off. Consistency in attendance plummeted. The Caucus decided that consistency, a known location, was most important for persistence in attendance, and opened its own rented headquarters at a storefront in Oak Park, next door to the former Panther headquarters, across the street from the local temple of the Nation of Islam.[131]

In its first decade the SABC and its offspring, the Sacramento Area Black Political Caucus, threw themselves into addressing the troubles of the world.

THE SABC IN ACTION DURING THE 1970S. During the 1970s the scope of the SABC's work was comparable to that of the NAACP and the Urban League, but as a new organization it was going through a more dynamic phase. As *sui generis* to Sacramento it may be representative of some features of Black political life particular to Sacramento.

I identified 70 SABC activities which constituted the corpus of the organization's work over the decade. They do not constitute a sample. They form a comprehensive collection whose few omissions result from lapses in the record but do not alter the character of the whole. The sources from which the activities are drawn include internal records such as organizational minutes and correspondence, position papers and public presentations. They also include the print media, interviews, and participant-observer experiences.

I define an activity as a task which may consist of one or more events. For example, holding weekly meetings is one activity. If weekly meetings were held every week in a year, that would be 52 events in one year alone, but *all* the SABC weekly meetings in the whole decade count as *one* activity. On the other hand, for the whole decade, the Caucus sponsored one conference for the local Black media. That single event is also one activity.

I slotted the events into 14 categories. An activity can be classified in one or more categories. For example, the activity of sponsoring a conference for local Black media can fall into the *categories* of political education, independent Black institutions, support of other organizations, and community organization — though the conference is counted as a single *activity*.

TABLE 2.7 CATEGORIES OF KINDS OF SABC ACTIVITIES DURING THE 1970s

Category	# of kinds of events	Rank among categories	% of total events
lobbying	22	1	16.79
political education	15	2	11.45
electoral	12	3	9.16
public advocacy	12	3	9.16
grievance representation	11	5	8.39
independent Black institutions	10	6	7.63
support of other organizations	9	7	6.87
protest	8	8	6.10
operating under color of public authority	7	9	5.34
self-support	6	10	4.58
cultural	6	10	4.58
national & state level	6	10	4.58
community organizing	5	13	3.81
boycott	1	14	0.76

Table 2.7 indicates the number, rank, and percent of each category in which the SABC conducted activities from 1971 through 1979.

By lobbying, I mean direct attempts to influence incumbents of government offices, whether elected or appointed, including civil service appointees. Such efforts included, but were not limited to persuasive, informational, and reward or punishment interventions.

Political education means efforts to inform and influence publics on political questions, whether the publics are officeholders, the media, or the general public.

Electoral activities included those directly associated with voting, whether they were trying to influence candidates or incumbents, endorsing candidates, public forums for candidates, fund-raising, GOTV, canvassing, working in campaigns, voter registration, or press conferences about elections. The SABC engaged in all those kinds of activities, most of them as the Sacramento Area Black Political Caucus, but some, such as voter registration drives and working on ballot measures, as the SABC.

Public advocacy was speaking or writing to public bodies with a view toward influencing public policy. This advocacy differed from lobbying in that it was always performed in a public forum. Sometimes written testimony was provided as well as oral testimony, and sometimes the written testimony was in the form of a letter to the editor or an op-ed piece.

Grievances constituted acting as the representative of an aggrieved person during grievance procedures. The Caucus acted in that capacity for employees of city and county government, school districts, various branches of the national government (particularly air bases), the poverty program, non-governmental organizations, and for private employers, as well as for people who had grievances over housing accommodations.

Independent Black institutions (IBI) meant supporting or building an institution run by Black people to serve the interests of Black people.

Support of other organizations consisted of lending direct support, either physical or material, to contribute to the well-being of another organization. Such an organization might or might not be an IBI.

Protest included mass demonstrations against public policy or acts of public servants.

Acting under the color of public authority meant carrying out Caucus policy through a position on an official governmental body, usually an appointed board or commission, including hiring and promotional boards and panels.

National and state levels dealt with Caucus involvement with decision-making bodies on the national and state levels.

Cultural activities were those concerned primarily with cultural matters, i.e., having to do with values, beliefs, and aesthetic expression.

Self-support had to do with maintenance of the organization. Such activities were meetings, fund-raisers, collecting dues.

Community organization meant encouraging and facilitating members of the African-descended population at large and specific sectors of the population to organize in order to identify and pursue their own objectives.

There was only one boycott in which the SABC was an active participant: the very first Caucus activity, the boycott of Breuner's.

These 14 categories and 70 kinds of activities meant literally hundreds, indeed, several thousand events.

Ranking categories of activities by number of kinds was one way of looking at what the organization was doing. It indicated the *kinds* of activities by frequency, but it did not indicate the number of events by kind, nor the amount of time per kind. A tremendous amount of time and number of events consisted simply of holding SABC meetings, including committee meetings, yet the category into which that kind of activity fell, self-support, tied for 10th ranking in terms of *number* of *kinds* of events. There were not that many *kinds* of activities the SABC did to maintain itself, there was simply a very large number of the same kinds of activities, a very large number that took a lot of time. Those activities were (1) holding meetings, (2) fund-raisers, (3) collecting dues, (4) becoming incorporated, (5) holding retreats, and (6) maintaining an office. There wasn't much variety, but it took a lot of time.

To look at how the organization was actually spending its time, to compare expenditures of time, I used the construct of the organizational year. The organizational year is based on counting the time the organization spent on an activity. For example, the organization worked all nine years on maintenance: holding meetings, collecting dues, and holding fund-raisers. It didn't spend nine years becoming incorporated, holding retreats, or maintaining an office. It spent a year on incorporation and obtaining 501 (c) 4 status. It held retreats for 9 years, but each one took only about 4 months to prepare for, execute, and follow up, or a total of 36 months over the 9 years, an equivalent of 3 organizational years. It maintained an office for 5 years which actually required continuous activity over each of the five years — paying utilities, rent, phone, and upkeep. The total of all the time spent on the 6 maintenance activities added up to 36 organizational years. It spent considerably less time on some other activities. It spent a month to secure the city's commitment to make repairs to a park in Oak Park. It spent a week forging a community effort to prevent the firing of the Human Rights director. Looking at how much time the SABC spent on specific activities provided a clearer understanding of how it distributed its time. This information is represented in Table 2.8.

TABLE 2.8 CATEGORIES OF SABC WORK BY
ORGANIZATIONAL YEAR OVER THE 1970S

Category	# of organizational years	Rank among categories	% of total of organizational years
self-support	36	1	17.82
lobbying	32	2	15.89
political education*	23	3	11.39
support of other organizations*	23	4	11.39
cultural	16	5	7.92
public advocacy*	14	6	6.91
independent Black institutions*	14	7	6.91
acting under color of authority	13	8	6.42
electoral	10	9	4.95
national & state	7	10	3.47
grievance	6	11	2.98
protest	4	12	2.00
community organizing	3	13	1.49
boycott	1	14	0.50
Total	202		100**

*Not a tie. Difference in rank based on organizational months and weeks not reported in this table.
**Slightly over 100 percent due to rounding.

Table 2.8 makes clear how the SABC was dividing its time. It spent more on maintenance, over 17.82 percent, than anything else. Lobbying, ranking 2nd, moved from first when looking at *kinds* of activities, was still an important category of activity, taking almost 16 percent of the organization's time. At 3rd and 4th, respectively, both in double-digit percentages, political education and support of other organizations received substantial amounts of time. Public advocacy, at 6th, drops behind cultural activities, which moved up from a tie at 10th, to 5th, in terms of time on task. Yet, disappointingly, for an organization self-consciously dedicated to community organizing, the SABC carried out few kinds of such activities (five), and spent little time doing them (3 organizational years) ranking 13th in amount of time spent. There was little activity — one boycott with its associated picketing — which could be considered militant, or an in your face kind of activity.

It is important to distinguish community organizing from working in the community. Much of what SABC did was in the community. Its office was in the community, in the heart of Oak Park. Many of its political education events were in the community. Cultural programs were frequently held in the community. Schule Jumamose, which the SABC supported, was in the community, as were other IBIs. Public advocacy frequently took place in the community. But being in the community is not organizing in the community. I have defined community organizing as "encouraging and facilitating members of the Black population at large and specific sectors of the population *to organize in order to identify and pursue their own objectives*." The SABC wasn't doing much of that.

CAUCUS INTERACTION WITH STATE GOVERNMENT. The Caucus' engagement with the California Legislative Black Caucus (CLBC) is worth discussing in detail, particularly with respect to one measure involving the internal politics of the California State Assembly. This instance indicates the kind of interface that often went on between ordinary Black people and the elites who represented them. They illustrate how everyday people attempted to assess and influence their spokespersons, as well as the absence of compelling structural links between them.

In 1978 Kevin McCarthy decided to run for Assembly speaker following the election of the incumbent, George Moscone, as mayor of San Francisco. Willie Brown challenged McCarthy for the seat. The California Legislative Black Caucus did not support Willie Brown. Most of its members supported McCarthy. To most Black people in California who followed state politics, this was incomprehensible.

One SABC member, Frank Jones, who was from San Francisco — Willie Brown's city — but who had moved to Sacramento with a job promotion, was outraged. He demanded that the Caucus investigate the reasons for this treachery and issue a report on its findings. As a result, the SABC conducted an examination of the contest for the speakership, including interviewing members of the CLBC.

The CLBC members appeared forthright. They did not attempt to cover up very significant differences between themselves and Willie Brown. While they thought Brown was an extremely competent legislator, far more capable than McCarthy, they didn't trust him. They cited all kinds of instances when Brown had promised one thing and done another, when he had betrayed CLBC members. They also cited differences between Brown and the Black legislators from Southern California. *All* the Black assemblymen except Brown were from Southern California. Only one, Assemblyman John Miller, the chair of the CLBC, was supportive of Brown. During this particular term no Black women served in the Assembly. The Southern California section met on a regular schedule, they said, while the whole Caucus met sporadically. The Southern California contingent had an agenda, while the CLBC as a whole did not. When Brown held a position of significant influence in the Assembly Democratic Caucus, chairman of the Ways and Means Committee, he did not use it to help Black members get the positions they sought.

They maintained that if Willie Brown won the speakership, he would not share leadership with other Black members. He thought he had their votes in his pocket and had no need to make any concessions to them. Moreover, he believed he had enough votes to win without them. They wanted to prove to him not only that he couldn't count, but also that he had a price to pay for treating them so cavalierly. McCarthy, on the other hand, was willing to negotiate with them. He was willing to appoint them as chairs of powerful committees. They had been able to negotiate such favorable terms with him, that though it appeared counterintuitive, their constituencies, *Black* people, would be better off with Willie Brown's not winning the speakership. Furthermore, Willie Brown didn't directly represent many Black people because his assembly district was not majority Black, and he acted accordingly. On the other hand, they all came from Black majority districts and were much more attuned to serving the interests of Black Californians.

The upshot was that Willie Brown lost the race to lead the Assembly and the members of the CLBC got the deals they had negotiated.

The SABC report concluded that the behavior of the Black assembly members — Willie Brown and the others as well — was a sorry display of blind ambition, individualism, and self-serving on the part of everyone involved, at the expense of the collective interest of the state's

Black population. Almost all of the Black legislators' interests were dominated by their own aspirations and the priorities of the Democratic Party. Not one of them placed the interests of Black Californians at the center of their concerns.[132] The Caucus report was an example of how ordinary Black people informed themselves and their constituents at the same time they failed to produce any significant change in the behavior of their sanctioned statewide leaders.

THE REACH OF SABC ACTIVITIES. Another arena in which the SABC engaged in considerable outreach was its television program. In cooperation with Pan African Studies at CSUS the Caucus got a grant from the California Council for the Humanities to produce a monthly program for a year. The Caucus interviewed the chief council for the Regents of the University of California, responsible for representing the university in the Bakke case. They brought in Hoyt Fuller, fresh from a trip to Brazil. In another arena, the Caucus sat on the Northern California Committee for the Sixth Pan African Congress. The full reach of Black politics was captured *within* the organization.

THE BLACK UNITY FESTIVAL. The SABC decided to sponsor a Unity Festival on the weekend of Juneteenth, Father's Day weekend. They situated it at lovely Miller Park, along the banks of the Sacramento River, next to the city's marina. There was comparatively little publicity. The organization made arrangements for a permit, acquired the requisite portable restrooms, secured barriers to help direct the flow of traffic. The Caucus developed a security team which met with the police department to coordinate managing the event with minimal impact on the general public's use of the park.

On the morning of the event Caucus teams arrived early and set up the security, barriers, signs, vendors, stage, microphones and speakers. A few Black families and groups of friends arrived early to claim picnic areas. Security made its liaisons with the SPD. The SABC had no idea of how many people to expect, maybe a few hundred with a good turnout. By noon most of the vendors and people scheduled for the early part of the program had arrived. The people who had staked out picnic areas were barbecuing; some were playing catch. Kids played kickball and tag. People socialized. There were plenty of parking places. The police had required the roads into and out of the park converted into a one-way loop. People could park, or they could drop people off, but they could drive in only one direction. Everyone entered the park at a single point and exited it at another point — no two-way traffic. At noon cars drove through the park at intervals varying from 100 to 300 feet apart throughout the three-quarter mile loop. About 12:30 P.M. traffic density began to increase. By 1 P.M. there were no parking places left in the park. Cars were bumper to bumper throughout the loop. Around 1:30 P.M. the commanding police officer made his way through the traffic to reach Oscar Starks, head of Caucus security. The officer said the street leading to the park was jammed with traffic to a distance of two miles. People had begun parking a mile away and walking. He wanted to know how many people the SABC expected. Oscar laughed. He said they hadn't expected as many as were already in the park. He had no idea how many were coming.

Around 2:15 P.M. a few Caucus members walked to a knoll affording a view of the park approaches and exits. While automobiles could enter the park by only one route, pedestrians could enter by both ends of the loop, one an entrance for cars, and the other, an exit. From the knoll, as far as the observers could see, on each approach, people on foot poured into the park. No one had seen anything like it. No one had ever seen so many Black people at the same time at a single site in Sacramento. Periodically, throughout the afternoon, people walked to the knoll and watched the flowing crowd. Sacramento had a Black population of 40,000.

The low-ball figure of the turnout was 10,000. Everyone was stunned. Nobody could explain it. The same phenomenon occurred every year until Miller Park was temporarily closed for a marina expansion. Nobody was ever able to explain it. Whatever the cause, the unprecedented size of the gathering at the first and all the subsequent Black Unity Festivals redounded to the benefit of the SABC. The Caucus gained immense credibility and political clout. Any organization which could summon up 10,000 people was a force to be reckoned with.

A SUMMATION. The SABC began as an attempt to form an umbrella Black organization for Black Sacramentans, a committee of the whole for African-descended peoples in the region. It brought together people from many and widely disparate points of view, and widely and disparate social circumstances. The effort to constitute the organization as a kind of "Negro Sanhedrin" failed. It was slow and cumbersome. It drew its members outside the issue-stance comfort zone of the most established Black organizations, placing strains on its internal cohesion. Robert Smith argues that the kinds of differences among Black people in the U.S. exhibited in the composition of the Sacramento Area Black Caucus are what make the unending struggle for "unity without uniformity" or a "minimum program" practically impossible. The differences between Black people are too great and too real for them — or their leadership — to be placed within a single organizational structure.

Cruse says: perhaps, but at least they can talk to each other, or they *should* talk to each other. The Sacramento Area Black Caucus in its formative period showed that Black people with deep and fundamental differences could not only talk together, but that in some circumstances they could act together and develop strategy and tactics in concert with one another *inside the same organization*. There *was* a kind of committee of the whole which functioned for a short time.

This quasi-government of a tiny slice of the Black Nation, to use Matthew Holden's terminology, was short-lived. The SABC became one more particular Black organization. Whatever its *early* days may have said to the feasibility of an all-inclusive Black organization, its longer trajectory gave that notion no support. The effort was not sustained, and if Smith is to believed, *could not be sustained.*

Nevertheless, the SABC was a clear marker that in Sacramento class and ideological antagonisms were not impassable barriers for cooperation and common action among people whose ancestors had come from Africa. Indeed, Smith and Seltzer make quite clear that the linked fate among Black people does not mean they come to the table for the same reasons, but that even in their diversity, the social forces at work in the U.S. bring them to the table *for different reasons*— but often in a position to champion the same objectives. We cannot minimize the deep social consciousness among many Black people which is emotional, affective, composed of matters of belief and feeling which often override more objective or rational motivations. They share deep social memories.

Though Caucus members were all very active as individuals, they felt almost a compulsion to come together — a compulsion not shared by their colleagues who were teachers, administrators, public service workers, students, clergymen, union members, and entrepreneurs, but who also were not sons and daughters of Africa.

The SABC used spaces controlled by Black people to further their objectives: the *Observer*'s conference room, the offices of the Greater Sacramento Area Economic Plan, the facilities of the Lincoln Christian Center, and, finally, their own office.

The SABC often won. Their boycott was successful. They got the city council to appoint more Black people to boards and commissions. They got the county to adopt an affirmative action program, and for all practical purposes it was the Caucus which appointed the first director of the county affirmative action program, Clyde Rainwater. They acted in concert with other Black organizations to get the city to appoint a citizens committee to investigate the police department's use of deadly force in the slaying of a promising Black teenager. They had their members appointed to public bodies where they could act with the authority of the state. They reeled off victory after victory. These successes sustained a remarkable *esprit de corps*.

They also hooked up with what was going on statewide, nationally, and internationally — the California Legislative Black Caucus, the Congressional Black Caucus, the National Committee to Overturn the Bakke Decision, and the Sixth Pan African Congress.

The Caucus, however, had almost negligible success at community organizing. It was a community organization. It was rooted in the community and based in the community — in Black neighborhoods. But its ability to organize the community was insignificant. The SABC was very good at playing to its strengths. It did a remarkable job at doing what its members were good at doing. Equally important is what it did not do, what perhaps it *could not* do.

Summary

Merely categorizing the Black organizations in Sacramento during the '70s points out the richness and diversity of this population. People organized on the basis of class and gender, and across class and gender. They organized for social, service, political, economic, professional, recreational, health, educational, religious, cultural, and informational reasons. They organized to mobilize. In each category there tended to be not a single orientation or focus, but multiple ones, often complimentary, but also contending, antagonistic, and even dismissive or ignorant of one another. People organized on the basis of place of origin whether that place was an airbase (Tuskegee, Brothers at Mather), or a city (River City). They organized on the basis of neighborhoods. They formed organizations for special causes and events.

Their organizations interacted — or did not — in myriad ways. Some organizations were ephemeral, others long-standing institutions. Memberships varied. Some could count their numbers in the hundreds, others by twos and threes. Memberships fluctuated.

In Sacramento, in the '70s, this study finds no grounds for considering Black churches a font of political activity. While there was some church involvement in the community's political life, its overall role was marginal. That the same thing cannot be said about church *members* points out a critical puzzle.

How did these intervening variables (Tarrow's term) between the individual and the state or formations such as political parties interact with each other to effect both the micro and macro political worlds? With a great deal of complexity. It is also clear that they had major effects both on individuals who either participated in them — *or did not* — and on the larger instrumentalities of politics and society.

During the 1970s Black political activity in Sacramento improved life circumstances for Black people. Those successes rode piggy-back on political activities of Black people throughout the country and the world. They defended gains in Black well-being, and carved out spaces in the political arena for Black people to act with agency.

There can be no doubt that the same and even greater levels of Black organizational activities were going on in cities and towns throughout the country. The details identified here indicate a national phenomenon. The Sacramento example alerts us to the richness we have in the national Black organizational base, a world so diverse, fecund, and dynamic that it begs for further and deeper inquiry.

TABLE 2.9 FUNCTIONAL CATEGORIES OF
BLACK ORGANIZATIONS IN SACRAMENTO, 1970–1999,
BY NUMBERS AND PERCENTAGES

Category	Number*	Percentage
Social	40	24.0
Service	22	13.3
Political	19	11.4
Professional	11	6.6
Economic	8	4.8
Youth	8	4.8
Informational	8	4.8
Religious	7	4.2
Cultural	5	3.0
Student	5	3.0
Mobilizing	4	2.4
Religious	4	2.4
Multipurpose	4	2.4
Recreational	4	2.4
Health	1	0.6

*Number of organizations active in each category, not actual numbers of individual organizations. As a result, the totals are not summed. Some organizations appear in more than one category.

TABLE 2.10 FUNCTIONAL CATEGORIES OF
BLACK ORGANIZATIONS IN SACRAMENTO,
1970–1979, BY NUMBERS AND PERCENTAGES
(ENHANCED POLITICAL COUNT)

Category	Number*	Percentage
Social	40	22.6
Political	30	16.9
Service	22	12.4
Professional	11	6.2
Economic	8	4.5
Youth	8	4.5
Informational	8	4.5
Religious	7	3.9
Educational	6	3.4
Cultural	5	2.8
Student	5	2.8
Mobilizing	4	2.4
Multipurpose	4	2.4
Recreational	4	2.4
Health	1	0.5

*Number of organizations active in each category, not individual organizations. As a result the totals are not summed. Some organizations appear in more than one category.

TABLE **2.11** SACRAMENTO BLACK WOMEN'S ORGANIZATIONS,
BY CATEGORY, 1970–1979

Category	Number
Sororities	6
Clubs	7*
Civic	6*
Masonic/Lodge	6
Auxiliary	3
Health	1
Total	29*

*2 are double-counted

TABLE **2.12** SACRAMENTO BLACK MEN'S ORGANIZATIONS,
BY CATEGORY, 1970–1979

Category	Number
Clubs	6
Masonic/Lodge	6
Fraternities	5
Total	17

Electoral Politics

While nationally Black people had achieved some degree of electoral success before the 1970s, most of those achievements were in majority Black districts, either within city councils, state legislatures, or the national Congress. There were some exceptions, such as the election to the Senate of Edmund Brooke in Massachusetts. Some Black mayors had been elected in majority Black cities. Occasionally, Black people were elected to at-large posts. Almost all electoral success had occurred outside the South. Nevertheless, for the large part, elective office, even high appointive office, was *terra incognita* for African descendants. Most Black people lived in places where they were neither elected nor appointed to political office, and where as constituents they were represented by white incumbents. That situation gradually began to change. We can see how those steps unfolded in Sacramento.

In the 1970s Black Sacramentans increasingly attempted to obtain elected and appointed positions. During the decade some positions normally filled by election were filled by appointment. Others, such as seats on boards and commissions, as well as administrative positions, were routinely filled by appointment. The principal local governments considered here are the Sacramento City Council, the Sacramento County Board of Supervisors, the Los Rios College Board of Trustees, and positions on various school boards. Some consideration is given to positions in state government with discernible impacts on Sacramento Black politics.

District Elections Begin

During 1970 Sacramento voters approved a change in the city charter which took the city from at-large city council representation to district representation, with the exception of the mayor, elected at large. The charter change was influenced by the Civil Rights Movement, drawing heavily on court decisions mandating that elections satisfy the provisions of the 14th Amendment requiring, in the language of the time, "one man, one vote." The more accurate term is "one person, one vote," but the substantive effect was the same. The push was to see that every segment of the population was effectively reflected in the state, that people had equal chances to be represented as communities of interest. In the redistricting proposal put before the Sacramento voters in 1970, and in all subsequent redistricting years, these constitutional principles dominated the popular political discussions as they did nationally.

The first city council chosen by districts was elected in 1971. The charter amendment provided that half of the seats in the '71 election were to be filled for four year terms and half for two years. The office of mayor was excepted. The mayor was to be elected to a full four year term. In every subsequent regular election all seats would be for full four year terms. The intent was to have half of the council up for election every four years to insure continuity. At no time after 1971 would the whole council be up for simultaneous election. Lot would determine whether the first term of two years would fall to odd or even numbered districts.[133]

Milton McGhee, the sole Black incumbent, who at the time of the 1971 election was vice mayor, ran for mayor. His opponent was the incumbent, Richard Marriot.

The city's two major Black neighborhoods, Del Paso Heights and Oak Park, were located, respectively, in Districts 2 and 5. One of the districts would elect a representative who would serve only a two year first term.

In District 2 the majority of the population was white, 23 percent of the residents were Black. There were six candidates in the primary, 1 Chicano, 2 Black, and 3 white. One of the Black candidates, Rosenwald "Robbie" Robertson, was the biggest vote-getter. He won 47.7 percent of the votes. His closest contender, Johnnie Bunch, a white candidate, got 16.4 percent of the vote. Robertson was a liberal Democrat. Bunch was an arch-conservative. The district was overwhelmingly Democratic.[134]

Robertson had maximized the Black vote in the primary. With 82 more votes he would have been elected in the primary. The other Black candidate had garnered more than 82 votes. The white vote had been scattered between the three white candidates, Robertson, and the Chicano candidate. Voter turnout in District 2 was the lowest in the city. Chicanos, while appreciable in numbers, were not politically active. The white population was poor and working class. Many of its members were Democrats in the mode of the then solid-South. The Black community in the Heights was the most politically active segment of the district.[135]

Bunch was inarticulate and a poor campaigner without much of a campaign organization. Robertson, as head of the United Christian Centers, had the backing of many prominent Sacramentans from outside the district, as well as the support of many politicians. Nevertheless, in racial terms, Robertson was looking at a 3 to 1 white to Black voter ratio in the district.[136]

As the general election approached, Robertson had a strong organization and a visible campaign. He avoided a contest on racial lines, saying the candidate with the best credentials should win.[137] There was no question that by meritocracy standards, he had the best credentials. His campaign generally followed the deracialization model that Jones, Clemons, and others have discussed. Robertson had great name recognition because of his extensive involvement in public affairs throughout the region. Bunch had little record to go on and almost no name recognition. His only prior involvement in politics had been participation in a petition drive for better law enforcement.[138] He had almost no outside support or endorsements.

Nevertheless, in the November election, Bunch tripled his vote total. He went from 636

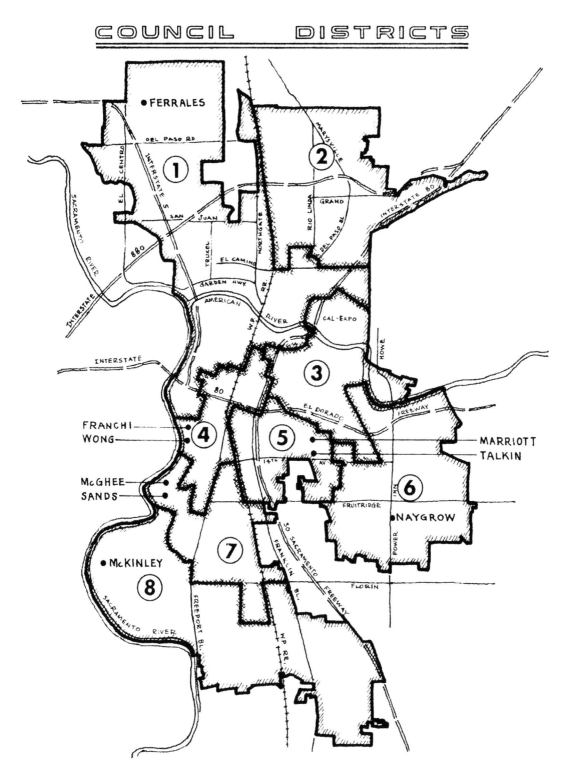

COUNCIL DISTRICTS

City council districts established in 1970 when Sacramento voters approved electing council members by district. The names connected to dots on the map are those of the incumbents at the time the ballot measure was approved. They reveal a principal reason for the voters' approval. Note that two incumbents live in each of 3 districts. Two districts were large areas where no council members resided.

in the primary to 1,885 in the general election,[139] more votes than Robertson had in the primary. Robertson, whose campaign strategy had been to maximize his primary turnout, picked up only two-thirds as many votes as Bunch did between elections. His total, however, 2,699 votes, gave him the victory.[140] The election presented the spectacle of a well-known, highly regarded, articulate, widely endorsed candidate of proven competence, running against a totally unknown of campaign-demonstrated incompetence. Without the racial difference, Bunch's achieving the votes he did would have been inconceivable.

Perhaps the most significant factor contributing to the election outcome was the feeling among Black people that they owned the district. They saw it as a Black space. They mobilized and turned out to enforce their ownership. Interestingly enough, many whites acceded to Black ownership. They, too, saw the district as a Black space. They stayed away from the polls in greater numbers than anywhere else in the city.[141]

District 5 was a horse of a different color. Included in the district were two neighborhoods with well-established identities, with other neighborhoods whose identities were less crystallized. The well-defined neighborhoods were Oak Park and Curtis Park. Both had white majorities. The district as a whole had an overwhelming white majority.[142] In Oak Park, in addition to a significant Black population, there was a significant Latino presence.[143] Both neighborhoods had scatterings of Asian residents, most of whom were of Japanese or Chinese descent.[144] Oak Park was primarily a poor and working-class neighborhood. Although a significant number of residents were homeowners, there was a large and increasing number of renters. It boasted two elementary schools. It was home to the city's oldest and most storied public high school, Sacramento High. Oak Park was popularly known as a Black neighborhood, dangerous, with a high crime rate. Black people were its most highly organized and mobilized population. As in Del Paso Heights, Black people tended to see the neighborhood as theirs, a Black space. Despite their majority, white people were not prone to public challenges of this assertion.

Curtis Park, on the other hand, not only had a white majority, it was almost exclusively white. It was a pleasant, tree-shaded, solid middle class neighborhood. It housed many young civic leaders. It had its own elementary school. Once Curtis Park had been adjacent to Oak Park. With the construction of the freeway system through Sacramento, just as Oak Park was turning from a middle class enclave into a working class neighborhood with a noticeable Black population, State Route 99 swallowed up the blocks that had joined the two neighborhoods, separating them like a walled moat.

Smart money predicted the battle for the representation of District 5 would be between Curtis Park and Oak Park. That proved to be the case. The ultimate winner was Phil Isenberg, a young white lawyer, a leader of the young Turks who had spearheaded the campaign to elect city council members by district, a liberal Democrat, and a Curtis Park resident.[145]

While Isenberg could win elections without Oak Park, he preferred not to. Additionally, though he could win elections without Oak Park, being an effective council member without Oak Park support would be close to impossible. It was the most volatile neighborhood in the city, well organized, and its denizens were not prone to biting their tongues or staying away from city hall when their dander was up. Isenberg nurtured relationships with Oak Park activists and with critical Black organizations such as the NAACP, the Urban League, and the SABC.[146]

Milton McGhee, the Black vice mayor under the at-large system, lost the mayoral election to Richard Marriott, the incumbent.

On November 23, 1971, at the first meeting of the new council, lots were drawn to determine whether odd or even numbered districts would hold elections in 1973. Odd numbered districts lost. They got two-year terms.[147]

School District Elections

During the 1970s, Black people continued to be elected to the DPHESD Board and began to run for election to the Grant Joint Union District Board, which encompassed the DPHESD.[148] A Black incumbent, Dr. George Stewart, a dentist, sat on the Los Rios College District Board. He was outspoken and controversial — championing Black causes and berating district and campus administrators for negligence of Black interests and needs — he made good copy, was often in the newspapers and on television, had great name recognition, and was returned to office by the voters.[149] He was not apparently Black. You couldn't tell by looking.

William Rutland was elected to the Sacramento City Unified School District (SCUSD) Board. He was the highest ranking Black civilian employee at McClellan Air Force Base.[150]

In running for city council, for school board seats, Black people began to develop skills, contacts, and experience in running political campaigns, and as political candidates.

Change in District 2

Robbie Robertson was one of the stars of the new city council. Regrettably, he died after only two years in office. Rather than hold a special election to fill the vacancy, the city council decided to appoint a replacement, and invited applications.

Not only in Del Paso Heights, but throughout the city, black organizations and activists mobilized. They came to the city council and testified, pressuring and intimidating the council to appoint a Black applicant. What they had won through organizing, mobilizing, and the ballot box, they were not disposed to see the council take by fiat. Crowds of Black people appeared at committee meetings and full council sessions whenever the matter was on the agenda. The council meetings became Black spaces suffused by Black narratives.

Dominated as the new council was by liberals, they were ill-prepared to challenge the mandate of an obviously united Black population. Though Black people agreed on the need to fill the seat with a Black person, they held no consensus on who that should be. Robbie Robertson had been an ideal candidate and councilman. It was clear that nobody was actually going to be able to replace him. None of the announced candidates came close to matching his credentials, connections, or abilities. Why the council picked who they finally chose remains a mystery. Herman "Ace" Lawson had been one of the original Tuskegee Airmen. At the time of his appointment he was a state civil service employee. By all accounts, including his nickname, "Ace" was a remarkable pilot. It is possible that his resume alone was enough to convince the council members that he was the one. He had completed a total of 133 combat missions over France, Greece, Germany, Czechoslovakia, Austria, Italy, Yugoslavia, and Romania. He flew P-40s, P-47s, and P-51s. A rarity for a Black person in his day, he was promoted to first lieutenant. He was flight leader, 99th Fighter Squadron, 332nd Fighter Group. As flight leader he never lost a pilot to enemy action. He was awarded the Distinguished Flying Cross, Award of Valor, Air Medals, Unit Citation Medal, and campaign medals. He survived two crashes due to engine failure, bailing out each time, once over the Mediterranean where he was rescued by the U.S. Navy. Before the war he had learned to build and fly gliders on his own. He learned to fly propeller driven aircraft at Fresno State College, where he was also Collegiate Light Heavyweight Boxing champion for two years, the first four year Black football player at Fresno State, and a letterman in Basketball and track. He did all this while he worked his way through college.[151] When he first applied for admission as a pilot to the Army Air Corps, although he already had his pilot's license and the Corps' need was desperate, he was told by the recruiter, "Get the hell out of here, Boy! The army isn't training any night fighters!"[152] Tuskegee gave him the chance to fly, and he took every advantage of it. He probably applied for the council position out of a sense of civic duty. He was not, however, well-suited to the office. He had no civic or political experience and apparently no interest in either. He had no idea of what the responsibilities of a council member were, and did not seem to learn. He may have seen the appointment as an honor in recognition of his achievement. He had no legislative agenda. He brought no issues to the council, did not understand those on the agenda or which others raised, and appeared generally uninterested. He did not know the council's procedures either at the beginning or the end of his term. When he came up for election in 1975, the challengers were legion. As a testament to his effectiveness on the council, he didn't make it out of the primary.

After the primary, the contestants who faced off in the general election were Charles Bradley, a Black community activist from the Heights; and Blaine Fisher, a white real estate broker who had many properties in District 2, including some in the Heights.[153] Fisher was in the solid-South mold of the Democratic Party.

Bradley was well known in the Heights. He had been active in the War on Poverty. He

had a broad base of support in the Heights and he was able to bring in workers from other parts of the city.[154] He had little money and no professional staff, but a young, enthusiastic cadre of returned students — recent college graduates — anchored his campaign. They ran as vigorous and efficient a campaign as their resources and experiences allowed. Bradley lost the election by 113 votes, 1971 to 1858. Fewer than 4,000 voters turned out for the Fisher-Bradley election, as compared with 4,500 for the Robertson-Bunch election.[155] With Fisher's election, Black people and the Heights lost control of District 2. No Black person sat on the Sacramento City Council.

Change in District 5

In District 5 another scenario developed. Isenberg was reelected in

Herman "Ace" Lawson was appointed to the city council in 1973 to represent District 2. Courtesy of the *Sacramento Observer Newspapers*.

1973. But in 1975 he decided to challenge Marriot in the mayoral election. Isenberg won. That left his council seat vacant. When the council met to talk about appointing a new council member, they were besieged by the organized Black population. Black people talked about how it was a disgrace that the Black population of the city, constituting 13 percent of the city's residents, had no representation on the city council. They argued that District 5 was a Black-influence district. They pointed to Blaine Fisher and said, clearly, no one could seriously argue that he represented Black people in the Heights or anywhere. They pushed the point that to maintain civic harmony, which Sacramento had seen precious little of, Isenberg's seat must go to a Black person.

Callie Carney was an Oak Park activist appointed to the city council in 1975 to represent District 5. She was later executive director of the Women's Civic Improvement Club. Courtesy of the *Sacramento Observer Newspapers.*

Probably the most egregious thing that had happened under the new council's watch was the police murder of Raymond Brewer. While that event stood out, it was representative of the generally strained relationship between the city's Black residents and its governing authorities, as well as the outright hostility between the Black population and the Sacramento Police Department.

Aside from the racial tensions in Sacramento, the majority could not in good faith turn their backs on such a large, organized, and loyal part of the Democratic Party. The Black people who spoke to the council when it was considering applications for the District 5 seat also made clear they did not want another honorific appointment. They wanted someone who knew something about *Robert's Rules of Order*, who had a political agenda, and a progressive one at that. They wanted someone with political savvy, who had traction with the movers and shakers in the area. The council named Callie Carney, a Black woman, as Isenberg's successor.[156]

Callie was a veteran of the War on Poverty. She had served as executive director of the Oak Park Neighborhood Council. She had been in the trenches working to prevent young Black men from falling into the clutches of the criminal justice system. She had become an influential activist in the Democratic Party. She was an eloquent and persuasive speaker who had legitimate credentials as a militant. She was often in the streets during the long hot summers and the police stormings of Oak Park.[157] She could fire people to rage or move them to tears. Her appointment was widely approved by the Black activist community.

School Board Politics Revisited

In the meanwhile, Black activists, principally in the SABC, the NAACP, and the Urban League, in tandem with Black educational organizations, Black administrators and teachers in the Sacramento City Unified School District (SCUSD), had become prominent actors in the district's internal politics. The highest Black administrator in the district was Dr. Ervin Jackson, an assistant superintendent in charge of inter-group relations. Black people who became involved in the district's internal politics targeted the appointment of a Black superintendent as a goal. William Rutland, the Black member of the school board, was an ally in that struggle. Eventually, the efforts of the Black coalition paid off when Dr. Edmond B. Forte was appointed as the district's first Black superintendent in 1973.[158]

Dan Thompson was elected to the city council from District 5 in 1977. Courtesy of the *Sacramento Observer Newspapers*.

Back to District 5

In District 5, after her appointment in 1975, Callie was up for her first election in 1977. She had the support of every Democratic leader in Sacramento. District 2 was overwhelmingly Democratic. No Democrat with any aspirations for a political future was going to challenge her, and none did. There was, however, a fly in the ointment in the person of Dan Thompson, a young Black entrepreneur, just out of college. Dan was a virtual unknown, but he had campaign experience. He had run against Isenberg the first time the council had been elected by district. Few people thought he had much of a chance, but he was embarrassing because he was a Black candidate challenging a Black incumbent, a popular Black incumbent. Dan Thompson won.[159] His electoral victory solidified District 5 as a Black district — despite having a large white majority.

Back to District 2

In Del Paso Heights as the 1979 city council election approached, Black leaders and activists got together to develop a strategy based on a clear pattern that had emerged ever since the city council had gone to district elections. In every single election, a Black candidate from the Heights had captured, by far, the largest vote in the primary election. First it had been Robbie Robertson. Robertson had gone on to win the general election, but in that election, an unknown, disorganized, and incompetent white candidate had tripled the vote he'd received in the primary. Robertson was an unusually attractive and competent candidate. In the next election, Charles Bradley had easily out-polled every other candidate in the primary, but had lost the general election.

The leaders in the Heights decided the most promising strategy was to shoot for a victory in the primary. Few people voted in the spring and the edge in organization and mobilization the Heights consistently produced could be enough to swamp the white candidates in the primary before the sheer mass of the white population, even with a marginal turnout, would enable it to garner a narrow margin of victory in the fall. The group decided to hold a Del Paso Heights convention to select one Black candidate for the primary election. All the Black people interested in running could try to win the convention's nomination, but whoever the convention picked would be the sole Black candidate for District 2. Before the white population had awakened for the fall election, the seat would be in Black hands. Every candidate who participated in the convention would have to agree to follow the rules — not to enter the contest if he did not win the convention nomination. It was quite a risk,

Rosenwald "Robbie" Robertson was the first Black person elected to the Sacramento City Council from a district. He was a Del Paso Heights resident, elected to represent District 2. Courtesy of the *Sacramento Observer Newspapers*.

but the candidate who won would have the united support of a proven politically efficacious community.[160]

All the Black candidates agreed to observe the convention rules. The event was well advertised and well attended. The battle for support was hard-fought and heated. In the end, Charles Bradley won the nomination and received the endorsement of all the other candidates.[161]

Bradley's team went all out in the primary. They conducted an extensive voter registration campaign. They contacted almost every Black person in the Heights who was unregistered and registered most of them. They also ran a GOTV effort that found a way to get every Black voter to the polls who was capable of going. Bradley won 49.3 percent of the vote. The incumbent, Blaine Fisher, captured only 40.4 percent of the vote, 300 fewer votes than Bradley.[162] Fisher was disgusted. He told the press, "Let District 2 have Bradley because that's it."[163]

Bradley had come only 0.7 percent + one vote from winning in the primary. He was 82 votes short, the same number that had prevented Robertson from winning his primary. The 82 votes were both good and bad omens, good because Robertson falling the same number short in the primary, had won the general election by a handsome margin, bad because in Robertson's election there had been two Black candidates in the primary and because Charles Bradley was not Rosenwald Robertson.

If Fisher lived up to his word and refrained from active campaigning in the general election, Bradley would win. The white vote would not turn out. Bradley ran a deracialized campaign.[164] Fisher, however, proved true to form. He had lied. He campaigned actively. He picked up 1,000 votes. Just as Bradley's brain-trust had feared, they had done such a good job in the primary they were able to squeeze out only 300 more votes for Bradley in the general election. Fisher was returned to the council by a margin of 278 votes.[165]

The Wider Arena of Electoral Politics

Within the SCUSD coalition Black organizations and employees were influential in the appointment of a Black principal, Adolphus McGhee, to lead Sacramento High School.[166] In Del Paso Heights, increasing numbers of Black people primed themselves to run for the Grant Joint Union High School Board. One of them, Josie Washington, was elected.[167]

By the late 1970s, Thomas Daughtery had become the first Black judge on the Municipal Court.[168] William Morgan was tapped as the 1st Black judge on the Superior Court.[169] Mrs. Sylvester Jennings was elected to the County Board of Education.[170] In 1972 the SABC had spoken to the city council about the absence of Black people on significant city boards and commissions. By the late 1970s, Roy Grimes sat on the City Planning Commission. Archalene Martin was the chair of the County Planning Commission. Grantland Johnson sat on the Regional Transit Commission.[171] Don Nance was director of the County Parks and Recreation Department. Bill Redmond was executive director of the County Welfare Department. Charles Thomas was the general manager of the Sacramento Regional Transit Authority. Walt Thompson was ombudsman for the City of Sacramento. Ray Charles was city fire marshal. Elza Minor was executive director of the Sacramento Economic and Training Agency (SETA).[172] In the education arena, James Bond was president of California State University, Sacramento (CSUS).[173] Louis Johnson was vice chancellor of the Los Rios College District.[174] Hazel Mahone was assistant superintendent for Adult Education in the SCUSD.[175] Jesse McClure was the dean of the School of Social Work at CSUS.[176] There were no fewer than six Black school principals in the area's schools.[177] The explosion in the number of Sacramento's elected and appointed Black officials during the decade was matched nationwide. Everywhere similar processes were at work.

State Government in Local Black Politics

In at least one significant respect the setting of Sacramento's Black population rendered a meaningful difference between its politics and those of most of the country's Black population. Sacramento is the state capital. That renders its politics similar to those of Black people who reside in East Lansing, Michigan; Springfield, Illinois; Richmond, Virginia; Albany, New York; and in some respects, Washington, D.C., as well as other capitals. With the city as the locus of state power, there is the potential for the government to open opportunities for local Black residents. In Sacramento, prior to the 1950s, that potential was not realized. As discussed in chapter one, the state government simply did not hire permanent Black employees. There were no elected Black officials in the state house. There were no Black people and there was no Black influence in state government. That situation began to change in the 1950s. During the 1970s it underwent a sea change. From that point on, residence in the state capitol did have an influence on the personal fortunes of a number of Black people. Indeed, many Black people moved to Sacramento for that very reason. Because California is the most populous state in the union, with the biggest budget, and the 9th largest economy in the world, the role of its location for the Black population in its capital approximates on a much smaller scale the role that Washington, D.C., plays for Black people there. By 1970 state government was a player in Sacramento Black politics.

During the decade, the lieutenant governor, Mervyn Dymally; the state superintendent of Public Instruction, Wilson Riles; and the director of the Department of Motor Vehicles, Doris Alexis, were all Black. Marion Woods was director of the Department of Benefits Payments. Leonard Grimes was California secretary of Agricultural Services. Alice Wright-Cottingim was chief deputy director of the State Department of Parks and Recreation. Rex Fortune was associate superintendent of Public Instruction. Patsy Fulcher was deputy assistant of the California Health and Welfare Agency. Lester Riggins was chief deputy director of the California Department of General Services. Dorothy Roby-Stevens was assistant director of the California Department of Corrections. Attorney Nathaniel Colley was chair of the California Racing Board. Herb Rhodes served on the California Unemployment Insurance Appeals Board.[178] That Black people would occupy such a panoply of government positions would have been inconceivable a decade earlier.

These Black officeholders were significant for Sacramento's Black population and for Black politics in Sacramento. They hired many Black people and appointed many to high ranking positions. Some were Sacramento residents. Others, once hired, came to Sacramento to live. These incumbents controlled significant budgets. They signed contracts and hired consultants, many of whom were Black. Black officials, including state legislators, mentored younger, less experienced Black people and made careers possible for them — in and out of public service.

The officeholders affected state policy. They supported initiatives which enabled Black people throughout the state to come together in Sacramento for meetings and conferences where they developed political ideas, policies, and action strategies. Those occasions provided opportunities for networking and identifying promising people in their midst. Black leaders in statewide office opened many doors for Black people to enter the public and private sec-

SACRAMENTO COUNTY STATISTICAL AREAS

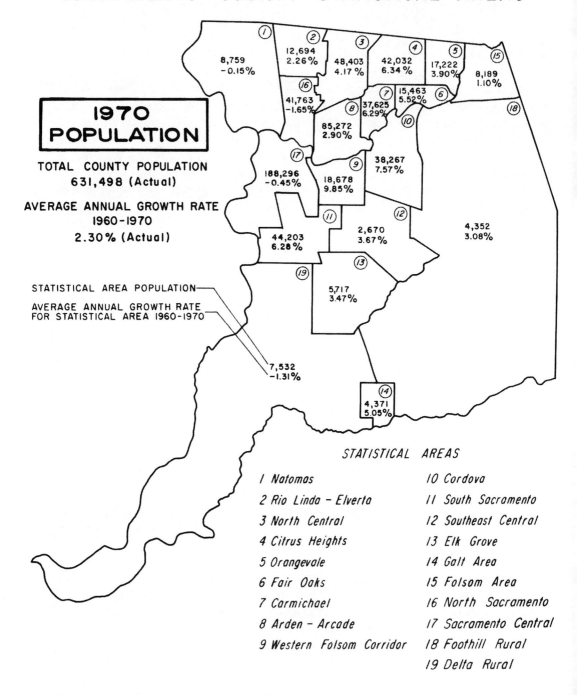

1970 POPULATION

TOTAL COUNTY POPULATION
631,498 (Actual)

AVERAGE ANNUAL GROWTH RATE
1960-1970
2.30% (Actual)

STATISTICAL AREA POPULATION—
AVERAGE ANNUAL GROWTH RATE
FOR STATISTICAL AREA 1960-1970

Map values:

① 8,759 −0.15%
② 12,694 2.26%
③ 48,403 4.17%
④ 42,032 6.34%
⑤ 17,222 3.90%
⑮ 8,189 1.10%
⑯ 41,763 −1.65%
⑦ 15,463 5.52%
⑧ 37,625 6.29%
85,272 2.90%
⑰ 188,296 −0.45%
⑨ 38,267 7.57%
18,678 9.85%
⑪ 2,670 3.67%
4,352 3.08%
44,203 6.28%
⑲ 5,717 3.47%
7,532 −1.31%
⑭ 4,371 5.05%

STATISTICAL AREAS

1 Natomas	10 Cordova
2 Rio Linda – Elverta	11 South Sacramento
3 North Central	12 Southeast Central
4 Citrus Heights	13 Elk Grove
5 Orangevale	14 Galt Area
6 Fair Oaks	15 Folsom Area
7 Carmichael	16 North Sacramento
8 Arden – Arcade	17 Sacramento Central
9 Western Folsom Corridor	18 Foothill Rural
	19 Delta Rural

PREPARED BY THE SACRAMENTO COUNTY PLANNING DEPARTMENT — JUNE 1971

Sacramento County Statistical Areas, 1970. The map shows Sacramento County population distribution at the time of the 1970 census. Note the declines in the most rural areas of the county and in the core city area.

tors both as individuals and organizational formations. Many more Black Sacramentans were able touch their fingers to levers of influence, power, and money.

Afterword

The nation's Black infrastructure was substantially augmented in the 1970s. In Sacramento an earlier structure of churches, masonic orders, men's and women's clubs, social clubs, the garbagemen's association, all anchored by the NAACP, was amplified by the creation of the BPP, BSUs, political and professional organizations, sororities and fraternities, arts and cultural organizations, an umbrella organization, and campaign committees. Collectively, they expanded the Black population's capacity to act. The period of organizational growth which began in the late 1950s, increased in the 1960s, and accelerated in the 1970s was not the product of developments in Sacramento alone, but of national and international changes. In the 1970s throughout the United States more spaces were developed where black people could interact, develop, and pursue their own initiatives, where Black narratives prevailed and Black memories were stored.

Broad Sources of Political Change

Population mobility played no small role in the country's ability to foster Black political development. Marion Woods, the major initiator of the Sacramento Urban League, was born and raised in Georgia. The Urban League was part of the heritage he brought with him. National initiatives created projects that stimulated Black political efforts. The War on Poverty structure came from a national legislative program. Black Sacramentans had the indigenous capacity to take advantage of it — but that there was something to take advantage of was a product of national, not local politics.

Black Student Unions arose out of the Black Power Movement. Hardy Frye came to Sacramento from the armed services and Mississippi. He brought his southern sensibilities with him. Mark Anthony Teemer returned from combat in Vietnam. He exchanged the Marine Corps' M-16 for the Panthers' shotgun. He didn't pick up the gun; he was already carrying one. He simply exchanged one for another. The professional class brought its sororities, fraternities, arts, cultural, and educational organizations, its professional associations. Maxwell Owusu came from Nigeria, Mugo Mugo-Gatheru from Kenya, John Shoka from Tanzania, Gabriel Bannerman-Richter from Ghana, Alexandre Kimenyi from Rwanda. The Sixth Pan African Congress delegation was the result of international momentum. The Nation of Islam and the Republic of New Africa were results of national outreach. Sacramento changed over the '50s and '60s, but the country changed, too, and so did the world. All those factors combined to create a perfect storm of organizational growth.

A Tipping Point

It is unlikely that before the late 1960s Black Sacramento would have had either the critical mass or the organizational specialization to respond to the Oak Park 4 as it did. Three decades earlier it had been a triumph to pressure the city to hire Black garbage collectors. Barely two decades earlier it had been a coup to compel the state of California to hire *one* full-time, permanent Black civil service worker — who happened to have the highest score on the state civil service exam.

In 1969 the Sacramento Police Department shot up the Black Panther headquarters with wanton disregard for human life or safety and launched a campaign of terror against Oak Park's Black male residents. By 1970, the city's African-descended population had the capacity to respond to those affronts in new ways.

The period immediately preceding the '70s produced a condition the '70s drew on heavily, a mobilized Black population. It was comparatively easy to form new Black organizations. Black people were ready for them. It was comparatively easy to get those organizations to take action. Black Sacramentans were eager to get involved in what Black people had done and were doing elsewhere. African people coming to Sacramento from all over the country and the world intended to keep doing what they had been doing elsewhere. There were *new* activities for Black people to immerse themselves in: political campaigns, elective office, Black Studies, Kwanzaa, Neighborhood Councils, Project Area Committees, *Rumble*, the Sacramento Area Black Caucus, the Panthers, the Nation of Islam, the Republic of New Africa. There was the California Legislative Black Caucus, a Black lieutenant governor, a Black mayor of Los Angeles, a Black state superintendent of Public Instruction. There were Black members of Congress and the state legislature. Black people in Sacramento held press conferences and members of the press knocked each other out of the way to cover them. Newspapers and television stations began hiring Black reporters. The local state university had a Black president. The federal expression of these trends was significant, particularly at McClellan and Mather Air Force Bases and the Sacramento Army Depot. There, high ranking Black military officers and civilians wielded considerable clout. Their policies, purchases, and contracts, created significant opportunities in the local economy. They provided career paths for Sacramento residents. There was something in the air, part of the *zeitgeist*, the spirit of the times.

Our Time Has Come

The *zeitgeist,* tipping points, produced results beyond our current abilities to explain — like the red, black and green decals that mysteriously appeared in the '70s. Black people put them on notebooks, in their windows, on their cars. No one seemed to know where they came from, why so many Black people had them, or what they meant. But there they were, ubiquitous. They were a mystery — like the Sacramento Black Unity Festival. The materialization of so many Black people at Miller Park had very little to do with the mobilizing capacity of the SABC. It was much more an expression of the spirit of the times, the mindset of everyday Black people.

Seizing Spaces and Making Them Black

The 1970s witnessed Black domination of the War on Poverty, nationally and in Sacramento. Black politics produced an Affirmative Action Office for the county of Sacramento with a Black director. Black people were placed on the city Civil Service Commission and a Black director of City Personnel was hired. Black politics drove the mayor to appoint a Citizens' Committee on Police Practices to investigate the SPD. Black political organizing, strategizing, and skill put a Black superintendent in charge of the Sacramento City Unified School District, a Black principal at Sacramento High School, and Black principals at elementary and middle schools throughout the district. Black politics delivered a Black school board in the Del Paso Heights Elementary School District, and Black superintendents. Black politics placed a Black member on both the SCUSD Board and the Grant Joint Union District Board.

Black politics resulted in the election of a Black person to the Los Rios Community College District. Les Gary (director of the Lincoln Christian Center) and Luke Connelly (a young lawyer, newly admitted to the bar, and fresh from the Black student struggles) used their skills in the service of Black politics so that when Sacramento voters amended the city charter to require the election of council members by districts, the final council maps resulted in two Black-influence districts. Ultimately, that districting, combined with other aspects of Black politics resulted in four Black people serving on the Sacramento City Council during the decade. Three Black judges were named to Sacramento Courts. Previously there had been none. Black influence resulted in the appointment of Black department heads in the city, county, special district, and state governments. Black people were appointed to all the major boards and commissions in the city and county. The SABC and the Sacramento Urban League produced their own television programs. The Sacramento NAACP produced its own radio program.

The Spread of Black Narrative

Political mobilization and activism provided more legitimacy for Black people as public spokespersons. News media covered Black press conferences. Reporters sought out Black leaders and organizers. When Black people spoke from their positions as lieutenant governor, state superintendent of education, departmental director, city council member, school board member, school district superintendent, school principal, university president, or university dean, they spoke with the imprimatur of office.

The Products of Black Officeholders

Perhaps the most direct impact of Black people in office was getting other Black people jobs and contracts. They hired Black people. They put Black people on interview panels. They implemented affirmative action. They publicized job openings to Black people. They solicited Black job applicants. In the SCUSD they sent teams of recruiters to historically Black colleges and universities. Black officeholders promoted other Black people into positions of authority. They mentored Black people. They informed Black businesses of contracts up for bid.

Overall, the widespread presence of Black officials throughout the political infrastructure resulted not in tens, dozens, or scores of jobs for Black people, but hundreds. The absolute numbers of Black people benefiting from these actions were substantial. Proportionately, however, they were few. Probably no more than 3 percent of the Black population benefited from this largesse. Nationally, that's over 600,000 people. A whopping 97 percent of the Black population received no direct benefits. Moreover, in Sacramento, many people who got jobs and promotions came to the capital from other places *for* the jobs. They were not long-term locals. This had the advantage of recruiting more trained and skilled Black people, but many stayed only long enough for their next promotion or better job offer, and the disadvantage of such external recruitment was that it reduced opportunities for long-term residents. Yet, statewide, and nationally, such combinations of vertical and horizontal movements produced more lasting benefits. In Sacramento the single greatest impact of Black officeholders was the several hundred jobs that went to Black people who otherwise would not have had them. Black incumbents were providing similar opportunities for their constituents in every hamlet, village, town, and city in the country. The national effects were proportionally more effective because wherever the occupants of such positions moved, they still remained within the Black population.

With respect to other accomplishments, we must face head-on the most powerful and ubiquitous — the most determining — conditions of Black life in the United States and Sacramento. Just as few African descendants served in the national Congress and were entirely insufficient to pass any piece of legislation or even get a bill out of committee, in Sacramento Black officeholders served one at a time on the city council, a body of nine incumbents; one at a time on the SCUSD Board, a body of seven incumbents; one at a time on the Grant Joint Union School District Board, a body of five; one at a time on the Los Rios Community College District Board, a body of seven. Only on the DPHESD Board did Black people constitute the majority — one of the smallest and poorest school districts in the county. Nevertheless, the differential impact of that majority circumstance is clear. The DPHESD had more Black superintendents, principals, and teachers than the much larger school districts which surrounded it. It had much larger Black non-teaching staffs. Every kind of employment opportunity was much more accessible to Black people in the DPHESD than in any other county school district. In the Heights, the curriculum, subject to state guidelines, was influenced by Black people. Unlike Del Paso Heights, most city and county policy bodies with any Black incumbents at all had only one. While they were certainly in positions to join coalitions — the point Browning, et al., make — their agendas were not the coalition priorities.

Among the non–Del Paso Heights situations, the Black Sacramento City Council members were in perhaps the most favorable situation. Most other members on that council were liberal Democrats, i.e., the coalition priorities would contain some elements of the Black agenda: affirmative action, the poverty program, revitalizing poor neighborhoods. Other elements of the Black agenda — police reform, work place discrimination, widespread affordable housing, and zoning — were more problematical. Where Black officials tended to be most effective, apart from providing jobs, was with major capital outlays in neighborhoods: community centers, swimming pools, libraries, elementary schools, and parks. This is the equivalent of pork barrel legislation at the national and state levels, a kind of legislation which most legislators are able to secure. They were also somewhat effective in addressing crises: the Oak Park 4, Raymond Brewer, the county jail, the police raid on the Nation of Islam. They were good at symbolic acts: the Dr. King holiday, and school and library naming.

It may be more revealing to indicate what they did not do. They did not contribute to lowering crime or incarceration rates for Black people, to reducing the *general* levels of unemployment and underemployment for Black people. They did not improve the housing stock available for Black people, the level of drug or alcohol addiction among Black people, or rehabilitation program accessibility for those who remained addicted. Despite their many successes in improving their positions within school district hierarchies, they did not improve the performance of Black children in the public schools or Black high school graduation rates.

As was the case for the country at large, the people who dominated Sacramento's life were those who employed the most liquid assets. The city government's resources were decidedly limited, particularly after the passage of proposition 13 in 1978 which reduced local property tax — the predominant source of local revenues — by 52 percent. As a result, those private persons and institutions with money determined what the city did. Developers were the principal source of funds — not only for local political campaigns, but also for the development of infrastructure. If they didn't put it on their drawing boards, it didn't get done. Like Washington, D.C., Sacramento had large areas occupied by government facilities not subject to taxation. These included not only the vast expanses devoted to state government, but also two major Air Force bases and an army installation.

Except on the most marginal levels, Black Sacramentans were not participants in the economic realms which controlled policy by default. People with assets financed political campaigns, housing, buildings, malls, supermarkets, roads, bridges, neighborhoods, business districts, manufacturing sites, new technologies, and infrastructure maintenance. For these undertakings Black people were merely spectators. For all practical purposes, a few were bench warmers who never got into the game.

Black Officeholders and Political Accountability

Except in the Heights, Black political officeholders did not belong to any effective Black accountability structure. They usually had nominal memberships in the NAACP, and occasionally the Urban League. They generally belonged to Black churches. They often belonged to Black fraternal or masonic orders. They attended candidate nights and interviews held by Black organizations. Outside the Heights they belonged to no Black organization which required them to be accountable to it. They had friends, family members, and acquaintances who were active in such organizations, but they themselves were not responsible to any.

In the Heights, DPHESD Board members were directly accountable to Black voters because the majority of the district's voters were Black. There were also active neighborhood organizations, such as the Good Neighbors Club, which held public officials accountable and sought specific policy objectives. Additionally, the Heights had created a convention to screen Black candidates for the District 2 city council seat. The Heights had long-standing influential, informal associations and networks. People used them to interact with policy leaders and convey opinions to them. No such dense and meaningful accountability structure existed anywhere else in the region.

There is another side of this accountability question and its correspondence to the national picture is much more explicit. It involves the Democratic Party. Many Black officials belonged to the Democratic Party. To receive party support (unofficial, of course, in Sacramento), they had to be responsible to Democratic policies and priorities. Such accountability afforded them access to the party's vast network of contacts and resources, and not only from the immediate area.

In short, the Black population had no institutional means for informing Black public leaders of their interests and priorities, or for holding them accountable, but the Democratic Party did. Nor was there any forum offering continual interchange between elected Black officials and their constituencies. For the most part, Black elected officials *had to* meet, bargain, talk, and interact with their non–Black peers *on* the city council, *on* the school boards, *on* the special district boards. There was no structure or procedure for such mandatory interaction among Black officeholders with each other. Except in the Heights, the staffs they worked with were largely of non–African descent. For the most part, the policy worlds Africans inhabited were non–Black and largely white. They were hegemonic spaces where hegemonic narratives and social memories prevailed.

One of Bill Lee's purposes in proposing what came to be the Sacramento Area Black Caucus was to create a venue to fill the gulf in interactions between Black leaders — a sanhedrin, a *formal* pseudo-government. That purpose was never fully realized, and was soon abandoned. The same kinds of experiments went on ceaselessly at the national level: the

National Black Political Party, the National Black Assembly, the National Black Leadership Roundtable, and countless Black summits.

Ordinary People

Black officials were able to implement some changes, but structural, procedural, and demographic factors limited their scope of action. The astounding feature of Black politics in the decade was that ordinary Black people were able to transcend structural, procedural and demographic factors to such a degree as to enable the breakthroughs that put more Black people into decision making positions where they could utilize the available options. Ordinary Black people made those options possible. To do that they drew on the upheavals of the Civil Rights and Black Power movements. They internalized the movements' perspectives and dynamics and applied them to their specific situations. The people who did that — who worked in the Poverty Program, the BSUs, the NAACP, the Urban League, the Panthers, the WCIC, the SABC, the Oak Park Community Legal Defense Fund, Schule Jumamose, the Sacramento Black Nurses Association — held no political office and had no titles in front of their names. They were everyday Black people. Their efforts were those of a leviathan.

CHAPTER 3

The 1980s

In Sacramento as in most of the United States, by the end of the 1970s the social move-ment that had carried over from the late '60s had been lost to Nixon, Watergate, and even-tually, Ronald Reagan. The Black politics of the 1960s which had been characterized by fierce challenges to the status quo, had morphed into more routine political forms, capped by the quest for elective office.

The diminution of such actors as SNCC, the Black Panthers, and Black Student Unions seemed to indicate a decline in activism among some sectors of young Black people, but not all. Indeed, activism among other sectors increased dramatically. They consisted of the very poor and most marginalized. Their activism featured gangs, drugs, and gun violence.

Their predations joined with the twin calamities of crack and AIDS, creating a perfect trifecta, or troika, of catastrophes for Black people, particularly Black young people. We might say the decade witnessed a cavalcade of disasters for Black people: the Reagan Revolution, Black youth gangs, crack, the criminalization of large sectors of the Black population, and AIDS. Black people had to face multiple catastrophes simultaneously. Their efforts to com-bat them were made all the more difficult by the collapse of the War on Poverty.

In this chapter, after paying homage to the passing of the War on Poverty, we first exam-ine the thrust of Black politics which captured the most attention during the 1980s, electoral politics. Afterwards, we look at Black organizations, collective mobilization, and state poli-tics. In this combination of approaches we witness the principal means Black people devel-oped to contend with a new world of sorrows.

[handwritten margin note: Electoral politics dominate black discourse in 1980s]

The War on Poverty

For all practical purposes, when President Carter left office, the War on Poverty ended. In Sacramento, in a desultory fashion, SAEOC and a few delegate agencies continued with John Robinson as SAEOC executive director. With revenue sharing, less and less money went into the structures, and they shortly withered away.

[handwritten margin note: War on poverty + SHRA]

Only the Neighborhood Project Area Committees (PACs), which had been incorporated into the Sacramento Housing and Redevelopment Agency, remained. They had become per-manent fixtures of Sacramento local government. No longer, however, did they have inde-pendent staffs. Their staff functions were assumed by the housing agency.

The disappearance of the poverty program not only took away significant Black spaces, it also deprived the Black population of a number of jobs, and a valuable source of job training and political apprenticeships. The poverty agencies had acted as direct conduits for both poor and middle class Black people into political internships. They were not replaced.

Many of the poverty warriors had moved on. Others were forced to scramble for their suppers, and still others were thrown back into the morass they had climbed out of. But the pipeline, the vehicles for self-improvement, the avenues for political involvement were all shut down. For those who had not been involved in the Poverty Program through the '70s, by the end of 1980, the door had been shut. For those still living in the target areas the state no longer offered a way out. Instead, Reagan provided a safety net so no one would hear heads crack and bones snap as people plummeted into hard times. The net caught them and held them above the abyss where they could writhe and squirm, but could not escape.

Electoral Politics

After Reagan's election in 1980, Black people asked themselves, *What are **we** going to do about this?* Two months before the presidential election, the National Black Assembly began to provide answers when it hosted the National Black Political Convention (NBPC) in New Orleans, August 27 to 29, 1980. The convention passed a resolution calling for the creation of an independent Black political party.[1]

The month of the election, only weeks after the polls had closed, November 21 to 23, 1980, 1500 delegates from all over the country met in Philadelphia. They approved the formation of the National Black Independent Political Party (NBIPP), and set up a mechanism, the National Organizing Committee (NOC), to put their resolve into effect.[2]

At work in the creation of NBIPP and many other Black political initiatives was the perception that the 1980 election had confirmed that items on the National Black Agenda were off the country's agenda. Black people would have to take care of them themselves.

That was as true in Sacramento as it was elsewhere. In Sacramento there were three clear indicators of these trends:

1. The SABC sent a delegate to the NBPC in New Orleans which passed the resolution calling for the creation of a Black political party.[3]
2. On October 15 to 18, 1980, the Pan African Studies Program at CSU Sacramento and the SABC co-hosted a conference entitled, "A Working Conference for a Black Political Party."[4] Attending were Harold Cruse, author of *The Crisis of the Negro Intellectual,* one of the most influential books on Black political thought to come out of the 1960s[5]; Dr. Maulana Karenga, founder of the Black organization, US, creator of Kwanzaa, and one of the country's most influential Black nationalists[6]; William Strickland, associate professor of political science in the W.E.B. DuBois Department of Afro-American Studies at the University of Massachusetts, one of the principal authors of the National Black Agenda adopted at the 1972 National Black Convention[7]; James Turner, a leader of the B.S.U. at Northwestern during the student uprisings of 1968 and director of the Africana Studies and Research Center at Cornell[8]; one of his colleagues from Cornell, Manning Marable, senior research associate of Africana Studies, already a prolific author, widely heralded as the next W.E.B. DuBois[9]; Omawale Satterthwaite, president of the Institute for the Study of Community Economic Development, councilman for the East Palo Alto Municipal Council, delegate to the 6th PAC[10]; and Ron Daniels, president of the National Black Political Assembly.[11]
3. The creation in Sacramento, prior to the existence of NBIPP, of a Black political party, the Party for the New Black Politics (PNBP).[12]

Before the 1980 election was even held, like their counterparts all over the country as indicated by those attending the working conference, the nationalist element of Sacramento's Black population was highly mobilized.

The Reagan election did not have the same effect on Black activists and politicians who were not nationalists, but it kept their antennae attuned to the nationalist aspect of their political perceptions. They were increasingly likely to engage in race-based strategies.

Redistricting in Sacramento

In 1981 the Sacramento City Council had to draw new council district lines based on the 1980 census. This would be the city's first redistricting since council districts were created. The council established a well-publicized and community-driven process. City staff offered redistricting kits for interested parties so they could create and submit their own proposals.[13] The council also scheduled open hearings for public testimony, presentation of plans, and discussion.[14] One hearing was held in each district. On the basis of community-submitted plans, testimony, and hearings, the staff was to submit a final proposal for the council's consideration. The council could approve or modify the proposal as it saw fit.[15]

The pc was virtually unheard of so most of the work was done manually on maps using hard copy census block tables. It was laborious and time consuming. The SABC took the lead in developing a comprehensive proposal on behalf of the Black population.[16]

The most striking revelation the 1980 census provided was a dramatic shift in the city's Black population. First, the Black population had increased substantially. The whole city's population had grown, but the Black population's growth rate had exceeded the city's. In 1970 Black people were 11 percent of Sacramento's population. In 1980 they were 13.3 percent.[17] Secondly, the major concentration of Black people had changed. In 1970 the two largest concentrations were in Del Paso Heights and Oak Park. In 1980 the largest concentration was in the southern part of the city in an area called Meadowview. In 1980 Meadowview was home to 25 percent of the city's African descended residents in five contiguous census tracts.[18] This finding was the focus of the caucus' redistricting plan.

[margin handwriting: Changing pd demographics 1970–1980]

The Sacramento City Charter provided that in setting district boundaries consideration shall be given to "community of interests of the districts, existing neighborhoods and community boundaries." Indeed, a California judicial review looked at a redistricting proposal specifically as it affected Black voters.[19]

SABC Initiatives

The SABC sought to develop a redistricting plan which would put this new community of interest into one council district. If the boundaries remained the same as they had been in 1970, the population would be divided between Districts 7 and 8. In 1970 when 7 and 8 had been formed, this Black population concentration had not existed.[20]

At the same time the SABC had to account for the tremendous change in Black population distribution, it also had to try to preserve the interests of Black people in District 2, Del Paso Heights, and District 5, Oak Park. The caucus wanted to be fair to other communities of interest as well, particularly Latinos and Asians. The SABC set out to develop a fair proposal that would also recognize and incorporate the new Black community.[21] The plan they produced was presented at an early redistricting hearing, and over time, with some adjustments, became the standard model presented by city staff, along with the rationale which

[margin handwriting: SABC balancing Act]

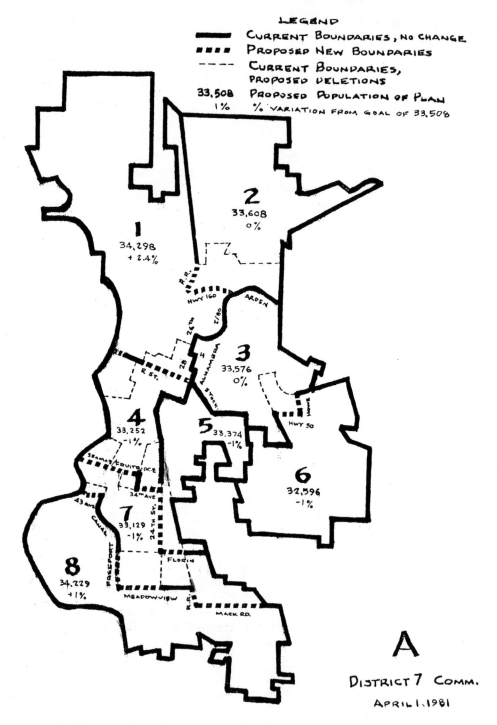

Proposed Reapportionment 1981. This was the last-minute map drawn up by the District 7 Committee and adopted by the city council. It split the Meadowview community in half. Almost half of the community is between Meadow View and Florin Roads, as seen on the map.

explained how it served the diverse population's collective needs. In every one of the five hearings, the new Meadowview community was kept intact within a single district.[22] In a summary meeting on April 16, all three possible district configurations kept the Meadowview community in a single district.[23]

ideal plan, but

A Fly in the Ointment

At the eleventh hour a letter was submitted to Councilman Thomas Hoeber, chairman of the Reapportionment Committee. Although dated April 1, the letter was not received until almost the close of the proceedings and the text acknowledged it had been delivered late in the process. It also recognized that what it suggested was unprecedented. It did so in this curious and almost unintelligible sentence concluding its second paragraph.

> However, since this Plan proposes changes to the District lines being considered at other meetings, we ask that this Plan be considered in total even though appearance is made only at the one meeting.[24]

This sentence might be accurately translated as follows: *Although we have not offered this plan earlier and it has not been considered on its merits by anybody else, and although there will be no chance to criticize or amend it, we recommend that you adopt it as it stands and cast aside all prior deliberations.*

It was signed by Thomas Chinn, for the District 7 Committee.[25] The new plan split the Meadowview population in half. It put 45 percent of the community in District 7, and 55 percent in District 8 — completely obliterating the *political* presence of this Black population.[26] The stated rationale for this plan was threefold:

new plan

1. Though District 7 has shrunk by 4,000 people and District 8 has grown by 18,000 people, there is no need to change the boundaries because the same neighborhoods exist as when the original district boundaries were drawn. The original boundaries were based on a comprehensive city plan. If the boundaries were redrawn, boundaries for all districts would have to be redrawn.

argument for not redrawing

The argument makes no sense. The whole point of the census is *to enable* redrawing district boundaries to make sure that the districts are as representative of the population as possible. *There is nothing wrong with redrawing the boundaries of all the districts. Indeed, that is what the redistricting requirement anticipates.*

2. District 7 is composed of 4 neighborhoods. Both council members who have been elected in the district reside in the same neighborhood. Obviously, the voters of District 7 are happy electing all members of the council from one and the same neighborhood. Expanding the boundaries of District 7 won't change that, because while voters even now can pick council members from 4 different neighborhoods, they don't. They pick them all from the same neighborhood.

The position defies reasonable interpretation. First of all, just because voters in the past have chosen to elect people from one neighborhood, even if the boundaries were to remain the same, it does not mean they would continue to do so. Secondly, with the boundaries changed, there would not only be more neighborhoods to choose from in selecting a council member, *different people would be making the choice*. Therefore, there is no possibility of predicting who they might choose.

3. Prior council hearings have recognized the need to expand District 5's boundaries for the purpose of increasing the chance of a Black or Hispanic representative of the district. Therefore, it is appropriate to make racial or national origin considerations in creating district boundary lines. In the case of District 7 the boundaries should not be changed because doing so would eliminate the possibility of electing an Asian–Pacific American from District 7.[27]

Item 3 falters on two grounds. First of all, it is misleading. The plan that survived all the rounds of deliberations up to that point, the one which kept the Meadowview district intact, did so by concentrating Black voters in District 8. That plan was deliberately designed to keep the Asian community of interest which was present in District 7 intact. The second error in item 3 is that it neglects to consider the *new* community of interest in Meadowview at all.

What then, *really* was the problem with keeping Meadowview intact and passing the plan developed and approved throughout the deliberative process? It would change District 7. Chinn and his committee were actually operating as a shill for Lynn Robie, the councilwoman from District 7. If the proposal which put all of Meadowview together in District 7 were approved, she would have to run against a Black opponent in a district which was over 30 percent Black and which would be a majority non-white district. To avoid that she had her committee submit a proposal which ripped Meadowview in half. It was this last-minute, aprocedural, spurious, ill-conceived, and speciously considered proposal which the city council approved.[28]

Dan Thompson, the sole Black member of the city council, moved the adoption of the first plan. He could not even get a second.[29] After his motion died for lack of a second, the council approved the back-alley proposal drawn up by the District 7 Committee. The council protected one of their own and effectively disenfranchised 25 percent of Sacramento's Black population. Had Meadowview been kept intact, it not only would have created a heavily Black-influenced district, it also would have created the only majority non-white council district in the city.[30]

The SABC was astonished and infuriated by the council vote. It had played by the rules, gone out of its way to be fair, and according to the rules of the game, had won. But, unbeknownst to them, the game was not being played by the rules; their opposition — who they had not even known existed — had not played fair or by the rules, had lost the game, but won the election.

The city council justified its decision by saying:

1. The approved plan provides for a 20 percent Black population in 4 council districts.
2. Preserving the Meadowview community intact would have resulted in non-compact districts.[31]

The *Sacramento Bee*, endorsing the council's decision, said the proposed District 8 which the council had not approved, was shaped funny.[32]

SABC Reacts

The SABC took its fury both to the city council and the Black community. The motion to approve Chinn's plan could be reconsidered if a council member who had voted for the motion moved to reconsider. Councilman Thompson voted against the motion, so he could not move to reconsider. It would have to come from another member of the council, all of whom — except Blaine Fisher — were liberal Democrats. The caucus position was clear: (1) the deliberative process had been junked, and (2) the approved plan was a mess and logically indefensible.[33]

As to the neatness of district lines or compactness of districts, the districts *weren't* that funny looking. Compared with districts all over the state, they were almost models of compactness. More importantly, a shape on a map, particularly a neat, clear, regular shape on a map, has nothing to do either with how people actually live in space or how communities of interest are physically laid out. To violate communities of interest by making neat lines on a map is to violate the whole purpose of districting and redistricting. The very point of the process every 10 years is to provide people equal representation. If that meant only that electoral districts need be numerically equal, redistricting would be no problem at all: just divide the population into the neatest, most compact equally populated districts without regard to the characteristics of populations within the boundaries.[34] That would be a travesty of representative government. Nevertheless, that is precisely what happens when communities of interest are slashed and burned to make neat lines on a map.

People don't live that way. There are train tracks, freeways, vacant lots, public parks, squiggly streets, rivers, creeks, junkyards, odd-shaped blocks, irregular parcels. Neat lines and compact shapes violate all that — *and have nothing to do with representing people.* The point of redistricting is not map-making, but providing democratic representation. The aesthetics of the map must yield to the interests of the people.[35] Anybody who fails to see that doesn't get the point of *representative* government. The Sacramento City Council didn't get it — or said it didn't.

Black people did. The SABC went to organizational meetings, churches, forums. Members tried to get representatives of the community to sue the city. They were even willing to build up a war chest to finance a suit.[36] There were, however, no local attorneys who would touch it, even though every politically informed African descendant knew the city council had held its Black population in contempt and sacrificed it for an incumbent's seat. About that there was no doubt.

After the ordinance establishing the new council districts went into effect and a new council was elected, Dan Thompson no longer represented District 5. Joe Serna, a Chicano, a professor of government and ethnic studies at California State University Sacramento, was elected.[37] No Black person sat on the city council. There is almost no doubt that had Meadowview been kept intact, a Black person would have been elected to the council. In one fell swoop, Lynn Robie had kept her seat and Black people had been kept out of elective office.

The Sacramento City Council had done to the local Black population what Ronald Reagan's election had done to the national Black population — cast its fate to the wind. In both instances Black people got the message.

Reagan's election was a symbol of disaster for most of the Black political community. They realized they had better develop some autonomous political initiatives. Organized Black nationalists were particularly energized to build an independent political capacity.

Many of them sought to build political autonomy through the National Black Political Assembly in its National Black Political Conventions of 1972, '76, '78, and '80.[38] The last one approved the call for the creation of an independent Black political party.[39] From that the National Black Independent Political Party (NBIPP) arose.

The hostility toward Reagan and the move to more race-centered agendas were not limited to nationalists. In March of 1981 the Sacramento Urban League sent a letter to the chief of the California State Police (who had jurisdiction over the State Capitol and the Capitol grounds), in an arena usually outside the Urban League's purview, to challenge the State Police granting a permit to the Ku Klux Klan to stage a rally on the State Capitol grounds.[40]

In December of 1981, the Sacramento branch of the NAACP, the SABC, Black Advocates in State Service (BASS), and the Sacramento Urban League held a joint press conference and sent a telegram to President Reagan.[41] At the press conference, they said in part,

> The millions of Black South Africans who are torn away from their families for long periods of time to labor in the bowels of South Africa's mines and to labor in South Africa's factories, fields, and homes are the most repressed people on this earth. And yet, this administration has refused to condemn apartheid and has refused to impose sanctions against the repressive South African government.[42]

> Given this posture by the Reagan administration, we can only conclude that the civil and human rights of Black people are not deemed important concerns of this administration. As an African people, the hosts of this press conference cannot accept this kind of hypocrisy.[43]

Earlier, in the spring of 1981 the SABC chair, Otis Scott, had published a more pointed statement in the *SABC Newsletter*: "In a word or two what the Reagan administration holds for Black Americans is HARD TIMES."[44]

Harold Washington

The sentiments and activities present in Sacramento were nationwide. Mel King was gearing up to run for mayor in Boston. Black nationalists and radicals were energized and gearing up right along with him.[45]

In Chicago Black nationalists were casting about for a Black candidate to challenge the Daley machine.[46] They settled on an incumbent, progressive member of Chicago's congressional delegation, Harold Washington.[47] Washington was an established figure in Chicago politics and no stranger to the mayoral election. He had run for mayor in 1977 and finished out of the money with only 11 percent of the vote.[48] There was little reason to think any differently about his chances in 1983. Yet Black people were tired of throwing their time, energy, and money behind white candidates only to be betrayed after electoral victory.

Washington was skeptical and reluctant.[49] A serious mayoral campaign was no light undertaking. He had responsibilities in Congress, and while nationalists were enthusiastic and serious, they had minimal electoral experience. They were hardly a rock on which to build a campaign. Washington did not want to play games with them, but he wanted them to be realistic. He told them to register 50,000 voters come back, then they could talk.[50] When they came back with 50,000 new registered voters, Washington said they'd need to register 100,000.[51] The nationalists came back with 180,000.[52] He sat down to talk.

The Harold Washington campaign became a national campaign. It was going to be hard to raise money from the Democratic Party fat cats. There was not only the condition that Washington was Black, there was also the reality that the two major candidates in the party were, respectively, the incumbent mayor and the namesake and son of Richard J. Daley. Washington wasn't even on the radar screen. He was, however, clearly within the lenses of African descendants *all over the country* who had been mobilized by Reagan's election.

Washington went east and west, north and south, attempting to shake the numerous but spindly Black money trees. Everywhere, he was greeted with overwhelming exuberance. What money those little trees held fell off. He even came to Sacramento where local Black politicos of every stripe went wild.[53]

On election day in Chicago, February 22, 1983, the Black troops came out. They carried on an unprecedented GOTV campaign in every Chicago Black neighborhood. Simultaneously, Jane Byrne and Daley ate up each others' votes. When the polls were closed and all the ballots counted, the news stunned the city. Harold Washington had won the Democratic primary! Black Chicagoans went wild. They literally danced in the streets. Together, they had done the impossible.[54] Black people throughout the country joined them in celebration. This was a Black victory, regardless of where Black people lived. The African descendant population was a *national* population and this was a *national* victory.

Normally, winning the Democratic primary is equivalent to winning Chicago's mayoral election. The problem was that a Black victory in the Democratic primary was not normal. It became immediately clear that the general election was going to be decidedly abnormal.

In Chicago's mayoral race, since the general election is merely a pro forma event, the Republican candidate is traditionally marked by a lack of distinction. Ordinary and even dismal characters who don't mind losing, and who expect to lose, pick up the Republican mantle and wear it for a season before watching it go down to crushing defeat. Chicago Republicans who are capable and interested in higher office, point for statewide office — in particular, U.S. senator or governor. The Republican mayoral candidate for 1983, Bernard Epton, a nondescript man with no substantial following, fit the norm. All that changed immediately after the primary. The results had hardly been announced when the leading alderman on the city council, Edward "Fast Eddie" Vrdolyak, who was also the chairman of the Cook County Democratic Party, *the leading Democrat in the city next to the mayor*, announced his support for the *Republican* candidate.[55] In any other circumstances this would have been unspeakable heresy. Under the circumstances of the Washington triumph, however, the alderman was joined by other Democratic aldermen and life-long Democrats all over the city who had scarcely been able to let the word Republican pass their lips.[56] Caught off guard by Washington's triumph in the primary, the leading Democratic members of the city council turned the general election into a race war. This was recognized by Black people from Maine to San Diego.

In Chicago, the Black nationalists, militants, and other inspired Black political workers went back into the trenches. The ecstasy of the primary victory elated the Black populace. People who had resisted earlier entreaties to stand up and vote voluntarily signed up to vote, many for the first time. Harold buttons became required wearing apparel for Black residents of the Windy City.[57]

Harold Washington went back on the road. He returned to Sacramento where he was hailed as a conquering hero. But everyone knew he faced a monstrous struggle. They dug as deeply into their pockets as they could. This was not just Harold's fight. This was not just Chicago's fight. This was a fight for the whole Black nation.

Run, Jesse, Run

An essay by Jesse Jackson appeared under the headline of *The Washington Post* in *The Guardian*, May 1, 1983, entitled, "Let a Black Democrat Run for President."[58] Jackson made a case for the legitimacy, timeliness, and appropriateness of a full-blown Black candidacy in the Democratic presidential primary. One could hear, in the background, "Run, Jesse, run!"

Not in Isolation

The Black electoral reaction to Reagan's election, often led by the least electorally-oriented Black activists — nationalists and radical leftists — was not limited to Boston, Chicago, or the stirrings around Jesse Jackson. It was also present in Sacramento, most notably in the person of Grantland Johnson.

Grantland Johnson

Grantland Johnson was raised in Del Paso Heights. Since his student days at American River College and Sacramento State he had been involved in the political life of the Heights. At Sacramento State he had been a central member of the school's dynamic and community-oriented BSU and PASU.[59]

When Grantland graduated from CSUS, he became active in the National Alliance Against Racism and Oppression. He went to Cuba as a member of the Venceremos Brigade. He traveled the country as an organizer for the National Committee to Overturn the Bakke Decision and he was a member of the organization's leadership structure. He was hired by Henry Lopez, Concilio's executive director. He had known

Active in the Pan African Student Union in the '70s, Grantland Johnson was elected to the Sacramento City Council from District 2 in 1983 and to the County Board of Supervisors in 1987. Subsequently, he was appointed western regional director of HUD by President Clinton, and director of the California Department of Human Services by Governor Gray Davis. Courtesy of the *Sacramento Observer Newspapers*.

Grantland from Grantland's student days and his work in the community.[60]

Grantland married another Heights resident, Charlotte Bolton, also a Sacramento State graduate. She was every bit as political as Grantland. They had one child, a daughter. Charlotte decided to run for the Del Paso Heights Elementary School Board (DPHESB). Grantland was actively involved in her campaign. She won. Subsequently, he worked on a number of other DPHESB campaigns, including a successful effort to defeat a recall attempt of two school board members he had helped put in office. He worked on both of Charles Bradley's campaigns for District 2, co-managing Bradley's second attempt. He also worked on two successful campaigns for Black candidates for the Grant Joint Union High School District Board. He managed the campaign of Sam Pannell, a Black candidate for District 7. Sam survived the primary, but lost the general election.[61]

Concilio recommended Grantland to the Sacramento City Council for appointment to the Regional Transit Authority Board of Directors. He was appointed. Eventually, he became board chairman. In that capacity he took an action which alienated a significant segment of Sacramento's Black petty bourgeoisie. He recommended and voted for the firing of the agency's executive director, Charles Thomas, a Black man. He also distanced himself from other members of the same component of the Black population when he publicly opposed the Black superintendent of the DPHESD, Dr. Charles Townsel.[62] According to this sector of the Black community, a Black person in any leadership position was, *ipso facto*, a good thing. This was a common sentiment among the country's Black bourgeoisie and certainly not unique to Sacramento.

After Blaine Fisher defeated Charles Bradley for the second time in 1979, a number of Heights residents told Grantland he should run against Fisher during the next round. Grantland had just begun life as a gainfully employed family man and was not receptive to the entreaties. In 1981, however, when Dan Thompson was not returned to the city council, and there were no Black city council members, others began to encourage Grantland to run. Among them were the mayor, other city council members, members of the California State Assembly, and a prominent Heights union leader. Grantland and Charlotte talked it over.[63] Grantland came to the conclusion that he was the only progressive in District 2 who had a snowball's chance in hell of beating Blaine Fisher. If he really wanted a progressive to fill that seat, he was the only feasible possibility.[64]

A Serious Limitation

The leading members of Sacramento's Black petty bourgeoisie would support Grantland neither financially nor as campaign workers. They regarded him as misguided. For one, he was a leftist. He called himself a progressive, but they saw him as a radical, a militant, while they featured themselves as moderates and liberals. Secondly, they saw his attacks on Charles Thomas and Dr. Townsel as betrayals of the race.[65]

Among members of the Black petty bourgeoisie Grantland's only stalwart supporters were the few progressives. Small in number and meager in resources, they were nevertheless at his disposal throughout the campaign. They attended and held fund-raisers for him, made public endorsements, walked precincts, registered voters, and spearheaded GOTV campaigns.

(handwritten margin note: Grantland supports & opposed)

Grantland knew that the broader Black bourgeoisie would not constitute one of his major support groups, so he had to develop plans for his campaign with that limitation in mind. His basic and repeated stance was that District 2 was neglected largely because it consisted mainly of poor and working-class people. To get decent services from the city, people in the district — despite their differences (largely racial) — had to work with each other on the basis of their *shared interests*. Voters in the district had to support people who would represent those interests to the city council — and if they did not — get rid of them.[66] In short, outside the Black precincts, Johnson ran a classic deracialized campaign.

The Campaign

During March of 1983, when Grantland's campaign office was set up in Leslie Campbell's family room, the campaign began in earnest. Leslie was on the board of the DPHESD. Grantland had worked on her campaign committee. They had been BSU members at Sacramento State together. Leslie had started college as a mature woman after she'd married, had a family, and divorced. Her oldest children were almost Grantland's age. Charlotte, Grant-land, and Leslie were the key members of his campaign committee.[67] The campaign was designed to be absolutely grassroots. The plan was to walk the whole district, door to door. Grantland wanted to follow the mass line: from the people, to the people.[68] His principal strategy within Black precincts was to secure them as his base and maximize their turnout.

The team had a lot of electoral experience. They knew the Heights and the district inti-mately. They had been major participants or candidates in nine election campaigns. They designed precinct work around reducing the universe they would concentrate on. They wanted to identify and focus on people who were likely to support Grantland — not only likely to be in favor of him, but who would actually vote for him. Serendipitously, fate had provided them with a remarkable instrument for achieving that goal. The gubernatorial election had ended just a few months earlier, in November of 1982. In heavily Black-populated areas the Demo-cratic Party had geared up an enormous effort for its candidate, Tom Bradley, the Black mayor of Los Angeles. Grantland's campaign had a list of precincts which had gone heavily for Bradley with high turnout rates. Those precincts, they reasoned, were theirs. Their job was to walk those precincts, identify individual voters who would vote for Grantland, and turn them out.[69]

The Bradley gubernatorial campaign had registered the highest number of Black Demo-cratic voters in the state's history. As a result, Grantland's campaign decided not to focus on voter registration, but on voter turnout. Nevertheless, because they walked the precincts so intensely, they added 500 voters to the rolls by the primary election.[70]

The overall strategy included consolidating Grantland's base in the Heights among Black voters. They wanted to make sure those voters knew Grantland wasn't taking them for granted. His campaign would begin and end with Black voters in the Heights. Throughout the cam-paign the committee worked the Heights more thoroughly than anywhere else.[71]

The campaign brain trust set up three categories of precincts: most likely, swing, and not likely. Black precincts were most likely. They were walked three times. Swing precincts were walked twice. Grantland walked all the most likely and swing precincts. Volunteers walked marginal precincts twice. People self-identified as voters received a stamped postcard, addressed to Grantland's campaign headquarters. It asked the respondent to identify major city-related problems in the neighborhood or district, and to identify their satisfaction or dis-satisfaction with the incumbent.[72]

Charlotte's sister had a personal computer, so much a rarity for the times the campaign referred to it as a mini-computer. To them, a computer was a mainframe, the giant structures housed in universities, major government agencies, and big corporations. All the district's vot-ers were entered into her computer. Mailings were targeted to likely Grantland voters and people who returned postcards. There was a significant response from the 2,000 postcards distributed. People identified weed-infested lots, junk cars, debris, stray dogs, and substan-dard buildings as their most frequent complaints. Grantland framed his campaign around those concerns and what he would do to correct them. He also blamed the incumbent for doing nothing about them.[73]

As a door-to-door campaigner Grantland was one of his own best assets. He often walked eight hours, going home only when it was too dark to pick out addresses. He listened. He talked. He didn't give rote replies. He encouraged dialogue. Like Bill Clinton, much later, he was a master at interchange with voters. The campaign used a buddy system. Workers went out in pairs. But Charlotte, Leslie, and others eventually recognized they had to send Grant-land out alone. He kept his buddies out too long, and he was wearing them out. His conversations were so effective that after he walked a neighborhood, residents felt free to call—not his campaign headquarters, but his house—and they frequently did.[74]

District 2 contained 3,648 Chicanos, 12.17 percent of the population. There were 6,811 Black people, 22.74 percent of the population. White people numbered 19,499, 65.09 percent of residents.[75] *Combined*, the Black and Chicano populations added up to half the white population. Even if Grantland got every Black and Chicano vote, whites could still outpoll them 2 to 1. In the primary Grantland had the advantage that there were four white candidates, including the incumbent. There was another Black candidate, George Washington, but his campaign wasn't comparable to Grantland's, and ironically, Grantland had better name recognition than *George Washington*.

[margin note: demo- makeup of District 2]

While it appeared likely to those in Grantland's campaign that he would be one of the two top candidates in the primary, the general election had always been a strong point for the surviving white candidate, particularly Blaine Fisher. In the general election overwhelming white numbers had been simply too great to overcome. There was, however, an anomaly between the voting and population figures. Registered white voters had on occasion outnumbered registered Black voters by as little as 51 percent to 49 percent, even though whites tripled Blacks in population.[76] Black people in the aggregate, in District 2, were much more disposed to register. Robbie Robertson had shown that if a Black candidate could maximize the Black vote when there was a minimum white vote and win a slice of the white vote, that candidate could win. It was this kind of differentiation in Black voter intensity and participation that gave Black candidates the effrontery to challenge the white incumbent. Black voters really acted as if they owned the district. White voters did not. While this situation would appear to challenge the conventional wisdom, we do not have enough national data at this level of detail to know that is the case. Certainly, the phenomenon of Black people claiming ownership of poverty neighborhoods even though they were in the minority would seem to indicate that this kind of ownership of unlikely political spaces is not an isolated instance.

For fund-raisers Grantland's campaign relied on a number of grassroots efforts and on personal and organizational donations. Late in the primary Grantland used one of his most innovative, productive, and controversial fund-raising ideas: contributions from the national transit community, reached through his contacts as chair of the Regional Transit Authority. This initiative produced a lot of money, but most of it came too late for the primary.[77]

[margin note: additional funds for Gen. Election]

Grantland finished first in the primary and Fisher second, 1532 votes to 1451. The 500 additional voters Grantland's campaign had registered proved vital. There was, however, bad news in the numbers. Fisher and Lyla Ferris, a white, environmentalist, liberal, yuppie candidate, had a combined total of 2521 votes. Grantland and the other Black candidate, George Washington, had a combined total of 1805 votes. The combination of *all* the white candidates had received 2949 votes, 62 percent of the ballots. Black candidates had received 38 percent.[78] It was clear Grantland was going to need more than Black votes to win. Another patented Fisher closing was in the offing.

[margin note: Primary results]

The General Election

The Johnson campaign went into phase 2. The transit money came into play. Grantland hired a professional manager, Rick Yanes. He was good and he had a record of working with progressive candidates. The deep pockets also enabled Grantland to hire two clerical workers. Yanes' first major accomplishment was securing a new office. Leslie's family room would not do. Yanes did something the volunteer committee, experienced as its members were, never

new
office
space
in
commercial
area

would have tried. He found a huge, vacant store on the major street in the district, Del Paso Boulevard, at its busiest intersection, sandwiched between a Safeway and a McDonald's. The original campaign crew never would have even looked at the site because of prohibitive costs. Yanes, however, made inquiries. He found that the site had been leased to a thrift store. It would not be able to move in until a week after the election. Yanes talked to the thrift people about a sub-lease at a cut rate. They agreed. They had nothing to lose. They even threw in office furniture as part of the deal.[79]

The place was mammoth. There was plenty of space for telephone canvassers, and room to lay out and assemble kits for walkers. There was space to arrange for separate areas to instruct new walkers while other work went on uninterrupted. There was also room for what came to play an inspirational role in the campaign: food. In this serendipitous development, the importance of consolidating Grantland's base showed its hidden strengths. One of the campaign's major emphases was getting Heights supporters involved in the campaign. The organization wanted volunteers to feel that the vast new headquarters belonged to them. Most people in the Heights, while they had solid voting records in both primary and general elections, didn't know anything about participating in a campaign other than voting. Grantland's organization intended to teach them. Many were older, afraid or physically incapable of precinct walking. Tasks were tailor made for them. Some did phone calling. Some assembled kits for walkers. The place was so big a day-care area for campaign workers' children was set up. A whole wall displayed the children's artwork. Some of it portrayed Grantland triumphing over Fisher. Some volunteers worked in the day care center. Others brought in food for volunteers. Not finger sandwiches. Pots of greens, beans, spaghetti, slabs of ribs, delicious sauces, peach cobbler, corn bread, fried chicken, pound cake, pies, cookies, gumbo. Many white volunteers got hooked. They'd never had many of the dishes. They rushed back for the gastronomical delights at the end of a day's walking. The headquarters' ambience was so great that workers literally had to be shooed out every night, usually around 11:30 P.M.[80]

The campaign amassed 300 volunteers. In the course of the primary and general campaigns Grantland covered every precinct in his base area three times. Volunteers walked each of them an additional two times. In the primary Grantland had won two thirds of the swing precincts. They were incorporated into the base. Grantland walked each of them three times, and the volunteers covered them two more times. The campaign made a deliberate decision not to try to register more voters but to concentrate on their reduced universe.[81]

The campaign featured a televised debate between Grantland and Blaine Fisher. Grantland was articulate, well-informed, bright, and conceptually clear. Fisher was inarticulate, uninformed, obtuse, and confused. All of that was made clear in the debate. It was comical. Fisher seemed to have been set up as a straight man for Grantland. Unfortunately, it was aired at a bad time, but it was very popular at campaign headquarters. On election night it was shown over and over as straight entertainment.[82]

The campaign mailings were based on Grantland's theme that the purpose of local government was to serve neighborhoods. Mailings were targeted to specific issues associated with each neighborhood through the postcard system. If a neighborhood had complained about stray dogs, the mailing explained what the city could do about stray dogs, why it hadn't done that, and committed Grantland, if elected, to cut down the number of stray dogs, using available means.[83]

On election day the campaign put 90 workers on the street for GOTV work. There were so many they had to be doubled up in some precincts. Fisher seized the lead in the absentee ballots. As the evening progressed, he kept it. At midnight Fisher still had the lead. Grantland's campaign workers who had come to celebrate jammed the headquarters. They became downcast. They saw the repetition of the old scenario, the insurmountable number of white voters. The office closed and workers went home with the count still going on, the results still discouraging. The day following the election Grantland still trailed. Incomprehensibly he was ebullient. The count in his base area was still out. When the final tally was in, Grantland had 3056 votes. Blaine Fisher had 2649. District 2 had elected a new city council representative.[84]

TABLE 3.1 SEPTEMBER 1983 DISTRICT 2 PRIMARY VOTE DISTRIBUTION BY CANDIDATE, VOTER TURNOUT AND PERCENTAGES BY PRECINCT

Prec	# reg	# vote	Vote %	Johns	Wash	Fish	Ferris	Hintz	Walter
27	1401	362	25.8	156	31	58	84	11	13
28	856	240	28.0	13	10	78	106	29	3
29	1088	284	26.1	15	9	93	126	27	9
30	147	39	26.5	4	1	14	7	3	5
32	1129	273	24.1	143	30	60	20	3	0
33	1119	342	30.2	245	32	19	19	0	0
34	1026	300	29.2	113	15	85	51	12	12
35	880	229	26.0	57	9	77	47	15	15
36	1260	310	24.6	50	8	95	104	18	20
37	294	79	26.8	37	12	12	10	1	1
38	1203	435	36.1	264	59	51	15	6	4
39	923	241	26.1	134	23	44	17	3	4
40	581	163	28.0	21	2	89	22	18	2
41	868	217	25.0	35	4	96	51	11	11
42	865	255	29.4	42	2	126	58	8	12
43	1128	318	28.1	57	10	136	74	8	22
44	521	159	30.5	21	1	70	42	5	17
45	1284	326	25.3	53	3	93	119	12	36
46	295	68	22.9	14	4	26	11	6	4
47	302	77	25.4	16	0	22	20	10	5
48	200	62	22.1	4	3	30	22	0	1
Other							1		
Totals	14445	4779		1532	273	1451	1070	215	213

TABLE 3.2 NOVEMBER 1983 DISTRICT 2 GENERAL ELECTION VOTE DISTRIBUTION BY CANDIDATES AND VOTER TURNOUT AND PERCENTAGES BY PRECINCT

				City Council Mayoral Seat			
Precinct	# reg	# vote	Vote %	Johnson	Fisher	Relles	Rudin
27	1137	350	30.7	241	92	164	148
28	1119	406	36.2	357	25	201	151
29	1197	523	43.6	437	55	225	208
30	147	47	31.9	13	30	33	13
31	1033	337	32.6	190	127	197	129
32	879	278	31.6	130	122	132	127

Precinct	# reg	# vote	Vote %	City Council Mayoral Seat			
				Johnson	Fisher	Relles	Rudin
33	1265	409	32.3	125	241	240	154
34	921	296	32.1	212	69	114	136
35	582	223	38.3	53	161	121	91
36	863	294	34.0	91	181	159	121
37	867	331	38.1	87	226	167	152
38	1134	423	37.3	162	246	262	143
39	519	207	39.8	66	129	129	66
40	1287	415	32.2	188	210	232	166
41	298	85	28.5	26	46	47	33
42	303	103	33.6	48	47	47	47
43	1398	475	33.9	312	147	293	164
44	858	305	35.5	101	195	101	116
45	1095	366	33.4	119	225	219	135
46	296	108	36.4	74	33	59	44
Other				1	1	0	2
Totals	17198	5980		3056	2649	3222	234

Election Analysis

There were 21 precincts in the primary election and 20 in the general. The precincts were numbered differently in the general election than in the primary, so that, for example, precinct 27 in the general election is not the same as precinct 27 in the general election. District 2 kept the same set of precinct numbers for both elections, but they were tacked onto the various precincts seemingly at random for each election.[85] In the primary Grantland won 7 precincts and lost 14. In the general he won 9 and lost 11. In his base area, in the general election he not only held his primary vote total, but picked up 753 more. He picked up 516 more than he and his Black opponent, George Washington, both had in the primary. Sixty percent (1823 votes) of Grantland's election total came from his base area. He got almost 300 more votes from his base area alone than he did from the whole district in the primary. He got 18 more votes from his base area alone than he and George Washington together got in the whole district in the primary. This was clearly a case of maximizing his base.

In winning two precincts he had lost in the primary he picked up 105 votes. In the eleven precincts he lost in the general election he picked up 702 votes, 648 more than he and the other Black candidate had received from those precincts in the primary. He collected 1031 votes in the precincts he lost, as opposed to 329 in the primary. Grantland picked up votes in every single precinct, ranging from an increase of 174 in a precinct within his base to a low of 9 in a losing precinct. He picked up as many as 135 votes in a precinct he lost. The lowest number of votes he gained in a precinct he won was 32, increasing by 300 percent the total he had received in that precinct during the primary, enabling him to win the precinct by one vote. In every precinct his vote totals exceeded his and Washington's combined in the primary election. He picked up 1524 new votes, falling 8 short of doubling his totals for the primary. His 3056 tally dwarfed the 1805 he and Washington together had totaled in the primary. He minimized his losses in the precincts Fisher won.

Fisher also picked up votes, a total of 1198. But while all the white votes together had polled 2949 votes in the primary, Fisher got only 2649 in the general. He lost 300 votes from the white primary total. Grantland, on the other hand, picked up 1251 votes over the Black candidates' primary total. In the general election, even if Fisher had won the same total number of votes as white candidates had won in the primary, Grantland's tally still would have exceeded his by 100 votes. Fifteen hundred more votes were cast in the general election than in the primary. Unlike Grantland, Fisher had fewer votes than the white primary candidates in the precincts he lost and even in some he won. This tendency was evident in the two precincts Grantland picked up. In the smaller one, white candidates won 154 votes in the primary. Fisher got 122 in the general. In each case, though Grantland won the precinct, he got fewer votes than the white totals in the primary.

The voter turnout was not high in any precinct. In the primary election, the numbers ranged from a low of 22.1 percent in a white precinct to a high of 36.1 percent in a precinct in Grantland's base area. In the general election the figures ranged from 28.5 percent in a white precinct to 43.6 percent in one of Grantland's base precincts. In addition to having turnout rates comparable to white voters, Black voters were registered at higher rates.

The figures in Table 3.1 indicate that in the primary the average voter turnout in precincts Grantland won was higher than in the ones he lost. The average turnout in his winning precincts was 28.27 percent as compared with 26.19 percent in the ones he lost. Because the Black population was registered at higher rates than the white population, the Black *voting* population *proportionally* exceeded the white voting population in two important respects: a) a greater proportion of the Black population was eligible to vote; and b) of that higher proportion, a larger percentage actually voted. This occurred in the face of the consistent findings in the literature that lower SES groups are less likely to vote than others in primary elections.

In the general election, Table 3.2, all voters turned out at higher rates than in the primary. The higher overall turnout for the general election, and particularly the increase among white voters may be partially explained by the condition that the mayoral contest received a great deal of media publicity. Even so, the highest turnout rate in District 2 was in the precinct with the greatest concentration of Black voters and in which Grantland's campaign had expended its maximum effort. Turnout in that precinct exceeded any other precinct's by almost 4 percentage points. The overall numbers between Fisher's precincts and Grantland's, with respect to voting rates, were almost indistinguishable, Fisher's voting at a 34.66 percent rate and Grantland's at a 34.52 percent rate. This almost unity between the two groups despite the condition that a higher proportion of the Black population was registered to vote, means that a higher percentage of the overall Black population than the overall white population actually voted. If we compare the vote totals in Fisher's precincts between the votes in the mayoral contest and the votes in the District 2 contest, we find that 50 fewer votes were cast in the District 2 contest. That drops the rate of voting in the District 2 contest in Fisher's precincts to 34.26 percent — under the rate in Grantland's.

The numbers run directly contrary to the popular wisdom that Black people neither register nor vote at the same rate as whites, particularly poor Black people.[86] Indeed, according to popular wisdom, a Black candidate would be wasting time trying to build a base on a poor, Black population that constituted only 23 percent of a district population. Commonsense would tell us that is a formula for defeat. That is why we do the research.

Grantland not only maximized his base area, he also minimized his loss in the white areas by putting his white workers into Fisher's precincts. While Grantland and his workers covered his base areas five times, his workers covered Fisher's areas twice. This enabled them to identify individual voters they could target in Fisher's areas. In the general election Grantland at least doubled his primary vote in every precinct he lost except one where he fell 2 votes short of doubling it. In one precinct (#29 in the primary and #45 in the general), he fell 1 vote short of increasing his total by a magnitude of 6, moving from 15 votes to 119. On the other hand, Fisher stayed out of Grantland's base altogether. There, a few Black people campaigned for Fisher, primarily associated with a group he had appointed to a redevelopment committee, but they largely limited their campaigning to lawn signs and coffee-klatches, and did not canvass.[87]

A Critical Weakness

A major weakness of Grantland's electoral strategy was that it had no ongoing *organizational* base. Grantland was a member of a close cadre of people who had worked together in the Heights. They did not constitute a formal organization. A campaign organization, consisting of people from many different organizations, and of people with no organizational affiliations, came together in the election, but it ceased to exist as soon as the election was over and the thrift store moved into its building. That is one reason for the kind of schizophrenic identification of campaign organizations in this study. They are sporadic. They do not contribute to a community's organizational infrastructure in a sustained way. They are task oriented, and the task is of extremely limited scope and duration. That is why Jesse Jackson's Rainbow Coalition offered another kind of possibility. That was the attraction of NBIPP. The organizers behind both efforts were looking at long-term results. They were not limiting their focus to specific elections. They were looking at creating institutions which could provide substantive political efforts over the long haul.

In practical terms Grantland was accountable only to himself and his conscience. Any program he pursued was essentially his program. While in order to be reelected or elected elsewhere he would have to please his constituency to a certain extent, realizing such an objective is not equivalent to pursuing a progressive agenda. Nor did his presence in office provide the kinds of leverages and entrees for an *organized* constituency which would arise were he part of an ongoing organizational structure — appointments, contracts, influence on decision makers.

This is a serious shortcoming. It is not of Grantland's making and he is not responsible for it. But the weakness for a progressive Black movement that this condition constitutes cannot be overlooked. There was, for example, no guarantee that the reservoir of experience developed in the Johnson campaign would be available for future elections, or even that the people involved in the campaign would ever hook up with each other again.

Nor is this a failing associated solely with the Johnson campaign. We saw it in the Harold Washington election, in the Wilson Riles, Jr., election. It is up to the activists who participate in such efforts — including the candidates — to remedy it. Black people cannot afford a politics of the individual. A progressive Black politics must be about the most oppressed of our population. For such a politics to be sustained, accountable, and minimize the dangers of co-optation, it must have an organized constituency which keeps the feet of its leadership to the fire. Leadership faces the real and present danger of leaning with the strongest wind. Unfortunately, the wind switches direction. It was a weakness of the Rainbow Coalition. Even though activists saw the coalition as an ongoing, mass based institution, it never developed a national leadership structure independent of Jesse Jackson. When he was not the candidate, there was none. In a sense, Black electoral politics often suffers from a Ralph Nader syndrome. The candidate is the campaign.

An Assessment

In Grantland Johnson's 1983 election to the Sacramento City Council, we had a case where Black voters felt empowered in their city council district. They felt it was theirs. In fact, that was part of the Black narrative — that District 2 was their seat and they were going to take it back — even though they were only 23 percent of the population. That feeling of empowerment was maximized and exploited throughout the district by linking Black voters to a candidate and a campaign organization that drew on that enthusiasm to run a superior campaign. Nor can that dynamic be divorced from the national mood which increasingly convinced Black people around the country that they had to take their political fortunes directly into their own hands.

Chicago

True to form, the Democratic Party's candidate, Harold Washington, won the mayoral election in Chicago. His victory, however, was not conventional. It was a cliffhanger, won only at the closing bell, and then perhaps solely because the Republican candidate flaked. It is very possible that Bernard Epton snatched defeat from the jaws of victory.[88] Washington won because of his own resilience and the gut-busting work of the Black population. It was not Democratic politics as usual which put Washington in the mayor's office. It was Black politics played at its finest and carried out till the very instant the polls closed that enabled Washington to slip through the narrow crack in the door before it slammed shut.

When Washington won the Democratic primary, white voters did not roll over. They rolled to the Republican Party in unprecedented numbers to prevent a Black capture of *their* city — which they definitely saw as a white, and *not* a Black, space. They knew that even if a Republican won the mayor's office, the Democrats still controlled the city council and the pick of the spoils. To defeat Washington they pulled out all the stops but could not overcome the number of white Democrats who could not bear to cross party lines. Some white Democrats did not vote at all. Others closed their eyes and held their noses as they voted for their party's candidate. Latinos sided with Washington. African people gave him a landslide. The combination of white Democratic loyalists, white Democrats who could not vote the Republican ticket, Latino majorities, and an unimaginable Black voting bloc was enough — barely — to bring him home.[89] Incontestably, the numbers of Black voters added to the rolls during Washington's campaign was the biggest single factor allowing him to win. He had only a 48,250 vote margin. He would not even have been in the ballpark without the almost 200,000 new Black voters registered for the election.[90] His greatest asset was an inspired Black population. On April 12, 1983, Chicago's voters chose a Black man to lead the Second City. The victory rested on the backs of ordinary Black people.

Sacramento

Five months after Washington's victory, Sacramento's second district sent Grantland Johnson to the city council. For the first time in six years a Black person was elected to the council. For the first time in two years a Black person sat on the council. A representational void was filled. In Sacramento the Black candidate had to overcome an even greater voter disparity than in Chicago. As in Chicago, that victory was made possible only by minimizing losses in white and Latino areas, but it rested firmly on the hypermobilization of the Black population. Black people outperformed their white counterparts by orders of magnitude. Grantland won because he was an outstanding candidate and because Black voters looked the opportunity in the eye and did not blink.

Both Washington and Johnson had shown that a Black majority constituency was not necessary to win a racially contested election. The sole *sine qua non* was a hyperorganized and super-engaged Black population. With those elements as a foundation, anything was possible.

Jesse Jackson

Shirley Chisholm had been a serious presidential candidate in 1972, but she had mounted nothing like a major nationwide campaign.[91] Jesse Jackson was sensitive to the political winds. The Democratic Party had lost the presidential elections of 1968, 1972, and 1980. Had it not been for Watergate, they probably would have lost 1976. Black people were the largest, most consistent block of Democratic voters. With the sole exception of 1964, the Democratic Party had not won a majority of the white vote since 1948.[92] Jackson believed the Black vote could best show its strength in Democratic primaries, and in so doing renegotiate its place in the Democratic Party coalition. As Jackson addressed Black audiences, they chanted, "Run, Jesse, run!" They were the motive force for his candidacy.

Jackson's campaign posed a dilemma for the fledgling NBIPP. NBIPP founders, as one rationale for its formation, had explicitly rejected the Democratic Party as merely the left wing of the U.S. conservative party. But Jackson was deliberately running in Democratic primaries. How could a Black *independent* party register Black voters into the Democratic Party to vote in Democratic primaries? This position was expressed by Central Committee member Kwaku Duren, from Los Angeles, who put his words into NBIPP's mouth when he wrote,

> NBIPP *is opposed* to Jackson's running as a candidate of the Democratic party ... we think the interests of the Black community ... can only best be advanced through an independent political campaign.[93]

On the other hand, JoNina Abron, from Northern California, and Far Western regional representative, argued,

> There is strong evidence that electoral politics is *the major* activity in the Black movement now. The position that our party takes on this question will ... determine the character and extent of our involvement in electoral politics in the period ... until November '84.[94]

This issue was to be hotly contested within NBIPP and led to serous organizational fractures. While JoNina eventually resigned her position on the Administration and Policy Committee to work on the Jackson campaign,[95] many other NBIPP leaders refused to cross the line to organize, campaign, and vote in a Democratic Party primary.[96] The party ultimately proved flexible on the issue and let members do as their consciences dictated.[97] That was a fortunate development for Sacramento where the Party for the New Black Politics served both as the local NBIPP chapter and as an independent organization. Most PNBP members registered as Democrats for the '84 Democratic primary and worked in the Jackson campaign. What they did after the Democratic Party convention, however, was another matter. Most put no effort into the Democratic campaign for the November election. After November, however, Black people in Sacramento, like Black people all over the country, had to face the hard reality that Reagan had been elected to a second term.

The Sacramento Valley Rainbow Coalition Organizing Committee

One Sacramento Black organization which developed during the 1980s was part of a much broader political effort: the Rainbow Coalition. The local organization did not die out at the end of the 1984 Democratic primaries, the 1984 presidential campaign, or even the 1984 November election which returned Ronald Reagan to the White House. Rather the contrary, the organization continued to grow and deepen following the 1984 election campaign.[98] It might seem problematic to consider the Rainbow Coalition a Black organization. It was intended, specifically, to be a rainbow organization: red, Black, brown, yellow, and white, gay and lesbian. It was to be the organization of all the locked out, centering on the needs and aspirations of the most locked out of all — the poor.[99] The poor were universal. They included people of every color. As white people formed the overwhelming majority of the population, there were more poor whites than anybody else. The Rainbow Coalition was intended to be broadly encompassing. In Sacramento, the leaders, the activists in the local Rainbow Coalition, the SVRCOC (Sacramento Valley Rainbow Coalition Organizing Committee), fit that description. Organized labor was present. Asians were particularly active. Latinos and white progressives were well represented. There were Native Americans and a solid representation of Black people.[100] How, then, might the SVRCOC be considered a Black organization? It can because of the definition I established at the outset. Its leadership was dominated by Black people, Black people constituted the plurality of its membership, and it was intended to serve the needs and interests of Black people.[101] It was intended to serve the needs and interests of others as well, but so were the NAACP and the Urban League, yet one would be hard pressed to omit them from the pantheon of Black organizations. At its root — all rhetoric, slogans, and initiatives not withstanding — it was Jesse Jackson's campaign organization. Without him it did not exist. He set the agenda and he was the motor driving the machinery. While the Sacramento organization was diverse and had primarily class-based programmatic goals, it was always bound to the will of the national organization. It was also inconceivable that the local organization could operate or take any significant policy stances without the concurrence of its Black leadership. No other element of the coalition was as indispensable. The coalition could function without any one or any subset of the others. But without Black participation it would have died. Black participation and consent constituted its *sine qua non*. The SVRCOC was a Black organization.[102]

While the SVRCOC, formally organized in 1986, had begun in 1983 with Jackson's first run for the nomination, the Sacramento campaign organization never ceased operating, and its membership constituted the core membership of the SVRCOC. In effect, the earlier organization simply changed its name and assumed the organizational form required by the national organization.

While the Rainbow Coalition was Jesse Jackson's campaign organization, the Sacramento contingent saw it as a vehicle for a much deeper level of organizational work. Its members were interested in progressive reform. They wanted to challenge the prevailing order, engage in mass mobilization, and drive a structured reordering of the society and its politics.[103] Most of its leaders and activists were progressives. They believed in some form of socialism. Their key goal was a more equitable distribution of wealth and power.[104] Jackson's emphases and those of the local Sacramento organization were every bit as much international as domestic.[105]

The SVRCOC was able to draw strength from, as well as give impetus to, the dynamics of local politics. The Rainbow Coalition constituted a pool of workers for local elections.

At the same time, its members' participation in local elections helped invigorate the coalition and provide its cadres with feet-on-the-ground political experience.

The Return of Grantland Johnson

Another aspect of the national political scene in 1987 was that Harold Washington was running for reelection as mayor of Chicago. The development of his campaign and his appearances in Sacramento stimulated the Rainbow Coalition, Jesse Jackson's run in 1988, and the SVRCOC. It kept Black politics on the front burner of Black activists around the country, including Sacramento.

Grantland Johnson was a beneficiary of this focus. By all accounts he was an effective and popular city council member. He was fully embraced by the Democratic Party. He actively engaged in coalition building. He had contacts and supporters in a wide range of publics. He was also well-connected and highly thought of in state and national political circles.[106] As a member of the city council, however, he suffered from a serious shortcoming. He could not make a living wage.[107] He was totally committed to his responsibilities on the council. That made the position a full-time job. A product of California's reform movement it the early 20th century, Sacramento's municipal government utilized the city manager form. The city's chief administrative officer was the city manager. The city council was envisaged as a broadly legislative body with most of the detailed vision and operations left to the city manager and the administrative staff appointed by the manager and serving at the manager's pleasure. Grantland's *full-time* council position yielded only $10,000 per year.[108] Charlotte was the family's principal financial provider. Grantland was coming up for reelection in 1987, but he feared he could not *afford* to be reelected. If he were, he would have to declare bankruptcy.

At the same time one of the most reliable members of the progressive Democratic coalition on the County Board of Supervisors, Ted Sheedy, faced a number of personal challenges which cast a long shadow over his political future. The county's progressive Democrats wanted to keep control of the seat, but the prospects looked dim. They began to engage in palavers about how to deal with the deteriorating situation. Some of them picked up hints that Grantland was thinking about not running again. If that were true, the election cycle would result in a double debacle. They began to come to the conclusion that there was one way to pull the chestnuts out of the fire, to turn looming disaster into a brilliant triumph. A few approached Grantland. They lamented with him the crushing financial hardship four more years on the council would impose on his family. They knew, however, he was a political junkie. They suggested there might be a way out of his financial nightmare without abandoning his political vocation. The position of county supervisor was fully salaried. The progressive incumbent who represented the supervisorial district Grantland lived in was not going to seek reelection. Grantland could run for his seat.[109]

The proposition was interesting but not terribly feasible as a solution to Grantland's woes. Black people constituted 5.9 percent of the county's population.[110] Everyone had seen what had happened to the immensely popular Black mayor of Los Angeles when he had run for governor against a lackluster, but white Republican opponent. White electorates didn't elect Black people. Though the population in Grantland's city council district was overwhelmingly white, they had not elected him. Black voters had elected him. White voters had simply refrained from defeating him. A majority of whites who had voted, voted against him. Even if Grantland made it through the primary in the county election, he had no prayer against a white candidate in the general election. While his district had a comparatively large non-white population, the numbers of white people in the district dwarfed them. Making it through the primary would only set him up for a slaughter in the general election.

Democratic big-wigs had been thinking over the same problem. The supervisorial district, they reminded him, is Democratic. We can make you the Democratic candidate. We can get the Democratic Central Committee behind you. We can get the state party behind you. We can get the Sacramento congressional delegation behind you. We can mobilize the whole party apparatus on your behalf. You have wide support among non-whites. You'll have the backing of organized labor. The Asians like you. Jews will support you even though they don't like your stance on Palestine. The Latinos — you worked for Concilio for heaven's sake — will back you. And we will have a Black voter turnout such as the county has never seen. They are a small percentage of the population — but they can constitute the margin of victory. You can win this election.[111]

They talked a good game, but Grantland was not a naif. There was one question they hadn't addressed, hadn't even raised. *Where's the beef?* It took a lot of dollars to elect a county supervisor. *Where's the money?*

He was told, you're going to get money from the party — the local, the state, and the national party. You're going to get money from the unions. Whatever political dollars Black people have, you'll get. Money should not be a deterrent. Grantland told them, this is a local election. I know local elections. Developers are the big money behind local elections. And I am the poster child of the local environmentalists. The major source of funding for this election is closed off from me. The party big-wigs told him, make one phone call. Don't give us your final answer. Make one phone call. They gave him the phone number of Angelo Tsakapolous, the major developer in Sacramento who supported the Democratic Party. Tsakapolous was the dean of philanthropists in Sacramento. In politics, if he chose, he could outspend almost any combination of other developers. Grantland made the call. When he got through the phone protocols to the direct line, Tsakapolous picked up. "Mr. Supervisor," he said. The money door was wide open.

Grantland threw his hat in the ring. The money door was open, but the odds were still against him. He would have to work relentlessly merely to prevent himself from being embarrassed. He did. He became the first Black person elected to the Sacramento County Board of Supervisors.

Black activists did yeoman's work in his campaign. Those closest to him were his old-time colleagues from the Heights and the progressives. He also had legions of other supporters from his work on the city council, from progressive organizations, and his coalition-building fixation. He may well have benefited from an energized base during a considerably off-year election. But unlike many other candidates, he had a significant base to energize.

A meaningful component of his progressive support was active in the SVRCOC. In fact, Grantland's campaign was a regular item on the SVRCOC meeting agendas.[112] Their participation in his election left them charged, triumphant, and highly motivated as they plunged into Jesse Jackson's 1988 campaign.

Two Faces of Electoral Politics

There was always a disconnect between Jesse Jackson and his fervent supporters on the left. There was an even greater disconnect between most Black voters and most Black elected officials. The latter of these gaps was most evident during the 1983 to '84 Jackson campaign.

Jesse Jackson, like most Black elected officials, was a loyal Democrat. The difference was

Jackson was willing to be a maverick. His run for the nomination was unauthorized, unapproved by the Democratic leadership. They strongly discouraged it. Black elected officials were dependent on the party leadership for their political careers. Most came from safe districts so they didn't have to worry about being reelected. What they had to worry about, once in office, were the favors the party would bestow on them. They were in no position to buck the leadership if they cared about their political futures. Jesse Jackson, who had not been elected to anything, had no debts to the party hierarchy. Its members had no control over his future, and no control over him. He was, rather, seeking to put them in his debt by claiming the allegiance of Black voters.

On the other hand, Jackson's most activist supporters were not loyal Democrats. Many of them had to change their registrations or even register for the first time to be able to vote for Jackson in the primaries. They wanted to buck the party, and if the party did not incorporate his goals sufficiently into the platform and party policy, to bolt the party and run independently, taking a potential Democratic victory margin with them. Jesse Jackson did no such thing, which was a great disappointment to the progressive wing of his supporters.

In 1984, despite his lack of support from elected Black officialdom, Jackson had carried 90 percent of the Black vote in the primaries.[113] That made two realities evident to Black officeholders: (1) they were out of touch with their base on the question of Jackson, and (2) they could not deliver Black votes for other presidential candidates. What was clear to them would also be plain to other political wonks. Their inability to deliver votes would not enhance their standing in the party. Only one obvious solution appeared to them — to follow their constituents into the Rainbow Coalition.

In California this tendency was most clearly represented at the statewide level in the annual meetings of BAPAC. BAPAC, the Black American Political Association of California, was Willie Brown's baby.[114] It was his attempt to build an institutional base for politics in California's Black population. It would operate not only as an instrument for mobilizing and implementing a Black political agenda, but could also serve as a PAC for Black Democratic candidates. It was a means of institutionalizing statewide grassroots support for the Black political establishment.[115]

Black politicians in the Los Angeles basin had no need for such an organization. They had their own effective and powerful operations. They had twice elected a Black mayor. They had elected Black people to lead other municipalities in the area. They controlled school boards, community college districts, and a higher percentage of statewide and legislative offices than their numbers warranted. Throughout the 1980s they sent a larger congressional delegation to Washington, D.C., than all the southern states combined. They sat as judges in the courts and on the Los Angeles County Board of Supervisors (without a doubt the second most powerful legislative body in the state). They had formidable fund-raising capabilities.

There was no counterpart for such an organizational infrastructure at the state level. The Bay Area had the formidable Black Women Organized for Political Action (BWOPA). It functioned as a political education organization, an organizing committee, a mobilizing organization, and a PAC.

As speaker of the California State Assembly, Willie Brown sought to build a statewide Black organization to undergird his position as a state leader. The San Francisco Assembly district which elected him to the state legislature was not even majority Black.[116] In effect, he had no Black political base. He sought to build one. Although he was a leader of the state Democratic Party, an independent Black political organization would make him less dependent on the party's primarily white leadership. Nevertheless, his Black organization would be an establishment organization, directly tied to Black political officeholders.[117]

BAPAC was a clear marker of how national political winds were blowing among the members of the state's Black establishment. In January of 1987 BAPAC invited Jesse Jackson to address its annual convention.[118] During the meeting a motion was introduced, spontaneously, for BAPAC to endorse Jackson for the Democratic Party's presidential nomination. It passed overwhelmingly amid jubilant celebration.[119] That endorsement was representative at the state level of activities at the local level which brought the SVRCOC into the same political campaign as Sacramento BAPAC. The two organizations represented unmistakably different visions for Black people in Sacramento, the state, the country, and the world, but they minimized those differences as they merged their efforts in Jackson's primary campaign. That kind of bridging-the-divide activity between Black leadership echelons was a characteristic of the 1988 Jackson campaign. It reflected the solidarity within the Black voting public. The cart was pulling the horse.

The Obvious

Black electoral politics in Sacramento were dominated by Grantland Johnson during the 1980s. He won election to the city council, defeating the incumbent in District 2. He became the first Black supervisor in the county's history. Additionally, he ran and participated in a number of other campaigns and worked with the local Rainbow Coalition. He became the guru for local Black politicians and aspiring Black politicians.

[handwritten margin note: Grantland dominated black political discourse of Sac in 1980s]

The Less Obvious

We would be mistaken, however, to assume that little else by the way of Black electoral activity was going on. Other Black candidates ran for city council. They simply were not elected. Black candidates ran for school boards, community college district seats, and special district seats. Many were elected. Black people were appointed to city and county boards and commissions, a number of them by Grantland, but by other elected officials as well. They were appointed to high-level administrative posts in state and local offices, and to the bench. They were appointed as school district superintendents, and a Black woman, Queen Randall, was appointed president of American River College. Any number of Black school principals were appointed. At CSUS and the local community colleges Black people were named deans and top-ranking administrators.

The broad Black electorate turned out in unprecedented numbers in Grantland's elections and for Jesse Jackson in the Democratic primaries in 1984 and 1988. People hosted fundraisers, gave donations, and engaged in routine political work. Black people were elected to the County Democratic Central Committee. Even Black Republicans formed their own organization.

An Assessment

Throughout the decade in Sacramento not more than one Black person served on either the city council or the Board of Supervisors at any given time. From the end of 1981, the end of Dan Thompson's incumbency on the Sacramento City Council, to the end of 1983, no Black person served on either body. From 1983 through the end of the 1980s one Black person served on either the city council or the Board of Supervisors. He was the same person: Grantland Johnson.

Both the national and local Black electorates recognized they were operating in a hostile environment. That condition was underlined by Reagan's victories in 1980 and 1984, by the elder Bush's win in 1988, by Tom Bradley's defeat by the non-entity, George Deukmejian, and by the defeats at the statewide level of Mervyn Dymally and Wilson Riles. Oddly enough, these electoral death-knells did not dim African-descendent electoral activity. On the contrary, they threw themselves into the Rainbow Campaign and the Rainbow Coalition. In Sacramento they charged into Grantland Johnson's races, and into a wide range of local contests. Instead of despair, they faced with resolve the all too apparent disdain exhibited toward them by their compatriots. In the electoral arena, the clearly conservative cast of the wider population threw Black people into ferocious activity. They tried to establish their own distinct and authentic voices as an electorate. In effect, their actions issued a proclamation to the dominant officeholders of the era, "You may represent the bulk of the population, but you don't represent us."

The same level of activity was apparent everywhere — on Jackson's coattails or not, Black people elected increasing numbers of representatives to Congress, state legislatures, mayor's offices, school boards, D.A.'s offices, judgeships, special districts, and even as governor of Virginia. These results were not due to some *deus ex machina*, but to the deep, hard, and sustained kind of work which took place in Sacramento. What we saw in the most widely publicized election results was merely the tip of the iceberg. It was an iceberg based on a national population with its own social spaces, narratives, and memory — one which saw itself and operated as a distinct community of interest.

Collective Mobilization

In the 1980s the most significant mass collectivization efforts in Black politics were in the electoral arena. In Sacramento they were associated with Grantland Johnson's campaigns for city council and the County Board of Supervisors, and with Jesse Jackson's runs for the Democratic Party's presidential nomination in 1984 and 1988. The other significant collective mobilization initiatives were elite mobilizations. In Sacramento they were associated with the Black Citizens' Activist Committee (BCAC), the Ad Hoc Committee for the Fair Administration of Justice, and the Black American Political Association for California (BAPAC).

Community Mobilization

Nationally, the peak electoral collective mobilization Black political efforts were associated with the creation of the National Black Independent Political Party and the Jesse Jackson political campaigns of 1984 and 1988. The Chicago mayoral campaigns of Harold Washington in 1983 and 1987 also claimed the national stage. Other local mobilizations of national significance took place in the Mel King campaign in Boston, the Ken Cockrell campaign in Detroit, and the Wilson Riles, Jr., campaign in Oakland. In Sacramento similar efforts took place far from the national spotlight.

GRANTLAND JOHNSON'S CAMPAIGNS. Grantland Johnson's electoral campaigns were representative of the effort required to produce a mass mobilization. Grantland made his final decision to run for the council in the summer of 1982.[120] The primary election was in June of 1983, almost a year distant. Grantland and his immediate support group worked from the summer of 1982 to November 1983 (the general election). He assembled help from campaign contributors, endorsers, planners, and workers during the first several months of organizing. He and his workers began hitting the streets in January of 1983. They developed campaign strategies, solicited contributions, developed mailers, and manufactured campaign literature (walking pieces, mailers, campaign signs, mail-in postcards). They canvassed neighborhoods, recruited people to put up signs in their yards, sought endorsements from the press, tracked Black voters, and registered voters as they walked. They set up phone banks, attended forums, candidate nights, courted organizational support, returned phone calls, and worked for press coverage. Once the primary was over, they hired a full-time campaign manager, established a new headquarters, recruited and trained new workers, mapped the precincts and walked door to door several times. All that effort was expended to mobilize people to do one thing: go to a polling place for a few minutes on election day to vote for Grantland Johnson. It took literally tens of thousands of hours of work and tens of thousands of dollars to get 1,532 people to vote for Grantland in the primary and 3,056 to vote for him in the general election. A commensurate effort was necessary in his 1987 election to the County Board of Supervisors.

The energy and resources expended were stupendous. It resulted in mobilization across class, race, gender, and party lines. Collective mass mobilization — even for such a routinized activity as an election — is not a walk in the park.

THE SACRAMENTO VALLEY RAINBOW COALITION ORGANIZING COMMITTEE. The Sacramento Valley Rainbow Coalition Organizing Committee (SVRCOC) was a mass mobilization that went on for six years. It began in 1983 with the first organizing efforts for Jesse Jackson's run for the Democratic nomination in 1984, and ended following the 1988 Democratic convention.

The campaigns, unlike Grantland's, were connected to a national movement. As a result, they drew on the publicity, interest, and momentum developed nationally. The SVRCOC ran a grassroots effort. As with the city council and supervisorial races, the whole focus was to get people to turn out to vote. The SVRCOC had its own progressive agenda and organizing strategy tied to the Rainbow Coalition, but the goal most effectively articulated and produced was turning out Jackson voters for the Democratic primary. In short, 6 years and untold numbers of hours and dollars were required to produce 2 days of mass voting, 4 years apart.

ASSESSMENT. Examining these events helps illustrate why effective collective mass mobilization is not an everyday occurrence. The social and political capital required to produce it is phenomenal — even when associated with a routinized event. The cost is not generally given sufficient consideration by analysts. When the occasion is not routine, but has to be created by the mobilizers themselves, the rarity of success — despite undeniable need — speaks to the magnitude of the challenge. The indispensable element — win, lose, or draw — is significant participation by everyday folk.

Activist Mobilization

THE BLACK CITIZENS' ACTIVIST COMMITTEE. After November of 1984, many Black activists, particularly progressives, turned their attention to what they could do to contribute to the internal capacity of the Black population. In Sacramento, one effort along those lines was the formation of the Black Community Activist Committee (BCAC).

The BCAC came out of a long series of community discussions organized by the Sacramento Local Organizing Committee of NBIPP. The Sacramento LOC hosted the first discussion in July of 1982 and entitled it, "Reagonomics and the Black Community."[121] Following Reagan's reelection in 1984, NBIPP sponsored another discussion, a conference named The Sacramento Area Black Activist Conference. The call said the 1984 election and events leading up to it made two points remarkably clear:

1. Neither the Republican nor Democratic parties were going to contribute much to Black people in the immediate future.
2. Black people were willing to do something for their own futures.

The call said,

> At the very least this conference should supply every participant with a list of organizations and contact persons in Sacramento, and with a list of concerns of this community's Black population, with some idea of what is being done — and not being done — to address them ... we hope that far more than the least expectation will emerge from our work. But that is up to each of us.[122]

The conference took place March 30, 1985, at the Oak Park Community Center (OPCC). Over 80 people from 11 neighborhoods and 23 organizations attended. It centered around two workshops, one on networking and the other on identifying concerns. The conference established a planning committee to implement the decisions arising out of the workshops.[123]

The networking workshop established four objectives:

1. To produce a newsletter within 30 days to summarize the work of the conference and to disseminate the newsletter as widely as possible in the Black population.
2. To develop a comprehensive directory of Black organizations in Sacramento.
3. To develop an annual calendar of events sponsored by Sacramento Black organizations.
4. To publish and disseminate the newsletter on a regular basis.[124]

The concerns workshop identified two objectives:

1. Establishing education, employment, and teen issues as the top priorities for problem solving in Sacramento's Black communities.
2. For the planning committee to convene Black organizations and individuals throughout the area which are addressing or would like to address the three priorities, in order to develop comprehensive and coordinated approaches to each.[125]

Additionally, the networking workshop identified 86 Black organizations and 13 elected and appointed officials.[126]

Thirty days later, April 30, 1985, the BCAC came out with the newsletter. It included four articles on the conference; basic information about BCAC, including contacts; listed the 86 organizations divided into 8 categories; the 13 officials; upcoming events in May; a calendar of events for the year, including a list of sponsoring organizations; and a request for information about future events.[127]

The educational convening took place on August 24 at the Oak Park Community Center.[128] It looked at pre-school through adult education, all school districts, and private schools.[129] In May of 1986 BCAC published the directory, titled *A Black Community Directory for the Sacramento Area*.[130] It included 168 businesses, 73 churches, and 83 organizations, for a total of 324 listings. It was the first directory published since the early 1970s when the Urban League had published one under the leadership of Dolores Bryant.

The Ad Hoc Committee for the Fair Administration of Justice

Another organization which arose in 1985 was the Ad Hoc Committee for the Fair Administration of Justice. This organization arose from a return by Sacramento's vindictive criminal justice system to the Oak Park 4. The committee was created "to promote the fair administration of justice in the Sacramento Superior Court Case # 70922, charging Mr. Akinsanya Kambon, aka Mark Teemer, with possession of a designated controlled substance and the carrying of a fire arm during the commission of a felony."[131]

Akinsanya Kambon, as Mark Teemer, was a member of the Oak Park 4. After the case against him and the other co-defendants was dismissed, he took stock of his situation and left town. He earned a master's degree in fine arts from Fresno State University. He went to Africa where he traveled widely both in East and West Africa. His primary mission, beyond grounding himself in his ancestral culture and civilization, was to study the lost-wax method of bronze casting under the tutelage of African masters. While he lived and studied in Africa, he was awarded an African name, Akinsanya Kambon.[132]

While he had recognized the wisdom of living far from Sacramento, he still had family in the city, including children. Periodically, he made lightning forays to his home town. If he stayed 24 hours or longer, the police learned of his presence and acted accordingly. Typical was the time his daughter was hit by a car. When Kambon rushed to the scene, he was arrested for assault.[133]

Such a visit led to his arrest for two counts of possession: (1) of a controlled substance, and (2) of a firearm while committing a felony (to wit, possessing the controlled substance).[134] At the time Kambon was on the Art Department faculty of California State University Long Beach. The police broke in as he sat in the living room of a friend's house. According to police, cocaine and a gun were in the house, hence his possession. They took pictures of him in the same room with the gun and the dope to establish his possession.[135] The district attorney took the fabrication to trial. The result was a hung jury. Undaunted, the D.A. took the case back to trial with the same results. It was when the D.A. announced he was taking the case back for a third trial that the Ad Hoc Committee was born.[136]

It was composed primarily of Black notables, including Sacramento's most influential Black minister of the period, Dr. Ephraim Williams of St. Paul Baptist Church. Dr. Williams wrote a letter to the district attorney on behalf of the Ad Hoc Committee. He requested an appointment for the whole group to meet with the D.A. concerning Akinsanya's case. He said, in part, "A third trial, in our eyes, seems to go beyond what is required to render justice to the community and the accused."[137] The D.A. agreed to meet with the committee.

Twelve members of the committee, including the Rev. Williams, attended the meeting. They told the D.A. they had reviewed the master calendar for the Sacramento Superior Court for the period of June 1983 through December 1984, 502 cases. In not a single case was there an instance of a hung jury where a defendant was subject to three trials. In only one case was there even a second trial of a hung jury case. In that instance, though the alleged offense was child molestation, the D.A. requested that charges be dismissed.

The D.A. listened and agreed with the committee's position. He looked at the twelve people and promised, in the interest of justice, he would not hold Kambon for a third trial.

A week later he wrote Dr. Williams to tell him he was taking Akinsanya Kambon back to trial. In addition, he was adding a third charge: perjury. He said he reviewed the trial record (*he hadn't before?*) and found Kambon's testimony illogical, contradictory, and perjurous. *Yet two juries had heard the very same testimony and had not been able to convict.* He said further that he had reviewed the evidence and it looked convincing. *But it was the same evidence that had already been presented twice.* He did not mention the *promise* he had made to the twelve citizens who had met with him. He did not admit he had lied.[138] Akinsanya Kambon was convicted in the third trial. For the Oak Park 4 and the community which had waged the struggle for their release, there was neither slumber nor sleep.

BAPAC. BAPAC, the Black American Political Association of California, was Willie Brown's attempt to build an institutional base for politics in California's Black population, one which would operate not only as an instrument for mobilizing and implementing a Black political agenda, but which also could serve as a PAC for Black Democratic candidates in the state. It was a means of institutionalizing statewide grassroots support for the Black political establishment.[139]

BAPAC was organized in regions and in specific communities within regions. The Sacramento chapter was in the northern region. It was composed of elected officials and appointees in the state government, state civil service employees, and local officials and high-profile activists. Its job was to follow the mandates of the statewide organization and to support local officials and organizations who sought help. It was another reflection of the widespread sentiment that even the Black elite could not rely on the dominant institutions: the Democratic Party, the state legislature, even constitutional office. To be able to have an independent and viable voice, they had to have a specific, institutional voice in Black communities.

Dr. Ephraim Williams: The Reverend Williams emerged in the 1980s as Sacramento's most politically influential and active Black minister. Courtesy of The Black Group.

Summary

In both mass and elite mobilizations the initiatives came from relatively small numbers of people. In Sacramento they were characterized by Grantland Johnson and his long-term cohort of friends in the Heights, the Democratic Party and progressive activists interested in grassroots organizing who joined the Jackson campaigns, Willie Brown and his supporters, the local contingent of NBIPP, and friends and supporters of Akinsanya Kambon. In each instance they had been stimulated by international, national, state, and local factors, including — centrally — the Reagan electoral victory in 1980. The kind of activity we see here, replicated across the country, led to increasing Black political capacity both electorally and in the growth of autonomous Black infrastructure.

While the initiatives rested on small numbers of people, effective action required greater numbers — in the case of elections, thousands; in the cases of the BCAC and BAPAC, scores. Even the Ad Hoc Committee required at least an even dozen. In all instances these were local people, grass roots. This was their work. People like them were doing the work up and down the country.

Black Organizations

This examination of Black organizations in the 1980s focuses on Sacramento with the understanding that similar developments took place all over the nation. In chapter two we explored a number of propositions, insights, and observations about Black political organizations. This treatment will serve primarily as a comparison with Sacramento Black organizations in the 1970s. Most obvious is the increase in number. The routine count shows 125 in the 70s, and 162 in the 80s, a 22.2 percent increase. Among the top 4 categories significant differences emerged. While the social organization category remained number 1, the n in that category declined, from 40 to 35. The n's for the service and political categories remained constant at 22 and 11 respectively. In the top 4, only the category of professional organizations increased, from 11 to 15. The professional category replaced the political category, by the routine count, as number 3. Because of increases in their n's, the economic and cultural categories tied with the political category for 4th position, each counting 11 organizations. Cultural organizations more than doubled, from 5 in the 1970s to 11 in the 1980s. They moved from 9th rank to 4th.

Other categories which declined were youth, religious, recreational, and mobilizing. A total of five experienced declines. Eight increased — information, education, student, health, and multi-purpose — in addition to professional, cultural, and economic. Health organizations quintupled, from 1 to 5. One new category was created, crime prevention.

Increased Diversity

By the enhanced political count, political organizations became the largest category, leapfrogging over service and social organizations, at 41, outnumbering the social category by 6 and the service by 19. More Black Sacramentans were running for more and more varied political offices. Between them, by the enhanced political count, the big 3 categories of social, service, and political organizations accounted for 66.8 percent of Black organizations as compared with 42.2 percent by the routine count. The big 3 in the 1970s accounted for 48.7 percent of organizations by the routine count; by the 1980s the same 3 organizations accounted for only 42.2 percent of the total. Replacing political organizations with professional organizations for the '80s still yielded a total for the three biggest categories of only 45.7 percent. By the routine count Black organizations were considerably less concentrated during the 1980s. In the 1970s only 4 categories had double digit figures. In the 1980s that number increased to 7. By the routine count the spread between the category with the largest number of organizations and with the smallest number decreased from 39 to 32. The smallest category increased from 1 to 3, and the largest decreased from 40 to 35. In the '70s the median number of organizations per category was 7; in the '80s it was 9. One whole new organizational category had been created. The configuration of the Black infrastructure had altered dramatically.

The Growing Significance of the Enhanced Political Count

The phenomenal increase in political organizations by the enhanced political count raises an intriguing question: were more political energies going into office-seeking than to other political functions? Observations from the '90s may shed light on this question.

The increase in campaign organizations does not include efforts associated with the Jesse Jackson campaigns because they were part of the routine count. Under the banner of the Rainbow Coalition they developed into a long-term organization. Routine Black political activity was not necessarily declining, rather its methods might have been changing, from protest to politics. The spread of Black organizational activity across a wide range of organizational categories was also reflected by declines in youth and mobilization organizations. The smaller number of mobilizing organizations suggests another indicator of from protest to politics.

These trends also might have foretold more ominous consequences. The organizations which would normally have been at the cutting edge of mitigating the social horror in the midst of the Black population were directly concerned with youth and mobilizing. At the same time youth and mobilizing activities were declining in the contexts I studied, they were increasing at exponential rates in the most desperate sectors of the Black population. That the Black population was not blind to these developments is suggested by the creation of three specific crime-fighting organizations. Yet it is possible that other kinds of organizations might have been better preventive agents. AIDS might have accounted for some of the increase in the number of health organizations.

Women's and Men's Organizations

Women's organizations decreased by 1. Men's organizations decreased by 4. Five women's organizations were lost and 4 were gained, a net decrease of 1. Five men's organizations were lost and 1 was gained, a net decrease of 4. Two new women's organizations, Sister Friends and the Birthing Project, were extremely significant. Sister Friends was a replacement for the Sacramento Black Women's Network, which continued in the 1980s and made its most dramatic achievements then, but which also exhausted much of its leadership. That exhaustion, toward the end of the decade, led key members to establish Sister Friends, a much less public network. The Birthing Project, a women's health organization, unleashed a virtual revolution in pre-natal and postnatal care which resulted in its founder, Kathryn Hall, receiving an Image Award. Women also created one health organization. Men did not create any health organizations.

The new men's organization, the Sacramento chapter of the 100 Black Men, was also a significant addition. It was the first men's organization during the two decades to operate as a civic organization. It was also a youth organization, as its principal functions were mentoring and providing scholarships. During the '80s, the Tuskegee Airmen's Association, which was of long-standing duration, began to operate more as a civic organization than primarily a club (a veteran's organization). It assumed dual functions. People born in Africa accounted for a new category of organizations composed of people who established organizational identities based on countries of origin, e.g., Association of Citizens and Friends of Liberia (ACFLI).

Organizational Persistence

By the routine count 27 of '70s organizations did not continue into the '80s. Ninety-eight '70s organizations persisted into the '80s, 77.6 percent. Not counting campaign committees, 64 new organizations originated during the 1980s, 39.5 percent of the total. Twenty-seven numerically replaced those that went defunct; 37 constituted the margin by which the '80s total exceeded the '70s. There was a gross gain of 64 organizations and a net gain of 37. Given the short duration of campaign committees and their extremely narrow focus, it would be misleading to characterize Sacramento's Black organizational infrastructure by the enhanced political count. It would not be misleading, however, to note their impact on the category of political organizations — coming close to quadrupling their number. Campaign organizations dramatically changed the conformation of Black political organizations in the 1980s. Nevertheless, no local campaign organizations (the Rainbow Coalition, as a national organization, falls outside this category) lasted the whole decade, while most other political organizations did. There is, however, an underlying conundrum with respect to campaign organizations. Many people in campaign organizations were involved in more than one. In effect, many people were continuously involved in political campaigns throughout the decade. Some had been involved throughout the 1970s as well. This gives more continuity to some campaign elements than might be superficially recognized. In some respects there might have been one or more *über*-campaign organizations spanning the decade.

Campaign organizations are no substitute for institutions of collective responsibility and accountability, as they are tied entirely to the candidate, may be considered creatures of the candidate, and have no broader political role, particularly with respect to the well-being of the constituency. While people who participate in campaign organizations may have the good of the constituency in mind, the campaign organization *per se* does not.

Organizations by Class

Twenty-one of the 24 working class organizations of the 1970s continued into the 1980s, 87.5 percent. There were no new Black working class organizations. The resulting total was 21, a net decline of 3. Eighteen mixed organizations of the '70s failed to carry over into the '80s, 37.5 percent. Thirty mixed class organizations present in the '70s remained into the '80s, 62.5 percent. Twenty-nine (46 percent) new mixed organizations yielded a net gain of 11 from the '70s to the '80s, 52 to 63. Twelve middle class organizations ended before the '80s, just over 25 percent. Almost 75 percent persisted. Thirty-six new middle class organizations began during the eighties, producing a net gain of 24, from 49 to 73. Three times as many new organizations were created in this category as disbanded. The upshot was that the total of middle class organizations, lower than that of mixed organizations in the '70s, surpassed the mixed total in the '80s.

Among the working class, mixed, and middle class organizations, only the working class declined. There was significant growth in the other two categories, and net growth in the middle class was particularly robust. In some ways these trends reflected demographic patterns, locally and nationally. The Black middle class was growing. The poor Black population was declining. Perhaps every bit as significantly, these were also neighborhood or spatial trends. The organized and continually organizing middle class was moving out of neighborhoods populated primarily by other Black people, and into neighborhoods where Black people were few and far between. Increasingly, Black organizations were not neighborhood organizations. They drew membership from broadly dispersed persons who did not necessarily see each other in their daily routines, but had to make special efforts to get together as organizational members.

Neighborhoods which remained primarily Black increasingly consisted of a narrow demographic, poor Black people. Organizational life tended to be much less dynamic in those areas. Organizations persisted in Del Paso Heights, in Oak Park, and new ones originated in Meadowview, but many such organizations were *in* the neighborhoods, not *of* the neighborhoods. The Women's Civic Improvement Club still had its center in Oak Park, but most members drove in for the meetings. The Good Neighbors Club still met in Del Paso Heights, but much of its activity was centered around running a Head Start program under state auspices, not in being an independent resource for the community. The Meadowview Improvement Association and Meadowview Community Action were vibrant groups, but given the great concentration of African descended people in Meadowview, a much broader and deeper Black organizational infrastructure would have provided more vitality across the far-flung neighborhood. The demise of poverty organizations, which were both *in and of* the neighborhoods, progressively diminished the organizational infra-structure in poor Black neighborhoods. In all these areas the emergent gang infrastructure was wide, deep, and energized. Its members were neighbors. They saw each other and interacted with each other every day. They lived together.

Crisis Organizations

Two crisis organizations were formed during the 1980s. One was formed by African-descended peoples. The second was formed by the police chief, but was entirely dependent on heavy participation from Black people. Additionally, there was a pre-crisis group which never amounted to an organization, but which had several meetings. The Black crisis organizations arose to face a problem which was national in scope: Black youth gangs. A-Gang was an organization formed in the Meadowview area by activist Joe Debbs. He started the organization when his nephew, not a gang member, was killed in a gang shooting. The Task Force on Black Youth Gangs was created by the Sacramento police chief to enlist the help of the organized Black population in finding ways to combat Black youth gangs and their effects in Sacramento. The other effort, which did not result in the formation of an organization was the prescient effort of Dr. Ervin Jackson of the Sacramento City Unified School District to create a holistic strategy to head off the Black gang problem before it started.

A-Gang was primarily oriented toward organizing residents in Black neighborhoods to find and implement solutions to the destructive elements of gang life in their own environs. This included working with the police department and other public entities, but its major emphasis was on getting Black people to deal with the question themselves where they lived. The Task Force on Black Youth Gangs used the police department to inform Black organizations about gang activities in various areas of the city, how to identify gang members, gang territories, gang signs, the use of graffiti, and gang activities. The police department also worked with the organizations to set up summer employment, job training, youth recreation, and educational programs as means of providing alternative activities for potential gang members and even gang members themselves.

In addition to these specific crisis organizations, the whole range of Black organizations, from fraternities and sororities, social clubs, civic organizations, and political organizations, expended significant autonomous efforts to address the crises in the Black population they identified, which — in order of the significance attributed to them — were Black youth gangs, crack, and AIDS.

Indicators of Black Organizational Persistence and Reach

Crisis organizations in the 1980s didn't utilize the dramatic forms displayed in the '70s: picking up the gun, taking over speaking platforms or classrooms, throwing speakers from the stage, mass demonstrations, boycotts, defiant marches, or picketing. Activities tended to be more genteel: forming campaign committees, attending meetings, following *Robert's Rules of Order*, writing reports, and testifying before public bodies. During the decade, William Julius Wilson's 1978 book, *The Declining Significance of Race*, gained much publicity and credibility.[140] The elections of the late 1980s, particularly the 1988 and '89 elections, received widespread attention from the ability of Black candidates to win in non–Black majority electoral settings. The phenomenon was later examined extensively in Georgia Person's 1993 edited collection, *Dilemmas of Black Politics*.[141] The Bakke decision spoke to the national propensity to avoid or minimize race-specific approaches to social conditions.[142] These considerations might lead one to speculate that Black organizational activity was in decline. While work styles indicate there was less fervor in Black organizational activity, the absolute numbers of Black organizations, increasing by approximately 25 percent, do not indicate a reduction in Black-based organizational activity. But what about organizations deeply rooted in race, founded specifically as Black organizations? A reduction in their numbers might indicate that to Black people *there was* a declining significance of race. There were 87 in the 1970s. There were 128 in the '80s, a net increase of 47 percent. This would not indicate a decline in race-based organizational activity.

There is, however, the possibility that fewer Black organizations of national or international scope persisted in the '80s. The data do not confirm that speculation either. The net number of those organizations increased from 41 to 52, an increase of approximately 25 percent. Neither a declining significance of race, deracialization, or the minimization of race-specific approaches on the part of Black people were reflected in the comparison of Black organizational life in Sacramento between the 1970s and 1980s. The direction was toward more Black organizational activity and more race-based organizational formation.

Trends

While the number of women's organizations declined in the 1980s, they still outnumbered men's organizations. While the decade saw the creation of men's civic organizations, women's organizations in that category quadrupled the men's. The number of working class organizations declined by a sixth. The mixed and middle class organizations increased dramatically. Black organizational life, vital in the 1970s, by the 1980s had become richer and more complex — though without the dynamism, energy, and mass involvement that had characterized it in the '70s. Much political effort was directed into electoral politics and its progeny: appointed office on commissions, boards, and public committees; hiring of Black professionals as administrators and consultants; and lobbying. CBOs became less influential. Black people who spoke as representatives of the state played more prominent roles both within the Black population and in the wider society.

demographic shift in Sac during 1980s growing AA pop.

The reduction in the number of working class organizations was accompanied by the greater dispersal of middle class and employed working class people across the Sacramento region, and the emergence of Black youth gangs in neighborhoods populated primarily by the Black poor. Black people who were middle or working class, who moved into the area from elsewhere, were likely to settle in areas outside of hardcore, poverty stricken Black neighborhoods. There was increasingly little indigenous Black organizational presence in impoverished Black areas to engage the most destructive phenomena in the neighborhoods. The Black underclass became more self-contained and isolated from other sectors of the Black population.

TABLE 3.3 FUNCTIONAL CATEGORIES OF BLACK ORGANIZATIONS
IN SACRAMENTO, 1980–1989, BY NUMBERS AND PERCENTAGES

Category	Number	Percentage
Social	35	21.9
Service	23	14.4
Professional	15	9.4
Political	11	6.9
Cultural	11	6.9
Economic	11	6.9
Informational	10	6.3
Educational	9	5.6
Multi-purpose	6	3.7
Student	6	3.7
Youth	5	3.1
Health	5	3.1
Religious	4	2.5
Recreational	3	1.9
Mobilizing	3	1.9
Crime Prevention	3	1.9

TABLE 3.4 FUNCTIONAL CATEGORIES OF BLACK ORGANIZATIONS
IN SACRAMENTO, 1980–1989, BY NUMBERS AND PERCENTAGES
(ENHANCED POLITICAL COUNT)

Category	Number	Percentage
Political	41	21.6
Social	35	18.4
Service	22	16.8
Professional	15	7.9
Cultural	11	5.8
Economic	11	5.8
Informational	10	5.3
Educational	9	4.7
Multi-purpose	6	3.2
Student	6	3.2
Youth	5	2.6
Health	5	2.6

Category	Number	Percentage
Religious	4	2.1
Recreational	3	1.6
Mobilizing	3	1.6
Crime Prevention	3	1.6

TABLE 3.5 SACRAMENTO BLACK WOMEN'S ORGANIZATIONS BY CATEGORY, 1980–1989

Category	Number
Sororities	6
Clubs	6
Civic	8
Masonic/Lodge	6
Auxiliary	3
Health	2
Religious	1
Total	31*

*5 double-counted

TABLE 3.6 SACRAMENTO BLACK MEN'S ORGANIZATIONS, BY CATEGORY, 1980–1989

Category	Number
Fraternities	4
Clubs	3
Lodges	5
Civic	2
Religious	1
Total	15*

*2 are double-counted

State Government

In the 1980s, due to the removal from office of the two statewide elected officers — Mervyn Dymally, lieutenant governor, and Wilson Riles, state superintendent of education — there were no statewide Black elected officials. The role they had played in Sacramento Black politics evaporated.

Willie Brown, however, became Speaker of the Assembly and wielded considerable power. Within Sacramento his primary role was as a mentor. He had many Black Sacramento residents appointed to office and hired to positions in the legislature on committee staffs, individual members' staffs, and as consultants. They developed valuable political experience and contacts and were to play increasingly significant roles in Sacramento local politics.

We may expect similar developments in other state houses, the national government, and even municipalities when the few but influential Black officeholders are removed from office or positions of influence or power. We certainly saw it when Republicans won majorities in the U.S. House of Representatives. Both the role and the treasury of the Congressional Black Caucus tumbled. The effects on Black staff, consultants, and dependent institutions were often devastating.

Afterword

The Context

The election of Ronald Reagan in 1980 marked the consolidation of the Republican Party's capture of the national government, a counter-reformation. That process had begun with Richard Nixon's victory in 1968, including the wholesale implementation of the southern strategy. The Republican Party targeted the Solid South as its electoral base, intending to shift the South's political identification from the Democratic to the Republican Party. The Democratic Party was identified as the party of Black people. Without having to say so explicitly, that made the Republican Party the party of white people. Liberal and Democrat became synonymous. Conservative and Republican became synonymous; i.e., Democratic became "bad," Republican became "good."

Watergate constituted the only obstacle in the path of the Republican march to complete victory — an obstacle, one might keep in mind, created by the Republicans themselves. Watergate and Watergate alone enabled the victory of Jimmy Carter in 1976. Carter, a southerner, was an impediment to the Republican Party's Southern Strategy as he carried his own state, Georgia, a critical key to a consolidated South.

The setback, however, did not deter the Republicans' visions or efforts to resurrect the solid South in their own image. Carter, however marginally, contributed to their success. He appointed a Black man, Andy Young, to the U.N. He gave Panama back to the brown people, whooped and hollered about human rights, and canceled the chance for national triumph by withdrawing from the Olympics in protest over the Soviet Union's human rights policies — thereby depriving himself of the celebration of national glory as the election season drew nigh — as opposed to the actual scenario where he was castigated and blamed for losing hostages to Iran.

Richard Nixon was the prophet, but Ronald Reagan was the true master of the southern strategy. He crafted the image of the Republican Party as the political home of the "good old boys." He knocked Carter out of the ring and claimed the political crown of the presidency.

To Black people Ronald Reagan's election signaled what the Compromise of 1877 had 103 years earlier. The country had thrown them to the wolves. It was turning its back on them.

The Response

What did Black people do? They did what they had done 100 years earlier. They turned inward. They looked to themselves for the future. The Civil Rights Movement, as disciplined, courageous, and even as radical as it was, rested on the hope, in the belief, that the country could and would *do the right thing*. The Black Power movement rejected that belief, hope, and assumption. Throughout the 1970s those two powerful strains of Black politics struggled with each other. By 1980 significant numbers of Black people concluded that although the Black Power movement might not hold the keys to the kingdom, it certainly possessed a valuable kernel of knowledge. Elijah Muhammad had stressed the imperative, "*Do for self.*" In the 1980s increasing numbers of Black people began to ask themselves what they could *do for self.*

Many embraced the work of the National Committee to Overturn the Bakke Decision. Some started celebrating Kwanzaa. Others began taking trips to Africa. An important element created NBIPP. Some railed against apartheid. They began publishing, *Essence, Black Enterprise, Black Issues in Higher Education.* They were practicing *do for self.* They drafted Harold Washington to run for mayor of Chicago. They ran an unprecedented campaign which elected him. They ran progressive Black candidates for city councils in Detroit and Oakland, and won both. They ran Mel King for mayor in Boston. Though they lost there, they put up a good fight. They began to chant, "Run, Jesse, run!" Black people had begun to pick their way through to a new vision of electoral politics. If we can't find anyone to speak for us, we'll speak for ourselves. *Do for self.*

All these tendencies were expressed in Sacramento. The Party for the New Black Politics, NBIPP, the *Rumble* Awards ceremonies, the Grantland Johnson city council campaign, the '84 Rainbow Campaign, a local South Africa divestment campaign, The Black Community Activist Committee — identifying Sacramento's Black resources — all were groping toward a praxis of *do for self.*

How national context fit in Sactown

The Uneven Contest

It is critical that we not delude ourselves. The Republican Party that encompassed the Solid South, which took over the White House in 1980 and the California Governor's Mansion in 1982, was a colossus of staggering proportions. It had at its disposal the wealth of the entire United States of America and California, respectively, including the meager portion that belonged to Black people. Beside it, the fractured, impoverished, and powerless African-descended population was a frail and sickly waif, in possession of no state power through which it might express a collective will. The Black Nation within a nation has been a theme in the literature and the political literature on Black people for a century. It is rarely stated explicitly, however, that this Black Nation is a stateless nation. The state which controls it surely is not its own; indeed, it is in the main directly hostile to it, and it has no state which *is* its own. This incongruity underlies an important thrust of political Black nationalism. The vast and potent force that was the Republican Party was not only distinct from the resource-poor Black population, it was directly oppositional to it. The Republican Party had deliberately assumed the responsibility to crush the political aspirations of Black people. To most Black people it was malign. Nor was it simply a malign *influence.* It was a malign *power* with the ability to define right and wrong, good and bad, and to impose its definitions.

Black people were incapable of resisting the rain of plagues it visited upon them: homelessness, diminution of custodial care, rivers of drugs, of guns, unemployment, crippled and crippling schools, AIDS, criminalization, rampant incarceration, and abandonment of the state's protections. African people in the U.S. were driven into the impossible position of trying to create and nurture their households at the same time they fought a raging and insatiable dragon whose sole and relentless purpose was to lay them low and devour them.

This is not hyperbole. First of all, in terms of population, whites outnumbered Black people roughly 188,000,000 to 26,000,000 according to the 1980 census.[143] This enumeration excludes other major population groups identified in the census because the intent here is to compare those *most* favored by the Republican Party rooted in the Solid South, with those *most* disfavored by the Republican Party rooted in the Solid South. There were approximately 162,000,000 more people of European descent (not counting Hispanics) than people of African descent (not counting Hispanics) in the U.S. in 1980. Compared to African descended people, European descended people virtually monopolized positions of authority, influence, power, and wealth in the country, including the leadership of all the country's major institutions, inclusive of the state at every level. The collective wealth of Europeans at roughly eight times per capita that of Africans was a staggering roughly 1,396,000,000 *times* greater than the collective wealth of African descendants in the U.S. Europeans owned almost 1.4 billion times the wealth of Africans in the U.S. Put another way, Europeans could afford (support, pay for, invest) 1.4 *billion* times more than Africans could. If, for example, Africans could afford on the average, $100 per year from their accumulated wealth to support political causes, the total African population could afford $2,600,000,000 (2.6 billion dollars). The total European population could afford 1.4 billion *times* that, or $1,087,390,000,000 (one trillion, 87 billion, 390 million dollars).[144] Who is going to win any battle where money is the weapon of contestation? But we add to that the European position in sheer numbers, in power, in influence, in positions of authority, in dominance of the national institutions and we find the metaphor of a raging, insatiable dragon, if anything, understated.

The Specific Struggle in Sacramento

Power is not neutral. Let us see what these generalizations and numbers on the national scene look like when they are played out in Sacramento.

Akinsanya Kambon, Mark Teemer, as a member of the Oak Park 4, was a perpetual target of the SPD. The court had absolved him of all charges. He had served his country in combat during the Vietnam War. From a poor Black family, he pursued higher education and fought against injustice. He could have been a living symbol of the possible in the U.S. Instead, he was a pariah to Sacramento's criminal justice establishment. He was arrested and incarcerated repeatedly on baseless charges — baseless because the charges were always dropped. He was a victim of serial police harassment. But in 1985 (fifteen years after the Oak Park 4) the police developed a case on him they finally believed they could make stick. The district attorney filed charges — for possession of a controlled substance and for possession of a firearm while in the commission of a felony, itself a felony offense.

The case went to trial and resulted in two hung juries. In Sacramento County, the prevailing practice was not to retry cases involving hung juries, even on the most serious felonies. In Kambon's case, however, the D.A.'s office indicated they were going to bring him up for a third trial. This was unprecedented. A gathering of 12 of the most influential and respected African-descended residents of Sacramento met in person with the district attorney. They made a convincing argument against a third trial. The D.A. agreed with it on the spot. He *promised* the assembled group that he would not go to trial a third time, that he would dismiss all charges.

Within a week he had not only instituted a third trial on the two counts, he had also added a third charge of perjury. That trial resulted in a conviction.

I wish to elucidate, quite specifically, the power differentials at play here. In the original case, the Oak Park 4, the entire Oak Park Black population and particularly young males had been subjected to a frenzy of police terror, intimidation, assaults, and incarcerations lasting *weeks*. Against this mob mentality the African population was defenseless. They had neither the money, the power, or the public goodwill to resist the savage disruptions of their lives. Akin to a deathless pogrom, the law enforcement atrocities abrogated not only their citizenship but their very personhood. The whole Black population was mercilessly subjected to this treatment. No one — no person, organization, institution, no gathering of outraged individuals — came to their aid. They were all offered up as sacrifices to the death of a white policeman.

There was never any basis for a case against the four defendants. There was no weapon, no fingerprints, no shell casings, no links of any kind between the defendants and Officer Bennett. The prosecution's star witness, indeed, its only substantive witness, was crazy. The judge had no choice but to throw the rotten mess out of court. Yet the defendants had been arrested, incarcerated, and held in confinement for eight months. Their lives — and the course of their lives — were meaningless. The police, the District Attorney's Office, and the broad white population of Sacramento treated them with contempt. As a result, though they had been exonerated of the charges against them, they could be — and were — pursued, harassed, and excoriated by the police and prosecutors for decades.

The broad Black population, the organized and the activist Black populations were all adamantly opposed to every aspect of this treatment and entirely incapable of doing anything to stop it. They tried — consistently and repeatedly — as in the case of the three trials on the same charges against Kambon, but they were an ant battling an elephant, and they were crushed.

We can look at a much more specifically political act: Sacramento city redistricting following the 1980 census. Black people became actively and deeply involved in the whole process. They discovered that since the last census 25 percent of the city's African-descended population had occupied contiguous census tracts. That spoke to a tremendous opportunity for them to have meaningful representation on the city council. With great intellectual rigor, creativity and perseverance, they created a map of city council districts which met constitutional muster, which preserved prior existing communities of interest, and which placed the newly emerged African-origin population in the same council district. Their analyses and discussions directed the whole redistricting process. In straw votes taken as the recommendation to the council developed, their plan gained the support of every important stakeholder, including the city staff and the city council itself.

At the eleventh hour, one member of the city council, upset because her home address would place her in a reconfigured council district, offered a redistricting plan vetted by no one except a kangaroo committee from her district. Dan Thompson, the lone Black council member, opposed the plan. No other council member did. The council voted to keep intact the district of one council member by effectively disenfranchising 25 percent of the city's Black population.

The decision was outrageous. But the only people who were outraged were Black. They did not count. The city underlined that reality by making sure that their votes did not count. This is the wanton, naked use of power to emasculate and bash Black people.

National policies had similar effects. Construction of new housing for the poor was virtually terminated. Custodial facilities which housed the Black mentally and emotionally damaged were closed. The former residents were turned out into the streets. Without housing, they stayed in the streets. There they became part of the market for, and joined other victims of, the drugs and guns which proliferated, unchecked, through Black neighborhoods. In fact, the national mood seemed to be — prefiguring Martha Stewart — if they kill themselves, *that's a good thing.*

Residents of poor African-origin neighborhoods, for the first time in their lives, saw people living in parks, condemned houses, cars, and abandoned cars, sleeping inside post office vestibules and on the steps of businesses closed for the evening. They saw people, sometimes families, pushing shopping carts filled with their belongings, up and down the streets — literally, the streets — as the streets were smoother than the sidewalks and some of the neighborhoods had no sidewalks.

For the most part Africans in Sacramento did not throw up their hands in despair. They kept most of their organizations going. Only single-gender organizations and working class organizations suffered declines. Both women's and men's organizations created new organizations while declining in total numbers. Men developed their first completely civic organization, the Sacramento Chapter of the 100 Black Men. Women originated an innovative approach to neo-natal and post-natal care, the Birthing Project. Black people created a new category of organization — crime prevention, establishing 3. They quintupled their number of health organizations. They grew the total number of Black organizations by 25 percent.

They went to the polls, they ran for office, and they were elected in unprecedented numbers. They participated in cross-racial and cross-class alliances.

The class configuration of African-descended population, like that of much of the country, changed. There were more buppies, more members of the at least *pseudo* middle class.[145] At the same time, traditional Black neighborhoods became increasingly poor, and upwardly mobile people of African ancestry more widely dispersed.

Africans were generally aware of the impact of Reaganism. That's why they built the kinds of organizations they did and practiced the kinds of politics they did. Some, reading the future in the Republican capture of the presidency and the governor's office, switched parties. That would net them, they believed, rare birds as they were, greater access to judicial and political appointments, more access to government contracts.

Black people moved into Sacramento in increasing numbers. Some flew gang colors and brought with them thug mentalities and automatic weapons. Some brought cutting-edge training and rare life experiences that were new and invigorating for the river city. Many were to play significant and even dramatic roles in the life of their new home.

The Reagan and Deukmeijian administrations, rooted in the southern strategy, amounted to acts of war on the Black population. In the words of Walter Mosely, "Always outnumbered, always outgunned."[146] But Black people were not finished. They were trying to learn, by practice, what *do for self* really meant.

The Path Not Taken

In many ways the search for ways to *do for self* meant discovering who self was. That was in part what was involved in the celebration of Kwanzaa, the trips to Africa, the creation of Black cultural vehicles such as *Essence* and in Sacramento, the *Rumble* Awards ceremonies. What does it mean to be an African people, and how do African people live in the world?

The principled opposition to the apartheid regime in South Africa resulted in part from some answers people discovered to that question. Answers were also expressed in the drafting of Harold Washington to run for mayor of Chicago, the chants of "Run Jesse, run!" They were in Mel King in Boston, Wilson Riles, Jr., in Oakland, and Ken Cockrell in Detroit. They were found in the creation of NBIPP.

In Sacramento answers were expressed in the same tendencies: the Party for the New Black Politics, which merged into NBIPP; the Working Conference for a Black Political Party; the candidacies of Grantland Johnson. They were expressed in Sacramento's involvement in the anti-apartheid movement. Grantland Johnson introduced a resolution for divestment in the city council.[147] They were expressed in Sacramento participation in the National Committee to Overturn the Bakke Decision (NCOBD) and in the SVRCOC.

Three of those efforts were particularly charged with the task of organizing the most oppressed and exploited sectors of the Black population: the NCOBD, NBIPP, and the SVRCOC. All three, at various levels of commitment, made the effort. All three failed. None of the attempts to build organizations rooted in the lumpen proletariat succeeded. Not one. The most effective mass mobilization done during the decade was Grantland Johnson's campaign for city council. This was an all-out, full press, mobilizing effort that worked. But it was mobilizing, *not organizing*. It left no structure, it left no bodies of underclass people able to work on their own and with others. Like the campaign committee which fostered it, it appeared for the election, and then was gone.

The principal failure of Sacramento Black organizations in the 1970s persisted in the 1980s. Nobody was effective at organizing among the locked out except the Cripps and the Bloods. Mobilizing, yes. Organizing, no. This is principally a class question. Lower class organizations declined. Neither mixed-class nor middle class organizations could mobilize the lumpens. There were no Black Panthers. There was no SNCC. There was no Garvey. There was no SCLC under King. Black neighborhoods were stratified. The people left in the poorest Black neighborhoods had no substantive connections to the Black infrastructure. They were as close to the Links, the Deltas, and the Black Chamber of Commerce as they were to the Shriners, the Sutter Club, and the Metropolitan Chamber of Commerce. This is part of the problem that Cathy Cohen addresses — who may actively participate in the *activity* of being Black? Who is legitimate as a Black political participant? Just as important is the question of *how* is one to be a participant in Black politics? *How* is one to participate in a Black youth organization that is explicitly political, as opposed to Cripps or Bloods? How is a person who is undereducated or either under- or unemployed to be a legitimate participant in Black politics? It is clear that by the end of the 1980s Black people in Sacramento did not know the answers to any of these questions. In fact they did not know the central question — how to organize the most destitute of the Black population? This was a national problem, as, indeed Sacramento's Black population was national and international. The California state capital was not the only place in the country struggling with Crips, Bloods, AIDS, crack, low Black graduation rates, and high Black incarceration rates, high Black unemployment and infant mortality. The blunders, breakthroughs, failures, and striking innovations of African descendants in Sacramento had their counterparts everywhere Black people lived.

African descended people, not just in Sacramento, but in the United States, are not going to be successful at organizing the most oppressed among them until we understand why politics excludes them so pervasively, and why most members of the lumpen proletariat do not understand political participation as a germane element of their lives. What are the disconnects and what is their character? Until we know this, the single factor which can be most efficacious in the development of Black political strength — the organization of our most impoverished, most exploited, and most oppressed — will elude us.

CHAPTER 4

The 1990s

As the 1990s began Black people throughout the country were immersed in a storm of misfortunes, many of which they attributed to the politics of the Reagan and Bush administrations. The administrations' intention to "starve the beast," cutting the funds available to government and subsequently its capacity to act, had resulted in severe cutbacks in public housing, state-sponsored custodial care, and infrastructure projects, and the abandonment of a living minimum wage. Additionally, many saw the government as complicit in the drug trade because of its policies toward Nicaragua and its illegal support of the Contras in that country. They pictured the so-called War Against Drugs as a war against Black people, which through enforcement strategies and the hyper-enforcement and penalization of offenses related to crack cocaine had criminalized large segments of the Black population. The initial failure to recognize and address the AIDS crisis fell heavily on the Black population as did general reductions in public health spending and research.

The policies at state and local levels had mirrored and re-enforced those coming from the federal government. California was the ringleader, having both initiated the tax revolution and elected Reagan governor, giving him the credentials for a successful presidential run. Rather than beneficiaries, many African descended people in the country saw themselves as victims of both electoral majorities and the state. Everywhere Black people sought strategies which could bring them some measure of relief from a nation they saw as providing an increasingly poisonous environment for them.

In Sacramento *electoral* politics were the venue to which the organized sectors of the Black population brought their greatest attentions. Chapter 4 begins with them. We move then to considerations of collective mobilization, Black organizations, and the role of state politics. Finally, we look back over the nineties for an afterword.

Electoral Politics

A discussion of Black electoral politics in Sacramento during the 1990s must start with the Sacramento Redistricting Project. The project emerged from the Summit on African American Concerns. The summit was Ida Sydnor's brainchild. She was the founder of Black Sacramento Christian Club Organizers (BSCCO), a youth organization which ran after school tutoring programs and paired middle and high school students with mentors. Ida was appalled by the conditions she saw engulfing her young people. They seemed to have been visited by a rain of plagues: drugs, gangs, and gang violence in particular. She reached out to the lead-

140

ers of the NAACP, the 100 Black Men, and the Urban League, urging them to join her in issuing a call to Black organizations throughout Sacramento to come together to develop strategies for meeting these challenges. The leaders all agreed. They sent out a joint call, and in early 1991 the Summit on African American Concerns was held. The summit constituted itself as an organization.

The 1991 Sacramento Redistricting Project

One of the topics heatedly discussed during the summit was the 1981 decision of the Sacramento City Council to split Sacramento's largest Black community. It was offered as evidence of the recurring theme, "Nobody respects us." Many contended, "We let them get away with it!" When the summit divided itself into committees, one of them was the Economic Development and Political Action Committee. While the committee title included the twin themes of economic development and political action, most people who volunteered for the committee were more interested in political action. When the Economic Development and Political Action Committee met on April 6, 1991, it selected James Reede, Jr., as chair.[1] Many people attending the committee meeting had been heavily influenced by the discussion conducted during the summit about the 1981 city council redistricting decision. To prevent a recurrence of the same fiasco, the committee decided to establish the 1991 Sacramento Redistricting Project, co-chaired by James Reede, Jr., and Robert Pernell.[2] Its objective was to monitor the city's redistricting process to insure that the African ancestered population in the southern part of the city did not "get disrespected" again.

Most of the key personnel in the 1991 Redistricting Project did not live in Sacramento in 1980 when the last census results had been reported. Among the new arrivals were Vincent Harris, Pam Haynes, and the committee chair and project co-chair, James Reede, Jr. They were eager to tackle the public affront that had Black activists fuming for a decade. They established four goals:

1. Monitoring the redistricting process of local jurisdictions subject to redistricting in Sacramento County: the City of Sacramento, the County of Sacramento, the Sacramento Municipal Utilities District (SMUD), the Los Rios Community College District, and the Sacramento County Board of Education;

2. Vigorously organize the African American community to advocate and support redistricting plans that empower the community and its allies;

3. Develop formal opinions and positions to be advanced by the 1991 Redistricting Project and inform the community about them; and

4. Utilize all the political and legal means necessary to defeat efforts to disenfranchise the African American community.[3]

In a report a month later, the Redistricting Project said, "The 1991 Redistricting Project intends ... (to serve) as one, *if not the primary*, channel of African-American community opinion"[4] (emphasis mine). This meant the Redistricting Project was the sole, legitimate voice of the entire Black community on this question. Indeed, the project's theme was, "With One Voice."[5] The purpose of this narrative, which became dominant in Black public spaces, was to pre-empt and intimidate any alternative Black perspective.

The report said further that the project "is organized as a specific, limited term initiative."[6] In short, it was task-oriented and it had only one task. The project required formal affiliations for organizations which wanted to participate. To do so, they had to: (1) designate someone as liaison to the project; (2) make a financial contribution to the project; and (3) agree to inform their memberships about the importance of redistricting. Each subscribing organization had to sign a resolution of affiliation. The resolution committed the board of directors to support the project, specified the financial contribution, designated a liaison, certified that a majority of the board of directors had voted for affiliation, and was signed by the president and secretary.[7]

Costs for affiliation ranged from a high of $250.00 for national organizations, large churches, and large nonprofits, to a low of $75.00 for neighborhood organizations.[8] One purpose of affiliation was to give the project a financial base. An even more important one was to create a buy-in by the whole range of Black organizations in Sacramento.[9]

The Project Goes to Work

The project organized itself into task forces. Some were numbers crunchers, designed to do the gut work of going over census and precinct data and developing detailed maps. The research and development effort was led by Lauren Hammond, a young Capitol staffer. Charles Wiggins, who was computer savvy, got all the data the city had to work on a map Sam Pannell created.[10]

Other task forces were concerned with public information and community outreach, with coordinating public testimony, and with monitoring the city council. The project was determined to know at all times where the council votes were — and to know what had to be done to change ones needing changing. In developing maps, numbers crunchers worked closely with old hands who knew the neighborhoods intimately. The census told one set of stories — ethnicity, SES, housing stock; the old hands told others — just how important a barrier — a railroad track or a freeway — was, what neighborhoods felt linked to others and why.[11]

The project met with the affiliates every Monday night.[12] The project workers themselves had a working meeting once every week whether there was nothing or a lot to do. They went over important developments, brought everyone up to speed, identified problem areas, made plans, and struggled over approaches.[13] This was a critical space for project members, a space where they engaged in narratives with one another, a space they used to develop, sharpen, and integrate their collective narrative.

One key to the continuity and effectiveness of the project was staff. The project actually had no staff. It was entirely a volunteer effort, led by Vincent Harris, assistant to the executive director of the Women's Civic Improvement Club (WCIC), Mrs. Callie Carney, the former city council member. Thus, though it had no formal staff, in Vincent the project had a staff person of the highest caliber who was willing to put in overtime as a professional, unpaid project staff member.[14]

The project was able to use WCIC computers, secretaries, and mailing operations. Similar facilities were sometimes available from the Urban League.[15] This was possible only because Black people controlled institutional space whose resources they could direct as they chose. Newsletters, reports, fliers, and letters could be and were turned out regularly and systematically using the resources of Black institutions. Black physical space enabled the distribution of published Black narrative.

This effort produced the best district plan the city had ever seen. It drove the whole city redistricting process. Try as they might, others, including the city staff, were never able to come up with a better plan, or even an equal one. The project's map was finished and in the hands of the city's staff before the city staff's own maps.[16] The project published a newsletter, *Civic Action: Redistricting News and Views*, which it distributed to its affiliates and at public redistricting hearings.[17] It was a valuable space, whose entire narrative was that of the Redistricting Project, space people literally could take home and to the job with them, spreading the project's narrative.

The plan had two essential components: (1) to have the city council adopt the project's map; (2) Districts 7 and 8 should be renumbered.

The two council districts between which Meadowview had been divided were 7 and 8. The council member representing District 7, Lyn Robie, announced prior to the beginning of the redistricting process that she would not run for reelection.[18] But there was a trick in her announcement. The city charter had been amended in 1989 to synchronize city council elections with state elections. All elections would have to take place in even numbered years. In order to maintain the principle of staggered elections, anyone serving in an odd-numbered district would have his term extended to 1994. Instead of retiring from the council in 1993, as originally elected, Robie would automatically continue in office until 1994.[19] There would not be another election in District 7 until 1994. The Redistricting Project took the position that District 7 should become District 8, and District 8 should become District 7. That would make the seat in District 8 up for election in 1992. The project argued that having District 8 up for election in 1992 enabled the most democratic process. Instead of a member not elected by the new constituency serving for two years before the newly constituted district could elect its own representative, the residents could elect the person to fill the newly drawn district immediately. To do otherwise would defeat the whole purpose of redistricting — to make sure the incumbent was as representative of the population as electoral mechanisms would allow. Otherwise, a fifth of the decade the seat would be filled by someone who hadn't been elected by district voters.

Although this was a powerful principled argument, it derived from the circumstance that the Summit on African Concerns and the 1991 Redistricting Project in particular had built a tremendous movement in Black neighborhoods throughout the city, especially in Meadowview. The activists wanted to carry their surge straight into the 1992 election. Delaying an election for two years might lose the advantage they had with a fully mobilized Black population. It would be possible to win the redistricting battle and lose the election.

Once the drafting task force had handed its work over to the city, the community outreach task forces turned people out for the public hearings. The project lined up people to speak who were tied to neighborhoods where hearings were held. People who had participated in the 1981 effort to keep Meadowview in one district testified about the blatant racism and favoritism in the 1981 process.[20] In community centers all over the city, wherever the hearings were held, the presentations received overwhelming supportive vocal responses from the audiences as city council members listened. In every neighborhood the majority of people in attendance, and usually the overwhelming majority, were African descended. As *Civic Action #2* described one hearing, " More than half the audience of nearly a hundred were African-Americans, *despite a change in the location of the hearing announced the day before*" (emphasis mine).[21]

The scene was repeated over and over. At the hearings in Meadowview, the largest turnout for any hearing (200), 90 percent of the audience was Black.[22] The project turned the public hearings into Black spaces dominated by Black narrative.

The project developed a close working relationship with the Latino Coalition for Fair Sacramento Redistricting, which eventually adopted the project's basic map.[23]

Just when it appeared the plan would steamroll to victory, a monkey wrench was thrown into the game by the Sacramento Asian-Filipino-Pacific Islander Coalition for Fair Sacramento Redistricting, which claimed the plan would crush its interests. The group was composed primarily of affluent Asians (mostly Chinese and Japanese) who felt their voting strength was being diluted by combining them in a district with poor Asians (mostly Vietnamese and Hmong). Their action constituted a stab in the back because the 1991 Sacramento Redistricting Project had worked closely with them all along, supplying them with the project's plan early on, consulting with them regarding modifications, and even supplying them with the project's data-rich computer discs.[24]

The Redistricting Project faced the decision of whether to attack the Asian plan. It would actually increase the Black population in District 8 from 30 percent to 33 percent, but it would break some Black people off from communities they felt they belonged to. The Redistricting Project leadership decided simply to note their opposition to the plan changes, but not fight them.[25] As a result, the project's map was modified to keep most of the affluent Asians in their own district.[26] The Asians also opposed the 1991 Redistricting Project on the other critical issue, renumbering. Despite the modification of the general plan to meet their objections, the Asian coalition did not want an immediate election. Its leaders approached the District 7 incumbent, Lyn Robie, who had retained her seat by opposing the incorporation of Meadowview into a single district in 1981. They told her if she opposed renumbering, they would support her for reelection. They reasoned if she opposed renumbering, the council could not counter the will of a sitting council member on her own district. When the votes were cast, the Redistricting Project learned the worst, renumbering had been defeated by a vote of six to three.[27]

Here, it turns out, the project's decision not to go to the wall over the shape of the Asian district was a good one. Most observers concede that had the project fought that battle, it could have won. But in choosing to yield the point it earned considerable goodwill among council members and other redistricting activists.[28]

The decision not to renumber was a serious defeat for the project. At a social event the week of the defeat, a number of project leaders, other Black activists, and officeholders mulled over the mixed result at the city council meeting. Collectively they decided not to accept the council's vote on renumbering.[29] They had tailored the whole redistricting process to fit their vision. They decided to try to get the city council to reverse itself. That would require someone who had voted against renumbering to move to reconsider. They had six chances. The project pulled out all stops. Project members who lived in districts of those who had voted against renumbering met individually with their council representatives. Tom Chinn was told that project members who lived in his district would pledge their lives, their fortunes, and their sacred honor to see to it he never won another election if he didn't vote to renumber.[30]

Political leaders in Sacramento were called upon to exert pressure on opponents of renumbering. Several Black Sacramentans exercised considerable weight in the local Democratic Party. They could call on their ties to Willie Brown. Grantland Johnson sat on the County Board of Supervisors. Influential Black Democrats could use their influence on the County Democratic Central Committee. Without the Black vote, even in the Democratic city of Sacramento, no one was guaranteed election. Democratic leaders at the state level and local activists were told, *We want this decision to be rescinded. If it is not, there will be serious consequences.* The project and its affiliates packed the city council meeting on October 5 when the renumbering issue was to be raised again.[31] The meeting became a Black space dominated by Black narrative.

Terry Kastanis, council member for District 8, who would be spared a reelection campaign in 1992 if the districts were renumbered, and who had voted against renumbering in the first go-round, moved to reconsider.[32] The motion was seconded and passed. Council Districts 7 and 8 were renumbered.[33] Phase one of the 1991 Sacramento Redistricting Project was over. There remained the winning of a city council election. The kind of acumen shown by the Redistricting Project was not unique to Black Sacramentans. In fact, many of the leaders and most productive members were recent arrivals. This kind of political spade-work was going on in Black jurisdictions all over the country. The municipal, state, and congressional Black electoral victories Black people won over the decade did not rise up out of whole cloth.

The 1992 Election

Largely as a result of the extensive organization and mobilization by the Redistricting Project, and totally contrary to the project's intentions, five of the six candidates who filed for the council seat in District 8 were Black. The sixth was a Latino.[34] District 8 now had a majority of non-white voters, but whites still constituted a plurality. Nevertheless, the only non–Black candidate was a Latino. Through organizing and mobilizing during the redistricting process, through ownership of the public narrative on the question for almost a year, the Black population had asserted its ownership of District 8 and, just as crucially, the other groups had acquiesced.

Only one of the six candidates had been intensely involved in the redistricting effort, Sam Pannell. The other candidates were Sherwood Carthen, minister of a large congregation in Meadowview; Velma Harrel, who had been involved in neighborhood activities, particularly regarding youth; Pat Shelby, a longtime activist in Meadowview; and Audry Smith, a consultant who had participated in the redistricting drive. The Latino candidate, Michael Reyna, was on the city planning commission, a traditional entry point to the Sacramento City Council.[35]

The most aggressive campaigns were led by Carthen, Pannell, Shelby, and Smith. In addition to being active and visible in the Redistricting Project, Sam had other advantages. He had long, deep roots both in Meadowview and throughout Sacramento. He had been president of the SAEOC Board of Directors in the 1970s. He had twice run for city council, in 1971 and in 1977. Grantland Johnson had managed his second campaign. He had also worked in Grantland's campaigns. He was very well connected in the world of Black activists and political junkies in general. His roots in the community were broad. He had been deeply involved in Little League: coaching, officiating, and getting baseball diamonds into neighborhoods. He was sociable and made contacts easily. He was a teacher and a counselor. He was well known and respected in the teachers' union and he had been president of Black Educators for Action (BEFA). He was blunt, outspoken, full of ideas, energetic, and articulate. He was an avid campaigner. Without saying so explicitly he raised the question of where were all these folks when the fight was being waged to make this election possible? I know where I was. Everybody knows where I was. But where were all these Johnny-come-latelies?

In the end Sam won. In Sam Pannell District 8 gained a voice on the council which was loud, aggressive, and would not back down. It would have been hard to imagine a more forceful advocate. Within the first 90 days of taking office he had worked with the police department to shut down 17 drug houses in the district.[36]

Other Impacts of the Project

While the Redistricting Project's greatest impact was on the Sacramento City Council districts, it affected other districts as well. True to its charge, it drew up plans and district maps for the Sacramento County Board of Supervisors, the Los Rios Community College District, the Sacramento County Board of Education, and SMUD.[37] Project members attended redistricting hearings for all those bodies, presented their proposals, and offered oral and written testimony.[38] Their work had a significant effect on every redistricting plan adopted and further implications that were to play out over the decade. In no instance, however, was the effect as pronounced as for the city of Sacramento because nowhere else in the county was the African population as densely concentrated. Since the other jurisdictions covered much larger areas, the intent of the project was to draw some districts which would be shaped to capture as many Black neighborhoods as possible; for example, not only Meadowview, but Meadowview and Oak Park, and if possible, Glen Elder; not only Del Paso Heights, but Del Paso Heights and North Highlands, and if possible, Lincoln Village. That way it was possible to maximize Black influence in specific districts rather than having the Black vote so dispersed it could have little impact anywhere. The goal was to create jurisdictions where candidates had to make appeals to Black voters.

Another effect redistricting efforts had was to make government jurisdictions visible which lay largely outside the radar screens of Black voters and potential candidates. People involved or informed by the process began to think of running not just for the city council, the Board of Supervisors, or local school districts, but also for the SMUD Board, the Los Rios Board, and the County Board of Education. They began to think about and investigate jurisdictions they'd never even thought about and in some instances never heard of — park and recreation, fire, and water districts; the Port of Sacramento, mosquito abatement, and irrigation districts. Their senses both of citizenship and the possibilities for participation expanded. This kind of greater information about electoral possibilities — nationally — is what helped drive Black electoral gains of every kind in the 1990s.

The project had other objectives. It sought to build operational unity, tying together Sacramento's far flung Black populations. It succeeded at that. While people tended to turn out best for the hearings in their own neighborhoods, some traveled across the city and even the county to be present at venues far from their accustomed grounds, and people from all the neighborhoods came together at the meetings in city hall. Secondly, the project wanted to build viable alliances with other non-white populations. It succeeded in doing that with Latinos. That had far-reaching effects because the Latino member of the city council, Joe Serna, was gearing up to make a run for mayor. He labored assiduously to see that the Black-Latino coalition worked in the redistricting process. He won his race for mayor and became a staunch ally of Sam Pannell. The project tried *almost desperately* to make the coalition with the Asians stick. In that they failed, which was not only deeply disappointing, but surprising, because many of the 1991 Redistricting Project members had worked effectively with Asian activists in the Sacramento Valley Rainbow Coalition Organizing Committee. They came to see the differences in the two experiences as reflections of class differences within the Asian population they had not sufficiently taken into consideration.[39] Finally the project intended to re-enforce the tradition within the city's African descended population of working across class lines *within* the African-ancestored population. That effort also prevailed, as at both public hearings and city council meetings Black people of every social stratification came together, though the troops of the project were almost all young, college-educated members of the Black middle class.

The Summit on African American Concerns Revisited

Of all the committees, projects, and task forces that came out of the Summit on African American Concerns, the 1991 Redistricting Project was the only one that bore fruit. Every one of the others withered on the vine. The nexus of Ida Sydnor's concerns — *the youth*, street gangs, violence, crime, catastrophic performances in the schools — persisted and worsened. Health problems did not abate. Unemployment and underemployment remained egregious.

The galling defeat Black people suffered in 1981 was magnificently avenged, but the root conditions persisted. *Even a brilliant local victory could not stem the gargantuan inertia of national and international forces.* That the Summit on African American Concerns fell far short of its aspirations speaks in part to the role of national politics, including national *Black* politics, and the limits inherent in them. Short of forceful and persistent allies, even the most brilliant Black leaders and the most effectively organized and highly mobilized Black populations cannot turn the course of the colossal ship of state.

Women on the Move

By 1970 women were well-entrenched in the first ranks of the community's Black leaders. Due to the blatant hypocrisies of life in the United States and the related complications of seeking public funding, in the 1950s the Negro Women's Civic and Improvement Club changed its name to the Women's Civic Improvement Club (WCIC).[40] By 1970 the leader of WCIC was, *ipso facto*, a leader of Black Sacramento.

In Oak Park, Blanche Hill and Callie Carney were well known as the African descended leaders *par excellence*. In Del Paso Heights that mantle fell on women such as Mamie Johnson and Essie Brown. Seen as leaders of wider scope were Virna Canson of the NAACP and her sister-in- law, Dr. Fannie Canson, who became the first director of Ethnic Studies at then Sacramento State College. Essie Brown also became a community-wide leader when she was named executive director of SAEOC. The same status was eventually conferred on Delores Bryant, executive director of the Sacramento Urban League; Doris Alexis, director of Motor Vehicles for the State of California; and Alice Huffman, chief deputy director of the California Department of Parks and Recreation. Many women had distinguished themselves as educational leaders: Dr. Hazel Mahone, first Black superintendent of the Grant Joint Union High School District; Dr. Virgil Price, a deputy superintendent of the Sacramento City Unified School District; and Dr. Carolyn Minor, Dr. Pauline Travis and Dr. Hortense Hurdle, school principals. Esme Williams was appointed dean of students at John Still Junior High School. Irene West in the hamlet of Elk Grove was carving out a distinguished career as a teacher and principal. Sally Scott was doing the same thing in the SCUSD. Josie Washington was elected to the Grant Joint Union High School District Board. Charlotte Bolton, Leslie Campbell, and other women were elected to the Del Paso Heights Elementary School District Board. Kathryn Lee, joint owner of *The Sacramento Observer*, was in the first echelon of the city's Black leaders. At the end of the 1970s the Sacramento Black Women's Network (SBWN) was founded, giving birth to a remarkable run of African-descended women leaders.

GRACE DOUGLAS, RUMBLE. Grace Douglas was a woman who became an institution. She returned to college with the wave of mature Black students who entered higher education in the fierce and heady days of the Black Power and Black Student Movements. She was a brilliant student who took courses in Pan African Studies and loved to write. Her children were leaving the nest. Her husband was a high-ranking administrator in the state civil service. When she graduated from Sacramento State College, she decided to follow her heart. She established a corporation called Rumble, Inc. Its purpose was to publish a local newsletter which was a cutting-edge publication of informed and well-documented opinion for African-descended people. It focused on Sacramento, but it covered the whole African world. She featured sharp writers who went on to make names for themselves in a number of fields. *Rumble* became required reading for Black Sacramento racial advocates.

She established the *Rumble* Awards in the 1980s which recognized outstanding achievement by African-descended people. Awardees were not limited to Sacramento, though the bulk of the awards each year went to locals. She established the *Black Market*, which was both a paper and an entrepreneurial venture. All these were invaluable Black spaces. When anybody in Sacramento's Black cultural, political, and civic community said the name Grace, everybody knew who the speaker meant. She had as much impact on Black awareness, networking, and dynamism as any other Sacramento Black institution.

THE GROWING LEGACY. In the 1980s increasing numbers of Black women were elected to school boards. Alice Lytle was named to the bench. Shirley Thornton became deputy superintendent of the State Department of Education. Queen Randall was tapped as president of American River College, and later superintendent of the Los Rios Community College District. Kathryn Hall created the Birthing Project, which brought compassion, imagination, and studied practice to the condition of pregnancies among young, single, Black women. Esther Nelson assumed leadership of the Sacramento NAACP branch.

The Sacramento Black Women's Network, originated in 1979, in 1988 began to host an influential two-day conference in March. It brought in distinguished, nationally known speakers, presented scholarships, and honored women of achievement.[41] It offered a singular opportunity for networking.

THE FRUIT OF THE 1991 REDISTRICTING COMMITTEE. By the start of the 1990s dynamic women leaders and organizations were the norm in Sacramento's Black politics. One woman had the final word on any significant Black political developments in the area: Virna Canson. Adding to this distinguished record, the 1991 Redistricting Project led Sacramento's Black women to set

Dr. William Lee, co-founder of the *Sacramento Observer*, with his wife, Kathryn, ultimately joint owner. Courtesy of the *Sacramento Observer Newspapers*.

forth on an unprecedented assumption of leadership roles. Ida Sydnor issued the call that gave birth to the Redistricting Project's parent organization. Within the project Lauren Hammond and Pam Haynes played defining roles.

Additionally, Hammond and Haynes were participants in a striking innovation, Africa's Daughters Rising. Most influenced by Fran Burton, a long-time state capital guru, Africa's Daughters Rising was a Black women's PAC. It was designed to influence local politics and to foster increased participation of Black women in the electoral arena. Africa's Daughters Rising became a powerful factor in the equation of Sacramento's Black electoral politics.

In the 1990s Black women in Sacramento no longer served only as frontline troops and staff for the Black struggle — though they continued in those roles — they also served as the commanding generals in every sphere of political life. They did so both by constituting and leading their own organizations, and by assuming direction of organizations formerly dominated by males.

Black Women for Political Action (BWOPA) served a similar role in the Bay Area. Maxine Waters led a tremendously influential women's organization in Los Angeles. All over the country Black women were moving from the staff to leadership. This, too, strengthened the Black hand in 1990s politics. The more visible role of Black women in political leadership was not a local phenomenon. It was national. Carol Mosely Braun, campaigning for the U.S. Senate in Illinois, came to California and Sacramento seeking support, as Harold Washington and Jesse Jackson had before her. Like them, she got it.

The Re-emergence of Black Elected Officials and Striving for Continuity

The first big electoral triumph in the 1990s was the election of Sam Pannell. For the first time in five years a descendent of Africa sat on the Sacramento City Council. That put a Black person on each of the two dominant political bodies in Sacramento simultaneously, Sam Pannell on the city council and Grantland Johnson on the Sacramento County Board of Supervisors. At the time no one knew how critical Sam's election would prove for Black electoral office in Sacramento. Grantland Johnson was soon to be tapped by the newly elected Clinton administration for the position of western regional director of the Department of Housing and Urban Development. His departure, once again, left only one Black person in the top echelon of elected officials.

Nevertheless, Black people continued to make inroads on school boards. At one point 3 of the 5 members of the Grant Joint Union School Board were Black — in a district with an overwhelming white majority. The Black board members all came from Del Paso Heights. Even under Republican administrations descriptively Black people continued to be appointed to the bench and — with fateful consequences — to the University of California Board of Regents.

Strike — While the Iron Is Hot

Sam Pannell's election in 1992 came largely on the heels of the redistricting effort of 1991 and the 1991 Redistricting Project. Pannell's election did not exhaust the momentum gathered from the project. Robert Pernell, one of the project's co-chairs, had been interested in running for office when he began working with the project.[42] His first interest was the city council, but like Pannell he lived in District 8 and he had no interest in challenging Pannell for a seat. As he worked in the project, he explored other possibilities. The project had developed a Black influence district in SMUD. Pernell decided to run for that seat. He won.[43] The 1991 Redistricting Project claimed another victory.

Because it was a PAC, Africa's Daughters Rising was increasingly contacted by candidates and would-be candidates for every kind of elective office. The organization's members relished their roles as king- and queen-makers, and some entertained the idea of assuming crowns for themselves.

One with such ideas was Lauren Hammond. She had been appointed to the County Planning Commission by Ila Collins, a member of the County Board of Supervisors, a woman who remained one of Lauren's stalwart supporters.[44] The position on the planning commission was a plum among the region's advisory bodies. There she was involved with long-term decision-making for the whole region. As a staffer for the State Senate she was familiar with the strategies and tactics of developing and enacting legislation, as well as the techniques of running campaigns. She had worked on many statewide campaigns. She had also worked on Grantland's and Sam's campaigns. She had been intimately involved in the 1991 project's political engineering. She thought she had something worthwhile to offer as an elected leader.[45]

When a vacancy opened up in the California State Assembly, Deborah Ortiz, who had replaced Joe Serna as the representative of District 5 on the Sacramento City Council, jumped at the chance. She won the primary and took the seat in the fall general election.

A special election was called to fill her seat in Council District 5. Lauren Hammond

lived in the district. She had plenty of time to think about what to do, especially after Ortiz won the Democratic primary. She was ready, but she was no fool. She tested the waters. She talked to people. She went to meetings.[46] She felt out other potential Black candidates. She had the crew from the 1991 Redistricting Project. She had Africa's Daughters Rising. She had a base. But as a candidate she was a neophyte, and the big guns might have other choices for the slot. As it turns out, they did. They had been grooming Genevieve Shiroma for elective office. The District 5 opportunity came up and Shiroma lived in the district. Her candidacy was a no-brainer. Shiroma had been set up by putting her on the prestigious Regional Transit Board, the position from which Grantland had gone to the city council. She was on the fast track.[47]

Nevertheless, Lauren Hammond threw her hat in the ring. She had one

Sam Pannell was the first person elected to the reconfigured and renumbered District 8. He died in office after election to a second term in 1996. Courtesy of the *Sacramento Observer Newspapers*.

advantage. She had been an active union member. She had participated in a long, hard strike against the *Sacramento Bee*. She didn't get the *Bee*'s backing, but she got the backing of the firefighters and police unions. She also got other union support. The *Bee* endorsed Shiroma, as did the County Democratic Central Committee, and every elected Democratic official except Sam Pannell.[48]

Hammond ran a meticulously organized campaign. Everyone who walked for her had a specific block grid. The worker was required to contact everyone in the grid, identify every Hammond supporter, get her literature out to everyone, and check during polling to see which of her supporters had voted and which had not. Another operation furnished rides to polling places. She developed a beautiful campaign piece which was used both as a mailer and a handout. It stressed the strong family background afforded by her parents, her education in Sacramento schools from high school through college, and laid out her agenda: safe neighborhoods; community policing; kids and schools; economic opportunity; supporting small neighborhood businesses, not liquor stores; personal service; a district office; and every neighborhood getting its share of city resources and services.[49]

Hammond walked as much of the district as possible. She lived in Hollywood Park, a working and middle-class neighborhood. She blanketed it. Her headquarters were there. She did not neglect any part of the district. She sought to identify her supporters and maximize their turnout, wherever they lived. While her campaign was not deracialized, it would be safe to call it a multicultural campaign. Hers was a Rainbow Coalition much closer to that of the SVRCOC than to Jesse Jackson's national efforts. Except in Oak Park and among her Black campaign workers, it was not a Black campaign.[50] To everyone's surprise except her own, she defeated the favorite and was elected to the city council. Since this was only an interim election, she had to face the prospect of going up against the Democratic Party favorite again when the seat opened up for a full term the coming year. But for the time being, for the first time in Sacramento's history two Black people sat on the city council. They had both come out of the 1991 Redistricting Project.

In 1996 Sam Pannell was elected to his second term. He was a very popular council member. He was friendly and jovial, but he was not easygoing. He was driven. He worked hard and he was on the go, 24/7. He had health problems. His weight fluctuated considerably, though it never really got down to aver-

Lauren Hammond was elected to the Sacramento City Council in 1997 to fill a vacancy, and she was re-elected in 1998 for a full term. Courtesy of the *Sacramento Observer Newspapers*.

age. He had blood pressure and heart problems, none of which slowed him for more than a couple of weeks. He had diabetes. What he did most was deliver for his district. He got the police to shut down drug houses. He got a Meadowview Community Center built.[51] He revitalized a commercial strip. He was recognized throughout Sacramento as one of the city's foremost leaders. He didn't make many enemies, not only because of his warmth, but also because people were afraid to be his enemy. If Sam were coming down the track and you didn't get on board, the best thing to do was jump out of the way. City council meetings were carried on public access cable TV and people tuned in just to watch and listen to Sam Pannell. He pulled no punches and threw plenty. He was fond of saying things like, "I'm just a country boy. I don't understand that. You've got to explain it to me, so I can get it." He'd say, "The rest of you (*referring to other members of the council*) may understand this. I don't. Why don't you make it real simple so I can understand?" He was a presence. He died in office, December 4, 1997.

In addition to the city suffering a great loss, his death created a vacancy on the city council. Sam's death shocked Sacramento. It shocked District 8. It shocked Meadowview. He had won reelection just 18 months earlier and no one was prepared to run. At that time no one *wanted* to run. People wanted to grieve. The city memorialized him by renaming the Meadowview Community Center the Sam Pannell Community Center. Meanwhile the council had to think about filling the vacancy. Too much time was left in Sam's term to fill the position by appointment. There would have to be a special election. For the political community the question was — who would fill Sam's shoes? Whose feet were big enough? The sad answer was, no one's.

Some people encouraged Bonnie Pannell, Sam's widow, to run. Most pronounced among them were Sam Walton, Sam's campaign manager; the Rev. Ephraim Williams of St. Paul Baptist Church, Sam's and Bonnie's pastor; and Greta Cannon, a Meadowview activist and advocate for senior citizens.[52]

Bonnie had no interest in the position and little interest in politics. She had always supported Sam in his political ambitions but she had little intrinsic interest in the subject. She'd been raised in Del Paso Heights. She was thoroughly a Sacramentan, though not political. Nevertheless, she decided to run. Her primary motivation was that if she were elected, she could finish out Sam's term. She could do that for him. Then if someone else wanted to run — more power to them. If she didn't win, it wasn't meant to be.[53]

Since she had no political experience, she relied heavily on her advisors who were primarily the people who had encouraged her to run. Sam had a list of supporters. She called everyone on the list, told them she was going to run, and asked for their support. Every single one gave it.[54]

The campaign proved much more mean-spirited and nasty than she could have imagined. A lot of the vitriol came out in community forums. Her opponents' main complaint against her was that she had no experience. This seemed absurd to her because none of them had experience at being a city council member either.[55]

Asking people for money was difficult. She didn't think she'd be able to, but she did. Sam's campaign organization was good. It had run and won two elections, and the people who'd said they'd help, did. She just tried to be herself.[56] She won. District 8 once again elected a Black candidate and realized the possibility created by the 1991 Redistricting Project. There were still two Black members of the Sacramento City Council, now both women.

The project's string hadn't run out, though. Lauren Hammond's seat was up for a full term. She would have to face the big guns again. Fate stepped in, assuming the form of Ila

Collins. She convinced Genevieve Shiroma not to run.[57] Lauren Hammond was unopposed. She walked into her second term and first full term. The seat was now truly hers, solidly back in the Black column.

Many people had been talking to Pam Haynes about running for office. She had the credentials. She had a B.A. in political science from UCLA and an M.A. in public policy from the Kennedy School at Harvard. She had been in the private sector for 20 years and an organizer for her union before she went to graduate school. She had worked in state government and on the 1991 Redistricting Project. She was a member of Africa's Daughters Rising. She had worked as an aid to Deborah Ortiz. She was well connected. She was articulate. Most frequently she was encouraged to run for the Sacramento City Unified School District Board. She lived in the district. She saw that board as too dysfunctional to be an option for her.[58]

Before she had gone to UCLA she had gone to Los Angeles City College and had received a good educational foundation

Pam Haynes was appointed to the Los Rios Community College Board of Trustees in 1994 to fill a vacancy, and elected in her own right in 1996. Courtesy of The Black Group.

there. She felt committed to the role of community colleges in California and decided if she were to occupy public office, it should be on the board of a community college. She didn't know that a member of the Los Rios Community College District Board had moved out of town and had to vacate a seat. The board had decided to fill the seat by appointment. Again, her friends encouraged her to apply. She did and was asked to make a presentation to the board. The Kennedy School had prepared her well for that. The board had also been sensitized by the redistricting process. The person who left the board had been Black. They wanted a Black replacement. Ultimately they picked Pam.[59] In 1996 when she finally had to run for the seat, she ran as an incumbent and won.[60] The 1991 Redistricting Project had struck again.

The Air Force brought James Shelby to Sacramento. He was stationed at McClellan Air Force Base. He and his family lived in Rio Linda, just north of Del Paso Heights. He was always involved in the community. He became president of the PTA at his son's school. He ran the Little League baseball team and a football team for kids. In 1976 he was elected to the North Highlands Park and Recreation District. Ila Collins appointed him to the Sacramento County Civil Service Commission in 1976. He ran for the Rio Linda School Board in 1978 and lost. Subsequently he moved to Citrus Heights. Grantland appointed him to the County Planning Commission, and later removed him. He was re-appointed by Dave Cox, a Republican. In 1986 he was appointed by the Board of Supervisors to a commission to do a study of consolidating the City and County of Sacramento — looking at whether to construct a municipal government equivalent to San Francisco, which is both the city and the county of San Francisco. The plan was not adopted. James decided to serve on the Citrus Heights Fire District.[61]

Meanwhile, he had left the Air Force and was working for SMUD. He also served on the Sacramento Urban League's Board of Directors. He was a friend of the executive director, George Dean. When the board started considering firing Dean, Shelby resigned. After Dean left the Urban League in 1988 — he took the same job in Dallas — members of the board and others encouraged Shelby to apply for the executive director position. He was reluctant. Volunteering for the league was one thing. Working for it was another. He had a high paying job at SMUD with great benefits. The league could offer nothing like that. But he had a commitment to the race, and finally his daughter talked him into applying. He did. He was selected. Immediately he became a high-profile actor in Sacramento. Shelby was active in the Harold Washington Democratic Club. As executive director of the Urban League he responded to Ida Syndor's call to constitute a Summit of African American Concerns. The Harold Washington contingent at the summit launched the Committee on Economics and Politics, subsequently the 1991 Redistricting Project. His was one of the facilities project members used for conducting their work.[62]

After the failure of the city-county consolidation, Citrus Heights, where he lived, began to investigate incorporating as a city. In California any such intentions have to be approved by a regional Local Agency Formation Commission (LAFCO). The process requires extensive research, public discussion, and clearly articulated positions. Among other things, LAFCO has to decide whether the proposed new government can constitute a viable jurisdiction, e.g., its tax base and other sources of revenue, possible conflicts with other jurisdictions, the impact on other jurisdictions, and the transition process. James became involved in all that and LAFCO eventually approved the incorporation of the city of Citrus Heights. James was encouraged to run for the new city council. The elections were at large, seats filled consecutively from the highest vote getter down. James ran 4th out of 12 candidates. He was seated on the 5 member council.[63] Another prominent actor in the 1991 Project had won public office.

State Electoral Politics

More damaging to Black prospects in Sacramento than anything happening on the local level were events in statewide politics. Electorally, California is an anomaly. Frequently, statewide elections are captured by Republicans — gubernatorial, senatorial, presidential, and propositions on the ballot. This has been particularly true since the passage of Proposition 13 in 1978 which opened the floodgates to Republican ideas and candidates. Yet in the state's congressional delegation and state legislature, both in the Assembly and the Senate, Democrats are almost always in the majority. This is explained only in part by the Democrats' control of the legislative

James Shelby was elected to the first city council in the newly incorporated city of Citrus Heights in 1998. He was also executive director and CEO of the Greater Sacramento Area Urban League, Inc. Courtesy of The Black Group.

process during redistricting. For one thing, no one can really predict where population will grow in the 10 years between the censuses — which means areas with a majority of Democrats the year the census was taken can have a majority of Republicans two years later — but, more importantly, redistricting serves more to protect incumbents than it does to secure dominance of a particular party. This condition was reflected locally in excluding one-half the Black population in Meadowview during the 1981 redistricting process to preserve the seat of an incumbent (*and the city council and its seats are nonpartisan*).

While there are more registered Democrats than Republicans in California, this condition has little impact on statewide elections which can just as easily go Republican as Democratic. It is only at the state legislative and congressional levels that this Democratic edge in registration seems to have much practical meaning. Recently, for several election cycles Californians have voted Democratic in presidential elections, but that seems to be more a function of particular candidates than it does of party registration or identification.

These idiosyncrasies in California voting at the state level meant that for virtually all the 1980s and '90s (16 years) the governor's office was controlled by Republicans and the legislature was controlled by Democrats. It also meant that when Republicans couldn't get their measures approved in the legislature, they went to the initiative process to get them placed in statewide elections. That's what happened with Proposition 13, and was to happen throughout the 1980s and '90s for measures which increasingly imposed a conservative agenda on the state.

That pattern enabled Pete Wilson to put Wardell Connerly on the University of California Board of Regents along with other conservatives which resulted in the abolition of affirmative action in the admission of students to the University of California. In 1994 it resulted in the passage of Proposition 187, an initiative designed to deny illegal immigrants social services, health care, and public education. Many Latinos were illegal immigrants and couldn't vote to combat the measure. Many who were legal immigrants were not citizens and couldn't vote; many who were citizens did not vote, so the Latino vote was marginal in a statewide election. The same was true for Asians. Due to antagonisms between Blacks and Latinos many Black people backed Proposition 187. Most Black leaders opposed Proposition 187 and warned their constituencies, "What's good for the goose is good for the gander"; if Latinos were being targeted by Proposition 187, targeting Black people couldn't be far behind. For the most part the warnings fell on deaf ears.

Those ears suddenly popped open in 1996 with the appearance of Proposition 209, which would end affirmative action in the state. Despite ferocious opposition from progressives, Black organizations, Latino organizations, women's organizations, Asian organizations, and even some business organizations, Proposition 209 passed overwhelmingly and eliminated affirmative action in California. Both Proposition 187 and Proposition 209 were challenged in the courts — with more effect in the case of Proposition 187, but largely to no avail.[64]

The stigma of Proposition 209 as a racist measure was removed by the presence of Wardell Connerly, an alleged Black man, as the chief spokesperson for the initiative. How could it be racist when a Black man was its principal advocate, and he categorically declared it was not racist? This, however, was a strange *Black* man who insisted he was not Black and only accepted the appellation because it was a general usage, not because it depicted him. He said he had traced his ancestry and it was mainly French, Scotch, Irish, and Native American, with a little Black thrown in. He would not accept the designation African American and said he had nothing to do with Africa or Africans.[65] The *Sacramento Bee* catered to his sensibilities and stopped referring to him as African American (the newspaper's term for African descended people) or Black, and referred to him instead as mixed race or of combined European, Native American, and African descent.[66]

The same year (1996) which issued in Proposition 209 also brought term limits to the California State Legislature. In 1990, Proposition 140, introduced largely to expel Willie Brown as speaker of the California State Assembly, had been approved by the California electorate.[67] Willie Brown held the speaker's office for more years (15) than any other person in the state's history.[68] It looked as if he would go on being speaker forever. He was a lock for reelection in his own district every year, and it looked as if Democrats were going to maintain their hold on the Assembly. As long as he wanted to be speaker, he would, and his position was commonly characterized as an affront to every white resident of the state. Through his funding operations he masterminded Democratic candidates and elections. Through his office he controlled the legislative process and dispersed favors at his whim. He was a force in national politics as well and garnered favors from the Clinton administration. Grantland Johnson could never have been appointed regional director of HUD without his approval. Plus, he was smart, arrogant, not reluctant to make fools of others, drove fast cars and wore Italian-tailored suits, and though he was a married man with a family, infamously had a taste for white women.[69] He was anathema, intolerable. His continued presence, lording it over the state legislature, was an obscenity. The only way to get rid of him was to change the constitution, and that's how he was finally termed out of office. The initiative established term limits for members of the state legislature, and when Willie had completed his allotted terms, he was out. He accepted his defeat graciously. He ran for mayor of San Francisco and won.

Electorally, the state of California had developed a very hostile attitude toward Black interests and Black people. That posture had penetrated to the local level which made the political victories garnered by the daughters and sons of Africa in the state's capital city the more remarkable.

Black fortunes were suffering similar declines around the country. The best evidence of this was the Republican takeover of the House of Representatives in 1994 and the Republican wins of a majority of governorships. Despite these transformative Republican victories, Black political initiatives and triumphs in restricted jurisdictions throughout the country continued unabated. It was during this period that Black people elected the largest number of representatives to the House of Representatives in the country's history, captured the largest number of state legislative seats in the country's history, and elected the largest number of municipal officials. The kinds of efforts that made this possible in Sacramento were afoot elsewhere. Ordinary Black people had thrown themselves into the fray, and with striking originality and unprecedented expenditures of energy had found ways to go beyond a holding action to establish institutions and networks which strengthened their collective position even during the nadir of politics for the Democratic Party.

Collective Mobilization

A Path for a Decade

Though not recognized in public discourse and paid short shrift by most scholarship, the 1990s was a breakthrough era for Black collective mobilization in the United States. Much of it took place in the electoral arena as indicated by the preceding section. Yet a good deal of it went on outside electoral politics. That this is not widely known is partially because except for peak events such as the Million Man March, it was not widely reported in the press. Scholarship, on the other hand, had standards which also obscured the deeper and wider political picture developing among the country's African-descended population. It ascribed significance primarily to very limited research categories: measurable findings at the national level; studies of iconic sites, such as Washington, D.C., New York City, Atlanta, and other big cities, including those with Black majorities, or Black mayors; and detailed and rigorous studies of very narrow sites on strictly defined questions. There were few deep and comprehensive analyses and syntheses of the total Black politics literature. Finally, a primary premise of this book is that very little work was done looking at the deep settings and structures peopled by ordinary Black folk and how they conducted politics within them. As a result, it was possible for both the press and academia to imagine and portray the Million Man March as an isolated event. Nothing could be further from the truth. The Sacramento example drives this point home.

In many respects the Summit on African American Concerns and the 1991 Redistricting Project characterized African origin Sacramento mobilization throughout the decade. They arose out of the same process, yet in themselves, one represented activist mobilization and the other, community mobilization. The summit was a clear case of activist mobilization. The Redistricting Project, arising out of activist mobilization, realized its purpose only through community mobilization.

Further Activist Mobilization

THE BLACK BOURGEOISIE AND THE "N" WORD. On February 4, 1994, the political cartoon on the editorial page of the *Sacramento Bee* featured a Ku Klux Klan character talking about Farrakhan. The Klan member said, "That nigger makes a lot of sense."[70]

Newspapers had no sooner hit porch steps than the *Bee's* switchboard was lit up by Black callers. Many canceled their subscriptions on the spot. The next day the paper printed some of the callers' concerns along with the newspaper's defense.

Dr. Nate White, president of the Sacramento NAACP, said,

> It perpetuates racism ... the Bee could have used a better choice of words — they should have said "this minister," "this Muslim," "this person," "this man." ... In light of all the racism in Sacramento this year, that was adding fuel to the fire. The black community took that as a low blow.[71]

With respect to the *Bee's* defense, including the cartoonist's (Dennis Renault) position, "If you're going to depict a Klansman, you say what a Klansman says,"[72] Dr. White said,

> The Klansman didn't draw the cartoon. The artist who drew that and put that caption under it is responsible for his actions. I got the message loud and clear — he said racism is alive. The *Bee* needs to stop and apologize to the Sacramento community, and stop printing stuff that perpetuates racism.[73]

James Reede, co-chair of the 1991 Redistricting Project, had become vice chair of the Sacramento Human Rights and Fair Housing Commission. He said, "It would be the word that the Ku Klux Klan would say, but that doesn't make it right to repeat it."[74]

James Shelby said the cartoon was

> a tragedy that should not have happened. I think the editorial board lacks the sensitivity and ethics in journalism that the newspaper has tried to portray in the community.[75]

Derrell Roberts, Oak Park activist and director of the Ray Robinson Community Center, said, "It really showed poor judgment on the part of the editorial page staff to allow that to run."[76]

Peter Schrag, editorial page editor, said the cartoon was "designed to show bigotry's ugly face. The *Bee* regrets any offense or misunderstanding it caused." He went on to say, "The main point of the cartoon is bigotry, no matter where it comes from."[77]

Black leaders demanded a meeting with the publisher, management, and the editorial staff. The *Bee* agreed. By then the howls of outrage from ordinary Black people had been going on for days — more subscription cancellations, calls, letters to the editor, complaints to other media outlets, getting the story into the state and national press.[78]

All the big Black guns showed up at the meeting: Nate White, NAACP; James Shelby, Urban League; James Reede, Human Rights and Fair Housing Commission; Sam Pannell, Sacramento City Council; Callie Carney, WCIC; The Black Chamber of Commerce.[79] It was reminiscent of the 1970s when leaders of Sacramento's flagship Black organizations saved Bob Tyler's job.

They demanded a formal apology from the *Bee* and the cartoonist. They demanded the editorial staff get some training on handling racially sensitive issues. They had plenty of recommendations about whom to hire to conduct the training. They demanded that the *Bee* hire more Black editorial staff, run more Black columns on its editorial pages, do more contracting with Black businesses, and learn lessons from the *Sacramento Observer*, possibly doing some joint venturing. The *Bee*, they said, could do more publicity, more marketing of Black sponsored events. The negotiations weren't protracted, but several meetings were required. In the end, the *Bee* gave in.[80]

State of the Race

The Sacramento Area Black Caucus, the National Black Assembly, the Summit on African American Concerns, were object lessons in the futility of attempting to form long-lasting umbrella or all-embracing Black community organizations. At the same time they were instructive about both the persistence and the effectiveness of such efforts. The formation of the SABC had led to major improvements in the strengthening and networking of Sacramento's Black infrastructure. Once it had ceased to be an all-inclusive organization, it had become a dynamic, sophisticated Black multi-purpose organization able to produce such wide-ranging efforts as a Black Unity Festival; significant increases in the number of Black people appointed to boards, commissions, and administrative posts; and the activation of communities to improve their neighborhood schools. The National Black Assembly, among other accomplishments, produced the National Black Agenda, which served as the template for the Congressional Black Caucus legislative program for decades. The Summit on African American Concerns produced the 1991 Sacramento Redistricting Project.

The paradox that the Black population had a propensity to form all-encompassing organizations, that they never lasted, and yet often had positive by-products, was a riddle the SABC wrestled with. Annually, it conducted a planning retreat. Some caucus members were familiar with the work of Harold Cruse and Robert Smith, documenting the failures of such all-inclusive efforts nationally. Cruse had pointed to the missed opportunities to form a National Black Council. Its purpose would have constituted a space where African descendants of every perspective and class could meet at least annually in one forum and discuss issues which were important to each of their constituencies, but where they wouldn't actually try to do anything

STATE OF THE RACE

Conference
Hosted by the Sacramento Area Black Caucus
at the Women's Civic Improvement Club
3555 3rd Ave
Sacramento, California

August 1st, 1998

State of the Race, 1998. Program cover (depicting Rosa Parks) for the first Sacramento State of the Race Conference, 1998.

STATE OF THE RACE

Second Annual Conference
Hosted by the Sacramento Area Black Caucus
at the Women's Civic Improvement Club
3555 3rd Ave
Sacramento, California

August 7th, 1999

Program cover for the second State of the Race Conference, 1999 (Dr. Martin Luther King, Jr., and El Haj-Malik El-Shabazz [Malcolm X]).

as a body. The precedent for such assemblies, initiated after Cruse's discourse, was the National State of the Race conferences headed by Ron Daniels.

During the 1997 retreat the SABC decided to sponsor a Sacramento State of the Race Conference in August of 1998. Its purpose would be to bring together Black Sacramento organizations from a wide range of fields to share what they had done, what they were currently doing, and what they anticipated doing in the future. The notion was this would enable them to become better informed about what was — and was not — going on in Sacramento, and to offer opportunities for collaborations or mutual support efforts, or just the ability to get out of each others' way.[81]

The idea was for the State of the Race Conference to become an annual event, a Black institution. The first conference was held August 1, 1998. Twenty-six organizations participated. The caucus also prepared a list of 138 organizations, businesses, and elected officials. It prepared another list of 54 faith-based congregations. It provided contact information for each organization. All the information was printed in the conference program. Twenty-three organizations provided their annual calendars, which were also included in the program. Another program feature was a monthly calendar of events derived from individual organizational calendars.[82]

In 1999 the SABC sponsored the 2nd State of the Race Conference on August 7. The second conference had an even wider reach. One hundred and sixty-seven organizations were listed and 38 provided organizational calendars; 56 faith-based congregations were listed.[83]

Several projects grew out of the State of the Race Conferences. One involved collaboration among public and private school educators and parents. Probably the most fruitful products were long-term collaborations across a wide range of activities between the SABC, the Sacramento Valley Black United Fund, the All African People's Revolutionary Party, the California Black Chamber of Commerce, Carol's Books, the Center for Community Health and Well-Being, and the Women's Civic Improvement Club. During the 1999 SABC retreat, the caucus scheduled the third annual State of the Race Conference for August of 2000. These State of the Race Conferences intentionally replicated Ron Daniels' work that was going on in other parts of the country. This was a national tendency.

Further Mass Mobilization

We have already seen mass mobilization at work in the 1991 Redistricting Project. It was, however, not the sole initiative of the kind over the decade. It was merely the first.

THE MARTIN LUTHER KING MARCH & ALD. Two celebratory events became annual occasions for a ritual assembling and convocation of African peoples. One was the January Martin Luther King, Jr., March. It consisted of a six mile march, a rally usually held at the state Capitol, and a Job Fair and Expo at the Sacramento Community Center. The other was African Liberation Day in May, organized by the All African People's Revolutionary Party (AAPRP). It also consisted of a march, usually around McClatchy Park in Oak Park, or two miles from McClatchy Park to Sacramento City College. It was followed by a rally, workshops, and a day of music, speakers, and vendors in the park. The Martin Luther King March had broad participation across racial groups and usually included city leaders such as the mayor, members of the city council, and members of the Board of Supervisors. Despite its ecumenical flavor, most of the participants were Black. The African Liberation Day events, on the other hand, targeted Black people and almost everyone in attendance was Black, though some featured participants were Native Americans or Irish revolutionaries. While African Liberation Day sometimes included efforts to develop or disseminate a political program, the MLK March, Job Fair, and Expo *were* the program. They were also celebrated in many other places: the ALD, nationally and internationally; MLK Day, all over the U.S. These almost ritual events contrasted sharply with other, less regularized forms of mobilization.

THE MILLION MAN MARCH. In mid–1994, the Honorable Louis Farrakhan started putting the word out that he was going to issue a call for a Million Man March on the

Capitol, in Washington, D.C. The reaction of most Black people, particularly Black men, was that it was outrageous. Wouldn't that be something if he could pull it off? They fantasized about the government's terror as a million Black men descended on the Capitol. At first, almost nobody took Farrakhan seriously — it's a great idea, but it will never happen.

Farrakhan scheduled the march for October of 1995. About a year out activities inside the Nation of Islam began to indicate that something really was going to happen. Nationally, only a small segment of the Black population was getting the message that something big was actually in the works. Much of the early interest was on the East Coast (close to Washington, D.C.), and in Chicago, the headquarters of the Nation of Islam. When Ben Chavis, former executive secretary of the NAACP, got involved, more people perked up. Farrakhan tapped Chavis to chair the Million Man March Committee.

By early March of 1995 preparations were well underway. Speakers were going around the country touting the effort; organizers were spreading out. The loci for the drive were the local mosques of the Nation of Islam. Sacramento was the home of Mosque # 73, led by Minister Abdul Rahman Muhammad. He put together a group called Friends of the Nation. As the march date grew closer, organizational activity at the local level grew more intense and formalized. Friends of the Nation gave way to the Local Organizing Committee (LOC) for the Million Man March.

The major work of the LOC was raising money for the march. The committee also publicized the march and recruited men to go. The Sacramento LOC did not reserve a bus or other means for Sacramento residents to travel. Each man made his own arrangements, including lodging in D.C., though the LOC facilitated networking for those needing a place to stay in D.C. and those planning to travel by auto.

By September enthusiasm for the march was high throughout Black Sacramento. Organizations placed it on their agendas. Local colleges held forums. Even those who knew they would not be going looked forward to see what would happen. Others scrambled to make last minute arrangements to travel to the nation's capital.

Once the march got on the country's radar screen — and until a month before the march Black people were the only major population group aware of it — an organized and heavy resistance was mounted. There had always been opposition within the Black population as many labeled it sexist, non–Christian, or led by a Black racist. Colin Powell said, "I was concerned my presence on the stage with Farrakhan would give him a level of credibility ... I would not like to have seen."[84] Willie Brown said, "I vehemently object to the racist and sexist comments uttered by the leader of this march."[85] The Black church was almost uniform in its opposition.

Scathing as some Black opposition was, opposition from outside the Black population was even more focused and intense. Jewish leaders criticized Farrakhan for being anti–Semitic. The country's leader, President Clinton, condemned Farrakhan's role as the march organizer.[86] None of that did anything to stem the tide.

While there was no official count of the number of men from Sacramento who went, from their familiarity with men they knew were going, and from self-reporting of others, the Sacramento LOC estimated that 85 Black men from Sacramento attended.

Many who attended returned with a mission.

Individual marchers went around the area offering testimony to local organizations and audiences and encouraging people to respond to the spirit of the Million Man March, organize, contribute to their communities, and end the madness. The Sacramento Urban League devoted an edition of its television program, *The Urban League Reports*, to the march and to a panel of marchers which conveyed the need to use the march to make concrete accomplishments. California State University Sacramento sponsored a forum of march participants attended by over 200 people.

Following all these events, the LOC sponsored a standing-room-only and overflow public forum. Many people spoke of initiatives they wanted to launch, ranging from after school programs and early childhood interventions to starting businesses and linking up with Africa and the whole diaspora. Many lamented their own inability to attend the Million Man March and longed for some event that would capture its spirit in Sacramento.

Those in attendance decided to capture the momentum by organizing a local event or march no later than February of 1996, and for the LOC to take the lead in constituting a committee to organize it. A score of people volunteered to participate on the committee. The Million Man Marchers had not returned empty-handed. They brought the fire back with them.

THE 1,000 MAN MARCH. Many of the people at the LOC Report back were women. Most of them had opposed the Million Man March. They had viewed it as sexist. Nevertheless, most of them had also been inspired by it. None of them, however, wanted a march or demonstration of any type in Sacramento which was gender exclusive. Nor, from all outward appearances, did males who volunteered.

The LOC issued a call for a planning meeting and disseminated it widely throughout the Black population. At the meeting the group decided to follow the model established by the 1991 Redistricting Committee. Organizations and individuals would have to establish a buy-in. They would have to make a financial contribution and commit their organizations or themselves to carry out the tasks necessary to conduct the event. They established that the committee would deliberately avoid sexism in its own operations, in publicity for the event, and in the event itself. They established two co-chairs, one female and one male. They established functional committees: finance, program, outreach, liaison with governments, publicity, and planning. The whole committee would meet weekly to carry on overall approval and direction of the work and to coordinate activities. The committee also decided to draw directly on the precedent and the momentum established by the Million Man March, and to label the event the 1,000 Man March. Outreach and publicity were to make clear that this was not a men-only march — that it was a family event, a men, women, and children event that was deliberately not exclusive but inclusive. The reasons for the title were made explicit — linking it to the Million Man March — with the accompanying goal that at least 1,000 of those present would be male — that men had the same responsibilities to Black empowerment as women. The date set for the event was Saturday, February 17.[87]

The SABC became the lead organization, as both co-chairs were SABC members.[88] Other draft horse organizations for the 1,000 Man March Committee, the name the planners adopted, were the Million Man March LOC, the Nation of Islam, the 100 Black Men, the All African Peoples Revolutionary Party, and the California Legislative Black Caucus. A number of other organizations were significant and consistent participants as were some unaffiliated individuals. The liaison committee, headed by the 100 Black Men, had the key task of arrangements with governmental authorities. Their work was greatly facilitated by the California Legislative Black Caucus. The committee had decided to follow the pattern established by the Million Man March and hold the event at the state Capitol. State officials, including the California State Police, with responsibility for the Capitol grounds, had to work with the committee to approve plans and security arrangements. Because the areas immediately adjacent to the state

Capitol were under the jurisdiction of the Sacramento City Police Department, planning also had to be coordinated with them.

The program committee's responsibilities included a sound system. They contracted for a state of the art setup. February falls in Sacramento's rainy season, so the committee was concerned about rain. The sound company said their system could handle a little rain, but if they thought the rain was going to be too hard or continue too long, they would have to pack up and leave. The committee took the gamble and decided that if the worst should happen, they could rent a system of lesser quality from local sound stores. The walk-throughs conducted before February 17 took the rain possibility into account and the availability of alternate systems was checked, but everybody hoped there would be no need to go to the fall-back plan. The committee had chosen a state of the art system for a good reason. They wanted the highest quality sound possible.

As the technicians and march organizers arrived in the pre-dawn darkness of February 17, the weather was mild for mid–February. The sky was clear, the temperature was in the mid-forties. People began assembling the stage. The sound company went to work setting up. Vendors were logged in and assigned places. Tenth Street, flanking the whole west end of the state Capitol, was closed off for the march. It gradually became lined with vendors. The Sacramento Black Nurses Association provided a first aid tent just south of the stage.

As with the Million Man March, it was still dark when the expensive sound system proved its worth. A mussein broke the still darkness with the Muslim call to prayer. "A-A-A-louah — Akbar!" The call's lyrical beauty hung in the air. After the mussein a Native American called on his ancestors to bless those who had gathered on their land for the march, and to bless all they would do that day. He was followed by Catholic priests and Protestant ministers invoking the support of their triune God.

With dawn the organizers and vendors were joined by the first marchers who began to trickle onto the Capitol grounds. The sky was a deep blue with a hint of gray to the southwest.

One of the events scheduled for early morning was a press conference inside the state Capitol. Speakers at the press conference were Ahjamu Umi for the AAPRP; Faye Kennedy, march co-chair, for the SABC; Dia Poole, staff for the California Legislative Black Caucus; Minister Abdul Rahman Muhammad from Mosque # 73 of the Nation of Islam; Minister Tony Muhammad, western regional minister for the Nation of Islam.

The march theme was "A Call to Action." The leaders shared the march mission with the assembled journalists.

The 1000 Man March serves as a historic catalyst for people of African descent to be actively engaged in their own destiny. In the spirit of unity; self-determination; self-love; and economic, social, and political empowerment, the goals of the 1,000 Man March are to:

- Encourage all people of African descent to be active in community based organizations.
- Assert that all of our organizations should be financially and self-determined from resources within our community.
- Promote the development of a common ground and respect for the diversity of opinion and purpose within our community, from the actions of individuals to the missions of organizations, and to
- Provide a secure voice and opportunity for those formally voiceless in our community.[89]

As the press conference wound down, reports reached the leaders that the patch of gray sky was expanding ominously.

As the spokespersons went back outside, the first raindrops fell. A couple of hundred people had assembled before the stage where they were being entertained by scheduled performers. A few people in the crowd reluctantly began to pull out umbrellas or cover their heads with hoods. March organizers went to the sound people to ask them what they thought. The crew chief said they were okay if the rain stayed as it was, but that if it got any worse, they would seriously think about pulling out. The whole sky was now gray, and the rain light, but persistent.

The organizers kept an eye on the crowd, on those still coming, on the sky, and on the sound people. The rain gradually increased in intensity. More umbrellas popped open. More heads disappeared under hoods. The crew leader from the sound company came up to the program committee chair. He said they couldn't risk their equipment. They were going to pull out.

The rain got heavier. The sky got darker. The key organizers decided to meet.

Once assembled, they all asked, "What are we going to do?" The sound system was being packed as they spoke. The rain was heavy and showed no signs of letting up. A few hundred people had gathered and more were straggling in. Would they stay, in the rain, for the whole day's program? With the rain coming down, would those who had planned to come later come at all? The program committee members said they could get an adequate sound system from Skip's Music. It would take about a half an hour to get it, another half hour to bring it back, and a final half hour to set it up; i.e., it would take an hour and a half to make another sound system operational. What would the people, standing in the rain, with no operational sound

Frank Withrow (left) and T'Chaka Muhammad (right), two activist poets, address the 1,000 Man March. Courtesy of the *Sacramento Observer Newspapers*.

"Carry it on!" Men assembled for the 1,000 Man March defy the elements. Courtesy of the *Sacramento Observer Newspapers*.

system, do? Should we cancel the event? Who are we to say, come hell or high water, we're going to try to keep you out in a rainstorm just because we've been stupid enough to schedule an event in the middle of the rainy season?

The more they talked — and they talked fast — the more they were convinced they couldn't make the decision by themselves. This was a community event — a collaboration between those who called for the march and those who responded. They decided to lay out the facts to the people who had come, and abide by their decision. Someone in the program committee had shown the foresight to bring a bullhorn. They took that, and went back out into the rain.

A lot of people had stepped back from the platform to stand under the trees. Still, there were several hundred people in the open, soaked. A committee member went to the podium at the center of a raised area set up on the stage. Speaking through the bullhorn, he pointed to the banks of speakers being carried away. He said human beings were waterproof, but the expensive sound equipment wasn't. He said the bullhorn was now the sound system; they could get another sound system, less powerful, but adequate. That would take another hour and a half. He pointed to the sky and said he didn't see a break in the rain or in the clouds. The committee had staged the march as a call to action, but there was no need to drown anybody. The committee would abide by the will of those assembled. Should we call it off or carry it on? A burst of sound, as if spoken with one voice exploded from the crowd.

"Carry it on!"

Black Californians Meet with Pete. Poster for Sacramento Black Activists' meeting with Governor Pete Wilson on a Black Agenda.

People raised their fists into the sky and turned their faces up into the driving rain.

"We're not moving!"

"We're not going anywhere!"

The organizer shouted, "The people have spoken!" A great roar went up from the crowd. A crew from the program committee raced off to Skip's Music.

The following speakers and performers used the megaphone. Despite the rain, people continued to trickle into the park. Vendors began to lose their worried expressions. An hour and a half after the assemblage had delivered its vote of confidence, the new speakers were up and operating. The clouds parted. The sun beamed through. Another great cheer went up. The rest of the day was glorious and bright, with the temperature in the mid-sixties.

By noon 5,000 people had gathered. They heard speakers, storytellers, poets. They watched dancers and drill teams. Awards were made to the *Sacramento Observer*, to Black reporters from the *Sacramento Bee*, *Sacramento News and Review*, KXTV, and KCRA television.[90]

Tony Muhammad, the keynote speaker, challenged people to get involved in organizations, in the Nation of Islam, in churches. He told them to make personal commitments to their families and community. He said, "The spirit of the Million Man March is alive and well and taking root in Sacramento!"[91] He told the Republican governor, Pete Wilson, he would have a price to pay for supporting the end of affirmative action, and ignoring the sorry plight of African people in California.[92] It proved to be true that just as a Democrat was returned to the White House in 1996, in the next gubernatorial election, the Democrats seized the governor's office for the first time in sixteen years.

As days and weeks passed, the enthusiasm generated by the march did not wane. Increasing numbers of people continued to engage in volunteer work, join organizations, become active in religious congregations, became more grounded in their families, and form new organizations. The spirit continued over into the 1996 elections which saw Sam Pannell reelected; Lauren Hammond campaign for a council seat, and eventually win; more Black people elected to local office; Black involvement in the presidential election, and later, in the 1998 statewide California elections. It also was instrumental in launching Sacramento's first State of the Race Conference.

The Million Man March was not stillborn. Its documented progeny in Sacramento were prodigious. Nor were they without siblings all over the republic. It is also clear that without the kind of groundwork laid down by the Black population at large such as this study documents — groundwork which was going on simultaneously in many places around the republic, and which definitely was not restricted to Sacramento — the phenomenon of a million African ancestored men arriving on the same day on the National Mall in Washington, D.C., would have been impossible.

ROBBIN WARE AND THE BLACK OMBUDSMAN. Robbin Ware was a long-time participant in Sacramento's racial struggles. During the most dynamic years of the Black Student Movement he was an engaged college student. He received a Master's of Social Work degree and became a master's social worker for Sacramento County. He joined the SABC and was elected chair. In that capacity he was instrumental in bringing a Smithsonian exhibit on Black women to Sacramento's Crocker Art Museum. He left the caucus to form a new organization, the California Black Cultural Assembly. The organization's name notwithstanding, it was active on both the political and cultural fronts. Robbin later became active in the Sacramento chapter of the NAACP and was elected president.

The branch got so many complaints about police misconduct that Robbin began tracking them. He talked with the police chief. He talked with members of the city council. Nothing happened. The police didn't change and the complaints didn't stop. Robbin was a veteran of the bitter antagonism between the Sacramento Police Department and African people in Sacramento: the Oak Park 4, the protests against the police murder of Raymond Brewer, the slaying of Milton Baker, the raids on the Nation of Islam Temple. He knew about the continued police retaliations against Akinsanya Kambon and other members of the Oak Park 4 — indeed, of the Oak Park 15. He was fed up.

With the sharp increase in crime beginning in the late 1980s and continuing into the '90s, Sacramento residents had increasingly demanded community-oriented policing (COP). The idea was to get police officers on a walking or cycling beat, to get them on the same sidewalks with the people, to get them to know and become familiar with neighborhoods, and to get neighborhood residents familiar with them. This had been one of the recommendations of the Citizens' Committee on Police Practices appointed to investigate the department after the police murder of Raymond Brewer. The police chief, however, had rejected the recommendation as outmoded, out of date from modern police techniques of squad cars continuously on patrol and rapid response. Yet over 20 years later, COP had become police state of the art technique. In fact, one of the major criteria when the city selected a new police chief in 1994 was a familiarity with and enthusiasm for COP. The new chief, Arturo Venegas, adopted COP, but labeled it POP, problem-oriented policing.

POP or not, the NAACP was still getting dozens of police complaints weekly. Robbin opened up the NAACP office for sessions where people could come in and air their complaints in person. The office was swamped. He kept talking to the police, the council, representatives of other organizations, and the media. The media picked up the story and followed it. It was hard to go a day without reading about his campaign in the newspaper or seeing a story about it on television. Nothing changed.

Robbin lined up scores of complainants who were willing to talk publicly about what had happened to them. He said, we're going to take this thing to city hall. He mobilized the local NAACP membership. He reached out to other organizations. He got a place on the city council agenda.

The night the city council met to hear from the NAACP, the chambers were packed with Black people. There were people who had been scheduled to speak, and there were people who had not been scheduled but wanted to speak. There were their friends and family members, their supporters. The NAACP was there in force. Other Black organizations turned out. People came just because they were tired of the SPD and its treatment of Black people. Others came to see the show.

Robbin got up and made the NAACP's case. He laid out the studies they'd done, the calls from Black people they'd received, the attempts to get a hearing from the police department and the council. Then he opened the floodgates: he let the people speak. When they had finished, there was no doubt that the city and the police department had a serious problem.

The NAACP and the Black speakers wanted a police review board. The Sacramento Police Officers Association (SPOA) was adamant: no. They had a process and a structure to deal with citizen complaints and bad-apple police officers, Internal Affairs. Black people hooted. The fox guarding the hen-house, the police policing themselves — what kind of sense does that make? We want an external body: an external, independent, autonomous body. We want citizen involvement. We want Black citizen involvement. After all, we're the ones being harassed.

The council members admitted Internal Affairs wasn't working. If it were working, we wouldn't have all these people here with real grievances. Robbin reminded everybody that the NAACP was very good at going to court. The courts had forced the county to build a new jail and the courts could be used against the city and its police department, too.

That night the serious discussions began about what to do to corral a runaway police force and to protect abused Black residents. The discussions — the proposals and counter-proposals — continued for a long time. The city's final solution — an ombudsman reporting to the city manager — pleased no one. The police wanted the investigation of complaints to remain entirely within the department. The NAACP and mobilized Black people wanted a citizens' review board which had significant Black membership. The council stuck to its decision and went about soliciting applicants. The man who was finally hired in 1999, Don Casimere, was a former police officer. He had been an ombudsman in Oakland, and he was Black. Robbin Ware and the NAACP had won a victory of sorts. It was not an unconditional surrender. It was a negotiated peace.

Electoral Community Mobilization

There were four significant Black electoral community mobilization efforts during the decade: Sam Pannell's two election campaigns, Lauren Hammond's campaigns, and Bonnie

Pannell's campaign. Sam's and Bonnie's campaigns centered around Meadowview, but involved Black people from the whole region. Lauren's focused on Oak Park, but it, too, brought in Black people from throughout the metropolitan area.

A Summary

The 1990s were dramatic years for mobilizing and collaborating among Black people in Sacramento: the Summit on African American Concerns and the 1991 Sacramento Redistricting Project, the Martin Luther King, Jr., March & Expo, African Liberation Day, the coalition formed to confront the *Bee* for its use of the "N" word, the Million Man March, the 1,000 Man March, the State of the Race conferences, the NAACP's struggle against police violence, and four election campaigns.

A lot of that dynamism was a reaction to other dramatic activities among Black people: crack, AIDS, youth gangs, gun violence, and brutal hip-hop. A good deal of the activity cited

Bonnie Pannell was elected to city council from District 8 in 1997 after her husband's death in office and re-elected in 2000. Courtesy of The Black Group.

in this chapter was to combat activity outside the scope of this book. In many senses, what I have discussed here is counter-organization, reaction to the devastation that some elements of the Black population were visiting on themselves and everyone else.

How extensive and intensive that counter-organization was is often overlooked. The Million Man March is often depicted as a blip on a radar screen, a big splash that went away, with no effect. That is not what we saw in Sacramento. It was part of a much broader wave of ongoing activism. Farrakhan's call didn't come out of a vacuum. The atonement element of the march came from the widespread feeling that Black people themselves, Black men, had acquiesced in the release of a virulent strain of behavior by their own people. They were willing and eager to atone for their dereliction of responsibility, to do something positive to initiate a renewal. Plus, the march itself did some building, some organizing, some deep reaching into the Black population. People responded to it. Yes, they went to D.C., but they had to make all the arrangements that got them there. Yes, they went to D.C., but they came back, with a mission, a spirit, and determination. In Sacramento that led to more collaborations among organizations and more organizing. It led to the development of continuing projects and relationships. It led to State of the Race conferences and facilitated organizing people to combat police violence.

Nationally, and in Sacramento, too, gang violence and murder declined substantially through the late '90s. To the extent the decline is explained at all, it is generally attributed to the policies of the Clinton administration. Undoubtedly, those policies had a good deal to do with it. But what about the mobilization of Black voters which contributed to Clinton's election? What about the roles of Black people within the Clinton administration? Grantland Johnson was one of them. There is, however, a broader dynamic that was going on *within* the Black population. What impact did it have? Are we to say it had none? There were the activities noted here. Within 90 days after taking office Sam Pannell had shut 17 drug houses in his district. There were many more initiatives going on within individual organizations, e.g., the Black Sacramento Christian Club Organizers, the Save Our Children Task Force Against Drugs and Gangs, and the 100 Black Men. The SABC, for example, held a march against gangs and drugs which ended up surrounding a coffin in McClatchy Park. Each marcher walked by the coffin single file and looked down into it. *They were looking into a mirror.* It symbolized how many Black people and many Black organizations saw their roles in the devastation being visited upon their neighborhoods — as their responsibility. They did a lot of things — in Sacramento and everywhere else — to combat the pestilence wreaking havoc among them. Do we have the evidence to say all that energy and effort was expended with no significant effect? We know most of the efforts Black people undertook went unreported in the wider media. If a tree falls in the forest and no one's around to write about it, or to photograph it, did it fall? I don't know, but the tree's on the ground, and the crime rate came down.

The Macro-Micro Link in Collective Mobilization: Who were the people who crafted these events, and what was the world they inhabited?

Here I look at the physical and mental terrain occupied by a collection of Sacramento Black activists during the 1990s. I refer to physical terrain as spaces, and mental terrain as narrative and social memory. My intention is to map out the connections between the activists' individual lives, the organizations to which they belonged, and the dynamics of political activism.

Conduct of the Examination

In late 1995 and early 1996, I identified 13 Black Sacramento residents who were active in Black organizations and public life. I asked each of them to be a respondent in an extended interview. They all consented. All were active at the local level, and some were active at the state, national, and international levels as well. They represented a significant component of the city's more race-conscious Black activists. Among them were leaders in various organizations cited throughout the study, and particularly in the organizations associated with collective mobilization in the 1990s: the SABC, the 100 Black Men, Sister Friends, the Black United Fund, the Women's Civic Improvement Club, the 1991 Redistricting Project, the Summit for African American Concerns, the All African People's Revolutionary Party, and Africa's Daughters Rising. They also included a school board member and an unaffiliated cultural activist. They are not a representative sample. They are examined for what their lives can tell us about the worlds of space, narrative, and social memory Black Sacramento leaders inhabited. Nine of the 13 belonged to organizations which by program were either nationalist or Pan African-ist. Interestingly, most of the respondents did not identify themselves according to such labels. All belonged to some organizations to which no other members of the group belonged. In some respects, the group was representative of most local elites in the U.S. They were edu-cated. They were all high school graduates. Eleven had college degrees, eight had advanced degrees. All were employed except one, who was retired. Their ages ranged from early thir-ties to sixty-plus. Four were women, nine men. All had been active participants in Black col-lective life for some time. The youngest had been active for the shortest period, four years. The others had been active considerably longer, from ten years to more than thirty.[93]

Findings

Respondents identified 69 spaces which they frequented, 35 Black and 34 non–Black or mainstream. Mainstream, in this instance, is not synonymous with hegemonic. Mainstream means only that the spaces were dominated by the great majority of the population, It does not mean anything about the narrative within them.

Each set of Black spaces and each set of non–Black spaces was divided into two cate-gories: dominant and non-dominant. There were, then, Black-dominant spaces and Black non-dominant spaces and mainstream-dominant and mainstream non-dominant spaces. A dominant space was one which more respondents participated in than its counterpart, and in which a majority of all respondents participated. For example, all thirteen participated in con-versations with colleagues. Thirteen participated in conversations with mainstream colleagues. Four participated in conversations with Black colleagues. That marks the space of conversa-tions with colleagues as a mainstream-dominant space. All thirteen participated in families. Thirteen participated in families which met the criteria of a Black space. None participated in families which met the criteria of a mainstream space. The space of families is a Black-dominant space.

For every space reported on in the study except one — families — all respondents partic-ipated in both Black and mainstream spaces. Each respondent reported that a majority of the members of her or his family was Black. In all other spaces there were respondents who engaged in both Black and mainstream spaces. For example, in the space of reading profes-sional journals, 11 of the 13 respondents were participants. Of the 11, 9 read mainstream pro-fessional journals and 5 read Black professional journals. Three of the 9 who read mainstream professional journals also read Black professional journals. Two of the 5 who read Black jour-nals did not read mainstream journals. Six of those who read mainstream professional jour-nals did not read Black professional journals.

MAINSTREAM SPACES. The respondents lived and operated in a world which was not dominated by Black perspectives and values. While 2 respondents read Black newspapers reg-ularly, 12 read mainstream newspapers regularly. The 2 who read Black newspapers also read mainstream newspapers regularly. Only 1 respondent read no newspapers regularly. Twelve of the 13 attended non–Black spaces for their regular newspaper reading. Ten of those who attended non–Black spaces for their newspaper fare did not regularly attend Black spaces for such information. Clearly, non–Black spaces dominated the newspaper reading habits of this group. Moreover, it is of further significance that the Black newspaper the respondents identified, the *Sacramento Observer*, was a weekly, while the mainstream newspapers were dailies. The influence of regular Black newspaper reading paled almost into insignificance.

In this instance, newspaper reading, two of the respondents were double counted because they read both Black and non–Black newspapers. The pattern of double counting appears in every spatial set except the one for families. In every other set there are some subjects who attended both Black and non–Black spaces. While the n for those who watched television programs was 15, that reflects 12 respondents. What's being counted are spaces. Respondents serve as markers for spaces. One watched no television and is not included in the total. Nine watched only mainstream television programs regularly, 3 watched both Black (3) and mainstream (3) programs regularly. The count of 9 + 3 + 3 = 15, is a count of the 12 respondents who watched television regularly.[94] The overweening influence of mainstream television as opposed to Black television is unmistakable. This pattern extends to specific subjects featured on television. Five were likely to watch television programs featuring Black subjects and 11 were likely to watch those dealing with other subjects.

In a society dominated by non–Black media these patterns are perhaps not surprising. These respondents, however, all made choices about whether to watch television at all. As indicated, one chose to watch no television. All had at least three alternatives to watching mainstream television: (1) not watching television; (2) watching only Black programs; (3) watching only programs which have Black people as subjects. Only one person made either of the three alternative choices.

Nor was the workplace a particularly felicitous arena for a preponderance of Black subjects. Four of this group were likely to talk with their colleagues about Black people, but all 13 were likely to talk with their colleagues about other subjects. This may have been more a function of the workplace than the proclivities of the respondents. However that may be, these subjects spent very little time talking about Black people in the settings where they spent most of their conscious time.

These were race-conscious Black activists, yet among them, six went to lectures or conferences dealing with Black people and eleven went to conferences or lectures on other subjects. Only three labeled their political positions as Nationalist or Pan Africanist. The others used labels more prominent among the wider public: liberals, moderates, radicals, leftists.

No form of Black publication was their principal reading fare. Five read Black journals or professional publications. Nine read mainstream journal or professional publications. Eight were likely to read articles about Black people. All thirteen were likely to read articles on other subjects. Radio fared little better. Six listened to Black radio programs. Nine listened to other kinds of programs. Six listened to Black radio stations. Nine listened to news radio stations. In ten specific categories of spaces in which the respondents participated, more participated in mainstream spaces than in Black spaces. When respondents participated in both Black and non–Black spaces they were not exposed solely to dominant spaces, but while some respondents were exposed *only* to non–Black spaces, *none* were exposed *only* to Black spaces. There is no doubt that, overall, non–Black spaces were dominant.

Only three participated in more kinds of Black spaces than non–Black. Nine participated in more kinds of non–Black spaces. One participated in the same number of each. These data do not indicate the amount of time spent in each space. Nor can they compare time spent at Black and non–Black spaces. They also cannot indicate the frequency of involvement in each space.

Respondents differed more widely in their exposure to kinds of Black spaces than to kinds of non–Black spaces. The respondent attending the most kinds of Black spaces (A) identified 27 out of a possible 35 types. The respondent with the lowest number (J) cited only 11 Black space types (a difference of 16). Yet within mainstream spaces, the person citing the highest number (J) named 24, while the person with the lowest number (K), named 17 (a difference of 7). For mainstream spaces both the modal and mean number of types was 20, yet only 3 respondents participated in 20 or more types of Black spaces.

These data make clear that most of the respondents did not live isolated lives, divorced from the mainstream and society in general. Their perceptions, beliefs, and values were influenced by a pervasive immersion in mainstream spaces.

For these findings to be significant, one has to assume significant differences between Black and non–Black spaces and the narratives afoot in them. One basis for the assumption is that the respondents were not random, they were race-conscious activists and much more likely to frequent Black spaces containing race-conscious narratives than the Black population at large.

BLACK SPACES. Ten Black spaces were frequented by at least a majority of the respondents. In three instances *all* respondents participated in them and did not participate in an equal number of corresponding mainstream spaces. In three others, 12 and 11 respondents participated (12 in one, 11 in two), marking these as Black spaces which dominated their mainstream counterparts.

Space number one (1) represents the majority of the family members as Black. All 13 subjects shared this space. All also shared spaces (2), majority of friends are Black, and (3) listen to Black music.

Measure (4), belong to Black political organization, was shared by 12 subjects. Measure (5), belong to an organization other than political which has a majority of Black members, and (6) read Black magazines, were shared by eleven people.

Measures (7) and (8) each included 9 respondents. They are (7), read books on Black subjects, and (8), attend Black theatrical productions.

The other two measures, (9) and (10), each claimed eight respondents. Nine is: seek out articles — in newspapers, magazines, and journals — on Black subjects. Ten is: go to Black movies. These ten activities constituted a collection of Black spaces filled with Black narrative, contributing to a social memory with specific Black components.

Other spaces, while not as dominant for the whole pool of respondents, served as significant sources of Black narrative and social memory. Six listened to Black radio programs and Black radio stations, belonged to Black religious organizations, attended lectures and conferences featuring Black themes, and attended Black nightclubs. Five belonged to Black cultural organizations. Four belonged to Black e-mail lists (this was in 1995 and '96), and four also belonged to Black social organizations. Three watched BET regularly. (This was the original BET). For most of these people who attended Black churches, listened to Black radio stations, belonged to Black social organizations, and attended Black conferences, the spaces and the narratives prevailing in them augmented those present in the ten dominant Black spaces. The additional exposures deepened and strengthened their social memories of the Black experience. One is unlikely to find such an intense exposure to Black spaces among activists from mainstream segments of the population.

BLACK NARRATIVES. In examining Black narrative I utilized three categories: symbolic Black narrative, implicit Black narrative, and explicit Black narrative. The categories arose out of informant responses. Below I discuss each category and its principal characteristics.

Symbolic. Food, dress, and hairstyle constitute this category. Ten participants favor soul food in various manifestations. One wears Afrocentric clothing as professional apparel. Seven designate their hairstyles as afro or "natural." Two more include a reference to afros or naturals as parts of their hairstyle descriptions. Symbolic representations are statements people make about their identity with their conduct, their appearance, and their lives. These symbolic statements specify *racial* identity.

Implicit. Here I designate spaces where Black narrative *might* take place. We cannot categorically assert Black substance in the narrative, but it is rational to assume a Black narrative. The friends and families categories warrant this designation.

All thirteen activists said a majority of their friends were Black. Six also said they talked with their friends about Black subjects. But what about the nine who said they talked with their friends about politics? When Black people talk with each other about politics isn't it likely that some of that conversation is about Black politics, about how Black people are affected by and affect politics? What about the five who said they talked with friends about social problems? Is it likely that some of that conversation centered on Black social problems? Given the people involved in these conversations — all or mostly Black — (some of whom are Black activists) it is likely that these spaces created by friendships primarily among Black people are also filled with narratives about Black people.

Only two respondents said they talked with family members about Black subjects. Ten said they talked with family members about family. The most frequent subject of conversation among family members was other family members. But given that all thirteen respondents said a majority of their family members were Black, weren't most of these conversations about family members conversations about Black people? They may not have had race as subject matter, but they did have Black people as subject matter. They were not talking about *any family in general.* They were talking about *specific families.* These would seem to be black narratives in Black spaces. They would contribute to the social memory of Black families.

While these examples with friends and families might be narratives about Black people conducted in Black spaces, they were not specifically and self-consciously focused on race. They were race-based narratives which are not *intentionally* race-based. They were race based by default, race-based because the society is entirely racialized, because of the inescapability of race as a defining condition in the society; i.e., as a matter of circumstance and not of choice, friends and family members will most likely be members of the same race. Michael Dawson, Katherine Tate, and Dianne Pinderhughes all comment on this set of circumstances.

Explicit. For those narratives which were intentionally, self-consciously race based, what was their substance, their subject matter? We get the most explicit designations of such matters from the reading lists. They include among other works of similar substance: *Rosa Lee*; a biography of Harold Washington; *My American Journey*, by Colin Powell; *We Have No Leaders*; Kweisi Mfume's autobiography; *Solomon's Song*; Andrew Young's *An Easy Burden*; *Black Betty*; *The Autobiography of Frederick Douglass; Two Nations*, by Andrew Hatcher; several books by bell hooks; *The Philosophy and Opinions of Marcus Garvey; A Raisin in the Sun*; a collection of Maya Angelou's poems. In short, these are substantive works, complex, multifaceted, books which deal with race in the U.S. in no superficial fashion. This is informative, analytical, high quality narrative.

The respondents chose to read these books, as opposed to reading no books at all. They are not light, escapist works. They are not comedy, celebrity biography, or romance novels. They deal with central race figures in serious ways, with Nobel Prize level fiction, with Pulitzer Prize level poetry, with the most serious kinds of political and racial ideas. In these books the panel of activists engaged substantive narratives which addressed the deepest racial problems in the country.

For magazines, the highest number of readers, five each, were those reading *Emerge, Black Enterprise,* and *Ebony.* The magazine with the next highest number of regular readers, four, was *Essence*. The respondents also read *Ebony Man, Black Schools,* and *Black Issues in Higher Education.* This was not lightweight reading. While *Ebony, Black Enterprise,* and *Essence* are Black mainstream publications, they do not parrot the dominant mainstream, and they tend to be more than fluff.

The Black movies they went to differed in seriousness, as did the non–Black ones. Some of the more serious ones were *Get on the Bus* (about the Million Man March) and *The Preacher's Wife.* On the other end of the spectrum were *The Nutty Professor* and *Set It Off.* Theatrical productions included serious fare: *Jar the Floor, Raisin in the Sun, The Colored Museum.* I don't know how to count *Othello.*

We are not privy to specific conversations of the respondents in Black spaces. Nor do we know the substance of the discussions in all the meetings they attended. But from what we do know, from the books, magazines, movies, and plays they attended, from the marches, demonstrations, rallies, and forums they participated in, and from selected organizational meetings, there are a number of salient observations we can make about the narratives to which we have access.

They include the recognition of a specific racial identity. They develop racial consciousness, emphasize a positive image of people of African descent, and stress the need for struggle to improve the condition of African people. They encourage cooperation between Black people, emphasize the achievements of people of African ancestry, and stress the importance of resolving conflicts between African peoples, including those centered around class and gender. They include cultural expressions which re-enforce specific racial identity and stress both politics and economics as means of maximizing Black power.

These respondents were race conscious. They self-consciously participated in race organizations, read race publications, attended race-based performances, and participated in race-inspired politics. They said they talked about race to others. It was important to them. It was at the forefront of their minds and it informed their actions. The narratives in which they participated, both as recipients and presenters, were race conscious and often race based.

The narratives encompassed whatever questions were current among members of the Black population, e.g., affirmative action, Ebonics, the Million Man March, Kwanzaa, Mumia Abu-Jamal, Geronimo Pratt, Juneteenth, welfare reform, employment opportunities, economic empowerment, the African diaspora. The activists experienced a world of information, analysis, and dialogue outside the mainstream, a world re-enforced in many venues.

Their world had no monolithic vision. The activists belonged to different organizations with different perspectives. They read different books and articles, went to different movies and plays. They had differing levels of exposure to both Black and mainstream spaces. They were individuals, each with her or his own take on the world. In one organization to which several respondents belonged, a close-knit, harmonious organization, two actively opposed the Million Man March. Two others attended it. There was no uniformity in this group.

There were, however, perspectives, streams of information, lines of analysis which fell outside those of mainstream U.S.A., and which enabled them to develop critiques and analyses with common elements. They were, in a way, hooked up with each other. They were reading books, magazines, and articles tuned to the same sets of concerns. They went to movies and plays centered around the same issues. They shared a common music and the sensibilities associated with it. They belonged to organizations focused on the same populations. Those populations constituted the bulk of their friends and family members. They went to similar marches, forums, and demonstrations. They were very active politically. They often knew each other by sight. While they were certainly well-exposed to the hegemonic worldview, they were in a better position to take issue with it than the population at large.

SOCIAL MEMORY. The social memory of these activists had complex origins and was multidimensional.[95] It was constructed from sources both mainstream and particular. While the most widespread particular sources were associated with African ancestry, there were others which were influential for some: socialist, Marxist, Christian, feminist. They contributed to the variation in social memory. There is no doubt, however, that very powerful social forces which were almost entirely rooted in the Black population had the most widespread effects — family, friendship, Black music. The social memory of the pool was heavily influenced by politics in that twelve of the thirteen belonged to political organizations and all thirteen were much more politically active than members of the population at large. Many of them — whether still members or not — were heavily influenced by the Black church.

Their social memories left them quite conscious of Black-owned businesses or institutions and predisposed them to patronize such establishments. As a group, they were much informed by the lives of Black leaders. They were also informed by Black writers.

Their social memories led them to identify with each other, and with other Black people. It drove them to join the organizations they did and to avail themselves of the informational sources they used. Those organizations and informational sources, in turn, re-enforced their social memory. Narrative and social memory were mutually re-enforcing. Together they placed these activists in the position of engaging in struggle, leading struggle, and utilizing opportunities to expand struggle. To them, the events they witnessed on a daily basis — either in person or in the news — dilapidated schools, high Black unemployment rates, high Black infant mortality rates, the O.J. Simpson trial — were not isolated, abstracted events. They were woof and warp of life in this society, deeply embedded in a social and historical context they believed they knew.

Assessments

Looking at these activists it is easy to understand the consistent gaps on almost every major issue, in poll after poll, year after year, between the Black and white populations. It is easy to understand the differences in racial group reactions to the Rodney King and O.J. Simpson verdicts. It is easy to understand how 1,000,000 Black men could have gathered at the National Mall in Washington, D.C., as a result of a call to arms barely heard by the general public until the zero hour and how a similar number of Black women could have assembled in Philadelphia with even less mainstream fanfare. It is easy to see how Black people got exercised over church bombings, hate crimes, police brutalities, and racial insults which barely touched the national consciousness.

In Sacramento the reaction to the police roustings that followed the murder of Officer Bennett in the 1970s; the arrest of the Oak Park 15, 7, 5, and finally 4; the criminalization of the four Black young men eventually put on trial because they were militants, even though they were the flower of the community, were strictly Black phenomena. The Grantland Johnson campaigns and the furor over the emasculation of Meadowview in the redistricting process in the 1980s were Black phenomena. In the 1990s, the 1991 Redistricting Project, Africa's Daughters Rising, and the capture of two city council seats by Black women, were Black phenomena. These events came about because of the deep context in which Black activists and those they mobilized were immersed.

In this country Black people, and Black activists in particular, inhabit two terrains. One is shared by the national population. The other consists of renegade, guerrilla spaces, where the tales told, the values learned, and the memories perpetuated are woven from an entirely different fabric. These activists were of a different mind and sensibility from the population at large, and while the mind and sensibilities they inhabited were multifaceted, they held important components in common.

Only by seeing them can we appreciate why in the 1990s there were over 100 more Black organizations in Sacramento than in the tempestuous 1970s. Only by seeing them can we come to a phenomenological grasp of the eruption of a Million Man March, a 1,000 Man March, a Black Sacramento Christian Club Organizers. Only by seeing their specific social memories can we see the 1991 Redistricting Project as a riposte to a stab that occurred a decade earlier, a riposte by people who had not even lived in Sacramento at the time.

People who were outside the loop, who were not hooked up as the respondents were — regardless of complexion or ancestry — were much more influenced by the narrative afoot in mainstream public spaces. Their social memory was different in kind from those of the people revealed here, who were both the front line commanders and the shock troops in the struggle against the persistent, demeaning enmity of the society which had enslaved them.

Mobilization and Mobilizers

The mobilizing events, elite and mass, examined in the first part of this chapter were initiated and led by the 13 people profiled here and those like them. They were not any Black

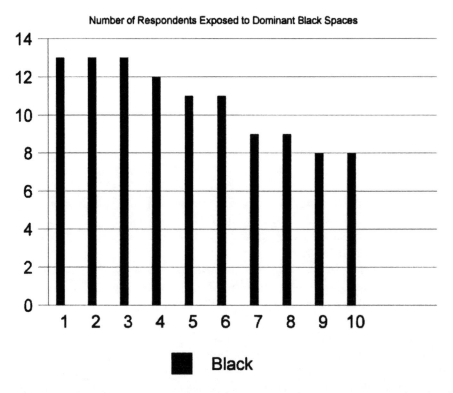

Figure 4.1 This graph depicts the number of dominant Black spaces participated in by all the respondents. It depicts the total number of activists who participated in each kind of dominant Black space. The *x* axis represents dominant Black spaces. The *y* axis represents number of respondents exposed. #1 on *x* axis represents families, 2 = friends, 3 = music, 4 = political organizations, 5 = magazines, 6 = other organizations, 7 = books, 8 = theater, 9 = articles, 10 = movies.

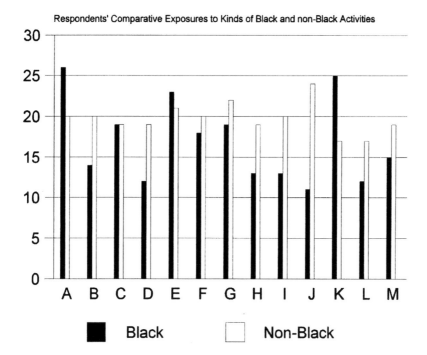

Figure 4.2 This graph depicts each respondent, identified as A through M, and the number of kinds of activities, both Black and mainstream in which each participated.

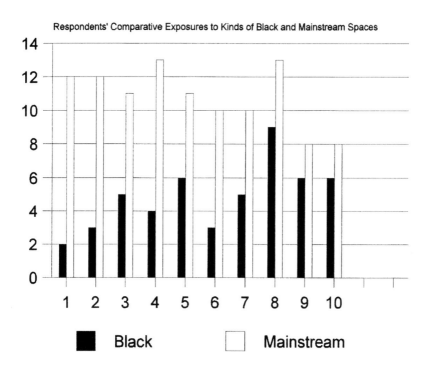

Figure 4.3 This graph depicts the number of respondents who were exposed to the kinds of spaces indicated in the graph, and in each kind of space compares the number of Black and mainstream spaces. Space 1 represents newspapers, 2 = TV programs, 3 = TV subjects, 4 = conversations, 5 = lectures, 6 = political, 7 = publications, 8 = articles, 9 = radio programs, 10 = radio stations.

people at random, but those who inhabited the spaces, joined in the narratives, and shared the memory documented here. Their counterparts could be found in almost every Black community in the country.

Black Organizations

Major Trends

Throughout this book I have used Black organizations as a proxy, as one powerful indicator of the directions and features of Black political activity. One of the reasons for the legitimacy of this approach is the collective character, the group character of political life. It is a dimension that aggregate analysis available from polling data accounts for, but inadequately. It is a dimension that institutional studies account for, but inadequately. In looking at the organizations themselves, who peoples them, what those members do, and how they do it, how they interact with each other — as well as with individuals and institutions — I contend we have a more substantial basis for a proxy of significant aspects of Black political life. When we consider, for example, the notions of the declining significance of race, the racial desegregation of life in the United States, the greater identification of Black people with the national population than with members of their racial group, the class interests of Black people trumping their racial interests, Black organizations provide a valuable window for assessing them. While it is extraordinarily difficult to get enough data nationally to make such assessments, the information is more accessible on the local level. Here we get a window on how Black organizations operate in their specific settings — and we do it over time.

During the 1990s the numbers of Black organizations in Sacramento grew rapidly. By the routine count the 232 Black organizations in the '90s exceeded the 162 in the '80s by 37.7 percent. The growth rate was higher than between the '70s and the '80s. The growth in campaign organizations, while at a lower rate than during the '80s, was still substantial, from 30 to 56, an increase of 86.7 percent. By the enhanced count, the political category numbered 82, keeping political organizations the largest category by that count. By the routine count political organizations rose from 11 to 26, still number 4 in the rankings. They were exceeded by service organizations (46), social organizations (44), and professional organizations (30). For the first time by the routine count, social organizations were not ranked number 1.

Working class Black organizations continued to decline. Part of the reduction was due to the disappearance of the anti-poverty agencies. Most homegrown Black working class organizations persisted, and one new one was created. But the anti-poverty structure which had mentored Callie Carney, Marion Woods, Essie Brown, Willie Hausey, Naaman Brown, Charles Bradley, Sam Pannell, and a host of others was no more. Mixed class Black organizations continued to grow, from 60 in the '80s, to 95 in the nineties. Growth also continued in middle class Black organizations, 73 in the '80s and 108 in the nineties.

Perhaps the most unexpected finding was the creation of four underclass organizations: the Health Care Workers Union, the People's Democratic Uhuru Movement, the Welfare Action Group, and Zulu Nation. Both the People's Democratic Uhuru Movement and Zulu Nation came out of the hip-hop movement. They were young people seeking positive directions for themselves and their generation, positive direction which was explicitly political. The other two organizations arose out of political struggles of very poor Black people, and were reactions to dominant political actors — the Health Care Workers Union at the local level, and the Welfare Action Group at both the local and national levels.

The '90s saw increasing numbers of Black organizations with national and international affiliations. There were thirty-two new ones. A significant number came from people from Africa or elsewhere in the diaspora. Organizations founded, specifically, as Black numbered 180, up from 122 in the '80s.

Women's organizations continued to outnumber men's, 37 to 14. They increased by six. Men's organizations declined by two. Women's civic organizations outnumbered men's, 13 to 3. Black males had 3 civic organizations, an increase of 1, but women's civic organizations grew by 5. Women's health organizations continued to increase. Women created two new kinds of single gender organizations: cultural and recreational. Men also developed a new recreational organization.

The Increasing Impact of Electoral Politics on Black Political Life

With two decades to look back on, the '90s offered an opportunity to see whether electoral politics occupied a much greater portion of the Black population's political work than in the past.

In the 1990s there were almost two and a half times more routine political organizations than there had been in either the '70s or the '80s. In both of those decades there had been 11. In the '90s there were 26. Not only that, but by the routine count, political organizations in the '90s counted for 9.8 percent of all organizations, as compared with 6.9 percent in the '80s. In the '70s they had been 11.4 percent. The varying number of political organizations made clear that their number was not related to population. The '70s and '80s both had the same number of political organizations, though the Black population grew considerably between the decades. The census recorded 36,418 Black people in Sacramento County in 1970, 58,951 in 1980, and 97,129 in 1990. In the '90s despite a substantial increase in the Black population — the 2000 count was 121,804 — the number of routine political organizations had grown much faster than the population.

High Growth Sectors

In the 1990s Black professional organizations continued to grow at impressive rates. So did Black cultural and health organizations. Youth organizations took a surprising leap in number. Many of the new youth organizations were not composed primarily of youth; instead they were composed mostly of mature people who focused on youth. Among such organizations were the Apricot Home School and the Black Sacramento Christian Club Organizers. There was, as mentioned above, an interesting new development in youth-constituted organizations — hip-hop, social consciousness based. Crime prevention organizations tripled. Most were youth-oriented. Economic organizations increased. Religious organizations rebounded. Many more organizations were based on country of origin.

Black Organizational Life Redesigned

The Black organizational infrastructure was assuming a new profile. Eight of the 16 categories had more than ten organizations in them, as compared with 7 in the '80s. In the '80s, outside the big 3 only 1 had as many as 15. In the '90s the big 3 had become the big 4 with rank-order rearranged, and 2 more categories had above 15 organizations in them. Additionally, in the '90s, no category had as few as 3 organizations. In the '80s there were three categories with only 3 organizations. In the '90s there were no categories with fewer than 5 members. Two categories had *increased* to five. One category had increased from 3 to 8. Another had tripled from 3 to 9. By the routine count the top 3 categories accounted for 45.2 percent of Black organizations, compared with 45.7 percent in the '80s, and 48.7 percent in the '70s. The median number for organizations per category in the '90s was 11, compared with 9 in the '80s, and 7 in the '70s.

Service, social, professional, and political organizations all grew during the decade, and while political organizations increased by almost 150 percent, professional organizations doubled, social organizations grew by 10 percent, service organizations increased by over 100 percent and outgrew even the exploding professional and political categories by 9 points. It took such extraordinary growth to place it atop the categorical standings.

Contrary to what is widely trumpeted in the media and in the popular consciousness, we may say, unequivocally, that not only were Black organizations not decreasing — they were *increasing* throughout the three decades. They were not only increasing, they were becoming *less* social and more instrumental, taking on arenas such as health and crime prevention, and professional interests.

The Declining Significance of Race?

Race in Sacramento, with respect to people of African descent, was not less significant than it had been in the past. If numbers of African-based organizations mean anything on that score, race was *more* significant with the passage of time. This finding seems completely counterintuitive. We *know* there were more middle class (or at least pseudo-middle class) Black people in the '80s than in the '70s, and more in the '90s than in the '80s. The culture and much of the scholarship tells us there were more people with assimilationist orientations. The one-drop rule was no longer a fixed standard for personal or racial identification. People had other options for identifying themselves; witness Wardell Connerly in Sacramento and Tiger Woods elsewhere. The courts and many states — including California — had decided race is such a non-factor with respect to equality of outcomes that affirmative action could be dismissed. Bill Cosby was widely hailed as one of the most popular men in the country. For a Black woman, Oprah Winfrey was gaining unprecedented popularity and influence. It would appear highly improbable that race could matter more in the 1990s than it did in the 1970s. Yet if 30 years of Black organizational formation in Sacramento tell us anything, it is that in some respects, race mattered more than ever. How could that be?

One way to account for it is by population growth. The Black population in Sacramento County had tripled over the period under examination. More people, more organizations. While that is a reasonable argument, it is less than convincing as a single explanation. During each decade significant numbers of Black organizations died out. As the significance of race decreases, there should be no need to replace dead organizations. The total should go down. In fact, this is precisely what we see with working class organizations. They were not replacing themselves. Their numbers decreased during each decade. If population growth alone results in the increase of the number of organizations, in a decade during which 25 percent of Black organizations ceased to exist, and the significance of race is declining, the creation of 25 percent new Black organizations would keep the total number fairly constant *because not as many are needed*. That is not what we see. With numbers arising solely from mixed and middle class Black organizations, from decade to decade the overall number of organizations *increased* substantially. More organizations were created than ended. The *range* of organizations also increased. New organizations were doing things neither former nor continuing organizations did. Moreover, increased population doesn't necessarily equate with an increase in numbers of organizations. We saw that clearly with the political category during the '70s and '80s. The numbers remained constant despite significant population growth. Organizations are not static. People move in and out of them all the time. People die. People leave the area. People lose interest. People switch organizations and create new ones.

Population growth is not equivalent to increases in numbers of organizations because people who are interested in organizational activity don't have to start new ones. They can join extant groups. We have looked at the phenomenon of people moving into a new area and looking for organizational homes. They don't have to reinvent the wheel. The U.S. population is much larger than it was in the early 1800s, but there are still two dominant political parties. The numbers of labor unions have declined despite massive population increases. Population increase does not equate with organizational increase, especially when a major factor stimulating organizational growth is reputedly on the decline.

A lot of African-descended people belong to non–Black organizations. Many belong to several non–Black organizations. Some do not belong to any Black organizations. Others belong to non–Black organizations and Black organizations. Some have multiple memberships in non–Black and Black organizations. It takes a tremendous amount of energy, effort, and time to form, join, and maintain organizations. The sketches of the Sacramento Area Black Caucus in the '70s and the Redistricting Project in the '90s are instructive on that point. Most people have families, loved ones, friends, jobs, hobbies, recreational pursuits. They have to sleep. They don't have a surfeit of time and energy to throw away frivolously. Does it make sense that enough people to maintain the Black organizational infrastructure documented in this study would commit so much of their lives to what they see as *no good reason*? Unlikely. What, then, are the reasons? Race may have something to do with it. If we follow the evidence where it leads us, what initially seemed counterintuitive is reached, by the sheer aggregation of data, as an inescapable conclusion. Race mattered at least as much in the 1990s as it did in the 1970s. If organizational numbers alone are an accurate indicator, it mattered more.

For confirmation on this point let us return to one critical set of organizations — those founded, specifically, *to be Black*. How many *originated* in the 1990s? Sixty-nine. This indicates a continuing and possibly increasing significance of race. Black people were *explicitly* expressing an orientation toward race-specific organizations.

A New Kind of Organization

In the 1990s a type of organization absent both in the '70s and '80s arose. It may be characterized as underclass, or lumpen. Its membership and leadership were predominantly underclass, and it served the interests of poor, marginalized Black people. The four which began in the 1990s were self-started. Two were connected to one mixed-class organization, the All African People's Revolutionary Party. Otherwise, they operated virtually in a world of their own, on their own. The other two, the Health Care Workers' Union, a professional organization formed primarily to attempt to engage in collective bargaining with the county, and the Welfare Action Group, organized by welfare eligible persons to address concerns about the Clinton administration's welfare reform and its implementation within Sacramento County. Outside of gangs, the Nation of Islam, and some storefront churches, the four were the only indigenous organizational presence in the Black underclass. They marked, however, a significant departure from the earlier decades when there were none. These organizations were not deeply entwined with other Black organizations. They were not part of Holden's quasi-government.

State vs. Extra-State Actors as Agents of Change

What do we see of quasi-state and pseudo-state tendencies in the 1990s? The Summit on African American Concerns comes as close to Holden's notion as we can imagine, with the exception that in Holden's formulation the consensus is inchoate. In the Summit on African American Concerns, the Black consensus took organizational form. It is entirely unlikely that a successful effort of the magnitude achieved by the 1991 Redistricting Project, one of the summit's progeny, could have been carried out by Black incumbents.

As in the 1970s and '80s, Black churches were not major agents of political change in Sacramento during the 1990s. Some churches and church leaders were. Foremost among them were St. Paul Baptist Church, under the leadership of Dr. Ephraim Williams; Antioch Progressive Baptist Church, headed by the Rev. Clarence Mitchell; St. Mark Baptist Church; the Rev. Height of St. John's Baptist Church; the Rev. Cecil Taylor of Kyle's Temple AME Church; as well as Allen Chapel AME. Most churches were not. Congregation members could be and were activated through other procedures and structures. That was clear in the case of the Million Man March and Sacramento's follow-up, the 1,000 Man March. Each was mobilized by specific organizations — not the area's churches.

Working within the constraints of the state and the Democratic Party, having to attune themselves to the political winds of electoral politics, political officeholders did not have the political freedom, nor were they allowed the vision, to function as creative change-agents as much as their friends and associates within the Black organizational infrastructure. This is not to say they played no significant roles. They did. They hammered out deals. They crafted means to implement reforms. They sought to fulfill their campaign promises. But their mobilizing efforts were primarily limited to their own campaigns. Their focus on the practicalities of nuts and bolts politics precluded their ability to see and act in the world anew.

TABLE 4.1 FUNCTIONAL CATEGORIES OF BLACK ORGANIZATIONS IN SACRAMENTO, 1990–1999, BY NUMBERS AND PERCENTAGES

Category	Number	Percentage
Service	46	17.4
Social	44	16.7
Professional	30	11.1
Political	26	9.8
Cultural	19	7.2
Youth	19	7.2
Economic	17	6.4
Health	11	3.8
Crime Prevention	9	3.4
Informational	8	3.0
Multi-purpose	8	3.0
Religious	8	2.7
Educational	6	2.3
Student	5	1.9
Mobilizing	5	1.9
Recreational	5	1.9

TABLE 4.2 FUNCTIONAL CATEGORIES OF BLACK ORGANIZATIONS
IN SACRAMENTO, 1990–1999, BY NUMBERS AND PERCENTAGES
(ENHANCED POLITICAL COUNT)

Category	Number	Percentage
Political	82	25.7
Service	46	14.4
Social	44	13.6
Professional	30	9.4
Cultural	19	5.9
Youth	19	5.9
Economic	17	5.3
Health	11	3.1
Crime Prevention	9	2.8
Informational	8	2.6
Multi-purpose	8	2.6
Religious	8	2.2
Educational	6	1.9
Student	5	1.6
Mobilizing	5	1.6
Recreational	5	1.6

TABLE 4.3 SACRAMENTO BLACK WOMEN'S ORGANIZATIONS
BY CATEGORY, 1990–1999

Category	Number
Sororities	7
Clubs	12
Civic	13
Masonic/Lodge	4
Auxiliary	1
Health	4
Religious	2
Cultural	1
Recreational	1
Total	45*

*8 double-counted

TABLE 4.4 SACRAMENTO BLACK MEN'S ORGANIZATIONS
BY CATEGORY, 1990–1999

Category	Number
Fraternities	5
Clubs	2
Masonic/Lodge	6
Civic	3
Religious	1
Recreational	1
Total	18*

*4 double-counted

State Government

In 1998 Governor Gray Davis picked Grantland Johnson as the director of the California Department of Health and Human Services. This was a cabinet level appointment of one of the state's largest departments. Grantland influenced the delivery of health and human services not only in Sacramento, but throughout the state. He also hired and promoted local Black people into high ranking positions in his department.

Willie Brown continued as Speaker of the Assembly through 1996. There he was a major influence on state policy, necessarily including Sacramento. He also remained active in hiring, promoting, and mentoring Black people. Through his efforts significant numbers attained important positions throughout state government. Other Black legislators made significant additions of Black people to their staffs.

In the 1990s Black people established influential consulting and lobbying firms which had both the state and local governments as clients. Black businesses also gained state contracts for delivering goods and services. The state government was the region's major employer of Black people. In a number of capacities Black Sacramentans became major players in state politics.

This kind of activity was going on throughout the country. People in statehouses and administrative posts were influencing policy. People in those positions were mentoring young Black leaders. They were moving on to Congress. They were sending trained people to work on staffs, political campaigns, and into local offices. All this was happening under the radar screen, not only of the mass media and pundits, but also of academics.

Afterword

I have argued that a major failing of the press and academia in the United States during the 1990s with respect to Black politics was the failure to recognize the degree of collective mobilization underway, a mobilization that was primarily the handiwork of everyday people. This is a somewhat puzzling argument in light of my accompanying finding that the great shortcoming of Black politics over the 1970s and 1980s, the failure to organize among the most oppressed people of African descent, persisted through the '90s. The argument is rendered more sensible by an understanding of the distinction I make between organizing and mobilizing. Below I make the distinction explicit. While the tendencies are national, my argument draws evidence and strength from the situation in Sacramento.

In Sacramento the great mobilization efforts of the 1990s — the 1991 Redistricting Project, the Million Man March, the 1,000 Man March, the challenge to the Sacramento Police Department, election campaigns (Sam Pannell, Lauren Hammond, Bonnie Pannell) — cried out for bottom-up organizing. It didn't happen. Only among the youth — People's Democratic Uhuru Movement, Zulu Nation — and constituencies arising in reaction to state policies — health care workers and welfare recipients — was organizing among the Black underclass fruitful. This was a sea change in improvement over the '70s and '80s, but still involved only the tiniest fraction of the Black underclass. The total of underclass organizations was four. That compares with a working class total of seventeen. The working class numbers were themselves minimal next to mixed and middle class organizations. The underclass number was, nevertheless, something as opposed to nothing. These data indicate that middle and working class Black people do not know how to organize the underclass. They tried, but failed.

Only the underclass successfully organized itself. We have a great deal of evidence on that from the earlier decades. Throughout the 30 years, the Nation of Islam, scores of storefront churches, and gangs did it. Those organizations are outside the purview of this study — but they were present and they were organizing the poorest and most déclassé of the African people.

Organizing and Mobilizing

I make a distinction between organizing and mobilizing. With enough popular momentum, the underclass can be *mobilized*. In the '90s we saw that repeatedly. Mobilization can be achieved through intense, short-term effort. Those mobilized have to put in only short-term and not necessarily intense effort. They have to be at a certain place at a specific time — *just be there* — or perform a specific act (such as voting) at a certain place, at a certain time. They don't have to establish long-term patterns of behavior, often requiring great effort and commitment. To marshal that kind of energy and concentration, people have to be highly motivated. They have to believe something positive can *and is likely to* result from their efforts. Or they simply have to enjoy what they're doing. In Sacramento, during the 1970s, '80s, and '90s, the Black working class and the Black middle class did not know how to motivate the poorest of the Black population.

While very poor Black people could be mobilized, there was not a sufficient organizational base for them to be mobilized as broadly, consistently, or as effectively as the Black working and middle classes. The Black lumpen organizations that arose during the 1990s sometimes worked in conjunction with working and middle class organizations, but there were only four of them. Each was specialized and did not involve a large segment of the Black underclass. Two were youth organizations and ill-disposed to work with conventional Black organizations of any kind, though they were at ease working with an unconventional Black organization — the AAPRP.

When there was a big mobilization in Sacramento, the effort was most successful when varied organizations mobilized their particular constituencies. For the most part, there were no underclass constituencies with a structural base. The underclass was unorganized, amorphous — except in the instances cited earlier. For a long time the considerable constituency of the Nation of Islam could not be reached for collective Black purposes because the Nation of Islam did not work with other Black organizations. That changed, but it was only change *within* the Nation that made the Nation's constituency accessible to other Black organizations. No efforts from outside could do it.

The Church

The Nation brought its constituency to the Million Man March, the 1,000 Man March, and city hall. They made a huge difference. If one large Black church turned out the same proportion of its congregation as the Nation, it could turn out 50 times the number. If the Nation turns out 50, a megachurch could turn out 2500. The numbers demonstrate the minimal level of Black church involvement in Sacramento's political life. The city had at least three megachurches. It had dozens of large churches. It had scores of small churches. Few were involved in politics. Those that were constituted a major resource for Black activists, but many congregation members would have been involved whether the churches were or not. The Million Man March was opposed by most Black churches — yet almost all of the million men were Christians. In Sacramento during the '90s intense political mobilization efforts went on despite, not because of, the Black church.

LESSONS. The deepest deficiencies in Sacramento's Black politics: (1) organizing the underclass and (2) involving the churches, were still full-blown in the 1990s. The sole glimmer of light was that the Black underclass built four organizations. Sacramento Black organizations' tendency of purposefully working across class lines was deepened to expand — however minimally — into cooperation with the organized underclass.

Continuing Tendencies

The 1991 Redistricting Project carried on the work of earlier decades seen in the BSUs, the SABC, and the SVRCOC, of working in coalitions and alliances with other racial groups. Even the AAPRP and the Nation of Islam self-consciously reached out to incorporate non–Black groups in some of their initiatives. This outreach did not make them any less Black nationalist or African-centered, but it did display broad visions of how to build human communities in Sacramento.

The Environment

The '90s bear powerful witness to the constraints imposed on Black politics in the U.S., and specifically in Sacramento. We may begin with Proposition 13, passed in 1978, which by the 1990s had become sacrosanct, a hallowed feature of California's and Sacramento's landscapes. What it meant was that public spending was severely limited. The policies that began to starve the beast almost two decades later at the national level had, by the 1990s in California and Sacramento, reduced the beast to a sniveling, mangy cur, begging for crumbs and handouts. California's famed freeway system had begun to crumble. The shining public school system was in shambles. Even the luster of the incomparable University of California had dimmed. Local streets, bridges, sewer systems, and water systems were falling apart. An illustration of these fiscal horrors was Serrano vs. Priest. The California Supreme Court had ruled in 1971 that financing California's public schools by taxes raised within individual school districts solely for the schools within each district violated the equal protection of the laws provisions of the 14th Amendment. The court ruled that California schools *must* develop a more equitable way of distributing property tax revenues to all the state's schools. The court sent the case back to Superior Court for factual determination. The central idea was not to drag down lavishly funded schools to the level of schools mired in penury, but to raise the levels of funding to the financially insolvent schools to match those of their more affluent neighbors. It would generate a renaissance in public education, a restoration of California's k-12 schools to eminence. The final ruling on the issues was delivered in 1976, and labeled Serrano II.[96] At the time Serrano II was handed down, the schools had just started their downward slide. At that brilliant moment, the churlish California electorate triumphantly approved Proposition 13, which cut local property taxes by a catastrophic 52 percent. Any hope for school reform was torn asunder.

One of the highest priorities of Black officials — elected and appointed — was egalitarian school reform. Proposition 13 not only made that impossible, it dashed the very *idea* to pieces. The Black struggle for meaningful improvement in the most impoverished public schools became a struggle in futility. Ronald Reagan had already eviscerated the state's mental health system, and once he became president, the country's public housing system. In California, by the 1990s, all that terrain had become scorched earth. There was no fiscal or ideological basis for recovery. The theme of tax reform, meaning tax cutting, had become sacred text. Taxes could not be raised. It didn't take long for that mantra to dominate the national arena with precisely the same effects. What Black people and Black officials faced in California they faced in every other state and in the national government.

Black politicians, as the element of the Democratic Party furthest to the left, were not even fighting a holding action. At best they were waging a fighting retreat. At worst — which was most of the time — they were trying to develop and implement strategies, on the run, to prevent a rout from becoming an all-out stampede. This condition intensified after the Republican conquest of the national Congress.

In the criminal justice arena California's solution was to criminalize as many Black people as possible, build more prisons, and throw Black people into them — at the same time that the rehabilitation system was ripped out of the correctional facilities. *Minimum* sentences of 25 years became routine. People who did no more than *buy* illegal drugs, or who were only present in the houses or even *neighborhoods* where illegal drugs were used, were cast into the dungeons of the prison authority for the rest of their productive years.[97] All Black people could do by means of opposing this madness was to rant and rave over the death penalty, which was not even the surface of the problem.

These conditions were national. While from 1960 to 1988, California sent more Black people to the U.S. Congress than all the states of the former Confederacy combined, the Congressional Black Caucus had no more prospect for the passage of meaningful reform legislation than it had of stopping the next earthquake headed down the San Andreas Fault.

In Sacramento, even for what little effect a city government could have on national calamities, what were Lauren Hammond and Bonnie Pannell to do out of a city council of nine? After 1992 no Black person sat on the County Board of Supervisors. Despite all kinds of Black school board members and administrators, the schools had no money. Every initiative that required resources was dead in the water. Local television channels established investigative departments which engaged in ludicrous games of "gotcha" with wasteful spending from the public trough, while the great evils — fiscal and otherwise — that truly needed investigating ripped through the country, the state, and impoverished neighborhoods. Gated — walled — communities became *en vogue*.

The legislatures, the courts, the executive — at the state and local levels as well as the national — were all co-conspirators and enablers in the disgraceful charade. What were Black people to do? Robert Smith and William Strickland have written extensively, with searing vision, about how the national structures, laws, procedures, and cultural mores operate as an oppressive and carnivorous monstrosity to the aspirations and well-being of African descended people in the U.S.A.[98]

The Products of Black Politics in This Context

A handful of developers had exponentially more influence on every significant political question in Sacramento than all the Black elected officials, appointed administrators, political activists, and organizations combined. To have even the most marginal effects on life in their city, Black Sacramentans, routinely, had to engage in extensive organizing and mobilizing, had to stage public demonstrations and spectacles. They had to show up *en masse* at city hall. They had to send aggregations of leaders to meet with the local media. Nobody else — no other population group — was doing anything like that. Most of these activities could not be carried out by elected and appointed leaders. Without the work of non-elected activists even the minimal effects produced could not have been achieved. As a result, the local Black population had to continually maintain, re-invent, and organize a massive infrastructure just to prevent being swallowed into the gluttonous and venomous maw of the wider population's agendas.

That such extreme efforts were necessary merely to avoid the disemboweling of the African-descended population helps explain the significant increase in the number of Black political organizations as identified by the routine count, even as the number of Black elected officials grew. The evidence does not support the contention that the need for routine black political organizations was reduced by the greater momentum for electoral politics.

We saw developments in the '90s we had not seen before: secular organization building among the Black underclass, including youth, and a broader Black population which mobilized against the worst scourges afflicting it — gangs, drugs, violence, and AIDS. From those efforts we saw some irrefutable effects. The '90s have served, at once, as an indicator of the capacities of African-descended people in Sacramento and the United States, as well as of the magnitude of the terrifying quagmire they inhabit.

CHAPTER 5

Conclusions

Our examination of Black politics from 1970 to 2000 shows, as noted in the introduction, that indeed, "something extraordinary was going on." By looking at Sacramento, we saw it in detail. What was it? Why wasn't it recognized by the masterful studies which cover the era? I contend it is because the studies minimized a critical component in the equation — ordinary Black people. They were producing the extraordinary.

Nor is it a mystery as to why this critical component in the study of Black political life was minimized. I return to Bill Strickland's critique cited at the end of the introduction. He proposed an answer to the question, "Why we need a revolutionary Black research agenda in the 21st century."[1]

To frame both the question and the answer he turned to the work of Dr. W.E.B. DuBois. He quoted DuBois's detailing what social scientists in the U.S. must do to conduct the kind of scholarship that a serious investigation of the aggregate life of Black people in the country requires.

> If they dally with the truth to humor the whims of the day, they do far more than hurt the good name of the American public, they hurt the cause of scientific truth the world over.[2]

Strickland explores why doing what DuBois proposed necessitates a revolutionary Black research agenda: "What DuBois's perspective represented and what it called for, implicitly, was a new history of America."[3] This new history is required because,

> The challenge ... is ... to try and gain a more accurate understanding of how the Republic has related actually, rather than mythically, to the Black presence in its midst.[4]

He goes on to say,

> The significance of DuBois's critique is that he saw America not as most Americans see it, but through his own racial lense, utilizing the second sight he had gained as a lifelong outsider in the land of his birth.[5]

The explorations of the social spaces, narratives, and memories inhabited by regular Black folk provided by this study help us to understand how they, too, saw life in the United States not as most of its people do, but through their own racial lenses. The vision thus obtained motivated them to act in significantly different ways from their counterparts. Looking at that behavior in great detail *forces us* into a revolutionary research agenda. It cannot consist of the same frames and data sets which dominate the conventional study of politics. Black politics, as I postulated in the introduction, is not white politics writ large. It is a different phenomenon. This research helps us to understand its particular lineaments.

Ordinary Black people had imbibed the lessons of Ella Baker, SNCC, the Mississippi

Freedom Democratic Party, BSUs — the notion of collective leadership. They had seen Medgar, Malcolm, Martin, Fred Hampton and Mark Clark cut down. They had seen Huey, Eldridge, and Assata Shakur chased out of the country. They knew the pitfalls of "The Leader." They acted collectively as a means of overcoming them.

In some senses the conservatives who trumpeted the tune that Black leadership had lost touch with the Black masses were correct. They did not, however, understand what they were saying and their attributions were far afield. They believed Black leadership was fighting the battles of the past — racial battles. They believed the Black population had gone beyond race and entered the color-blind society. The evidence documented in this study indicates the opposite. The Black population, first of all, was fighting — whatever the leaders might have been doing. Nor was their struggle based on a perception of a meritocracy or a color-blind society. It was rooted in the perception of a deeply racist, oppressive and exploitative society which highly privileged whiteness and viciously punished blackness. In order to build a place for themselves and their progeny they not only had to carry on the activities that all people must — maintaining their livelihoods, their families, participating in conventional political life, they also had to expend tremendous energies and resources creating an alternative world, including an alternative politics. They believed the meritocracy, the color-blind society, saw no need for the causes which were most important to Black people.

In Sacramento ordinary Black people drew up redistricting maps to maximize Black political participation in 1970, 1981, and 1991. All through the country they were doing similar things in pursuit of one person, one vote. Ordinary Black people organized, mobilized, and fought for the freedom of the Oak Park 4, just as they did for Huey, Angela, George Jackson, and Bobby Seale nationwide. They stormed city hall and demanded that the city face up to the police murder of Raymond Brewer — as they had done in similar situations in New York City, Los Angeles, and scores of cities cited in the Kerner Commission Report. By the thousands they attended the Sacramento Black Unity Festivals as they did similar events in every part of the United States.

Black people joined the NAACP, the Urban League, the Women's Civic Improvement Club. They created the SABC, the 100 Black Men, the Sacramento Black Women's Network, Africa's Daughters Rising. They challenged attacks on the Nation of Islam. They marched for a holiday for Dr. King. They stood out in the rain for the 1,000 Man March. They transformed city council districts in Sacramento — and all over the country. They gave rise to an ombudsman to monitor the Sacramento Police Department. They created police review boards in other cities.

The role of Ordinary Black people in the big picture is plain. Harold Washington did not want to run for mayor of Chicago. Grassroots people literally dragged him into the race by registering 180,000 new Black voters. Ordinary Black people chanted, "Run, Jesse, run," while Black leaders got in line behind Mondale. Black leaders came on board only in 1988 when it was evident that the Black electorate was going to back Jesse no matter what Black leaders did.

One million everyday Black men responded to Farrakhan's call for a Million Man March. Grassroots Black people organized their own local summits on Black gangs, drugs, violence, and AIDS. They formed community organizations to fight gangs and crime. They brought gang truces to Los Angeles. Hip-Hop youngsters organized to speak the truth to their own generation. While Black leaders kowtowed to Clinton, Black care workers organized against the demolition of social welfare.

Not only was the tail wagging the dog, it was *dragging* the dog — which was facing in the opposite direction — kicking and screaming into the future. For thirty years ordinary Black people organized, mobilized, talked together, worked together, and built together. Whatever the populations David Putnam studied were doing, Black people were not bowling alone.

Social Spaces, Narrative, and Memory

Social spaces, narrative, and memory open important avenues to understanding how Black people were able to fight the tide, deprived as they were of capital — social as well as the more conventional variety — proportionately few in numbers, and almost entirely outside the parameters of the national dialogue. In the '70s both activists and the Black population at large drew heavily on social memories from the Civil Rights and Black Power movements. They used spaces they controlled to develop and promote their own narratives. They seized hegemonic spaces at critical times and permeated them with Black narrative. These tendencies continued through the '80s and '90s. In Sacramento Black people were able to transmit social memories of Sacramento to new comers who took them as their own. Black uses of social spaces, narrative, and social memory enabled African descendants to focus on race as a tool for political organization and mobilization. People who apparently had little in common used race as a vehicle for forging cooperative action.

Black Organizations

The level of Black organizational activity throughout the 30 years began at a high level and increased over time. Despite an overall increase in population, working class organizations decreased. The growth among mixed and middle class organizations was almost exponential. Only in the '90s did a small number of underclass organizations emerge. Part of the difference in organizational numbers by class may be a function of the increase in the number of middle class Black people accompanied by a decrease in the Black working class. There is no ready explanation for the sudden emergence of a few underclass organizations during the '90s. With respect to the middle class, it is clear that in the '70s when the middle class was only emergent, the organizational infrastructure necessary to support a robust middle class did not exist and had to be built. During this period, while many Black people may have availed themselves of the opportunity to join non–Black organizations, that did not relieve them of the motivation to create and join new and extant Black organizations. They increased the number of organizations which were *intentionally* Black. Black organizational variation matched the increasing complexity and diversity of the African-origin population. These processes were underway nationwide.

Electoral Politics

During the 30 years covered by this study, Black electoral activity increased dramatically. In 1970 the number of Black legislators at any single level and at all levels combined was negligible. Black voters did not vote and were not expected to vote at the same rate as others. They did not often run for elective or appointed office. By 2000 they had undergone a sea change. For their presences in public places to have transformed so dramatically, *Black people themselves had to undergo remarkable changes.* The Black population in 2000 was a different Black population from the one in 1970. In many respects, *these were not the same people*. This detailed, longitudinal study helps us to understand how they were not.

In the 120 years of Sacramento history prior to 1970, only one Black person had ever been elected to the Sacramento City Council, and that did not happen until the 1960s. In the 30 years from 1970 to 2000, eight Black people served on the city council, six of them elected. From the middle of the '90s on, two Black people sat on the Sacramento City Council simultaneously. The newly formed city, Citrus Heights, elected a Black man to its first city council. Before the 1980s no Black person had ever served on the Sacramento County Board of Supervisors. Grantland Johnson was elected in 1987 and served into the 1990s. From the 1970s through 2000, Black people were elected and appointed to every level of government in the region, including the municipal, superior, and juvenile courts. In no earlier era had any Black people served on the bench. The same exponential rate in the increase of elected and appointed Black people occurred nationally.

In Sacramento, except for positions on the DPHESD Board, all Black candidates ran in jurisdictions that were overwhelmingly non–Black. Black percentages of jurisdictions outside the Heights never exceeded 33 percent and that figure was reached only in Meadowview. In other *Black-influence districts* Black people did not exceed 25 percent and in most instances were much lower. This meant that almost all Black political campaigns incorporated some variation of *deracialization*. Except in the Heights, Black candidates never made race an issue. Even in the Heights they rarely did because most of the candidates were Black and so was most of the electorate. Generally, Black candidates made appeals to generic problems within jurisdictions. Some emphasized class solidarity. Others ran on a multicultural theme. In no case did Black candidates stress or identify race as a significant factor to the general population. In Black venues — spaces, narratives, social memories — the case was entirely the opposite. There people organized and mobilized almost entirely on the basis of race. Black people in Black neighborhoods knew why they were voting, organizing, and mobilizing — to support the Black candidate. In most instances, however, *this did not mean just any Black person*. The candidate had to be correct on the racial question — known to identify as a Black person and also to be a supporter of progressive stances. Black candidates concentrated Black campaign workers in Black neighborhoods and non–Black workers in others. Black people came from throughout the region to work in jurisdictions where progressive Black candidates ran for office. For the Black population the campaigns were always very much racialized. For the general campaign, however, race never raised its unseemly head.

In *at large elections* Black people generally fared well. If a sufficient number of seats were up for election, there were generally enough candidates for concentrated Black ballots to elect one or more Black candidates. This was seen most frequently in school board elections which often filled seats at-large. In jurisdictions where representation was based on districts, Black activists tried to make sure there were *Black-influence districts*. They were not always successful, but they always made an all-out effort during redistricting to maximize Black populations in selected districts. Within Black-influence districts Black candidates were much more successful than population figures would project. Black people were elected to the Sacramento City Council in three separate council Districts — 2, 5, and 8. In not one of those districts was there a Black majority. In District 8, there was a non-white majority, but a white plurality. Black people were only 33 percent of the population. In Districts 2 and 5 there were white super-majorities. Nevertheless, Black people dominated District 2 in the first half of the '70s and the second half of the '80s, District 5 in the second half of the '80s and the second half of the '90s, and District 8 throughout the '90s. On the County Board of Supervisors, all the districts were white-super majorities, yet a Black candidate was elected to the board. On the County Board of Education, the Los Rios Community College District Board, and the Sacramento Municipal Utilities District Board, all the districts were white super-majorities, yet Black candidates were elected to the first two throughout the '80s and '90s, and to the third throughout the '90s. Increasingly, this counter-intuitive performance of Black candidates was found in localities throughout the United States. No small part of that result can be attributed to the unremitting and dogged work of everyday Black folk.

Collective Mobilization

All three decades featured significant episodes of Black collective mobilization, both activist and mass. Black collective mobilization impacted politics and the character of Black life everywhere in the U.S., including Sacramento. Indeed, I have contended that in the 1990s Black collective mobilization was more pronounced than it had been during the 1960s. One of the differences between the periods was that in the '60s it was remarkable. In the 1990s it was not. The popular perception was that there was less of it. This representation is what Strickland referred to as *mythical* rather than *actual*. The actual numbers lead us to a conclusion that is completely counter-intuitive. Not even in the '60s was there a Million Man March, Million Woman March, or Million Youth March.

In Sacramento Black collective mobilization marked the Black population as a factor to be accounted for in every significant political decision. It influenced the appointment of two Black people to the Sacramento City Council during the '70s and the appointment of a citizens' commission to restrain the police department. It resulted in the election of Grantland Johnson to both the city council and the Board of Supervisors. It had wide ranging effects in the criminal justice system, in enfranchising the biggest concentration of Black people in the region, opening of new electoral and appointed positions to Black people, and to significant cross-class and cross-neighborhood collaborations among Black people. It resulted in dramatic increases of Black women in leadership positions.

State Government

The primary role of Black people in state government for Black Sacramento was providing jobs. In the '70s, with Black people holding significant statewide offices, funds were available for statewide networking and policy consultation. The job connection placed many Black Sacramentans in powerful governmental positions which they used to leverage home-town politics. As Black people were ousted from statewide office, state government influence in local Black politics diminished. Nationally, the Republican Contract with America, taking over the House of Representatives, and later the Senate, had similar repercussions for Black people, as did Republican wins in various statehouses.

The Black Church

The Black church did not play a prominent role in Black politics. Individual churches and ministers contributed to political efforts, but by and large, even without church-based activities, most of the political activities documented in this study would have gone on with similar results. There is no doubt that had Black churches been fully engaged in political life that Black political outcomes would have been much more favorable than they turned out to be. The human and material resources of Black churches far exceeded those of any other sector or combination of sectors in the African descendant population.

The Contexts of Black Politics

Wealth

We know the median wealth of national Black households varied during the period of this study from less than 5 percent to 12.2 percent of the white median. Median white household wealth ranged from 38 to 6 times greater than the Black median. The great variation is accounted for because of the extremely low median wealth of the Black population. That gives relatively small dollar amounts a large impact on Black-white wealth ratios.[6] We get a truer picture of the comparative picture of wealth by looking at the median *financial* wealth of the two populations. In financial wealth we are looking at disposable wealth.

From 1970 until the end of the 1980s (20 of the years under consideration), the median financial wealth of the national Black population compared to that of the white population was 0. In other words, Black financial wealth did not reach 0.1 percent of white wealth. By 1992 the ratio was 0.7 percent (white disposable wealth was 99.33 percent times that of Black disposable wealth). By 1995 Black disposable wealth had reached 1.1 percent of whites.' It had risen to 3.2 percent by 1998. This upward trend was not one way. By 2000 comparative Black financial wealth had begun to decline.[7] These figures in themselves are troubling enough as 1–1 comparisons. Collective wealth, however, tells us the true disparities between the two populations. In Chapter 3 we took the conservative figure of white per capita wealth exceeding that of Black people by 8 times. Since there were more than six times as many white people as Black people, that meant that collectively white wealth exceeded Black wealth by magnitudes exceeding a trillion. In short, the Black population could spend almost *nothing* compared to what the white population could spend. This portrays the true wealth disparity between the two populations, the political differential in a country where money means almost everything.

The figures point out what Black people have done with so little. It is almost inconceivable that they could have accomplished what they have with so few resources. The outcomes we see, achieved in the face of such monumentally differential material resources, are too improbable for even the wildest magical realism fiction to propose. Readers would find the scenario *unbelievable*.

Power

Sacramento serves as an instructive example of the power differential between white and Black populations in the U.S., particularly since the Black percentage of the population in Sacramento approximated the national percentage throughout the 30 years. In the period from 1970, when only one Black person sat on a governing body in the city (other than the Del Paso Heights School District Board), to 2000, when two Black women sat on the city council, a Black men sat on the Citrus Heights and Elk Grove City Councils, a Black man had occupied a seat on the County Board of Supervisors, the bench held multiple Black incumbents, school boards and special district boards had many Black incumbents, and Black people held high administrative positions in every sector of local government, there had been such a drastic change as to make the face of local government virtually unrecognizable.

This *appearance* is deceiving. It leads us to the mythical propositions about meritocracy and a color-blind society. We can see why it is mythical by examining how much it affected the *exercise* of power. In the whole 30 years, on only two public policy-making bodies did Black people constitute a majority at any time: the Del Paso Heights Elementary School District Board, and the Grant Joint Union High School District Board. The DPHESD was populated by a majority of Black students and was the poorest district in the county. Other than those two sites — both in the same neighborhood — on every other policy-making board in the county, whatever Black people were present were in such small numbers as to be unable to determine the course of policy. Additionally, for most of the period, Sacramento lay under the thrall of the conservative mindset which governed the state. The policy posture of the state's general population was entirely in line with the southern strategy crafted by Richard Nixon and mastered by Ronald Reagan, which by the middle nineties had come to dominate the whole country.

As a corollary representation in the national government we may look at the Congressional Black Caucus. The numbers in the Congressional Black Caucus between 1970 and 2000 were starkly different. They had quadrupled. Yet the 2000 Congressional Black Caucus was just as incapable of passing the National Black Agenda (adopted by the CBC as its legislative agenda) — or any part of the National Black Agenda — as any Congress in the 1970s. The increase in numbers did not translate into meaningful increases in Black policy achievements. In part that was true due to increasingly Republican administrations, Congresses, or both. It was certainly influenced by the conservative agenda that became the template of national politics. Yet, regardless of the reasons, the effects of the structural and procedural — as well as the ideological components of national politics were such that Black people's most pressing concerns were buried.

Black people lived and operated in a completely hostile environment. In Sacramento, a Black teenager was murdered by the police department, an act the legal system deemed as falling within the purview of officer discretion. A young Black man was murdered by two young white men in front of multiple witnesses and the perpetrators, identified, were not even arrested. Four promising young Black men were bound over, held for almost a year without bail, and brought to trial on death penalty charges on the testimony of a felon *who was insane*. The largest Black population in the city was gerrymandered to deprive it of political agency for a decade. The region's dominant newspaper published a political cartoon that said, "That nigger makes sense." Every school district in the region demonstrably failed in the education of Black children. After the late 1970s the local press began to treat Black political activities with benign neglect. Except in the most extreme circumstances they would not cover them. To local readers — Black, white, or others — it was as if there weren't any. The Sacramento City Police Department maintained an ongoing practice of intimidating, harassing, and brutalizing Black people. HIV/AIDS was allowed to run rampant throughout Black neighborhoods. Black people were thrown into prisons at the same time that programs for rehabilitation were removed. Custodial facilities for the insane were closed. Public housing was drastically reduced. Hundreds of Black people in Sacramento, including whole families, were driven into homelessness. Without any legislative restraint the entertainment industry promoted gangsterism into iconic status in poor Black neighborhoods. Remedies such as affirmative action for the feral oppression and racism Black people had been subject to for centuries were outlawed. Black employees of the State of California received "adverse actions" (discipline) and dismissal at three times the rate of white employees.[8] Yet public employment was the job sector most open to Black people and where they had the best chances for career advancement.

Public airwaves became the property of right-wing reactionaries and pulpits for the southern strategy. Black studies — indeed, everything Black — became branded with the taint of political correctness. Black people were labeled a special interest and therefore political anathema. The state police conducted firing practice on "running nigger targets." Any one who spoke up specifically for Black interests became labeled as supporters of "descriptive representation," a clearly backwards and even racist perspective. This is the external environment in which Sacramento's Black population lived and engaged in political struggle. When they chanted, "No justice, no peace," they were not voicing a threat or a course of projected action. They were reciting the conditions of their lives. Only a "revolutionary Black research agenda" enables us to see and understand this.

The question which must arise to the thoughtful person is, given the extraordinarily subaltern, demeaned, despised, and impoverished condition of this population, how were they able to accomplish as much as they did?

The Tremendous Expenditure of Black Energy and Effort

The sheer depth and magnitude of the energy and effort expended by Black people to wage political struggles can be touched on by revisiting two organizations profiled in the study, the SABC and the 1991 Redistricting Project. They were both comparatively small organizations. The SABC had between 25 and 30 active members in the '70s, when they were profiled. Those active members, however, were not all the same people. Many came and left. The Redistricting Project was approximately the same size during its brief existence. In short, the lion's share of work produced by these organizations fell on the shoulders of a tiny segment of Sacramento's Black population.

As to the substance of the SABC's work, for the '70s I identified 70 kinds of activities divided among 14 categories. Over the decade members of the SABC engaged in 202 organizational years of work pursuing the organization's objectives.

The 1991 Redistricting Project met twice a week for 10 months. All the organizational maintenance had to be carried out, as well as the research, keeping the affiliates up to speed, and maintaining good relations with them. In addition the project had to establish relationships with all the bodies undergoing redistricting, including both elected representatives and staffs. Its members had to meet with them consistently. The project established relationships with individual members of the press as well as issuing press releases and holding press conferences. People had to engage in community outreach, not only to affiliate members, but also to churches, non-affiliate organizations, and neighborhood activists and residents. The project published a newsletter and reports. It developed, published, and circulated its plan. Members developed relationships with Latinos and Asians and held joint meetings with them. Once the public hearings began, project members presented reports at them, organized citizen testimony, and beat the bushes to turn people out. In the critical renumbering battle, project members talked to powerful Black and Democratic leaders at the county and state levels, met individually with Sacramento City Council members, and sought support from their Latino allies. This was round-the-clock work carried out non-stop for almost an entire year.

The kind of effort illustrated by the work of these two organizations was replicated across the breadth of Black organizations in Sacramento during the 30 year span. Almost all of them had significant projects toward which they expended stupendous energies and significant material resources.

This workload took a terrible toll on organizational members. Yet it was repeated year after year, by organization after organization, and the work was dramatically increased from the beginning to the end of the period. It enabled Black people to do what no other population did There were no comparable initiatives from any other racial group *in any single arena* to those that Black people developed *across the whole spectrum* of local politics. No other constituency battled as openly or as dramatically with the police department. No other population appeared at city hall *en masse* with such explosive concerns. No other constituency organized as boldly across the whole educational spectrum. No similar aggregation of people from other racial groups commandeered public spaces as deliberately. None had such an impact on the redistricting process or the war against violent street crimes. No other population extended itself to such limits for its collective well-being.

The Periodic Effort to Establish Umbrella Organizations as Energizing Impulses

When I began this study I was convinced of the folly of attempting to form umbrella or all-inclusive Black organizations with action agendas. They always fail. The African descended population is too large, diverse, complicated, and antagonistic for such organizations to work. To try to create them and make them work is a waste of precious time, energy, and money. It is folly of the highest order to continually attempt to duplicate failed attempts.

I believed it was possible to form comprehensive Black organizations of the type Cruse contemplated, "Negro Sanhedrins," where Black people of every class and persuasion share information and conduct discussions. But to expect such a hodge-podge of people, many of whom bear great animosities against one another, to be able to accomplish anything of substance is delusional. Nevertheless, the quest for Black unity is almost universal. Black people pray for it, cry for it, plead for it, and work for it. The results are always the same. The organizations crash or transform themselves into something less than intended.

This study pointed out what I had not discerned, that the efforts to forge Black unity are extraordinarily stimulating, invigorating, and energizing for Black people. They are renewals. They often arise from everyday Black folk and electrify them. They release the creative imagination: the SABC, the National Black Assembly, the Shirley Chisholm presidential campaign, the Rainbow Coalition, the Grantland Johnson campaigns, the Summit on African American Concerns, the 1991 Redistricting Project, the Million Man March. The soul needs nutrition. The struggle for unity is perhaps one of its greatest sources.

The struggle for racial unity is also a way ordinary Black people identify with each other. They are not blind to their income, wealth, gender, class, educational, sexual preference, occupational, generational, and residential differences. But they sense a commonality, some provided by social memory, some provided by social narratives. They seek to overcome their differences to achieve a unity of purpose, a unity they feel has been wrenched from them. That there never was such a unity is inconsequential. It is the aspiration which is compelling.

Unrealized Potential

Between the years 1970 and 2000 the political achievements of Black people, not only nationwide, but also in Sacramento, were phenomenal and virtually unheralded. The magnitude of their accomplishments arose from the circumstances of their lives: they were a despised minority amid a hostile majority possessing incomparable wealth and power. Even though this study categorically demonstrates that African people in Sacramento and the country at large were able to do more with less, it also suggests further areas to tap.

Community Organizing

Perhaps the most complete failure African descended people in Sacramento experienced during the last three decades of the twentieth century was their inability to organize among the lumpen proletariat, the very poor. Yet the promise is readily apparent in the Nation of Islam. As it moved from an introspective, self-contained organization to one more broadly engaged with the world, and specifically the Black world, it wrought wonders: the Million Man March, the 1,000 Man March, active participation in presidential and local elections. In Sacramento it was a dynamic and energizing force. Activists were able to draw on hithertofore untapped human reservoirs whose awesome potential is accented by the recognition that the Nation is only one of many potential pipelines to it.

Faith Based Organizations

The church can participate effectively in political life. That is established by the ones which do. Religious organizations that were apolitical or anti-political can become politicized — witness the Nation of Islam. There is also an extraordinary precedent for this change in the white evangelical movement. None of that potential was realized in Black Sacramento or in the Black church nationally.

Accountability and Responsibility of Black Elected Officials

The organization in the United States to which the largest number of Black elected officials are accountable is the Democratic Party. That was true in the last third of the 20th century in Sacramento, even though all the Black people who were elected held non-partisan positions. Almost none were directly accountable to any Black constituencies. Only in the DPHESD where a majority of the voters were Black were elected policy makers directly responsible to a Black electorate. In other jurisdictions, most of the non-partisan political contributions to Black candidates came from Democrats. If they had political aspirations beyond the local arena, approval would have to come from the Democratic Party. The Black population at large had no organizational ligatures they might use to bind Black candidates or incumbents to them. They had no razors to free them from bondage to the Democratic Party.

Divide Between the Black Electorate and Black Elected Officials

The lack of institutional links between Black elected officials and the Black electorates which they purportedly serve, particularly links which can be used both to constrain and

empower Black elected officials, accounts in large part for the divide between the Black electorates and Black officialdom. The gap was most obvious at the national level in the 1984
Democratic presidential primaries. The major reason why the Black Democratic establishment joined the Rainbow Coalition in 1988 was because of the Black electorate's refusal in
1984 to follow their leaders away from the Rainbow Coalition. That had been terribly embarrassing to Black leaders. In 1988 they were determined neither to be embarrassed again, nor
to reveal as they had in '84 that they were utterly incapable of delivering the Black vote. They
raced to catch up with the Black electorate while pretending to lead it.

In Sacramento the divide found at the national level did not show up in the local Rainbow Coalition, as most Sacramento elected Black officials were in it early, some before it even
formally existed. In that respect, virtually all Black people in Sacramento, elected or not, were
little people. The divide however was not *absent* in Sacramento. It showed up most vividly
in the failure of Black leaders to grow successors, to provide political mentorship to new gen-
erations of Black leaders. No one, for example, replaced Grantland Johnson in District 2 or
on the County Board of Supervisors. Though Lauren Hammond had Black political mentors, she had none who had occupied elected office in Sacramento. For her first term, Bonnie
Pannell was elected essentially as Sam Pannell's widow. Most Black activists recognized the
need, even incumbents did, but no collective body could *require* incumbents or candidates to
meet the challenge.

Demographics and the Black Population in Sacramento

In 2000 Sacramento's Black population was four times the size it had been in 1970. This
increase was not the result of simple addition. Conceiving of it as being four times the population is a much better indicator of the character of population change than thinking of it
as triple the original population added onto the base. In 2000, comparatively few of the
36,000 Black residents of the city in 1970 still lived there. Many had died. Many had moved
away. Their number was *replaced* by others who were born or moved in later. Far more than
the 80,000 new Black Sacramentans in 2000 were actually new, as most of the original population was no longer there. An overwhelming number of Black Sacramentans had no ancestral ties to the place. In many respects this was *entirely* a new population. That they attended
the same schools, joined the same churches, worked in the same buildings, lived in the same
neighborhoods, and joined the same organizations as their predecessors gave the appearance
of continuity. In many respects they inhabited the same physical world even though significant
aspects of the city had altered radically. We may make the same observations about the national
Black population. Even though the 2000 population was almost entirely different from the
1970 population and inhabited transfigured spaces, thinking of it as a continuous population
is not entirely an illusion.

They shared an identity with those who had preceded them. They referenced the same
neighborhoods as earlier inhabitants. The meanings of neighborhood names had not drastically altered. Their conversations, their memories, *which were often not their own memories at
all,* joined them to people long gone. They were able to draw on an old tradition as if it were
their own, tune it to their contemporary reality, and through the combination attempt *to continue* the work to build a new world.

A Summation

A major purpose of this study has been to discover how, after the end of the Civil Rights and Black Power movements, despite deep and organized resistance, Black material and political gains persisted. I think the study has made a major contribution to understanding that phenomenon. We have seen what Black people were doing politically both nationally and in Sacramento, and what their efforts produced. We have also seen what they did not do, and as in the case of the underclass, some of the obstacles which prevented them from achieving more.

We have also seen the severe structural, perceptual, material, and affective constraints which limited them. Without substantial changes in the context they inhabit, it appears unlikely they will ever liberate themselves from a collective subaltern position. Their achievements in both their national and local circumstances have been nothing short of heroic, but we must remind ourselves that even Achilles had his heel. What we see with African people in the U.S. is a cruel Gordian knot. Race is what has put them in this despised condition. Yet race has been the most formidable tool for liberating them from it. How this conundrum may be resolved, alas, is a task beyond the capability of my generation.

It is clear, however, that between 1970 and 2000 most of the initiatives and most of the work of wrestling with this conundrum arose from ordinary Black people. They — what they do and how they do it — must remain central to our scholarship.

Chapter Notes

Introduction

1. Two of the most prominent are Robert Smith and Adolph Reed. See, particularly, Robert Smith, *We Have No Leaders: African Americans in the Post-Civil Rights Era* (Albany: State University of New York Press, 1996); Adolph Reed, *Class Notes: Posing as Politics and Other Thoughts on the American Scene* (Minneapolis: University of Minnesota Press, 2000); and *Stirrings in the Jigg: Black Power in the Post Segregation Era* (Minneapolis: University of Minnesota Press, 1999). For a notable exception see Linda Williams, *The Constraint of Race: Legacies of White Skin Privilege in America* (University Park: Pennsylvania State University Press, 2003). Yet her focus remains on high-level developments and effects of policies. Other titles which indicate the popularity of the subject include Frederick C. Harris, Valeria Sinclair-Chapman, and Brian D. Mackenzie, "Macrodynamics of Black Political Participation in the Post-Civil Rights Era," *The Journal of Politics* 67, no. 4 (November 2005): 1143–1163; and Ollie Johnson and Karin Stanford, eds., *Black Political Organizations in the Post-Civil Rights Era* (New Brunswick, NJ: Rutgers University Press, 2002).

2. Smith and Reed, though in agreement on the point, are not in agreement as to why.

3. In addition to Smith and Reed emphasizing phenomena on overarching levels are the Chicago and Michigan schools of Michael Dawson which use national opinion samples with exploded Black population samples. See, particularly, Dawson, *Behind the Mule: Race in African-American Politics* (Princeton, NJ: Princeton University Press, 1994); and Katherine Tate, *From Protest to Politics: The New Black Voters in American Elections* (New York: Russell Sage Foundation and Harvard University Press, 1993, 1994). On the judiciary, see, for example, *New Perspectives in American Politics, The National Political Science Review* 1, the section "Symposium II: Black Americans and the Constitution," pp. 114–132.

4. Rufus P. Browning, Dale Rogers Marshall, and David H. Tabb, *Protest Is Not Enough* (Berkeley: University of California Press, 1986), p. 17: "Minority groups were almost totally excluded from city politics in the early 1960s." In addition, a lot of their analysis is linked to what they label incorporation—the ability to effect policy—which they find varied greatly from city to city, as well as over time.

5. National Institutes of Health, National Human Genome Research Institute, http://science.education.nih.gov/supplements/nih1/genetic/guide/genetic_variation.htm, November 30, 2006: "Research results consistently demonstrate that about 85 percent of all human genetic variation exists *within* human populations, whereas about only 15 percent of variation exists *between* populations" (Bryan Sykes, *The Seven Daughters of Eve* [New York: Norton, 2001]).

6. Melissa Nobles, *Shades of Citizenship: Race and Census in Modern Politics* (Stanford: Stanford University Press, 2000).

7. *Ibid.*; see also Rhett Jones, "Black and Native American Relations Before 1800," *Western Journal of Black Studies* 1, no. 3 (September, 1977): 157, 159.

8. Frantz Fanon, *Black Skin, White Masks* (London: Pluto Press, 1986).

9. Nobles, *Shades*; Edward E. Telles, *Race in Another America: The Significance of Skin Color in Brazil* (Princeton, NJ: Princeton University Press, 2004); Gevanilda Santos and Maria Palmina da Silva, eds., *Racismo no Brasil: persepcoes da discriminacao e do preconceito racial no seculo XXI* (Sao Paulo: Editora Fundacao Perseu Abramo, 2005).

10. Melissa Harris-Lacewell, *Barbershops, Bibles, and BET: Everyday Talk and Black Political Thought* (Princeton, NJ: Princeton University Press, 2004), articulated a similar point of view with respect to how Black ideology in everyday talk is influenced, developed, and utilized.

11. For example, Wilma King. *Stolen Childhood: Slave Youth in Nineteenth Century America* (Bloomington: Indiana University Press, 1995): "Infant mortality rates were high," p. 9, "51% of the deaths among the non white population occurred in children nine years of age and under," p. 10, i.e., 49 percent did not survive even childhood.

12. According to photius.com http://www.photius.com/wfb.1999rankings/population_ohtml, there are 237 populated territories in the world. Of those 31 have larger populations than the African descended population of the U.S., and 205 have smaller populations. Out of 50 African countries listed, 5 have higher populations, and 44 have smaller populations.

13. Harris-Lacewell, *Barbershops, Bibles, and BET*, and Michael Dawson, *Black Visions: The Roots of Contemporary African-American Political Ideologies* (Chicago: University of Chicago Press, 2001), explore this

proposition from two related but different perspectives in their considerations of Black ideology.

14. Anthony Marx, *Making Race and Nation: A Comparison of the United States, South Africa, and Brazil* (Cambridge: Cambridge University Press, 1996).

15. Taney in the Dred Scott decision, "It is too clear for dispute that the enslaved African race were not intended to be included," and further, "It would not in any part of the civilized world be supposed to embrace the negro race, which, by common consent, had been excluded from civilized governments and the family of nations."

16. *Ibid.*, and Marx, *Making Race.*

17. Homer Plessy was a legally Black man who appeared white. People of his class and color had deliberately chosen to violate the law in Louisiana that required segregation by race on the state's trains. Plessy was chosen to represent the group by attempting to sit in the white section. In order that the conductor, to follow the law, would deny Plessy the seat, the group had to inform the conductor that Plessy was Black. Otherwise he would not have known.

18. Harris-Lacewell, *Barbershops, Bibles, and BET.* Her idea of Black talk is a well-reasoned and coherent way of thinking about these behaviors.

19. Taylor Branch, *At Canaan's Edge: America in the King Years, 1965–1968* (New York: Simon and Schuster, 2006), pp. 337–338.

20. Browning, et al., *Protest Is Not Enough*, pp. 86–90, 92.

21. Matthew Holden uses the term "quasi-government." Though he means something different from what I mean by "pseudo-government," he refers to a kind of consensus on political issues among Black elites in particular locales. Matthew Holden, Jr., *The Politics of the Black Nation* (New York: Chandler, 1973).

22. It is hard, for example, to imagine that Wardell Connerly's politics are Black politics, though his pattern fits what Harris-Lacewell calls Black conservatism. Connerly, however, doesn't consider himself Black. How can a man who does not feature himself as Black, and who adamantly denies promoting racial politics of any sort, be considered a practitioner of Black politics? It seems to me that people such as Connerly and Alan Keyes, who profess not to be practicing Black politics and who certainly are not intending to focus their efforts for the benefit of Black people as a categoric group, should not be considered as engaged in Black politics solely on the basis of their ancestry.

23. "Welcome to America's Most Diverse City," ""America's most integrated city." www.timecom. The article, "Welcome to America's Most Diverse City," appeared in the August 22, 2002, edition of *Time Magazine*.

24. While a number of writers are quite explicit concerning this subject, e.g., Mack Jones, "A Frame of Reference for Black Politics," in *Black Political Life in the United States*, Lenneal J. Henderson, ed. (San Francisco: Chandler, 1972). Dawson, *Behind the Mule*, and *Black Visions*; Cathy Cohen, *The Boundaries of Blackness: Aids and the Breakdown of Black Politics* (Chicago: University of Chicago Press, 1999); Melissa Harris-Lacewell, *Barbershops, Bibles, and BET*, they do not explicitly locate the broader subject matter of Black politics.

25. Recently, a number of scholars have addressed this problem of complexity explicitly with respect to Black politics. See Ricky K. Green, *Voices in Black Political Thought* (New York: Peter Lang, 2005); Dawson, *Black Visions*; Cohen, *The Boundaries of Blackness*; Harris-Lacewell. *Barbershops, Bibles, and BET*; Todd Shaw, symposium editor, "The Changing Boundaries of Blackness," *National Political Science Review* 11, 2007, Georgia A. Persons, ed., pp. 3–16.

26. I have explored these concepts in a number of articles and one book. See David Covin, *The Unified Black Movement in Brazil, 1978–2002* (Jefferson, NC: McFarland, 2006); Covin, "Black Activists During the Ebb Tide of a Social Movement," *National Political Science Review* 8, 2001; Covin, "Narrative, Free Space, and Communities of Memory in the Brazilian Black Consciousness Movement," *Western Journal of Black Studies* 21, no. 4, 1997; Covin, "Social Movement Theory in the Examination of Mobilization in the Black Community," *National Political Science Review* 6, 1997. My own thinking on the subject has been most heavily influenced by Richard Couto, "Narratives, Free Spaces, and Political Leadership," *The Journal of Politics* 55, no. 1, 1993; and *Ain't Gonna Let Nobody Turn Me Round: The Pursuit of Racial Justice in the South* (Philadelphia: Temple University Press, 1991); Sarah Evans and Harry Boite, *Free Spaces: The Sources of Democratic Change in America* (New York: Harper, 1985); Doug McAdam, *Political Processes and the Development of Insurgency, 1930–1970* (Chicago: University of Chicago Press, 1982); Aldon D. Morris, *The Origins of the Civil Rights Movement, Black Political Mobilization, Leadership, Power, and Mass Behavior* (Albany: New York State University Press, 1984); James Scott, *Domination and the Arts of Resistance: Hidden Transcripts* (New Haven, CT: Yale University Press, 1990); and Scott, *Weapons of the Weak: Everyday Forms of Peasant Resistance* (New Haven, CT: Yale University Press, 1985); Sidney Tarrow, *Social Movements, Collective Action, and Politics* (New York: Cambridge University Press, 1994); and Tarrow, *Politics and Reform: Collective Action, Social Movements, and Cycles of Protest*, Cornell Center for Independent Study, Western Societies Program Occasional Papers, no. 21, 1989.

27. Cathy Cohen (Cohen, 1999) has conducted a dense examination of the Black politics of AIDS. Her focus, however, is on a single (albeit complex and wide-ranging) issue. It is also a national examination, with particular emphasis on New York City. Her work is representative of much fine political science that focuses in detail on the complexity of a single policy area. The instant study is similar in its level of detail but considerably different in that it looks at a whole political universe, geographically, and over thirty years. Also, Minion K.C. Morrison's book, *Black Political Mobilization: Leadership, Power, & Mass Behavior* (Albany: State University of New York Press, 1987), is a similar comprehensive and detailed study, but its focus is on majority Black settings in the South.

28. William Strickland, "DuBois's Revenge: Reinterrogating American Democratic Theory ... or Why We Need a Revolutionary Black Research Agenda in the 21st Century," *SOULS* 10, no. 1, 2008.

Chapter 1

1. John Hope Franklin, *From Slavery to Freedom* (New York: Knopf, 1967), p. 113.
2. Lawrence B. De Graaf and Quintard Taylor, "Introduction," in Lawrence B. De Graaf, Kevin Mulray, and Quintard Taylor, eds., *Seeking El Dorado: African Americans in California* (Seattle: University of Washington Press, 2001), p. 6.
3. *Ibid.*; Clarence Caesar, *An Historical Overview of the Development of Sacramento's Black Community, 1850–1983.* Master's thesis, California State University, Sacramento, 1985, p. 8.
4. Caesar, 1985, p. 11.
5. Personal communication with Joe Moore, October 16, 2007.
6. De Graaf and Taylor, 2001, pp. 10–15; Willi Coleman. "African American Women and Community Development in California, 1848–1900," in *Seeking El Dorado: African Americans in California*, p. 101.
7. De Graaf and Taylor, 2001, p. 11.
8. Coleman, 2001, p. 102.
9. Grace Carter Douglas. "A Historical Study of the Women's Civic and Improvement Club," in *The Griot: An Anthology of African Necromancers*. Grace Carter Douglas, ed. (Sacramento: Rumble, 1988), p. 14.
10. De Graaf and Taylor, 2001, p. 10.
11. *Ibid.*, p. 11.
12. Coleman, 2001, p. 103.
13. *Ibid.*, pp. 100–102; DeGraaf and Taylor, 2001, pp. 8–11.
14. De Graaf and Taylor, 2001, pp. 9–10; Coleman, 2001, p. 107; Caesar, 1985, pp. 37–39.
15. Coleman, 2001, p. 109.
16. *Ibid.*
17. De Graaf and Taylor, 2001, p. 12.
18. *Ibid.*
19. *Ibid.*, p. 15.
20. *Ibid.*, p. 12.
21. Caesar, 1985, p. 132.
22. *Ibid.*, p. 129.
23. *Sacramento Observer, A Long Look Back*, November 1973, "Mrs. Netta Sparks," p. LL-36.
24. *Ibid.*; and *Ibid.*, "Simmie Franklin, p. LL-15; "Douglas McFarland," p. LL-22; "Rev. Solomon Nelson," p. LL-52; "Dr. Roscoe Brewer," p. LL-64.
25. Caesar, 1985, p. 132.
26. *Ibid.*, p. 110.
27. "Netta Sparks," p. LL-36.
28. *Ibid.*
29. Caesar, 1985, p. 133.
30. *Ibid.*
31. *Ibid.*
32. *Ibid.*
33. *Ibid.*, p. 135.
34. De Graaf and Taylor, 2001, p. 22.
35. Douglas, 1988, p. 14.
36. *Ibid.*, p. 18.
37. *Ibid.*, p. 23.
38. *Sacramento Observer, A Long Look Back*; Douglas, 1988, pp. 13–39.
39. Caesar, 1985, p. 118.
40. *Ibid.*, p. 120.
41. *Ibid.*, pp. 109–135.
42. De Graaf and Taylor, 2001, p. 11.

43. Caesar, 1985, p. 37.
44. *Ibid.*, p. 115.
45. *Ibid.*, p. 118.
46. "Netta Sparks," p. LL-36.
47. *Ibid.*
48. *Ibid.*
49. *Ibid.*
50. Caesar, 1985, p. 128.
51. *Sacramento Observer, A Long Look Back*, "Mrs. Gladys Canson," p. LL-13.
52. *Ibid.*, "Douglas McFarland," p. LL-22.
53. *Ibid.*; and "Dr. Roscoe Browning," p. LL-64.
54. *Sacramento Observer, A Long Look Back*, "Dr. Roscoe Browning."
55. Caesar, 1985, pp. 138, 147, 148.
56. *Ibid.*, pp. 147–148. Businesses included a liquor store, two restaurants and a hotel.
57. See map following page 38.
58. For example, in unincorporated areas with significant Black populations, such as North Highlands, Rancho Cordova, and the Fruitridge Pocket, there was no policy making body where Black residents' concerns and interests were substantively represented. There was no city government to represent them, and the Black population in the county was sufficiently limited that there was no need for any incumbent or candidate to pay it extensive attention. There was no county supervisorial district with even a 10 percent Black population.
59. Grantland Johnson interview (2001).
60. *Sacramento Observer, A Long Look Back*, "Mrs. Nona Henry," p. LL-16; "Mrs. Missouri Nash," p. 50–51.
61. *Ibid.*, "Mrs. Johnnie Ruth Luster," p. LL-20.
62. *Ibid.*, "Nathaniel S. Colley," p. LL-78.
63. *Ibid.*, "Dr. Kenneth Johnson," p. LL-78.
64. *Ibid.*, "Nathaniel S. Colley, Esq." p. LL-66.
65. Marion Woods interview (2001).
66. The Observer Newspapers, *Colorful Reflections* (Sacramento: Observer Newspapers, 2003), p. 11.
67. Gloria Abernethy, personal communication, Sacramento, California, April 26, 2008.
68. Huey P. Newton, with J. Herman Blake, *Revolutionary Suicide* (New York: Harcourt Brace Jovanovich, 1979), pp. 150–151.
69. Grantland Johnson interview (2001).
70. *Ibid.*, and Harvey Frye interview (2000).
71. Fred Foote interview (2000).
72. *Ibid.* Margaret Washington Creel went on to get her Ph.D. in history from the University of California at Berkeley. She is the author of *A Peculiar People: Slave Religion and Community Culture Among the Gullahs*, a prize-winning study which is the foundational work in its field. She was the historical consultant for the film *Daughters of the Dust* and other films. At the time of this writing she is professor of history at Cornell University.
73. At UCLA the struggle to control the Black Student Union was literally fought out between the U.S. organization and the Black Panthers. A resulting shootout resulted in the death of John Huggins, a Panther.
74. See Michael Mitchell, "Blacks and the *Abertura Democratica*," in *Race, Class, and Power in Brazi*,. Pierre-re-Michel Fontaine, ed. (Los Angeles: Center for Afro-American Studies, 1985), pp. 111–115; Anthony W.

Marx, *Making Race and Nation: A Comparison of the United States, South Africa, and Brazil* (Cambridge: Cambridge University Press, 1998), pp. 264–266.

Chapter 2

1. In the third edition of *From Slavery to Freedom*, John Hope Franklin entitles the last section, chapter 31, "The Negro Revolution. John Hope Franklin, *From Slavery to Freedom: A History of Negro Americans.* 3rd ed. (New York: Knopf, 1967). See also Louis Lomax, *The Negro Revolt* (New York: Signet Books, 1963).

2. James D. Wilson, *American Government: Institutions and Policies.* 2nd ed. (Lexington, MA: Heath, 1983), p. 475; Sacramento Area Economic Opportunity Council (SAEOC), Ad Hoc Committee Minutes, October 18, 1970; SAEOC, CAA Plans and Priorities, CAP Form 81, Funding Year F — January 1, 1971–December 31, 1971, list of SAEOC programs and delegate agencies; SAEOC & SF Regional EOP Offices, Memorandum of Understanding for Program Year F: January 1, 1971– December 31, 1971.

3. Wilson (1983), p. 475; SAEOC, Ad Hoc Committee Minutes, 1970; SAEOC, CAA Plans and Priorities, January 1, 1971–December 31, 1971.

4. Daryl D. Enos, "An Evaluation of the Neighborhood Councils," 1967, Table, p. 16.

5. *Ibid.*, Table, p. 18.

6. *Ibid.*, Table, p. 19.

7. *Ibid.*, Table, p. 20.

8. *Ibid.*, Table, p. 22.

9. SAEOC Executive Board meeting, Minutes, December 29, 1970.

10. Wilson (1983), p. 475; SAEOC, December 29, 1970; *Sacramento Union*, "FONO Wins Round in Power Struggle," August 11, 1970, p. 4; *Sacramento Bee*, "U.S. Probes Reports of State OEO Harassing Poverty War Efforts," November 18, 1970.

11. *Sacramento Observer*, "Sacramento's most influential Blacks," December 1977, p. 35.

12. Hardy Frye interview, 2000.

13. SAEOC, Partial, untitled statement issued by Naaman Brown, 1969, p. 1; Washington Neighborhood Council, Fact Sheet, 1969, p. 1.

14. Washington Neighborhood Council (1969), pp. 1 & 2; SAEOC, Partial untitled statement, 1969.

15. Washington Neighborhood Council (1969), p. 2.

16. *Ibid.*

17. *Ibid.*, p. 3.

18. SAEOC, CAA Plans and Priorities CAP Form 81, p. 7.

19. *Ibid.*

20. SAEOC, *Sacramento Community Action News*, "FONO Announces Second Housing Project," October 1970, p. 11.

21. Enos (1967), pp. 22–30.

22. *Ibid.*

23. Marion Woods Interview, 2000.

24. *Ibid.*

25. *Ibid.*

26. *Ibid.*

27. *Ibid.*

28. *Ibid.*

29. *Ibid.*

30. *Ibid.*, personal observations; Rufus P. Browning, Dale Rogers Marshall, and David H. Tabb, *Protest is Not Enough* (Berkeley: University of California Press, 1986). The authors held a reception in Sacramento after their book was published. Callie was feted there.

31. Charles E. Jones and Michael L. Clemons, "A Model of Racial Crossover Voting: An Assessment of the Wilder Victory," *Dilemmas of Black Politics: Issues of Leadership and Strategy*, Georgia Persons, ed. (New York: HarperCollins College Publishers, 1993), pp. 128–146.

32. *Sacramento Observer*, "Oak Park 4 Supplement," October 1, 1970.

33. *Ibid.*

34. *Ibid.*, May 14, 1970.

35. *Ibid.*

36. *Ibid.*, "Oak Park 4 Supplement," October 1, 1970.

37. *Ibid.*, May 14, 1970.

38. *Ibid.*, letter to the editor, 1970.

39. *Ibid.*, May 14, 1970,

40. *Ibid.*

41. *Ibid.*, May 14, 1970.

42. *Ibid.*, June 19, 1970, p. 1.

43. *Ibid.*, p. 2.

44. *Ibid.*, June 4, 1970, p. 3.

45. *Ibid.*, June 25, 1970, p. 1.

46. *Ibid.*, June 4, 1970, p.3; June 16, 1970, p. 21.

47. *Ibid.*, June 16, 1970, p. 21.

48. *Ibid.*, August 6, 1970, p. 2.

49. *Ibid.*

50. *Ibid.*

51. *Sacramento Bee*, December 29, 1971, p. B2.

52. *Ibid.*

53. *Ibid.* December 29, 1970, p. B2.

54. *Ibid.*

55. *Ibid.*

56. *Ibid.*

57. *Ibid.*

58. *Ibid.*, December 30, 1970, p. B2.

59. *Ibid.*, January 9, 1971, p. A2.

60. *Ibid.*

61. *Ibid.*, January 14, 1971, p. C2.

62. *Ibid.*, January 15, 1971, p. C2.

63. *Ibid.*

64. *Ibid.*, January 22, 1971, p. B3.

65. *Ibid.*, January 29, 1971, p. B2.

66. *Sacramento Bee*, January 29, 1971, p. B2.

67. *Ibid.*

68. *Ibid.*; samplings of *The Sacramento Observer*, longitudinally, provide specific representations of all the features mentioned above.

69. Michael Dawson, *Behind the Mule: Race and Class in African-American Politics* (Princeton, NJ: Princeton University Press, 1994), p. 77.

70. "Citizens Committee on Police Practices, A Member's Perspective," *Rumble* 1, no, 1 (June 1973): 1, 2–4.

71. Anyone who has ever witnessed this kind of takedown in the street recognizes that the command, "Halt," is rarely used. More typical is, "Get your ass down, motherfucker! Get on the ground, goddamn it, or I'll kill you! I'll blow your motherfuckin' head off! Get on the ground, goddamn it!" This and variations on it are yelled simultaneously by numbers of policemen. In this case the target of these shouts was a 15-year-old boy who had never been exposed to anything like it.

72. *Rumble*, June 1973, pp. 2–4.

73. Clarence Caesar, *An Historical Overview of the Development of Sacramento's Black Community, 1850–1983* (Unpublished thesis, California State University, Sacramento, 1985), p. 235.

74. Sacramento Area Black Caucus, "Why is the Black Caucus Going to the City Council to Accuse the Police Department of Discriminatory Acts Against Black People?" Undated public statement and flier issued by the SABC, June 1974; "Police Assaults the Nation," flier, author unknown, May 1974; "Letter from the Black Community of Sacramento to Minister Benjamin of the Nation of Islam," April 26, 1974.

75. Grace Douglass, "Rapping," *Rumble* 1, no. 34 (September 1979): 1.

76. *Rumble* 1, no. 32 (April 1979): 6.

77. Indeed, Mr. Smith was even able to get support from District 2's almost reactionary city council member, Blaine Fisher. Letter from Blaine Fisher, dated January 12, 1977, endorsing "the effort to make Martin Luther King Day in California, a State Holiday."

78. Rod Bush, *The New Black Vote* (San Francisco: Synthesis, 1984); Harold Cruse, *The Crisis of the Negro Intellectual* (New York: Morrow, 1967); Cruise, *Plural But Equal* New York: Morrow, 1987); James Jennings, *The Politics of Black Empowerment* (Detroit: Wayne State University Press, 1992); Robert Smith, *We Have No Leaders: African Americans in the Post–Civil Rights Era* (Albany: State University of New York Press, 1996); Ronald Walters and Robert Smith, *African American Leadership* (Albany: State University of New York Press, 1999); Aldon D. Morris, *The Origins of the Civil Rights Movement: Black Communities Organizing for Change* (New York: Free Press, 1984); Minion K.C. Morrison, *Black Mobilization: Leadership, Power, and Mass Behavior* (Albany: State University of New York Press, 1984); Charles Payne, *I've Got the Light of Freedom* (Berkeley: University of California Press, 1996); Doug McAdam, *Political Process and the Development of Black Insurgency, 1930–1970* (Chicago: University of Chicago Press, 1982).

79. Sidney Tarrow, *Social Movements, Collective Action, and Politics* (New York: Columbia University Press, 1982).

80. Jerrold G. Rusk, for example, in his review essay on the landmark study by Sidney Verba and Norman H. Nie, *Participation in America: Political Democracy and Social Equality* (New York: Harper & Row, 1972). Verba and Nie suggest they seem to feel little need to draw on the voluminous group literature. They omit that variable from their consideration. Jerrold R. Rusk, "Participation in America: A Review Essay," *American Political Science Review* 70, no. 2 (June 1976): 584–585.

81. For samples see: Frederick Barth, ed., *Ethnic Groups and Boundaries* (Boston: Little, Brown, 1969); Steve S. Messner, and Scott South, "Structural Determinants of Intergroup Association: Interracial Marriage and Crime," *American Journal of Sociology* 91, no. 6: 1409–30; Edward Telles, "Racial Distance and Region in Brazil: The Case of Marriage Among Color Groups," *Latin American Review* 28: 141–62; Robert McIver, *The Web of Government* (New York: McMillan, 1947); Mira Komarovsky, "The Voluntary Association of Urban Dwellers," *American Sociological Review* 11, 1946: 686–698; Pan Hare, Eda F. Borgetta, and Robert Bales,

eds., *Small Groups*, rev. ed. (New York: Knopf, 1965); George C. Homens, *The Human Group* (New York: Harcourt, Brace, 1950); Sherif Muzafer, "Experiments in Group Conflict," *Scientific American* 195, no. 5 (November 1956): 54–58; V.O. Key, *Politics, Parties, and Pressure Groups* (New York: Random House, 1942).

82. See, as examples, E.U. Essein Udom, *Black Nationalism: A Search for Identity in America* (New York: Dell, 1964); Ollie A. Johnson III and Karin Stanford, eds., *Black Political Organizations in the Post-Civil Rights Era* (New Brunswick, NJ: Rutgers University Press, 2002); Nancy J. Weiss, *The National Urban League* (New York: Oxford University Press, 1974); Charles Jones, ed., *The Black Panther Party Reconsidered* (Baltimore: Black Classic Press, 1988).

83. Tarrow, 1982.

84. Matthew Holden Jr., *The Politics of the Black Nation* (New York: Chandler, 1973), p. 3.

85. *Ibid.*

86. Milton Morris, *The Politics of Black America* (New York: Harper & Row, 1975), p. 208.

87. Frederick C. Harris, Valeria Sinclair-Chapman, Brian D. Mackenzie, "Macrodynamics of Black Political Participation in the Post-Civil Rights Era," *The Journal of Politics* 67, no. 4 (November 2005): 1143–1163.

88. Morris, 1975, p. 208.

89. Cited in Hanes Walton, *Invisible Politics: Black Political Behavior* (Albany: State University of New York Press, 1985), p. 260.

90. *Ibid.*, p. 254.

91. *Ibid.*, p. 260.

92. Smith, 1996, p. 87.

93. *Ibid.*

94. *Ibid.*, p. 124.

95. Leland T. Saito, *Race and Politics: Asian Americans, Latinos, and Whites in a Los Angeles Suburb* (Urbana: University of Illinois Press, 1998).

96. Holden, 1973, p. 4.

97. Walton, 1973, p. 245.

98. *Ibid.*, p. 260.

99. Morris, 1975, p. 260.

100. *Ibid.*

101. Holden, 1973, p. 3.

102. Tate, 1994, p. 93.

103. *Ibid.*

104. *Ibid.*, and table, p. 94.

105. *Ibid.*, p. 94.

106. *Ibid.*, p. 93.

107. *Ibid.*

108. *Ibid.*

109. Dawson, 1994, p. 10.

110. Browning, Marshall, and Tabb, 1984, p. 245.

111. *Ibid.*

112. Dawson, 1994, p. 50.

113. *Ibid.*, p. 58.

114. 1970 Block group data, by census tract.

115. Culture Collection, Sacramento, California, December 2005, personal communication.

116. Dawson, 1994, p. 50.

117. Grantland Johnson letter, undated. The letter serves as an illustration of this point, though in unusual circumstances. The letter was addressed to "Interested Parties." It was written when Grantland was running for election to the County Board of Supervisors. It announces the resignation of his campaign consultant

(campaign manager) and the appointment of a new one. This was a polite way of indicating he had fired his campaign manager.

118. Holden, 1973, p. 3.

119. *Ibid.*

120. Dr. Eugene Spencer Jr., letter dated June 29, 1973. Dr. Spencer, in his capacity as president of the Sacramento Urban League, was writing to Mayor Richard Marriott. He says, in part, that "various community organizations ... contacted you to investigate the matter ... after which the Human Relations Commission fully restored the Executive Director to his office."

121. The reference is in 1970 dollars.

122. This is not as strict a definition of single-gender organizations as is optimal. All of the organizations in the table originated as single-gender organizations, and most remained so. Some, however, such as the Women's Civic Improvement Club and the Tuskegee Airmen had members of both genders by the end of the 1970s, though in each case, the founding gender heavily predominated, the leadership was dominated by the founding gender, and the objectives remained as the founders had established them. It seems appropriate to classify these exceptions as they were originally designated not only because they were founded as single gender organizations, but also because they remain under the province of a single gender.

123. Counting California, Data Extraction Results, Census of Population, 1970, 2nd count, U.S. Department of Commerce, Bureau of the Census Data and Technical Assistance, University of California Berkeley, 2004 (November 30, 2006).

124. See, particularly, discussions in Charles M. Payne, *I've Got the Light of Freedom: The Organizing Tradition and the Mississippi Freedom Struggle* (Berkeley: University of California Press, 1996); and Joanne Grant, *Ella Baker: Freedom Bound* (New York: Wiley, 1998).

125. Sacramento Area Black Caucus, "Why is the Black Caucus Going to the City Council to Accuse the Police Department of Discriminatory Acts Against Black People?"; "Police Assaults the Nation"; "Letter from the Black Community of Sacramento to Minister Benjamin of the Nation of Islam."

126. Robert C. Smith and Richard Seltzer, *Race, Class, and Culture: A Study in Afro-American Mass Opinion* (Albany: State University of New York Press, 1992), pp. 29–31, 44–46, 86–88, 92–100, and especially 127–128.

127. Holden, 1973, pp. 3–8.

128. Cruse, 1987, p. 127, 128–134.

129. Author's personal observations.

130. The narrative in this section is based on the author's personal observations.

131. Sacramento Area Black Caucus, Summary Compilation SABC Revitalization Workshops, "Political Committee," October 24, 1975.

132. "Local Focus and Issues," *Rumble* 1, no. 11 (January 1975): 4–5; and notes taken during SABC interviews of assembly members Leon Ralph and Julian Dixon.

133. *Sacramento Bee*, November 3, 1971, pp. A1 and A24.

134. *Sacramento Bee*, September 22, 1971, p. B1.

135. *Ibid.*

136. *Ibid.*, November 3, 1971, pp. A1 and A24.

137. *Ibid.*, September 22, 1971, p. B1.

138. *Ibid.*

139. *Ibid.*, November 3, 1971, pp. A1 and A24.

140. *Ibid.*

141. This and all subsequent turnout and voter registration figures for primary and general elections were furnished by the Sacramento County Clerk's office.

142. David Covin, "Social Movement Theory in the Examination of Mobilization in a Black Community: The 1991 Sacramento Redistricting Project," *National Political Science Review* 6, 1997, p. 96. Census information by population and dwelling units by census tract.

143. Covin, 1997, p. 96.

144. Counting California Data extraction results, census of population, 1970, 2nd count. In 1970 the only East Asians listed were Chinese, Japanese, and Koreans. There were approximately 9,800 Japanese, 9,400 Chinese, and fewer than 300 Koreans. University of California Data Archive and Technical Assistance, University of California at Berkeley, (distributed 2004).

145. *Sacramento Bee*, n.d.

146. Letter from John Lindsey, Political Committee of SABC, undated (circa 1973). Also reported in letter of October 8, 1976, to various community activists after Isenberg was elected mayor.

147. *Sacramento Bee*, November 24, 1971, p. B1.

148. David Fontaine, interview, December 24, 1985, Sacramento, California.

149. *Sacramento Bee*, "Los Rios Trustee Stewart Invested in South Africa," August 24, 1979; Art Campos, "Trustees: Popular Courses Shifted from SCC to ARC," *Sacramento Bee*, March 22, 1979, p. 3. The Observer Newspapers, "Sacramento's 100 Most Influential Blacks," December 1977, p. 39; *Rumble* 1, no. 32 (April 1979): 3.

150. Marion Woods, interview, 2000; The Observer Newspapers, "Sacramento's 100 Most Influential Blacks," December 1977, p. 38.

151. Charlie Cooper and Ann Cooper, *Tuskegee's Heroes* (Osceola, WI: MBI, 1996), p. 33.

152. *Ibid.*, p. 69.

153. Grantland Johnson, interview, August 20, 1985.

154. *Ibid.*

155. Sacramento County Clerk's Office.

156. The Observer Newspapers, "Sacramento's 100 Most Influential Blacks," December 1977, p. 38.

157. Hardy Frye, interview, 2000.

158. Donald E. Hall, assistant superintendent, Sacramento City Unified School District. Letter dated October 8, 1973; Edward B. Fort, superintendent; Edward B. Fort, Sacramento City Unified School District superintendent. Letter dated September 3, 1974.

159. Covin, 1997, p. 98.

160. *Ibid.*, pp. 99–100.

161. *Ibid.*, p. 100.

162. Sacramento County Clerk's Office.

163. *Sacramento Bee*, October 1, 1979.

164. *Ibid.*

165. Sacramento County Clerk's Office.

166. *Scorpio Reporter, July 4th, 1876–1976, Souvenir Bicentennial Issue.*

167. The Observer Newspapers, "Sacramento's 100 Most Influential Blacks," December 1977, p. 39.

168. *Ibid.*, p. 35.

169. *Ibid.*, p. 38.

170. *Ibid.*, p. 37.

171. *Ibid.*; and Grantland Johnson, interview, August 20, 1985.

172. *Sacramento Observer*, December 19, 1977, p. 35.

173. *Ibid.*

174. *Ibid.*, p. 37.

175. *Scorpio Reporter, July 4th, 1876–1976, Souvenir Bicentennial Issue.*

176. *Ibid.*, and *Sacramento Observer*, December 1977; also author's observation.

177. *Sacramento Observer*, December, 1977.

178. *Scorpio Reporter, July 4th, 1876–1976, Souvenir Bicentennial Issue*; *Sacramento Observer*, December 1977; also author's observations.

Chapter 3

1. Geraldine Gregory, "What is the National Black Independent Political Party?" National Black Independent Political Party, 1980; National Black Independent Political Party, "Attend the Los Angeles Organizing Committee Conference, July 25," p. 3.

2. National Black Independent Political Party, Minutes, National Black Political Party Convention, Plenary Session, November 23, 1980.

3. The author was a member of the delegation.

4. Pan African Studies, California State University, Sacramento; Sacramento Area Black Caucus; California State University Visiting Scholars Program, "The Sacramento Working Conference on The Black Political Party, October 15–18, 1980," Conference Program, 1980.

5. Harold Cruse, *The Crisis of the Negro Intellectual: From Its Origins to the Present* (New York: Morrow, 1967).

6. Pan African Studies, California State University, Sacramento, et al., 1980, p. 5.

7. *Ibid.*

8. *Ibid.*

9. *Ibid.*, p. 7.

10. *Ibid.*, p. 6.

11. *Ibid.*

12. The Party for the New Black Politics was organized in early 1980. It published a monthly newsletter, *The Speaking Drum*, edited by Alexandre Kimenyi. The first issue was published by September 1980, almost three months before the National Black Independent Political Party organizing conference took place.

13. Thomas Chinn, letter dated April 1, 1981, addressed to the Honorable Thomas R. Hoeber, Chairman, Reapportionment Committee, City Council of Sacramento.

14. SABC position paper, May 1981; Les Gary, letter to Otis Scott, April 10, 1981; District 7 Committee, "A Proposed Reapportionment Plan for City Council Districts," April 1, 1981; Human Rights Commission, "Workshop on Reapportionment," March 30, 1981; Ernest R. Hawkins, Registrar of Voters, letter to Thomas R. Hoeber, Chairman, and Members, Sacramento City Reapportionment Committee, March 18, 1981.

15. Human Rights Commission, March 30, 1981; SABC, May 1981.

16. SABC , May 1981.

17. *Ibid.*

18. *Ibid.*

19. Sacramento City Charter, Section 23.

20. SABC, May 1981.

21. *Ibid.*

22. *Ibid.*

23. *Ibid.*

24. Thomas Chinn, April 1, 1981.

25. *Ibid.*

26. SABC, May 1981.

27. All 3 positions are found in District 7 Committee, April 1, 1981, pp. 8–9.

28. SABC, May 1981.

29. *Ibid.*

30. *Ibid.*

31. *Ibid.*

32. *Ibid.*

33. *Ibid.*

34. *Ibid.*

35. *Ibid.*

36. SABC, "Sacramento Area Black Caucus Legal Challenge to the Sacramento City Council's Redistricting Decision," June 1981.

37. Joe Serna's background was interesting. He was raised as a farm worker in California's central valley. He worked his way through college and graduated from Sacramento State College and the University of California, Davis. He became an organizer for the United Farm Workers under Cesar Chavez. He served in the Peace Corps and spent two years in South America. He was an intern for Black assemblyman Mervyn Dymally, who became lieutenant governor. Dymally was one of Serna's principal mentors. Serna became active in Sacramento Chicano, Democratic, and electoral politics, working in many campaigns during the 1970s.

38. NBIPP, "Questions and Answers on the National Black Independent Political Party." Dayton, 1980.

39. NBIPP, "Attend the Los Angeles Organizing Committee Conference, July 25." The party was formed during the organizing conference, November 21–23, 1980, in Philadelphia.

40. George Dean, president, Sacramento Urban League, Inc., letter, dated March 31, 1981.

41. Sacramento Branch NAACP, SABC, Black Advocates in State Service (BASS), Sacramento Urban League, telegram sent to President Ronald Reagan, December 29, 1981.

42. Organizational joint statement, December 29, 1981.

43. *Ibid.*

44. SABC, "From the Chair, *Newsletter*, Spring 1981.

45. James Jennings, "Boston: Blacks and Progressive Politics," in *The New Black Vote: Politics and Power in Four American Cities*, Rod Bush, ed. (San Francisco: Synthesis Press, 1984), pp. 269–290.

46. Robert McClory, "Up from Obscurity: Harold Washington," in Melvin G. Holli & Paul M. Green, eds., *The Making of the Mayor: Chicago, 1983* (Grand Rapids, MI: Eerdmans, 1984), p. 14; Abdul Alkalimat and Doug Gills, "Black Power vs. Racism: Harold Washington Becomes Mayor," in Bush, 1984, pp. 84–87.

47. McClory, 1983, p. 14; and Alkalimat and Gills in Bush, 1984, pp. 84–85.

48. Alkalimat and Gills in Bush, 1984, pp. 84–85.

49. Chicago Public Library. "Facts about Harold Washington, 42nd Mayor of Chicago." (1/18/2007).

50. McClory, 1984, p. 14.

51. Alkalimat and Gills in Bush, 1984, p. 85.

52. *Ibid.*, p. 88.

53. Black American Political Association of California (BAPAC), "Keeping it Together," 10th Anniversary Program, October 1988, p. 23.

54. It was not impossible, however, according to Washington's campaign objective, "80–80." That was to get an 80 percent Black voter turnout, and to capture 80 percent of the Black vote. He didn't actually reach his goal, but the astronomical increase in Black voter registration over what it had been only two years earlier — 200,000 voters — meant that he didn't have to reach the 80 percent turnout total to achieve his objective because there were just so many more Black voters than anyone had imagined. As it was, he turned out 73 percent of the Black vote and won more than 80 percent of the Black voters who turned out. Paul M. Green, "The Primary: Some New Players — Same Old Rules," Holli and Green, 1984, pp. 31–32; Michael B. Preston, "The Resurgence of Black Voting in Chicago, 1955–1983," Holli and Green, 1984, p. 48, has Washington receiving 352,100 out of the 482,344 Black votes cast in the primary (83 percent). As for dancing in the street, see Alkalimat and Gills in Bush, 1984, p. 121.

55. Wikipedia. "Harold Washington," en.wikipedia. org/wili/Harold_Washington. How insignificant the Republican vote in Chicago was can be established by the percentage of voters who asked for Democratic ballots in the primary — 98.6 percent. Only 1.4 percent voted in the Republican primary. How could such a party be expected to contest the general election? Green, 1984.

56. Wikipedia. "Harold Washington."

57. Alkalimat and Gills in Bush, pp. 106, 119.

58. Jackson, 1983.

59. Grantland Johnson, interview, August 20, 1985.

60. *Ibid.*

61. *Ibid.*

62. *Ibid.*

63. Charlotte Bolton, interview, November 19, 1985.

64. Johnson interview.

65. *Ibid.*

66. *Ibid.*

67. Leslie Campbell, interview, November 19, 1985.

68. Johnson interview.

69. *Ibid.*

70. *Ibid.*

71. *Ibid.*

72. *Ibid.*

73. *Ibid.*

74. Bolton interview; Campbell interview.

75. The figures came from analyses of the census tracts and partial census tracts included in District 2. Maps and precinct identification were developed from census bureau figures by the Sacramento Council of Local Governments (SACOG). Numbers were computed by the author.

76. *Ibid.* This particular ratio appeared in the 1979 Bradley-Fisher primary.

77. Johnson interview. Johnson indicated that contributions from transit-connected fund-raisers totaled

$25,000. Almost all of that money came in after the primary. The campaign spent $45,000 by the general election. Final expenditures amounted to $65,000. It is clear that the transit contributions were critical from the standpoint of financing the campaign.

78. See Table 3.1.

79. Johnson interview.

80. *Ibid.*

81. *Ibid.*

82. David Fontaine, interview, December 24, 1985; Bolton interview; Grantland Johnson interview.

83. Johnson interview.

84. *Ibid.*

85. David Covin, "The New Black Vote in Sacramento: The Impossible Dream?" Presented at the National Conference of Black Political Scientists meeting, Chicago, April 2–4, 1986, pp. 39–40.

86. Austin Ranney, "Trust and Representation in Presidential Primary Elections," *American Political Science Review* 65, no. 1 (March 1972): 27; William H. Flannigan, *Political Behavior and the American Electorate* (Boston: Allyn & Bacon, 1968), p. 12; Frank J. Sorauf, *Party Politics in America* (Boston: Little, Brown, 1968), p. 219; an excellent discussion of a generous set of considerations in the literature along with a fine bibliography is found in Philip E. Secret and James B. Johnson, "Political Efficacy, Political Trust and Electoral Participation: A Longitudinal Analysis," *The Western Journal of Black Studies* 9, no. 2 (Summer 1985): 74–83.

87. Johnson interview.

88. Don Rose, "How the 1983 Election was Won," *The Making of the Mayor: Chicago, 1983*, Melvin G. Holli and Paul M. Green, eds. (Grand Rapids, MI: Eerdmans, 1984), p. 120: "Epton dropped out of sight during most of the campaign's final weekend"; p. 123, "It is ... safe to say that a white candidate other than Epton, running a less strident campaign, might have wound up mayor."

89. *Ibid.*, pp. 121–124. This is also the consensual finding of most sources. On p. 124, however, Rose provides an accounting by Ward that brings the point home.

90. Alkalimat and Gills in Bush, pp. 119–120; Michael B. Preston, "The Resurgence of Black Voting in Chicago: 1955–1983," in Hollis and Green, 1984, p. 48. Dempsey Travis puts the figure at 230,000. Dempsey Travis, *Harold, The People's Mayor* (Chicago: Urban Research Press, 1989), p. 151.

91. While Chisholm was on the ballot in many states, she did not have the treasury to mount a truly national campaign; only 25 percent of the Black delegates to the 1972 Democratic Convention were Chisholm delegates. Smith, 1996, p. 54.

92. Chuck Stone, "The Negro Vote: *Ceteris Paribus*," *Black Political Life in the United States*, Lenneal J. Henderson, Jr., ed. (San Francisco: Chandler, 1972), pp. 133–149, especially p. 138. Stone examines Black partisan voting from 1948 through 1967 (though he looks at the Roosevelt years and earlier as well).

93. B. Kwaku Duren, *Statement on the Discussion of a Black Presidential Candidate*, October 17, 1983, p. 3.

94. JoNina Abron, Memo to the Central Committee, NBIPP, re: "1984 Presidential Elections — Issues for Consideration," June 3, 1983, p. 2.

95. JoNina Abron, Memo to NBIPP Administrative

and Policy Committee re: "Resignation as Co-Chair, National Program Development Committee, Future of the Bay Area NBIPP," April 17, 1984.

96. A review of some of these questions can be found in Ron Daniels, "Some Perspectives of an NBIPP strategy for 1984," submitted to the National Program Committee, as per assignment, n/d. Also see B. Kwaku Duren, October 17, 1983.

97. In the absence of an explicit policy decision, this is what happened. For example, Ron Daniels, who in 1984 was NBIPP's national co-co-chairman, by 1988 was co-co-chairman of Jesse Jackson's campaign.

98. National Rainbow Coalition, *Build the NRC: National Rainbow Coalition* (n.d.). "The success of the Rainbow Campaign of '84 led to our transition into a national grass roots progressive political organization."

99. Paul Taylor, "Jackson Working to Add Constituencies to 'Rainbow,'" *Washington Post*, April 20, 1986. "He (Jackson) wants to patch together a multiracial coalition of economic 'outs.'"

100. Sacramento Valley Rainbow Coalition, roster, January 1, 1986. At this period of organizing, in late 1986, the leadership roster included 7 whites, 4 Latinos, 8 Blacks, 4 Asians, and one Native American: 12 men and 12 women.

101. As indicated in note 100 above, Black people were a plurality of the leadership. See also, SVRCOC, *Rainbow Neighborhood Organization* (internal document). In a report to the SVRCOC, 3 high priority areas for organizing and work were identified. Del Paso Heights was the highest priority, p. 4; Oak Park was the second priority; West Sacramento, primarily a white area, was the 3rd priority. Meadowview was identified as meeting more demographic criteria than West Sacramento, but was not identified as the 3rd highest priority because it had no members on the organizing committee. Hence, the two top priority neighborhoods were Black, the top two of the top three. Additionally, another Black neighborhood would have been identified as one of the top three had it any organizers available. Of the other 4 potential target neighborhoods out of literally scores of possibilities, 2 were Black, one was Black-Latino, and the fourth was white, p. 5. In short, the top priorities the SVRCOC identified for organizing and political work were overwhelmingly Black. Descriptively, the top 3 were Black.

102. National Rainbow Coalition, Inc., "Summary of the Bylaws of the NRC," 1986. II. E. "The 'Congressional District' shall be a unit of the 'State Chapter.' An NRC 'State Chapter' or NRC 'Congressional District' cannot endorse any candidate for political office without first obtaining the prior written approval of the NRC Board." The SVRCOC consisted of multiple congressional districts; the 2nd, 3rd, 4th, and 5th California Congressional Districts.

103. SVRCOC. Rainbow Neighborhood Organization. "These are the criteria ... with the recognition that our purposes in organizing the Rainbow Coalition are not exclusively or primarily electoral, that they are intended to build an organizational base among the locked out which can contribute to the kind of political and social restructuring necessary in the effort for a more just society domestically and a more peaceful international order," p. 2.

104. This was most clearly expressed by the charac-

terization of the Democrats and Republicans as members of one party, the left and right wings of the capitalist party—this, even though Jesse Jackson was running to capture the nomination of the Democratic party. In a flier for a house meeting, October 16, 1986, to learn about the Rainbow Coalition, for example, 2 of the 5 initial talking points read as follows: "Bored by politicians who only represent the wealthy and the white?" "Like to have an alternative to Ronald Reagan, the Democrats, and the 'one-party' system?"

105. SVRCOC. "Bring Together All Stripes of our Rainbow," Founding Conference of SVRC, September 27, 1986, Program; "Rainbow Coalition as Catalyst for Free South Africa Movement"; "Foreign Policy Through the Prism of the Rainbow Coalition"; "Help Build the NRC for Peace Abroad and Justice at Home," flyer, SRC.

106. A few examples of his supporters illustrate the point. See Grantland Johnson, interview, 2000: Joe Serna, city council member, later to be mayor; the Sacramento Black Chamber of Commerce; Fire Fighters Local 39; the California Legislative Black Caucus; Democratic Clubs, e.g., the Fannie Lou Hamer Democratic Club; Phil Isenberg, former city council member, mayor, and member of the State Assembly; Vic Fazio, member of Congress; the Natomas Community Association; Sheriffs' Officers Association; Lloyd Connelly, Superior Court judge; BAPAC; Wilson Riles, Jr.; and Robert Matsui, member of Congress.

107. Johnson interview, 2000.

108. *Ibid.*

109. *Ibid.*

110. U.S. Census Bureau, U.S. Census, 1980.

111. Johnson interview, 2000.

112. SVRCOC agenda, July 1986; August 1986; September 1986; SVRC Founding Conference Program, "The Significance of the Grantland Johnson Campaign: Political Realignment in Sacramento?"; SVRCOC Minutes, September 1986.

113. Smith, 1996, p. 242. Smith cites a 95 percent of the Black vote figure for Jackson during the 1988 primaries.

114. The Black American Political Association of California, *10th Anniversary Convention, Souvenir Booklet*, Sacramento, California, October 14–16, 1988, p. 7: "He (Willie Brown) not only agreed to convene the first meeting but decided to host it in his hometown, San Francisco."

115. *Ibid.*, p. 11, "October 12–13, 1979, The 1st State Convention." The text reads, "The convention organizers had ... set a ... precedent for all subsequent BAPAC conventions—the establishment of an agenda that both showcased California's Black elected officials and also facilitated interaction between them and grassroots political activists." Page 13: "BAPAC leaders were given the charge to organize chapters in major cities throughout the state."

116. *Ibid.*, p. 15.

117. That is clear, p. 7, "the meeting call was issued by Assemblyman Willie J. Brown, Jr. It went to all black elected officials, all appointees of Governor Jerry Brown, and distinguished religious and community leaders." Statewide conveners listed, p. 11, included Brown; a bishop; state legislators; high ranking administrators; Dr. Carleton Goodlett, the newspaper publisher; other

Black publishers, including Bill Lee of the *Sacramento Observer*; school district superintendents; Ron Dellums; Wilson Riles, Jr.; county supervisors; and university deans. Fourteen Sacramentans were on the list out of the total of 59 (23.7 percent). One of them, by then a prominent lawyer and real estate broker, a decade earlier had been one of the young lawyers whose first case was the Oak Park 4, Joseph Cooper. He also filed the documents to incorporate BAPAC.

118. BAPAC, 1988, p. 33.

119. *Ibid.*, p. 27.

120. Grantland Johnson interview, 1985.

121. Program, "Reaganomics and the Black Community," presented by the Sacramento Organizing Committee of the National Black Independent Political Party, July 28, 1982, 7–9 P.M.

122. Black Community Activist Committee (BCAC), "In Memory of Blanche Hill and Byron Robertson," The Sacramento Area Black Activist Community Conference, n/d., p. 1.

123. *Ibid.*

124. *Ibid.*, p. 2.

125. *Ibid.*, p. 3.

126. *Ibid.*, p. 2.

127. BCAC, *Newsletter*, # 1, April 30, 1985.

128. BCAC, Announcement, "Black Education in Sacramento," Saturday, August 24, 9 A.M.–5 P.M., Oak Park Community Center, n/d.

129. *Ibid.*

130. BCAC, *A Black Community Directory: For the Sacramento Area.* Sacramento, May 1986.

131. Ad Hoc Committee for the Fair Administration of Justice, Bylaws, Article 2, section 1.

132. Personal communications, Akinsanya Kambon.

133. *Ibid.*

134. *Ibid.*

135. Ad Hoc Committee for the Fair Administration of Justice, Bylaws, Article 2, section 1.

136. Ad Hoc Committee for the Fair Administration of Justice, Letter to Board of Supervisors, Sacramento County, September 23, 1985.

137. Rev. Ephraim Williams, Letter to James Daugherty, Sacramento County district attorney, July 22, 1985.

138. John Daugherty, district attorney, letter to Rev. Ephraim Williams, August 9, 1985.

139. The Black American Political Association of California. *10th Anniversary Convention Souvenir Booklet*, 1988, p. 11, "October 12–13, 1979, The 1st State Convention." The text reads, "The convention organizers had ... set a ... precedent for all subsequent BAPAC conventions — the establishment of an agenda that both showcased California's Black elected officials and also facilitated interaction between them and grassroots political activists." P. 13: "BAPAC leaders were given the charge to organize chapters in major cities throughout the state."

140. William Julius Wilson, *The Declining Significance of Race* (Chicago: University of Chicago Press, 1978).

141. This concept was explored by 6 chapters in the section "Deracialization and the Strategic Calculus of Black Politics," most pointedly in the article by Charles Jones and Michael L. Clemons, "A Model of Crossover Voting: An Assessment of the Wilder Victory," in *The*

Dilemmas of Black Politics: Issues of Leadership and Strategy. Georgia Persons, ed. (New York: HarperCollins, 1993), pp. 128–146.

142. In Sacramento the effort to fight this trend was represented in the 1970s by the National Committee to Overturn the Bakke Decision. The decision was not overturned. As a result, the limits of affirmative action programs were greatly circumscribed under the dictum that race was not a structural barrier to entrance to professional schools, that only individual exclusions based on race could be considered as factors of admission. Race could be considered only in combination with other factors in admissions decisions. This judgment was an unambiguous statement that the courts found race no longer operating as a systematic impediment to the welfare of Black people in the aggregate.

143. These numbers are taken from the 1980 census and generously rounded to make my arithmetic easier. U.S. Census Bureau, U.S. Census, 1980.

144. Calculations provided by Dr. Lloyd Gavin, emeritus professor of mathematics, California State University of Sacramento.

145. "Buppies" (Black Urban Professionals, a take-off from "yuppies," young urban professionals). I say *pseudo* middle class deliberately, as the wealth of a Black family with an annual income of $50,000 was equivalent to the wealth of a white family with $10,000 annual income. The Black middle class was clearly a class of a different color.

146. Walter Mosely, *Always Outnumbered, Always Outgunned* (New York: Norton, 1998).

147. Grantland Johnson, "Divestment Ordinance," Memorandum, to mayor and council members. September 2, 1986.

Chapter 4

1. Vincent Harris, *1991 Redistricting Project*, Sacramento, Summit on African American Concerns, May 4, 1991.

2. *Ibid.*, p. 2.

3. *Ibid.*

4. *Ibid.*, p. 3.

5. *Ibid.*, p. 4.

6. *Ibid.*

7. *Ibid.*, p. 5.

8. *Ibid.*

9. Harris, January 10, 1993.

10. Pam Haynes interview, December 1992.

11. Harris, 1993; Haynes interview, 1992.

12. Harris, 1993.

13. *Ibid.*

14. *Ibid.*

15. *Ibid.*, and Haynes interview, 1992.

16. Harris, 1993.

17. *Ibid.*

18. The 1991 Redistricting Project Organizing Committee, "1991 Redistricting Project Progress Report — City Council Update," Memo to 1991 Redistricting Project Affiliates. October 2, 1991, p. 4.

19. Section 152 of the Sacramento City Charter, "Elections," Adopted October 10, 1989.

20. 1991 Redistricting Project. *Newsletter*, # 2, p. 2.

21. *Ibid.*, p. 8.

22. *Ibid.*
23. *Ibid.*, p. 3; Harris, 1993; Haynes interview, 1992.
24. Haynes interview, 1992.
25. Harris, 1993.
26. *Ibid.*
27. The 1991 Redistricting Project Organizing Committee, October 2, 1991, p. 7; Harris, 1993.
28. Harris, 1993.
29. The author was present and witnessed these conversations.
30. Haynes interview, 1992.
31. *Ibid.*; Harris, 1993; author's observations.
32. *Ibid.*
33. *Ibid.*
34. *The Sacramento Observer*, "Election Special," May 21–27, 1992, p. 1.
35. *Ibid.*
36. Obituary, Samuel C. Pannell, December 8, 1997.
37. Harris, 1993; Haynes interview, 1992.
38. Harris, 1993.
39. *Ibid.*
40. *Ibid.*, p. 26.
41. See, for example, "Between Us Sis'tuhs IV, Sharing, Striving, and Achieving," Program of the Fourth Annual Conference of the Sacramento Black Women's Network, Friday, March 27, and Saturday, March 28, 1992.
42. Vincent Harris, interview, January 10, 1993.
43. *Ibid.*; Haynes interview.
44. Lauren Hammond, interview, 2000.
45. *Ibid.*
46. *Ibid.*
47. *Ibid.*, and author's observations.
48. Hammond interview, 2000; also "Lauren Hammond, Sacramento Scrapbook," campaign piece. Lauren's prominent endorsers are listed on p. 8, the back page. Prominent persons not on this list endorsed Shiroma.
49. "Lauren Hammond, Sacramento Scrapbook."
50. Author's observations.
51. Eulogy, Sam Pannell, December 8, 1997.
52. Bonnie Pannell, interview, December 2005.
53. *Ibid.*
54. *Ibid.*
55. *Ibid.*
56. *Ibid.*
57. Hammond interview, 2000.
58. Pam Haynes interview, May 2006.
59. *Ibid.*
60. *Ibid.*
61. James Shelby, interview, September 24, 2004.
62. Haynes interview, December, 1992.
63. Shelby interview.
64. "California's Proposition 187 and Its Lessons."
65. Wardell Connerly, Roundtable discussion, Sacramento, California, February 1995.
66. *Sacramento Bee.*
67. James Richardson, *Willie Brown: A Biography* (Berkeley: University of California Press, 1996), p. 358, "Voters approved Proposition 140…. The measure was aimed directly at doing what Republicans had failed to do: end Willie Brown's speakership." And the author, Richardson, is no Willie Brown fan.
68. Willie Brown was speaker for 15 years. Even the legendary Jesse Unruh served only 7, one-half the length of Brown's reign.

69. See Richardson, 1996, especially pp. 333–366.
70. Dennis Renault, opinion cartoon, *The Sacramento Bee*, February 4, 1994, p. B6.
71. Stephen Magnani, "Bee Cartoon on Bigotry Provokes Reader Protests," *The Sacramento Bee*, February 5, 1995, p. B2.
72. *Ibid.*
73. *Ibid.*
74. *Ibid.*
75. *Ibid.*
76. *Ibid.*
77. *Ibid.*
78. Personal communication to author.
79. *Ibid.*
80. *Ibid.*
81. The accounting of the SABC deliberations are from the author's experiences as a participant-observer.
82. "The Sacramento Working Conference on the Black Political Party," October 15–18, 1980.
83. SABC, State of the Race, "Conference Program," August 1, 1998, pp. 3–5.
84. Herbert A. Sample. "Black men's day to feel like a million," *The Sacramento Bee*, October 17, 1995, p. A12.
85. *Ibid.*
86. *Ibid.*
87. The Observer Newspapers, Section B, October 26–November 1, 1995, p. B1.
88. Except as indicated otherwise by footnotes, this reportage of the 1,000 Man March comes from the author's experience as a participant-observer.
89. The Observer Newspapers, "The Thousand Man March," Section H, *March Special*, February 1996, p. H5.
90. *Ibid.*, p. H2.
91. *Ibid.*, pp. H8–9.
92. *Ibid.*, p. H8.
93. All of the interviews were conducted at political gatherings — either public or organizational. One set of interviews was conducted at an organizational retreat. Another took place at a public forum, a third was conducted at a rally in a park, a fourth was taken at the Martin Luther King Jr. March and Expo. The final set was done at the 1,000 Man March. The respondents answered 37 questions, both open-ended and closed. They were given great leeway in their responses as the intention was to learn what they really did. The interviews' major objective was threefold: (1) to elicit an understanding of the major Black and non-non–Black spaces frequented by each respondent; (2) to identify the character of Black narrative to which the respondents were exposed, in which they participated, and to identify where such narratives took place; and (3) to identify the character of social memory among the respondents. While the respondents were asked no direct questions about social memory, the character of some elements of their social memories can be inferred both from the social spaces they frequented and the narrative operative in those spaces. For example, the All African People's Revolutionary Party promotes a social memory which is African-centered, which points to the exploitative role of capitalism, and which links African people throughout the world. The 100 Black Men promotes a social memory that emphasizes the traditions and responsibilities of Black men, especially to young

Black males. The questions were designed to find out with respect to any activity, whether the respondent participated only in Black spaces, only in non–non–Black spaces, or both. For example, if a respondent indicated the activity of reading newspapers, did the respondent read only Black newspapers, only non–non–Black newspapers, or both? In some activities they participated only in Black spaces — interacting with family, for example. In other spaces some participated in only non–non–Black spaces, reading professional journals, for example. In still others they participated in both Black and non–non–Black spaces, watching television programs, for example.

94. 9 (only mainstream) + 3 (only Black) + 3 (both Black & mainstream) = 15.

95. These comments on social memory are derived more from the literature and from general observations of the respondents than on specific measures.

96. *Serrano v. Priest.* Cal.3d 728 (1976).

97. Personal communication with San Francisco Municipal Court judge, Lilian K. Sing; Sacramento, October 1990.

98. Robert Smith, *We Have No Leaders: African Americans in the Post–Civil Rights Era* (Albany: State University of New York Press, 1996); and "System Values and African American Leadership," *SOULS* 10,

no. 1 (2008); William Strickland, "Dubois' Revenge: Re-interrogating American Democratic Theory … or Why We Need a Revolutionary Black Research Agenda in the 21st Century," *SOULS* 10, no. 1 (2008).

Chapter 5

1. William Strickland, "DuBois's Revenge: Reinterrogating American Democratic Theory … or Why We Need a Revolutionary Black Research Agenda in the 21st Century," *SOULS* 10, no. 1 (2008): 33.

2. *Ibid.*, p. 33–34.

3. *Ibid.*, p. 34.

4. *Ibid.*, p. 35

5. *Ibid.*, p. 37.

6. Lawrence Michael, Jared Bernstein, Sylvia Allegreto, *The State of Working America 2004/2005* (Ithaca, NY: Cornell University Press, 2005), pp. 285–286. This reference was provided by Dr. John Henry, professor of economics, California State University of Sacramento.

7. Michael et al., p. 286.

8. State Personnel Board, "Disproportionate Effect in Disciplinary Actions in State Service." Sacramento, January 6, 1988.

Bibliography

Abernethy, Gloria. Personal communication. Sacramento, CA, April 26, 2008.

Abron, JoNina. Memo to the Central Committee, National Black Independent Political Party. "1984 Presidential Elections — Issues for Consideration." June 3, 1983.

_____. Memo to National Black Independent Political Party Administrative and Policy Committee. "Resignation as Co-Chair, National Program Development Committee, Future of the Bay Area NBIPP." April 17, 1984.

Ad Hoc Committee for the Fair Administration of Justice. Bylaws.

_____. Letter to Board of Supervisors, Sacramento County, CA, September 23, 1985.

Alkalimat, Abdul, and Doug Gills. "Black Power vs. Racism: Harold Washington Becomes Mayor." In *The New Black Vote: Politics and Power in Four American Cities*. Edited by Rod Bush. San Francisco: Synthesis Publications, 1984.

Barth, Frederick, ed. *Ethnic Groups and Boundaries*. Boston: Little, Brown, 1969.

Black American Political Association of California. "Keeping it Together." 10th Anniversary Program. October 1988.

Black Community Activist Committee. "In Memory of Blanche Hill and Byron Robertson." Program, The Sacramento Area Black Activist Community Conference, n.d.

_____. "Black Education in Sacramento." Announcement, n.d.

_____. *Newsletter* no. 1, April 30, 1985.

_____. *A Black Community Directory: For the Sacramento Area*. May 1986.

Bolton, Charlotte. Interview. November 19, 1985.

Branch, Taylor. *Parting the Waters: America in the King Years, 1954–63*. New York: Simon and Schuster, 1988.

_____. *Pillar of Fire: America in the King Years, 1963–65*. New York: Touchstone, 1999.

_____. *At Canaan's Edge: America in the King Years, 1965–1968*. New York: Simon and Schuster, 2006, pp. 337–338.

Brown, Willie L. *Basic Brown: My Life and Our Times*. New York: Simon and Schuster, 2008.

Browning, Rufus P., Dale Rogers Marshall, and David H. Tabb. *Protest is Not Enough*. Berkeley: University of California Press, 1986.

Bush, Rod. *The New Black Vote: Politics and Power in Four American Cities*. San Francisco: Synthesis Publications, 1984.

Caesar, Clarence. *An Historical Overview of the Development of Sacramento's Black Community, 1850–1983*. Master's thesis, California State University, Sacramento, 1985.

Campbell, Leslie. Interview. November 19, 1985.

Campos, Art. "Trustees: Popular Courses Shifted from SCC to ARC." *Sacramento Bee*, March 22, 1979, p. 3.

Center for Individual Rights. www.cir-nsa.org/cases/prop209_info.html

Chicago Public Library. "Facts About Harold Washington, 42nd Mayor of Chicago." www.chicagopubliclibrary.org. Accessed January 18, 2007.

Chinn, Thomas. Letter. April 1, 1981.

"Citizens Committee on Police Practices, A Member's Perspective." *Rumble* 1, no. 1 (June 1973): 1–4.

Cohen, Cathy. *The Boundaries of Blackness: Aids and the Breakdown of Black Politics*. Chicago: University of Chicago Press, 1999.

Coleman, Willi. "African American Women and Community Development in California, 1848–1900." In *Seeking El Dorado: African Americans in California*. Lawrence Brooks De Graaf, Kevin Mulroy, and Quintard Taylor, eds. Seattle: University of Washington Press, 2001.

Connerly, Wardell. Roundtable discussion. Sacramento, CA, 1995.

Cooper, Charlie, and Ann Cooper. *Tuskegee's Heroes*. Osceola, WI: MBI, 1963.

Couto, Richard. "Narratives, Free Spaces, and Political Leadership" *The Journal of Politics* 55, no. 1, 1993.

_____. *Ain't Gonna Let Nobody Turn Me Round: The Pursuit of Racial Justice in the South*. Philadelphia: Temple University Press, 1991.

Covin, David. *The Unified Black Movement in Brazil, 1978–2000*. Jefferson, NC: McFarland, 2006.

_____. "Black Activists During the Ebb Tide of a Social Movement." *National Political Science Review* 8, 2001.

_____. "Narrative, Free Space, and Communities of Memory in the Brazilian Black Consciousness Movement." *Western Journal of Black Studies* 21, no. 4, 1997.

_____. "Social Movement Theory in the Examination of Mobilization in the Black Community." *National Political Science Review* 6, 1997.

_____. "Reflections on Dilemmas of African American Leadership." *Dilemmas of Black Politics: Issues of Leadership and Strategy*. Georgia A. Persons, ed. New York: HarperCollins College Publishers, 1993, pp. 15–37.

_____. "The New Black Vote in Sacramento: The Impossible Dream?" Presented at the National Conference of Black Political Scientists Meeting, Chicago, April 2–4, 1986.

Counting California. Data Extraction Results, Census of Population 1970, 2nd count. U.S. Department of Commerce, Bureau of the Census Data and Technical Assistance, University of California at Berkeley, 2004 (November 30, 2006).

Cromwell, Martin F. "Informational Hearing on Disciplinary Action in State Service." Memorandum to State Personnel Board. January 5–6, 1988.

Cruse, Harold. *The Crisis of the Negro Intellectual: From its Origins to the Present*. New York: William Morrow, 1967.

_____. *Plural But Equal: Blacks and Minorities in America's Plural Society*. New York: William Morrow, 1987.

Culture Collection. Personal communication. Sacramento, CA, December 2005.

Daniels, Ron. "Some Perspectives of an NBIPP Strategy for 1984." Submitted to the National Program Committee, as per assignment. N.d.

Daugherty, John, District Attorney. Letter to Rev. Ephraim Williams, August 9, 1985.

Dawson, Michael. *Black Visions: The Roots of Contemporary African-American Political Ideologies*. Chicago: University of Chicago Press, 2001.

_____. *Behind the Mule: Race in African-American Politics*. Princeton, NJ: Princeton University Press, 1994.

De Graaf, Lawrence B., and Quintard Taylor. "Introduction." In Lawrence B. De Graaf, Kevin Murray, and Quintard Taylor, eds. *Seeking El Dorado: African Americans in California*. Seattle: University of Washington Press, 2001, p. 6.

Dean, George. President, Sacramento Urban League, Inc. Letter. March 31, 1981.

District 7 Committee. "A Proposed Reapportionment Plan for City Council Districts." April 1, 1981.

Douglas, Grace. "Rapping." *Rumble* no. 34, September 1979, p. 1.

Douglas, Grace Carter. "A Historical Study of the Women's Civic and Improvement Club." *The Griot: An Anthology of African Necromancers*. Grace Carter Douglas, ed. Sacramento: Rumble, 1988.

Duren, B. Kwaku. *Statement on the Discussion of a Black Presidential Candidate*. October 17, 1983.

Enos, Daryl. "An Evaluation of Neighborhood Councils." 1967.

Evans, Sarah, and Harry Boite. *Free Spaces: The Sources of Democratic Change in America*. New York: Harper, 1985.

Fanon, Franz. *Black Skin, White Masks*. London: Pluto Press, 1986.

Flanningan, William H. *Political Behavior and the American Electorate*. Boston: Allyn & Bacon, 1968.

Franklin, John Hope. *From Slavery to Freedom*. New York: Knopf, 1967.

Fontaine, David. Interview. December 24, 1985.

Foote, Fred. Interview. 2000.

Fort, Edward B. Superintendent, Sacramento City Unified School District. Letter. September 3, 1974.

Frye, Hardy. Interview. 2000.

Gary, Les. Letter to Otis Scott. April 10, 1981.

Grant, Joanne. *Ella Baker: Freedom Bound*. New York: Wiley, 1998.

Green, Paul M. "The Primary: Some New Players — Same Old Rules." In *The Making of the Mayor: Chicago, 1983*. Melvin G. Holli and Paul M. Green, eds. Grand Rapids, MI: Eerdmans, 1984.

Green, Ricky K. *Voices in Black Political Thought*. New York: Peter Lang, 2005.

Gregory, Geraldine. "What is the National Black Independent Political Party?" NBIPP, 1980.

Hall, Donald. Assistant superintendent, Sacramento City Unified School District. Letter. October 8, 1973.

Hammond, Lauren. Interview. 2000.

_____. "Lauren Hammond, Sacramento Scrapbook" (campaign promotional piece).

Hare, Pan, Eda F. Borgetta, and Robert Bales, eds. *Small Groups*. Rev. ed. New York: Knopf, 1965.

Harris, Frederick C., Valeria Sinclair-Chapman, and Brian D. Mackenzie. "Macrodynamics of Black Political Participation in the Post–Civil Rights Era." *The Journal of Politics* 67, no. 4 (November 2005): 1143–1163.

Harris, Vincent. *1991 Redistricting Project*. Sacramento: Summit on African American Concerns, May 4, 1991.

_____. Interview. December 2, 1992.

_____. Interview. January 10, 1993.

Harris-Lacewell, Melissa. *Barbershops, Bibles, and BET: Everyday Talk and Black Political Thought*. Princeton, NJ: Princeton University Press, 2004.

Hawkins, Ernest R., Registrar of Voters. Letter to Thomas R. Hoeber, Chairman, and Members, Sacramento City Reapportionment Committee, March 18, 1981.

Haynes, Pam. Interview, December, 1992.
_____. Interview, May, 2006.
Henderson, Lenneal J. Jr., ed. *Black Political Life in the United States*. San Francisco: Chandler, 1972.
Holden, Matthew Jr. *The Politics of the Black Nation*. New York: Chandler, 1973.
Holloway, John B. *Red Tails Black Wings: The Men of America's Black Air Force*. Rev. ed. Las Cruces, NM: Yucca Tree Press, 1997.
Homan, Lynn M., and Thomas Reilly. *Black Knights: The Story of the Tuskegee Airmen*. Gretna, LA: Pelican, 2003.
Homens, George C. *The Human Group*. New York: Knopf, 1965.
Human Rights Commission. "Workshop on Reapportionment." March 30, 1981.
Jennings, James. *The Politics of Black Empowerment*. Detroit: Wayne State University Press, 1992.
_____. "Boston: Blacks and Progressive Politics." In *The New Black Vote: Politics and Power in Four American Cities*. Rod Bush, ed. San Francisco: Synthesis Press, 1984.
Johnson, Grantland. Interview. 2001.
_____. Interview. August 20, 1985.
_____. "Divestment Ordinance." Memorandum to Mayor and City Council Members. September 2, 1986.
Johnson, Ollie, and Karin Stanford, eds. *Black Political Organizations in the Post-Civil Rights Era*. New Brunswick, NJ: Rutgers University Press, 2002.
Jones, Charles E., and Michel L. Clemons. "A Model of Racial Crossover Voting: An Assessment of the Wilder Victory." In *Dilemmas of Black Politics: Issues of Leadership and Strategy*. Georgia Persons, ed. New York: HarperCollins College Publishers, 1993, pp. 128–146.
Jones, Charles, ed. *The Black Panther Party Reconsidered*. Baltimore: Black Classic Press, 1988.
Jones, Mack H. "A Frame of Reference for Black Politics," *Black Political Life in the United States*. Lenneal J. Henderson, Jr., ed. San Francisco: Chandler, 1972.
Jones, Rhett. "Black and Native American Relations Before 1800." *Western Journal of Black Studies* 1, no. 3 (September 1977): 157, 159.
Kambon, Akinsanya. Personal communications.
_____. www.thegallerykambon.com
Key, V.O. *Politics, Parties, and Pressure Groups*. New York: Random House, 1942.
King, Wilma. *Stolen Childhood: Slave Youth in Nineteenth Century America*. Bloomington: Indiana University Press, 1995.
Komarovsky, Mira. "The Voluntary Association of Urban Dwellers." *American Sociological Review* 11, 1946, pp. 686–698.
Lewis, David L. *King: A Critical Biography*. Baltimore: Penguin Books, 1970.
Lindsey, John. Letter from Political Committee of SABC. Circa 1973.

Lomax, Louis. *The Negro Revolt*. New York: Signet Books, 1963.
Magnani, Stephen. "Bee Cartoon on Bigotry Provokes Reader Protests." *The Sacramento Bee*, February 5, 1995, p. B2.
Mailman, Stanley. "California's Proposition 187 and its Lessons. *New York Law Journal* (January 3, 1995): p. 3. www.ssbb.com/article1.html.
Marx, Anthony. *Making Race and Nation: A Comparison of the United States, South Africa, and Brazil*. Cambridge: Cambridge University Press, 1996.
McAdam, Doug. *Political Process and the Development of Black Insurgency, 1930–1970*. Chicago: University of Chicago Press, 1982.
McClory, Robert. "Up From Obscurity: Harold Washington." In *The Making of the Mayor: Chicago, 1983*. Melvin G. Holli and Paul M. Green, eds. Grand Rapids, MI: Eerdmans, 1984.
McIver, Robert. *The Web of Government*. NY: McMillan, 1947.
Messner, Steve S., and Scott South. "Structural Determinants of Intergroup Association: Interracial Marriage and Crime." *American Journal of Sociology* 91, no. 6: 1409–30.
Michael, Lawrence, Jared Bernstein, and Sylvia Allegretto. *The State of Working America 2004/05*. Ithaca, NY: Cornell University Press, 2005.
Mitchell, Michael. "Blacks and the *Abertura Democratica*." In *Race, Class, and Power in Brazil*. Pierre-Michel Fontaine, ed. Los Angeles: Center for Afro-American Studies, 1985.
Moore, Joseph. Personal communication. October 16, 2007.
Moore, Shirley Ann Wilson. *To Place Our Deeds: The African American Community in Richmond, California, 1910–1963*. Berkeley: University of California Press, 2000.
Morris, Aldon. *The Origins of the Civil Rights Movement: Black Communities Organizing for Change*. New York: Free Press, 1984.
Morris, Milton. *The Politics of Black America*. New York: Harper & Row, 1975.
Morrison, Minion K.C. *Black Political Mobilization: Leadership, Power, & Mass Behavior*. Albany: State University of New York Press, 1987.
Mosely, Walter. *Always Outnumbered, Always Outgunned*. New York: Norton, 1998.
Muzafer, Sherif. "Experiments in Group Conflict." *Scientific American* 195, no. 5 (November 1956): 54–58.
National Black Independent Political Party. Minutes. National Black Independent Party Convention, Plenary Session. November 23, 1980.
_____. "Attend the Los Angeles Organizing Committee Conference, July 25." N.d.
_____. "Questions and Answers on the National Black Independent Political Party." Dayton, 1980.
National Institutes of Health, National Human

Genome Research Institute. http"//science.educa
tion.nih.gov/supplements/nihlgenetic/guide/gene
tic_variation.htm.Accessed November 30, 2006.

National Rainbow Coalition. *Build the NRC: National Rainbow Coalition.* N.d.

Newton, Huey P., with J. Herman Blake. *Revolutionary Suicide.* New York: Harcourt Brace Jovanovich, 1979.

Niv Ram. "Local Focus and Issues." *Rumble* 1, no. 7 (April 1974).

Nobles, Melissa. *Shades of Citizenship: Race and Census in Modern Politics.* Stanford, CA: Stanford University Press, 2000.

Pan African Studies, California State University at Sacramento; SABC; and California State University Visiting Scholars Program. "The Sacramento Working Conference on the Black Political Party, October 15–18, 1980." Conference Program.

Pannell, Bonnie. Interview. December 2005.

Party for the New Black Politics. *The Speaking Drum.* September 1980.

Payne, Charles. *I've Got the Light of Freedom.* Berkeley: University of California Press, 1996.

Persons, Georgia A., ed. "The Politics of the Black 'Nation': A Twenty-Five Year Retrospective." *National Political Science Review* 8. New Brunswick: Transaction, 2001.

_____, ed. *Dilemmas of Black Politics: Issues of Leadership and Strategy.* New York: HarperCollins College Publishers, 1993.

Photius.com. http://www.photius.com/wfb.1999 rankings/population_ohtml.

Pinderhughes, Dianne M. *Race and Ethnicity in Chicago Politics: A Reexamination of Pluralist Theory.* Urbana: University of Illinois Press, 1987.

"Police Assaults the Nation." Flier. Author unknown. May 1974.

Preston, Michael B. "The Resurgence of Black Voting in Chicago, 1955–1983." In *The Making of the Mayor: Chicago, 1983.* Melvin G. Holli and Paul M. Green, eds. Grand Rapids, MI: Eerdmans, 1984.

Rainbow National Coalition, Inc. "Summary of the Bylaws of the NRC." 1986.

Ranney, Austin. "Trust and Representation in Presidential Primary Elections." *American Political Science Review* 65, no. 1 (March 1972).

Reed, Adolph. *Class Notes: Posing as Politics and Other Thoughts on the American Scene.* Minneapolis: University of Minnesota Press, 2000.

_____. *Thoughts on the American Scene.* Minneapolis: University of Minnesota Press, 2000.

_____. *Stirrings in the Jigg: Black Power in the Post Segregation Era.* Minneapolis: University of Minnesota Press, 1999.

Renault, Dennis. Opinion cartoon. *Sacramento Bee,* February 4, 1994, p. B6.

Richardson, James. *Willie Brown: A Biography.* Berkeley: University of California Press, 1996.

Rumble 1, no. 1 (June 1973).

_____, no. 7 (April 1974).

_____, no. 11 (January 1975).

_____, no. 32 (April 1979).

_____, 34 (September 1979).

Rusk, Jerrold R. "Participation in America: A Review Essay." *American Political Science Review* 70 (June 1976): 584–585.

Sacramento Area Black Caucus. "Why is the Black Caucus Going to the City Council to Accuse the Police Department of Discriminatory Acts Against Black People?" Public statement and flier. N.d.

_____. Notes. Interviews with assembly members Leon Ralph and Julian Dixon. December 1974.

_____. Summary Compilation SABC Revitalization Workshops, "Political Committee." October 24, 1975.

_____. Position Paper. May 1981.

_____. "Sacramento Area Black Caucus Legal Challenge to the Sacramento City Council's Redistricting Decision." June 1981.

_____. State of the Race. "Conference Program," August 1, 1998.

_____. State of the Race. "Conference Program," August 7, 1999.

Sacramento Area Economic Opportunity Council. *CAA Plans and Priorities, CAP Form 81,* Funding Year F: January 1, 1971– December 31, 1971. List of SAEOC programs and delegate agencies.

_____. Ad hoc committee minutes. October 18, 1970.

_____. Executive Board meeting minutes. December 29, 1970.

_____ and San Francisco Regional Educational Opportunity Program Offices. *Memorandum of Understanding for Program Year* F: January 1, 1971– December 31, 1971.

_____. Partial, untitled statement issued by Naaman Brown, 1969.

Sacramento Bee. December 29, 1970.

_____. December 30, 1970.

_____. January 9, 1971, p. A2.

_____. January 14, 1971, p. C2.

_____. January 15, 1971, p. C2

_____. January 22, 1971, p. B3.

_____. January 29, 1971, p. B2.

_____. September 22, 1971, p. B1

_____. November 3, 1971, pp. A1 and A24.

_____. "Los Rios Trustee Steward Invested in South Africa," August 24, 1979.

_____. October 1, 1979.

Sacramento Black Women's Network. Between Us Sis'tuhs IV. Program of the Fourth Annual Sacramento Black Women's Network Conference. Friday, March 27, and Saturday, March 28, 1992.

Sacramento Council of Local Governments.

Sacramento County Clerk.

Sacramento Observer. May 14, 1970.

_____. June 4, 1970.

_____. June 16, 1970.

_____. June 10, 1970.

_____. June 25, 1970.

_____. August 6, 1970.

_____. December, 1977.

_____. Election Special. May 21–27, 1992.

_____. "FONO Announces Second Housing Project." Sacramento Community Action News. October 1970, p. 11.

_____. Oak Park 4 Supplement. October 1, 1970.

_____. "Sacramento's Most Influential Blacks." December 1977, p. 35.

Sacramento Observer. *A Long Look Back.* November, 1973, "Douglas McFarland."

_____. "Dr. Kenneth Johnson."

_____. "Dr. Roscoe Brewer."

_____. "Mrs. Gladys Canson."

_____. "Mrs. Johnnie Ruth Luster."

_____. "Mrs. Missouri Nash."

_____. "Nathaniel S. Colley."

_____. "Mrs. Netta Sparks."

_____. "Mrs. Nona Henry."

_____. "Solomon Nelson."

Sacramento Organizing Committee of the National Black Independent Political Party. "Reaganomics and the Black Community." Program, July 28, 1982.

Sacramento Valley Rainbow Coalition. Roster. January 1, 1986.

_____. Rainbow Neighborhood Organization.

_____. "Bring Together All Stripes of our Rainbow." Founding Conference of SVRC. Program. September 27, 1986.

_____. "Rainbow Coalition as Catalyst for Free South Africa Movement." N.d.

_____. Agenda, July 1986.

_____. Agenda, August 1986.

_____. Agenda, September 1986.

_____. Minutes, September 1986.

Saito, Leland T. *Race and Politics: Asian Americans, Latinos, and Whites in a Los Angeles Suburb.* Urbana: University of Illinois Press, 1998.

Sample, Herbert. "Black Men's Day to feel like a million." *Sacramento Bee*, October 17, 1995.

Scorpio Reporter, July 4th, 1876–1976, Souvenir Bicentennial Issue.

Scott, James. *Domination and the Arts of Resistance: Hidden Transcripts.* New Haven, CT: Yale University Press, 1985.

_____. *Weapons of the Weak: Everyday Forms of Peasant Resistance.* New Haven, CT: Yale University Press, 1985.

Secret, Philip E., and James B. Johnson. "Political Efficacy, Political Trust and Electoral Participation: A Longitudinal Analysis." *The Western Journal of Black Studies* 9, no. 2 (Summer 1985).

Serrano v. Priest. Cal.3d 728 (1976).

Shaw, Todd. "The Changing Boundaries of Blackness." *National Political Science Review* 11, 2007: 3–16.

Shelby, James. Interview. September 24, 2004.

Sing, Lilian K., San Francisco Municipal Court Judge, personal communication, October 1990.

Smith, Robert, "System Values and African American Leadership." *SOULS* 10, no. 1, 2008.

Smith, Robert C. *Racism in the Post-Civil Rights Era: Now You See It, Now You Don't.* New York: State University Press, 1996.

_____. *We Have No Leaders: African Americans in the Post-Civil Rights Era.* Albany: State University of New York Press, 1996.

Smith, Robert C., and Richard Selzer. *Race, Class, and Culture: A Study in Afro-American Mass Opinion.* Albany: State University of New York Press, 1992.

Spencer, Dr. Eugene, Jr. Letter. June 29, 1973.

Stone, Chuck. "The Negro Vote: *Ceteris Paribus.*" In *Black Political Life in the United States.* Lenneal J. Henderson, Jr., ed. San Francisco: Chandler, 1972.

Strickland, William. "DuBois's Revenge: Reinterrogating American Democratic Theory ... or Why We Need a Revolutionary Black Research Agenda in the 21st Century." *SOULS* 10, no. 1, 2008.

Sykes, Bryan. *The Seven Daughters of Eve.* New York: Norton, 2001.

Sorauf, Frank J. *Party Politics in America.* Boston: Little, Brown, 1968.

State Personnel Board. "Disproportionate Effect in Disciplinary Actions in State Service." Informal Hearing. January 6, 1988.

Tarrow, Sidney. *Politics and Reform: Collective Action, Social Movements, and Cycles of Protest.* Cornell Center for Independent Study, Western Societies Program Occasional Papers, no. 21, 1989.

_____. *Social Movements, Collective Action, and Politics.* New York: Columbia University Press, 1982.

Tate, Katherine. *From Protest to Politics: The New Black Voters in American Elections.* New York: Russell Sage Foundation and Harvard University Press, 1993 and 1994.

Taylor, Paul. "Jackson Working to Add Constituencies to Rainbow," *Washington Post*, April 20, 1986.

Telles, Edward E. *Race in Another America: The Significance of Skin Color in Brazil.* Princeton: Princeton University Press, 2004.

_____. "Racial Discrimination in Brazil: The Case of Marriage Among Color Groups." *Latin American Review* 28: 141–62.

The 1991 Redistricting Project Organizing Committee. "1991 Redistricting Project Progress Report — City Council Update." Memo to 1991 Redistricting Affiliates. October 2, 1991.

The Observer Newspapers. "Sacramento's 100 Most Influential Blacks." December 1977.

_____. *Colorful Reflections.* Sacramento: Observer Newspapers, 2003.

_____. Section B. October 26–November 1, 1995, p. B-1.

_____. "The Thousand Man March." Section H, March Special. February 1996.

Travis, Dempsey. *Harold: The People's Mayor.* Chicago: Urban Research Press, 1989.

Udom, E.U. Essein. *Black Nationalism: A Search for Identity in America.* New York: Dell, 1964.

United States Census Bureau. Census, 1980.

Venturi, Gustavo, Gevanilda Santos, and Maria Palmira da Silva. *Racismo no Brasil: percepções da discriminação e do preconceito racial no século XXI.* São Paulo: Editora Fundação Perseu Abramo, 2005.

Walters, Ronald, and Robert Smith. *African American Leadership.* Albany: State University of New York Press, 1999.

Walton, Hanes. *Black Politics: A Theoretical and Structural Analysis.* Philadelphia: Lippincott, 1972.

_____. *Invisible Politics: Black Political Behavior.* Albany: State University of New York Press, 1985.

_____, and Robert C. Smith. *American Politics and the African American Quest for Universal Freedom.* New York: Longman, 2000.

Washington Neighborhood Council. Statement. 1969.

Weiss, Nancy J. *The National Urban League.* New York: Oxford University Press, 1974.

Westbrook, Shelby, ed. *Tuskegee Airmen, 1941–1945.* Chicago: Tuskegee Airmen, 2003.

Whitaker, Mel. "Blacks Form 'Tribunal' for Police, Court Acts." *Sacramento Bee,* pp. A1 and A8, n.d.

Wikipedia. "Harold Washington." http://en.wikipedia.org/wili/Harold_Washington.

Williams, Rev. Ephraim. Letter to James Daugherty, Sacramento district attorney. July 22, 1985.

Wilson, James D. *American Government: Institutions and Policies.* 2nd ed. Lexington, MA: Heath, 1983.

Wilson, William Julius. *The Declining Significance of Race.* Chicago. University of Chicago Press, 1978.

Wisham, Solon Jr. Letter to Lou Kemp, chairman, SABC, dated May 8, 1974.

Woods, Marion. Interview. 2001.

Women's Civic Improvement Club. Women's Civic Improvement Center, 1936–1986. 50th Anniversary Program. Sacramento 1986.

Index